W9-CLF-650

Mass Media and Mass Man

second edition

P 92
.U5 C3
1973

Mass Media and Mass Man

second
edition

Alan Casty
Santa Monica College

HOLT, RINEHART AND WINSTON, INC.
New York   Chicago   San Francisco
Atlanta   Dallas   Montreal   Toronto

INDIANA
PURDUE
LIBRARY
JAN 1976
WITHDRAWN
FORT WAYNE

Copyright © 1968, 1973 by Holt, Rinehart and Winston, Inc.
All rights reserved
Library of Congress Catalog Card Number: 72–83319
ISBN: 0–03–083452–x
Printed in the United States of America
   56   090   98765432

Preface

Since the first edition of *Mass Media and Mass Man* was published, study of the mass media has proliferated—both in education and society. In fact, the acceleration, the ubiquity, the changeableness—whether fashionably fickle or significantly fresh—of the new approaches and analyses seem to partake of the special flavor of the media. They echo that intensity of delivery and response that is so central a part of man's paradoxical encounter with the mass media. Since the media and the approaches to study of them are in such constant flux, this new edition contains many new selections—many more than a traditional, preacceleration revision would have—that reflect current developments. But at the same time, certain fundamental approaches have been maintained in new or previously used selections, and the same basic format of the first edition has been retained.

I have made two modifications of that format. This edition includes material *about* the media only; in applying the approaches and methods of analyses included here, it is more valuable, I feel, for the reader and viewer to interact with media materials in their original contexts. I have also not attempted to emulate the sensory impact of the media; what we have here are thorough, tightly organized, thoughtfully considered examples of old-fashioned, and still-valuable, linear communication.

More importantly, a third major part has been added to the original two parts—Mass Media and Culture and Mass Media and Information.

This—Part 1: Mass Media and Society—deals with aspects of the social impact of media, with social issues that blend, overlap, or interrelate the other two categories. But the majority of the selections, in Parts 2 and 3, still emphasize one or the other of the two major roles of media, as processors and conveyors of culture or of information. In this dual role, the mass media create and shape not only the values, tastes, attitudes, and the art and entertainment experiences of their audience, but also the patterns of fact and opinion about the perception and interpretation of the world of that audience. Obviously, communication of information does produce values, attitudes, and emotions that are intricately connected to those communicated by art and entertainment; conversely, art and entertainment do provide facts and produce opinions. Still, as the selections show, there are extremely important distinctions and differences of emphasis in the two roles; it is equally important to analyze these separately as a means of building a more meaningful final synthesis about our encounters with the mass media.

The subsections in each major part are a further tool of organization in pursuing this analytical approach. In each part, Section I gives the overview. From a variety of perspectives—journalism, criticism, political science, sociology, psychology, anthropology—these readings give the backgrounds and suggest the major contemporary theories and approaches. Section II (not included in Part 1) then implements these theories and approaches with discussions of individual media; Section III furnishes more personalized critiques and interpretations of specific cases, issues, and media events.

The materials and their organization can guide the reader to a greater understanding of such significant media matters as the roles and influences of the media, their methods and performances, their relationship to political life and private life, to the public and to individuals. With this guide, he can sharpen his skills as a member of the media audience, learning to make more valuable use of the media, to read and view intelligently and sensitively, and to judge with valid critical standards the performances of the media.

The student reader and viewer is also a writer. These selections can act as models or subject matter for his own writing about the media, as well as provide a valuable sampling of writing styles and rhetorical strategies. In addition, Part 4 supplies questions and topics and a bibliography for further study, analysis, research, and writing. In it, both sets of materials are organized to match the categories of the parts and sections of the text; but since all such categorizing is somewhat artificial, a little over-all skimming and cross-checking should prove one further aid in moving from analysis to synthesis.

I am grateful to all those whose comments and detailed critiques of the first edition have lead to many of the general and specific improvements in this edition. I would like specifically to thank, here publicly: Ronald Gottesman, the University of Wisconsin; T. J. Ross, Fairleigh Dickinson; Frank Miceli, Jersey City State College; Clyde Tracy, Meramec Community College; William B. Martin, Tarelton State College; Sarah Beth McCurdy, Louisiana State University; Carol Doig, Shoreline Community College.

A. C.

Santa Monica, California
November 1972

Contents

PART 4: FOR FURTHER STUDY, ANALYSIS,
AND RESEARCH

INDEXES

Mass Media
and
Society

I. Backgrounds and Perspectives

If the mass media affect society and social values, they build this effect through their impact on individuals. These individuals—all of us—may not be the victimized mass—alienated, fragmented, powerless against the tyrannical forces of the media—envisioned by earlier media critics. But neither are they, *we*, immune from the influences of the predominant systems of communication and our encounters with them. The common denominator of these contemporary systems—whether print, electronic, verbal, visual, or aural—is that they are designed for mass audiences. For all their differences, they possess similarities in the patterns of their procedures, the forms of their delivery, their content, and their degree of intensity. And for all of our individual idiocyncrasies and defenses, we do interact with this mass situation of communication. To the degree that our values and attitudes, our very perceptions of the world and ourselves are shaped by the unique qualities of this mass communication experience, its processes and impacts, we are, indeed, mass man.

All of the selections in this book serve to delineate these qualities, processes, impacts; the two pieces in this opening section provide an overall initial definition of the ways in which media interact with and affect individuals and society. In the selection from their important basic book on the processes of mass communication, William Rivers and Wilbur Schramm supply a lucid condensation of the classic explanation of this interaction in the areas of culture and information. In his article, Paul Baran then conjectures about the way technological advances and modifications of the current systems will both intensify and change this basic interaction and influence important phases of our personal, social, and political lives.

The Impact
of
Mass Media

William Rivers and Wilbur Schramm

Most of us depend upon mass-communication products for a large majority of all the information and entertainment we receive during life. It is especially obvious that what we know about public figures and public affairs is largely dependent upon what the mass media tell us. We are always subject to journalism and incapable of doing much about it. We can see too little for ourselves. Days are too short and the world is too big and complex for anyone to be sure of much about the web of government. What most of us think we know is not known at all in the sense of experience and observation.

We get only occasional firsthand glimpses of government by catching sight for a moment of a presidential candidate in the flesh, by shaking hands with a Senator (or talking with one while he absently shakes hands with someone else), by doing business with the field offices of federal agencies, dickering with the Internal Revenue Service—all the little bits and pieces of contact with officialdom that are described, too grandly, as "citizen participation in government."

We learn more at second hand—from friends, acquaintances, and lecturers on hurried tours, especially those who have just come from Washington or the state capital and are eager to impart what they consider, perhaps erroneously, to be the real story of what is going on there.

Yet this is sketchy stuff, and it adds only patches of color to the mosaic. The expanse of our knowledge of public affairs must come from the mass media. There simply are no practical alternatives. The specialists are, for the most part, in the same condition as the lay citizen. The professor of political science who devotes six months to studying municipal government in France will develop from the experience a more precise knowledge which he can pass on to his students when he returns to the classroom, and to his colleagues through scholarly articles. But in the context of the vast

From pp. 14–28 in "The Impact of Mass Communication" from *Responsibility in Mass Communication,* rev. ed., by William L. Rivers and Wilbur Schramm. Copyright © by the National Council of the Churches of Christ in the U.S.A. Copyright © 1957 by The Federal Council of the Churches of Christ in America. Reprinted by permission of Harper & Row, Publishers, Inc.

sweep of happenings over the world, his study is narrow—and by the time he returns to deliver his lectures and write his articles, the contemporary study he made is part of yesterday. Like the layman, he must learn of today through the mass media. Clearly, all of us live in a synthetic world, and the synthesis is fashioned largely from information supplied through mass communication.

This is one of the chief functions of mass communication, then: It *helps us to watch the horizon*, much as the ancient messenger once did. No longer depending on the running messenger or the distant drum, we watch the horizon through news bulletins or on-the-scene broadcasts or advertisements of opportunities.

Mass communication *helps us to correlate our response* to the challenges and opportunities which appear on the horizon and to *reach consensus* on social actions. In a real sense, tribal actions and town meetings have given way to mass communication, which enables us to read the rival arguments, see the rival candidates, and judge the issues.

Mass communication *helps us to transmit the culture* of our society to new members. We have always had teaching at the mother's knee and imitation of the father—and we still have. For thousands of years we have had schools of some kind. But mass communication has entered into this function by supplying textbooks, teaching films and programs, and a constant picturing of the roles and accepted mores of our society for both native Americans and immigrants. A large group of immigrants were once asked, "How did you first learn what American life was like?" Some of them had received letters from relatives, but their chief source was the picture magazine. "How did you get your first English lessons?" They answered, "From your movies."

Mass communication *helps entertain us*. The ballad singer, the dancer, and the traveling theater—even the pitchman—had gone on television, radio, and films. The storytellers of old are chiefly in print.

Finally, mass communication *helps sell goods and services*, and thus keeps our economic system healthy. We once listened for the town crier's advertisements, the word-of-mouth tidings of bargains, the bells of the traveling store-wagon—none very different from the practices of tribal times. Now we read the ads in newspapers and magazines, see them on television, and hear them on radio.

Does it make a difference that we now see so much of the world through the mass media? Marshall McLuhan and Harold Innis, the Canadian philosophers and critics of communication, argue that it certainly does. Oral cultures, they say, were time-bound; the people with power were those who could remember the past, its laws and lessons. When man invented printing, he moved into a space-bound culture. There was no longer any need to worry about remembering the past, for its records could now be stored conveniently on paper; the men with power in a media culture are those who know the most about the present and have the facilities to manipulate it. Before the age of printing, man saw the world with all his senses, three-dimensionally, realistically. Through printing, he saw it only with his eyes, and in an abstracted, linear, sequential form. Printed language very probably acts as a filter for reality. It gives some of its own form to life. Television, on the other hand, is a step back toward the oral culture. It merely extends man's eyes and ears, and lets him see reality much as he used to before Gutenberg. This is what McLuhan means when he says that television is "retribalizing" us.

We may now be at one of the great turning points of communication history. With machines that bring us incomparably more information, from farther away, than ever before, we are again becoming accustomed to looking at the distant environment without the interpretive filters of print. For some years now we have become accustomed to seeing our candidates on television rather than merely reading about them. We participated as a nation, by means of television, in the tragic events of November, 1963, and in similarly terrible events of 1968. The Vietnam war is the first war we have seen extensively on television.

For four centuries, until recently, we followed reality from left to right across a printed page. Most of our codes and standards of reporting on the environment have been formed from our experience with print. Are they still applicable to the audio-visual reporting on which we increasingly depend?

The media themselves thus have an effect, and the way we use them, the messages we put through them, also have an effect. Let us review some of the things we have learned about how communication has an effect on people.

We might begin with a homely little scene:

Mrs. A looks suspiciously at her husband, who is deep in a detective story while she is telling him the neighborhood news. She concludes her story abruptly: "And the horse ate up all our children."

"That's fine, dear," he says after a moment.

"Henry, did you hear a word I said?" she demands indignantly.

"No, dear," he says absently, turning the page.

Communication has to clear four hurdles: it must (1) attract attention, (2) be accepted, (3) be interpreted, and (4) be stored for use.

In this sad little story—it might happen to any of us!—the process of informing failed to clear the very first hurdle: it did not get attention. Millions of messages of all kinds die similarly. All of us go through life surrounded by messages, so many more than our senses can attend to or our nervous systems handle that we must defend ourselves by paying attention—or perceiving—selectively.

One way to determine how individuals select information is to think of a "fraction of selection," which might be represented as

$$\frac{\text{expectation of reward}}{\text{effort thought to be required}} = \text{likelihood of selection}$$

The likelihood that a receiver will attend to a message is enhanced when the reward is greater and the effort smaller. This helps to explain why television has made such a dent in movie attendance (less effort is required to enjoy programs at home), why jamming does not entirely stop the listening to foreign short-wave broadcasts (some listeners want very badly to hear them), and why the use of public libraries falls off so sharply after the teen years (the effort becomes much greater). The limitation of this approach is that it implies a rationality that does not always bulk large in the process of selection. Surely much selection is accidental: A person quite often "just happens" to be where he can attend to a given message. Some selection is impulsive. Much is the result of role patterns or habits learned from obscure experience. It is important to remember, however, that over the years a person tends to seek the kinds of communication that have rewarded him in the past—his favorite television programs, his favorite columnists, the advisers he trusts. He has, therefore, a built-in expectation of reward developed from looking in certain places. Beyond that, he tends, other things being equal, to select the cues to information which are close at hand and easy to find in the glut of communication.

Advertisers and other professional communicators try to make their messages appear more rewarding by appealing to the needs and interests of their intended audience—some of the appeals, like the beauties who advertise soft drinks, are quite remote from the rewards their users are actually likely to enjoy from accepting the product. They try to lure acceptance by making their messages stand out with large headlines or color or pictures or cleverness or repetition, and by saturating the channels. They also try to present their messages so as to eliminate noise and interference. One technique is to build in redundancy where it is necessary. When points are obscure, repetitions and examples are used to make them clear. In international news cables, important words are often repeated to negate the possibility that they will be garbled in transmission: "WILL NOT—REPEAT NOT—ACCEPT TERMS," the cable reads, and no editor ever upbraids a correspondent for that kind of redundancy.

Once the message has been presented as well as possible, the sender can do little more than be alert to feedback from the receiver. A skilled speaker, for example, can "read" his audience and adjust his communication accordingly. Although it is no longer possible to sharpen the message that has been sent, he can still add to it or correct it. And there is always the next time.

Then it rests with the receiver. If he attends to the message, he must decide whether to accept it. His acceptance will depend largely on the apparent validity of the message and on his judgment of the sender's credibility or prestige. A well-known experiment in attitude change once used a series of messages about the President of the United States which varied from very favorable to very unfavorable. One of them said that the President favored communism. The experimental audience laughed and refused to accept that message because of its lack of face validity. On the other hand, many readers would accept a rather shocking news item in a distinguished newspaper like the *New York Times* because of the *Times*'s reputation for accuracy.

A person who accepts a message will interpret it as his stored-up experience and his built-in values dictate, for he can interpret only in terms of the responses he has learned. We tend to interpret new experience, if possible, in ways that fit with old experience and accepted values. This, of course, sometimes leads to distortion—often to selecting the parts of a message that fit comfortably and discarding the rest.

How this works is suggested by a well-intended communication which went awry when a certain educational administrator was subjected to very serious charges by a local newspaper. A distinguished academic committee investigated and reported that the charges were without foundation. There had merely been, the committee members reported, "a failure of communication" in the administrator's department. They saw this as a vindication of the administrator (after all, what department has not sometimes suffered communication failures?). But the newspaper paid little attention to the acquittal, and trumpeted for weeks the fact that the committee had found a "failure of communication" involving the administrator. Ultimately, the administrator resigned. The chagrined committee members realized that they (the senders) and the newspaper (the receiver) had approached that communication with different purposes. They had thought to explain the trouble and to indicate that it was not serious. The newspaper, however, was out to get the administrator, and simply seized upon that part of the message that would further its purpose.

The process of informing, then, is not at all simple. In fact, it involves so many problems and pitfalls that the constant flow of relatively accurate information in human society may seem almost miraculous. Here is another little scene:

"What do you think T. S. Eliot really meant by 'The Hollow Men'?" asks Miss A, who is a high school senior.

"I don't know," her brother answers. "Why doesn't he write so that there's no question what he means?"

"It wouldn't be any fun if he did," says Miss A.

This exchange indicates the different ground rules which operate when the goal of the communication process is entertaining rather than informing. True, entertaining communication must get over the same hurdles. The message must be presented so as to be interpretable within the experience of the audience; it must appeal to audience needs and interests; and it must, so far as possible, be designed to avoid the hazards of noise and interference. That is, it must gain attention, be accepted, and be interpreted. Feedback is at least as important in entertainment as in informing; in live entertainment it is the crucial element—the artist fits his act to his audience, or he fails—and in media entertainment it is so important that broadcasters spend millions of dollars every year to learn about their audiences. The chief difference lies in the unwritten contract between sender and receiver. In informational communication, the sender is to be a good reporter, and the audience is to bring to the experience a reality-seeking and reality-testing mood. Entertainment, however, requires of the receivers a certain willing suspension of disbelief. Instead of reacting skeptically to anything that checks poorly with their picture of reality, members of the entertainment audience must be willing to go along with a story or a spoof or a joke, or to agonize and rejoice with a character who never lived or never could live. Instead of expecting simple, clear, unambiguous writing, they may be pleased with a certain level of artistic ambiguity and a host of latent meanings.

The entertainer may be expected to be more concerned with form than is the informational communicator. *How* he writes or speaks or moves is expected to give pleasure. He is usually imaginative rather than utilitarian, prizes rich writing over clear writing, and must expertly turn a phrase or build a scene. In short, although informational communication may be artistic, and although entertainment communication may present a picture of reality, the thrust of informing asks for the skill of the reporter, and the thrust of entertaining asks for the skill of the artist.

The receiver of entertainment communication is expected to be willing to identify with one or more of the characters, put himself in their places, feel with them. In poetry and modern painting, he is expected to enjoy ambiguity rather than be frustrated by it. Indeed, there is reason to believe that resolving ambiguities is one of our most pleasurable experiences, perhaps because so much pride is involved. One who understands James Joyce's *Ulysses* certainly develops a measure of pride. One who understands a joke is almost surely pleased, at least in part, because he "got it." (And it may be that jokes which must be explained cannot be funny because the necessity to have them explained robs the listener of his pride.) But it is also true that the question "What did the author mean?" is shunned by most modern writers and many modern teachers in favor of "What did the author mean to *you*?" . . .

Like informational communication, persuasive communication must get the message through, but that is rarely enough. To accomplish any substantial change, persuasion must control a psychological process in the receiver. It must set in motion some psychological dynamics by which the receiver will, in effect, change himself. In the example just given, the communication got through and set something going, all right, but it was the wrong thing.

It is not necessarily difficult to implant new attitudes or encourage new behavior in a new area, of course. If our first contingent of astronauts should return from the moon with an account of dangerous and hostile little green men, we would be easily persuaded to view this new threat with alarm. After all, we do not now have much in our mental files on the subject of moon men. However, if we had long known of the moon men and had long held attitudes toward them, changing the attitudes would be difficult. For when a strong area is attacked directly, the message is likely to be rejected or distorted.

Consider the situation in which persuasion occurs. Unlike entertainment and instructional communication, persuasion involves no contract between sender and receiver. The sender is on his own. He must choose the information and package it to fit his goals. He may attract attention by entertainment (the programs accompanying the commercials), by saturating the perceptual field (big type, loud commercials, parades, rallies), by big names and big events. He can advance arguments, make threats, offer rewards. *Caveat emptor!*

The receiver comes with his defenses up, prepared to be skeptical. He has experienced persuasion before. He asks, "What is there for *me* in this message?" He comes with a set of needs he wants to satisfy. He already has a set of beliefs and attitudes; some are relatively flexible but many he is prepared to defend stubbornly. He comes with a set of personal relationships and loyalties, and he feels deeply dependent on many of them. He comes with a set of perceptions of opportunity and threat in the environment and is not prepared to change them without persuasive evidence. On balance, the persuasion situation is a buyer's, not a seller's, market.

The receiver's needs, his beliefs and attitudes, his personal relationships, and his perception of the environment are all interdependent. A substantial change in one is likely to bring about a change in others. If, for example, the astronauts should bring back a convincing account of hostile moon men, this would substantially change our perception of the kind of threat that exists in our environment. In turn, this might lead us to think of other earthlings as allies rather than as enemies or competitors; to reorganize our goal patterns and our priorities for using resources; to rethink our concepts of the universe and of man's position in it.

The process of persuasion, so far as it is primarily a *communication process* (as distinguished, for example, from the use of force), consists of introducing information which leads the receiver to reappraise his perception of his environment, and through that to reappraise his needs and his ways of meeting them, or his social relationships, or his beliefs and attitudes. Perhaps the closest we have come to the kind of change that might be brought about by discovery of dangerous little moon men is the notorious panic caused by Orson Welles's radio broadcast, in 1938, of a dramatization of "The Invasion from Mars." The more susceptible listeners believed that invaders were actually sweeping all before them. Suddenly, their environmental support seemed to be crumbling, and with it their confidence in law and order and national power. Their need for self-preservation took control, and they fled to the hills.

Although the conscious use of threats to arouse the need for self-preservation can initiate a process of change, this has been shown to be a two-edged sword. In a famous experiment, researchers were somewhat surprised to find that lesser threats concerning tooth decay accomplished more than strong threats to send their experimental subjects to the toothbrush and the dentist. Later experiments showed that when the threat was too unpleasant, and especially when the cure was remote or difficult or uncertain, the whole topic was often repressed—swept under the rug. This may have been one of the reasons why the campaign against cigarette smoking was relatively ineffective. The prospect of lung cancer was so frightening, the cure so uncertain, the entire relation of smoking to cancer so befogged by counterclaims, that it was easier to change an old habit slightly (switching to a filter) and repress the picture of cancer than to make greater changes. (One of the most dramatic changes in product marketing did result from the campaign against cigarette smoking. Nonfilter cigarettes, which had always led the filters in sales, fell well behind.) Apparently, threats must be made in a low key unless one can offer a clear and certain remedy. Advertisers are usually careful to offer a carrot even as they brandish the stick: They suggest the horrors of bad breath, but they emphasize that it can be purged with Little Miracle Mouthwash, and that social joys are then available.

A change process can be triggered by altering a receiver's perception of his social relationships. Every salesman tries to establish himself as a friend of the prospective buyer. Many of the most successful evangelists place a new convert in a group of believers at once so that his decision will be socially reinforced. Many advertisements hold out the implied hope of being able to join an admired group—"men of distinction" or the sponsors of a paricular cause or the effervescent "Pepsi Generation."

One of the patterns which the Chinese have been reported to use in attempts at brainwashing involves both removing old social support and providing new support. A military captive is removed from his officers—and thus from his authority structure—and ultimately from his fellow P.O.W.'s—his friendship group. He is allowed to receive no mail from home, and is told that other captives have informed on him. These actions remove the social support for the values and behavior patterns the Chinese hope to change. Then the captive is placed in a small group where other captives are studying communist doctrine and writing "confessions" of their former "errors." He is rewarded and socially supported for every step he takes in the desired direction, and encouraged to build new friendships among converts. Obviously, so radical a change as persuading a soldier to give up his loyalty to his country is not accomplished very often, but the process is strong: (1) it undermines confidence in existing social relationships and (2) offers new relationships that (3) reward one for desired opinions and behavior.

Another tactic is to build cross pressures. If a man can be convinced that two groups he values, or two advisers he trusts, disagree completely on the point at issue, he will be vulnerable to a suggestion that seems to offer a way out of the conflict.

One of the most powerful processes available to persuasive communication is what we might call the strain toward consistency, Human beings strive for balance between what they know and believe and do. Suppose, now, that a persuasive message can push its way into cognitive areas that are relatively lightly defended. And suppose that this new information is out of balance with the present position, but not so far out of balance as to be rejected. For example, suppose it says that some admired individual or group holds a position that is inconsistent with the person's present position; or that a new position is not really inconsistent with his own, but rather a development of it. Then there is some reason to hope that the individual may reorganize and change some of his more strongly held positions in order to attain consistency.

On the Impact
of the New Communications Media
upon Social Values

Paul Baran

INTRODUCTION

The challenge of describing the manner in which new electrical communications are modifying society and its values resembles the one facing an ant approaching an overripe watermelon: it is appetizing but overwhelming. The task is more a career than a paper. Not having comprehensiveness

Reprinted, with permission, from a symposium "Communications: Part I" appearing in *Law and Contemporary Problems* (Vol. 34, No. 2, Spring 1969), published by the Duke University School of Law, Durham, North Carolina. Copyright, 1969, by Duke University.

as a possible choice, we must settle for consideration of only a few of the directions of change which are being and will be wrought by electrical communications. To retain perspective on what follows the reader should remember that the evolving electrical communications technology is only one factor—though a major one—among many bringing on a markedly changed society. The all-pervasive nature of the more powerful communications media is unique, especially when we use the term "electrical communications" in a broad sense to include efficient use of computers and the automation of mechanical systems, both of which would be impossible if it were not for the new communications technology.

To see better where we may be going, let us assume that the technological developments in this field which seem theoretically possible today are in fact accomplished in the future. If we use the future as a vantage point we can speak from a stance which will permit us a better vision of ourselves as a society. To do otherwise is to be too close to the phenomenon. We would be like the puzzled ant who, bobbing on a leaf in a storm, wonders what is happening to his world.[1] We seek to learn where our leaf is falling—or at least to learn the nature, magnitude, and direction of the winds of change.

But before we can take this broader view, we should at least attempt to satisfy our proclivity toward the more narrow—toward identifying specific developments in communications technology which even today suggest coming changes.

THE CHANGING COMMUNICATIONS TECHNOLOGY

Listing such developments is not difficult. Nor would it be difficult to combine them to produce the outlines of a scenario for change. Six points in particular would stand out in this scenario:

1. The full range of new communications services suggested by even the more wide-eyed people in the field generally appears to be technically possible (if one is not overly fussy about cost).

2. If cost is a matter of initial concern, comfort is restored by noting that prices of most systems components are rapidly dropping.

3. Lack of bandwidth is not the problem most believe it to be. All the transmission bandwidth one would ever want, together with lower cost communications terminals, computers, and similar hardware, appear to be in the cards.

4. Technology is rarely a binding constraint for new communications applications in the future.

---

[1] The recurrence of the ant simile may suggest both the author's perspective on his subject and his apprehensions about our future society.

5. There are more serious, *self-made* constraints—lack of entrepreneurial effort, copyright laws, common carrier regulations, antiquated frequency allocations, and the like—most of them institutional issues. But even man succumbs to reason. And as he does, these impediments will erode or diminish.

6. Avoiding the question of precise dates of availability, discussions of the implications of the new communications services possible may proceed without excessive concern for technological detail.

It takes only a limited imagination to visualize the new services. Yes, we probably will have person-to-person, large-screen TV in every home. Yes, we almost certainly will have data banks and similar products of progress. Yes, we will, if we wish, have the completely portable wrist watch telephone always with us, even in our most private retreats, for those among us whose time is so important that none can be wasted in doing only one thing at a time. Rather than dwell upon the technical details of such wonderful technological blessings to mankind, consider instead their social effects—for example, the portable telephone that rings at just the wrong time, and with a wrong number.

THE MESSAGE IS MORE IMPORTANT THAN THE MEDIUM

We Are What We Eat

Some nutritionists hold that the physical structure and well-being of an individual are to some degree determined by the food he eats—particularly at the earliest stages of body growth. There is a parallel in the observation that children grow socially. And this growth is to an increasing degree being derived from the mass media—especially the visual mass media. The value formation process proceeds most rapidly at the earliest stages of life. Here there are no fixed values to modify, only new ones to be added.

In our culture we tend almost completely to ignore the scope, effectiveness, and all-pervasive social conditioning that occurs to the younger recipient of the constant barrage from the mass media. This point, which can be disputed only in its particulars, is one we shall come back to from time to time in what follows.

The immediate changes that we will discuss will include those brought about by such services as the checkless-cashless society, the bookless library, the electric plug in the home that provides access to all the world's knowledge, and similar overpublicized possibilities. The changed life patterns that may result are both more obvious and less significant than the subtle changes in society's value structure inadvertently wrought by those whose interest is to keep the channels occupied and not to worry overmuch about content.

Message Versus Medium Effects; Random Versus Programmed Values

It is helpful to distinguish between media effects and message effects. For example, when TV arrived, children spent a little less time reading and sleeping. This was a *medium* effect. But when teeny boppers watch the Beatles or Ed Sullivan's program one year and fathers wonder why in hell their sons won't get a haircut five years later—this is a *message* effect.

Our historic insensitivity to message effects is unfortunate. It may be the single most important factor in determining the future value structure of our society. There are several reasons for this almost universal apathy. Cause and its delayed effects are not unambiguously related; the effects are nonlinear. And we tend to hold an almost unquestioning belief that control of our media is synonymous with loss of a constitutionally guaranteed freedom proclaimed first and foremost in the Bill of Rights.

A child who watches murder on TV rarely acts out his lesson. But there is a growing, gnawing doubt about what *may* be happening to the child's later sensitivity to violence. But it is not clear. It is like cigarette smoking. At one time, we had reason to suspect that it probably wasn't good for you. But in the absence of "proof-positive," as the cigarette commercials once said, though in a different context, the right to smoke cigarettes remained "good." And public policy seeks to promote that which is "good." Even today, when our knowledge is more complete, the overwhelming predominance of medical evidence makes an insufficient case to reverse past beliefs. There is an escalation of the level of proof required to modify earlier decisions. Collective minds reconsider neither easily nor rapidly. While the new communications have the potential to fill the child's (or adult's) input communication channel to capacity well before we realize what has happened, we have yet to see a public appreciation that the remedy—restructuring beliefs—will be very much more difficult than creating them initially.

The Coming Showdown

As a society we face a period of a loss of innocence when it dawns upon us that individuals are programmed to behave with a set of values acquired primarily in very early youth, and that even today the greatest input component to the formation of these values is by electrical communications. This day will not occur until we seriously consider the nature of the message between the lines of TV and other fare. Only then will we appreciate the full significance of programming designed foremost for the commercial benefit of advertisers and its impact upon the resulting fundamental values of the following generation of society. This day is probably not near because someone will first have to prove beyond a shadow of a doubt (1) that our value system is acquired and not God-given, (2) that it is very much subject to societal guidance through communications, and (3) that tampering with it is not as bad as leaving it alone.

We face a dilemma. We as a nation prefer a laissez-faire attitude toward content control of our media. This attitude may be a response to our awareness of repugnant dictatorial governments and religions which perpetuate themselves by blatantly distorting facts and conditioning values by control of information. We thus wish to believe that any development of values by accident is better than any indoctrination by governmental intent. Yet the hidden messages inflicted upon the very young are not at all random. They are sufficiently correlated (in the mathematical sense) that they possess the necessary consistency and frequency to form a potent conditioning force for value indoctrination. Of course, we are not *certain* of the precise nature and extent of the values being inculcated, and we therefore tend to regard program content as if it were neutral in its impact.

In the following we shall consider some of the new forces of change upon various sectors of society. We shall concentrate on communications *media* phenomena rather than *message* phenomena of the sort we have just been discussing. While the capability of message transfer is markedly increased over anything that we have yet seen, it is still the *content* of the message that will more substantially determine how future new electrical communications will change our life. But this cannot be understood without a better insight into the new electronics media themselves.

SOME VIGNETTES OF CHANGE

The following sketches suggest the nature of changes occurring, caused in large measure by the new communications. No attempt is made to be all-inclusive.

International Relations

THE END OF THE ALL-EVIL ENEMY   TV has breached the privacy needed to conduct an old-fashioned, highly dedicated war. The war in Vietnam is probably the first instance where this country faced an enemy not universally composed of all-evil men. Few American political leaders have ever been anxious to fight a war. To ask that it be fought in a goldfish bowl may be asking too much of them in the future.

THE END OF EFFECTIVE STRATEGIC MILITARY SECRECY   Electrical signals emanating from the communications networks of each major country are fair game for remote satellite antennae. Most of the strategic military effectiveness of a closed society's secrecy is lost through transmitting information over electrical communications channels. Electrical communications channels tend to be leaky. Further, the new mass communications media which allow the public access to a wide diversity of viewpoints have made maintenance of military secrets virtually impossible. Military procedures and national laws have yet to acknowledge this reality.

DEVELOPED COUNTRIES TOGETHER—UNDERDEVELOPED APART   The new communications capacity is not uniformly distributed. Like world wealth, "them that got, get." Conversely, those that have little may expect to get less. The more highly developed nations are also those with this new, powerful communications capacity. The underdeveloped nations have relatively less. Hence, the developed and underdeveloped nations have another divisive force to spread their interests farther apart.

National Affairs

MERCHANDISING POLITICAL CANDIDATES   Within the last thirty years, man has wrested more understanding of the techniques to change people's minds voluntarily than is found in all the tomes or rhetoric of recorded history. In a world where "technological fallout" is highly regarded, the short and obvious jump from selling soap to selling politicians will be natural and swift. Even today we see commercial organizations which will substitute, for a fee, their own pre-tested words for those of a candidate. The success of these organizations in winning an election has yet to be acknowledged by those responsible for preservation of our election process. It is embarrassing to a democracy to admit that the thirty to forty percentage points determining the outcome of a major election can be bought from public relations firms—firms that are not famous for their prudent selectivity or high ethical concerns. With better communications and computers these distorters of reality have increasing power to create candidates and to reach new heights, or depths, of subtle demagoguery: Starting with lots of money, they can buy an actor, add makeup, program him with a computer-prepared script based upon the populace's latest fears (earlier induced by the same mass electrical communications), and broadcast ten-second film clips ad nauseam until the polls predict success.

THE DEMONSTRATION IN LIEU OF THE VOTE   This coupling of financial and electronic resources to win elections has a possibly not accidental parallel in the new use of the violent demonstrations as a force to subvert representative democracy. One game is for the rich, while the other is open to all irresponsible comers, but both reflect the understanding that to preserve or to change institutions requires political power.

In a highly communicative world, access to the communications broadcast resource is partially equivalent to political power. The temptation for national governments to exercise power by controlling the communications media is old stuff—but not in the United States. However, the sale of TV time for political advantage is equivalent to a conversion of economic power into political power. Similarly, TV's insatiable appetite for visible dramatic news provides the mechanism whereby the demonstration—or, more accurately, the staged riot—can convert political zeal and energy into political support by galvanizing sympathies or inspiring fears and guilt.

TV news today is a form of entertainment. Entertainment seeks audience size. The visually dramatic overweighs balance and importance. The staged riot is remarkably cheap for the rioters. In "cost effectiveness" jargon it allows a maximum return of political power at lowest dollar investment cost if the issues of long-term societal costs are ignored. By its nature the tactic of staged riot seems reserved for minority use, though the majority has an analogous advantage in the availability of free and purchased TV time for its own activities.

A NEW DIFFICULTY IN ACHIEVING NATIONAL COHESION   A stable national government requires a measure of cohesion of the ruled. Such cohesion can be derived from an implicit mutual agreement on goals and direction—or even on the processes of determining goals and direction. With the diversity of information channels available, there is a growing ease of creating groups having access to distinctly differing models of reality, *without overlap*. For example, nearly every ideological group, from the student underground to the John Birchers, now has its own newspapers. Imagine a world in which there is a sufficient number of TV channels to keep each group, and in particular the less literate and tolerant members of the groups, wholly occupied? Will members of such groups ever again be able to talk meaningfully to one another? Will they ever obtain at least some information through the same filters so that their images of reality will overlap to some degree? Are we in danger of creating by electrical communications such diversity within society as to remove the commonness of experience necessary for human communication, political stability, and, indeed, nationhood itself? Must "confrontation" increasingly be used for human communication?

National political diversity requires good will and intelligence to work comfortably. The new visual media are not an unmixed blessing. This new diversity causes one to hope that the good will and intelligence of the nation is sufficiently broad-based to allow it to withstand the increasing communication pressures of the future.

THE TEMPTATION OF INSTANT PLEBISCITE   Today, most politicians rely on political polls to some measure. There is a potentially unwholesome communications development possible in the improvement of techniques to carry on such polls. We could, if we wish, have the technical capability to poll instantaneously all interested TV viewers to obtain an opinion profile on any issue put before the nation. What underlies the concern about such a development is the almost religious belief among some that everything shown between the commercials on TV is the truth. The subtle differentiation between the image of reality and reality itself is too easily lost when only parts of an issue are selected for presentation. TV writers worship simplicity as a factor contributing to audience size, but a well-staged TV show can nevertheless make many people believe not only that what they have seen is the truth but that they have seen the whole truth. Further, TV audiences probably select themselves on something other than a random or representative basis. These doubts about induced or inherent biases on the part of an electorate assembled by television suggest the dangers of immediate-response polling. From a distance, the restoration of the town-meeting principle by electronic ingenuity may seem to be a normal extension and improvement of the democratic process. But the short fuse of quick response does not allow room for error or for accommodation of majority and minority rights.

We will probably not move into the electronic plebiscite overnight. But the technology is near for a drift in this direction in an evolutionary manner. For example, instant electronic polling on TV will be economically useful for both advertising agencies and politicians in designing their campaigns, and without legislation to prohibit polling the views of large groups, it will seem natural to increase sample size to larger and larger audiences. If there are pushbuttons, they will be pushed, and if some do not have buttons, they will feel underprivileged and impotent. The next step, pushbuttons for all, becomes a plausible evolutionary development, and the last step—if nothing is done to prevent such an outcome—is probably to connect the pushbuttons to the action machine. Our present lack of appreciation of the dangers of this form of political representation is a reminder of our generally poor understanding of the potentialities of electrical communications and their effects on democratic processes.

Local Government

THE END OF THE BOUNDARY-WALLED CITY   With an increasing number of the tasks of the work day performed over communications circuits, there is a lessening need for people to congregate together to conduct the business of the world. The circle in which potential person-to-person conversation is possible increases when physical presence is not required. All who speak the same language in the world of electrical communications become neighbors, regardless of geographical distance. A new worldwide city of ideas is created whose boundaries do not coincide with the historic limits of the city. Tall office buildings will no longer be required as proximity becomes less and less a function of geography. The new communications capability will blur the distinction between urban and suburban existence.

The eventual large-scale substitution of communications for transportation is sufficiently predictable to require total re-examination of our concept of the city and its growth. When the full impact of the substitution is felt, it could mean the elimination of much which the city of today offers, indeed of its very *raison d'être*—ease of communications and transportation and access to more people and activities than is possible in a less dense area. Present cities could become as uneconomic and as anachronistic as the small farm in the era of the mechanization of agriculture. Left almost solely to the uses of those who cannot fully participate in the communications revolution the cities may become more poverty-ridden than we currently anticipate. Those whose assets are tied to the large city may have a more precarious investment than they realize.

LACK OF A FEEDBACK CHANNEL   Techniques to inform the public about what the government is doing are improving. Even today we overload or satiate most citizens with information on what the mayor is or is not doing. This is *downward* communication. One of the most pressing communications needs is for a good *upward* channel. For example, the slum dweller who listens and sees the mayor talking to him on television lacks any effective channel of communication upward to ask the mayor why his garbage has not been collected, or why the dope peddlers are so thick in his apartment lobby that he can hardly get into his own apartment.

This flood of news flowing downward and the felt lack of an upward channel of reply can be expected to worsen in the near term. We need an information feedback channel to assure the citizen that his specific message (not the group response) has, in fact, been received by the power structure. Failure to supply such a channel would appear to guarantee alienation from the political process. No one has yet seriously considered providing the ombudsman junction electrically. Yet in the large cities it may be the only realistic course open.

Vocational Pursuits and Power Structures

THE EROSION OF ROUTINE ADMINISTRATIVE AND CLERICAL FUNCTIONS The nature of employment is changing. An increasing portion of the average employee's day is spent on information transfer, and less on the physical production of goods. Better electrical communications and computers could allow increasing automation of administration and clerical functions. Many middle and lower middle management personnel may be expected to follow the clerks and production workers on their way out as their information-gathering and dissemination functions are assumed by computers linked to the outside world by the new communications. This is not to say that unemployment will result, only that major shifts of employment patterns will occur. New jobs will open as old ones disappear. For example, consider the following:

ELIMINATION OF THE MIDDLEMAN IN THE INFORMATION PROCESS Many of today's jobs are concerned with distorting information presented to the consumer. Slippery-tongued salesmen survived the invention of electrical communications, although their functions have been somewhat altered in the electronic age. The newer electrical communications between producer and consumer can reduce the need for some such middlemen. For example, the new electrical capability could allow precise price, specification, and delivery information to be given directly to the consumer by the computer, thus eliminating the need for some of today's salesmen. If so, the salesmanship of the future will have to be much more subtle—as puffing will be more readily subject to checking. In the future we will have the technical capability—whether or not it is used is another matter—to obtain the facts needed for better product comparison than today. We may even anticipate that manufacturing organizations will choose to sell products directly to the individual consumer, utilizing two-way TV connections and reducing the role of the army of intermediaries. New product comparison services, which can be addressed at the time of the selection decision, can be made economically viable with the new communications.

There is a remarkable number of other jobs that might be eliminated or modified by reliable, cheap communications and a well-programmed computer. Even an entire profession could be made obsolete. For example, the pharmacist, who in this age largely relabels packages or medicines, now serves little useful purpose other than as a check on the physician's honesty, a job that computers might adequately perform. Computer diagnosis and patient monitoring, often carried out by distant computers accessible by communications networks, may greatly change medical practice, perhaps eliminating nurses' jobs and freeing doctors for other pursuits.

Communications developments also threaten the "middle management" of society's past value-setting organizations: the clergy and the teachers. Even today the local clergyman does not seem nearly so all-knowing as he did during the last century. The diversity and often greater wisdom exhibited by a plurality of alternative commentaries on morals—on the radio and TV—is powerful competition. The work of the clergyman, as a distributor of moral wisdom, and of the teacher, as dispenser of education, has to some degree already been displaced by electronic channels. If it were not for their continuing service as an "upward" communications channel, many of these would have already been forced to turn to other endeavors. In the future, we may expect to see representatives of the familiar old professions, but their actual roles may have drastically changed from that of esteemed professionals.

One wonders if career choices of the young are adequately informed by an awareness of the impact of the new communications and the computer.

THE RICHEST MAN IN THE FUTURE WORLD As communication development evolves, more decision functions will be placed upon computers tied together as a common communications network. Financial success may in the future come to depend more upon the the brilliance and imagination of the human who programs the computer than upon any other single factor. The key man in the new power elite will be the one who can best program a computer, that is, the person who makes the best use of the available information and the computer's skills in formulating a problem. In a world where knowledge is power, and where communications mean access to power, he who can most effectively utilize this access will be in the driver's seat. Some persons (primarily computer programmers) claim that the richest man in the world in the year 2000 will be a computer programmer. This may sound outlandish, but few really good programmers laugh when they consider this assertion.

Education and Leisure

REVISED ROLE OF THE SCHOOL—ADMITTING TO THE BABY-SITTER ROLE   The new communications media, coupled with computers, will be capable of presenting more subject matter than the student can ever be fed in conventional schooling. However, this does not mean the demise of the conventional school and the substitution of the home TV screen. The teacher can still perform functions which we have not yet learned to automate, such as baby-sitting. Few parents will willingly pass up such cheap, safe baby-sitting services. It remains to be seen whether teachers will assume a greater role in the interpersonal educational experience and thus avoid technological obsolescence. Here, the human teacher has advantages that cannot be matched by a communications device.

THE NEW LEISURE   If historic trends continue, most individuals will have more disposable time and income. Some students of this trend look toward the computer/communications network to absorb the surplus hours and dollars. Recreation via communications lines may turn out to be a major use of the computer of the future. TV games could allow the viewer to participate by telephone/TV, thus enlarging the audience from a few chosen from the in-person audience to all the viewers, perhaps with an intensification of interest.

This new capability for masses to interact in gamelike fashion with a remote computer occurs at a time when the ability to flood people "downward" with information has exploded. Recreation via computers will be one of the few "upward" channels open to all. There is a strong emotional need for the feedback channel in most "electrical communications crowds" to allow people to interact with something.

THE SMALL GROUP BROADCAST   In this new world, individuals with common interests but who are geographically separated can "come together" to discuss or share topics of mutual interest. Everyone, no matter how small his physical community, will be potentially a part of an audience having a more specialized interest than any that can be assembled in any large city today. With the improving communications capability in the future, it will be economic to have smaller and smaller audiences for specialized programs. As institutional barriers to "pay-TV" are overcome and channel space becomes available, untapped markets will be reached, with benefits for all. In addition to theater, ballet, opera, "art" films, lectures, and other activities having less than mass appeal, who knows? We may have small groups around the country using electrical communications of the future to share a common interest in some particularly novel form of pornography. Don't dismiss the idea completely. Nature abhors an empty communications channel.

LIVING WITH THE INFORMATION OVERLOAD Excessive communications could mean a world of too many acquaintances, too few friends, an absence of tranquility, and a life of motion, frantic even by today's standards. Just as the nation is becoming intolerant of air, water, and noise pollution, the next generation may regard information overload not as a God-given process but as a controllable price of civilization. There are signs today of increasing concern for privacy and freedom from intrusion by undesired communications. Some believe that a desire exists for filtering and protective devices to cope with the deluge of requests for attention. For example, selectable telephone ringing signals could allow a caller to say that his call is not urgent, in the event the called party is in the tub, or otherwise occupied.

Without such efforts toward adjustment, we might find a revulsion developing toward an excess of communications. Before this happens, we can hope that those who supply communications channels appreciate the all-pervasive nature of their service and develop new filtering techniques.

POSTSCRIPT

The new communications is like fire, neither villain nor hero. While its role will depend on how it is used, not understanding how it works is indeed equivalent to playing with fire, for its potential for both good and harm is awesome. As an observer, I must confess I am becoming uncomfortable. This may be too powerful a social force to be left to chance in the hope that it will not be abused.

II. Critiques and Cases

The influence and impact of media upon man and society have created sharp crises, and accompanying sharp debates, over advertising and the handling of violence and a greater degree of sexual freedom and license in all media. Besides their timely relevance, arguments on these issues can serve to illustrate the ways in which basic processes of the media operate in concrete cases.

Marya Mannes' article on advertising has a double value. For it not only brings into striking focus the important relationship between commercial patterns and the role and identity of women, but it also casts a wider net in defining some of the more subtle dangers and dilemmas inherent in the advertising process. Similarly, Joseph Morgenstern's look at the current acceleration of violence in both television and movies poses long-range questions and reveals dilemmas pertinent to the nature and extent of media impact and influence.

While Stanley Kauffmann and Alexander Bickel differ in their positions toward pornography, it is important to note their areas of agreement, as well as the precise distinctions that separate their final positions. Both positions take into account the modifications in the vicarious experience of sex produced by the mass nature of today's media, but Bickel uses the differences between the public and private experience as the basis of his advocacy of some degree of control.

Television Advertising: the Splitting Image

Marya Mannes

A bride who looks scarcely fourteen whispers, "Oh, Mom, I'm so *happy!*" while a doting family adjust her gown and veil and a male voice croons softly, "A woman is a harder thing to be than a man. She has more feelings to feel." The mitigation of these excesses, it appears, is a feminine deodorant called Secret, which allows our bride to approach the altar with security as well as emotion.

Eddie Albert, a successful actor turned pitchman, bestows his attention on a lady with two suitcases, which prompt him to ask her whether she has been on a journey, "No," she says, or words to that effect, as she opens the suitcases. "My two boys bring back their soiled clothes every weekend from college for me to wash." And she goes into the familiar litany of grease, chocolate, mud, coffee, and fruit-juice stains, which presumably record the life of the average American male from two to fifty. Mr. Albert compliments her on this happy device to bring her boys home every week and hands her a box of Biz, because "Biz *is* better."

Two women with stony faces meet cart to cart in a supermarket as one takes a jar of peanut butter off a shelf. When the other asks her in a voice of nitric acid why she takes that brand, the first snaps, "Because I'm choosy for my family!" The two then break into delighted smiles as Number Two makes Number One taste Jiffy for "mothers who are choosy."

If you have not come across these dramatic interludes, it is because you are not home during the day and do not watch daytime television. It also means that your intestinal tract is spared from severe assaults, your credibility unstrained. Or, for that matter, you may look at commercials like these every day and manage either to ignore them or find nothing—given the fact of advertising—wrong with them. In that case, you are either so brainwashed or so innocent that you remain unaware of what this daily infusion may have done and is doing to an entire people as the long-accepted adjunct of free enterprise and support of "free" television.

"Given the fact" and "long-accepted" are the key words here. Only socialists, communists, idealists (or the BBC) fail to realize that a mass

Reprinted by permission of Harold Ober Associates Incorporated. Copyright © 1970 by Marya Mannes.

television system cannot exist without the support of sponsors, that the massive cost of maintaining it as a free service cannot be met without the massive income from selling products. You have only to read of the unending struggle to provide financial support for public, noncommercial television for further evidence.

Besides, aren't commercials in the public interest? Don't they help you choose what to buy? Don't they provide needed breaks from programing? Aren't many of them brilliantly done, and some of them funny? And now, with the new sexual freedom, all those gorgeous chicks with their shining hair and gleaming smiles? And if you didn't have commercials taking up a good part of each hour, how on earth would you find enough program material to fill the endless space/time void?

Tick off the yesses and what have you left? You have, I venture to submit, these intangible but possibly high costs: the diminution of human worth, the infusion and hardening of social attitudes no longer valid or desirable, pervasive discontent, and psychic fragmentation.

Should anyone wonder why deception is not an included detriment, I suggest that our public is so conditioned to promotion as a way of life, whether in art or politics or products, that elements of exaggeration or distortion are taken for granted. Nobody really believes that a certain shampoo will get a certain swain, or that an unclogged sinus can make a man a swinger. People are merely prepared to hope it will.

But the diminution of human worth is much more subtle and just as pervasive. In the guise of what they consider comedy, the producers of television commercials have created a loathsome gallery of men and women patterned, presumably, on Mr. and Mrs. America. Women liberationists have a major target in the commercial image of woman flashed hourly and daily to the vast majority. There are, indeed, only four kinds of females in this relentless sales procession: the gorgeous teen-age swinger with bouncing locks; the young mother teaching her baby girl the right soap for skin care; the middle-aged housewife with a voice like a power saw; and the old lady with dentures and irregularity. All these women, to be sure, exist. But between the swinging sex object and the constipated granny there are millions of females never shown in commercials. These are—married or single—intelligent, sensitive women who bring charm to their homes, who work at jobs as well as lend grace to their marriage, who support themselves, who have talents or hobbies or commitments, or who are skilled at their professions.

To my knowledge, as a frequent if reluctant observer, I know of only one woman on a commercial who has a job; a comic plumber pushing Comet. Funny, heh? Think of a dame with a plunger.

With this one representative of our labor force, which is well over thirty million women, we are left with nothing but the full-time housewife in all her whining glory: obsessed with whiter wash, moister cakes, shinier floors, cleaner children, softer diapers, and greaseless fried chicken. In the rare instances when these ladies are not in the kitchen, at the washing machine, or waiting on hubby, they are buying beauty shops (fantasy, see?) to take home so that their hair will have more body. Or out at the supermarket being choosy.

If they were attractive in their obsessions, they might be bearable. But they are not. They are pushy, loud-mouthed, stupid, and—of all things now—bereft of sexuality. Presumably, the argument in the tenets of advertising is that once a woman marries she changes overnight from plaything to floor-waxer.

To be fair, men make an equivalent transition in commercials. The swinging male with the mod hair and the beautiful chick turns inevitably into the paunchy slob who chokes on his wife's cake. You will notice, however, that the voice urging the viewer to buy the product is nearly always male: gentle, wise, helpful, seductive. And the visible presence telling the housewife how to get shinier floors and whiter wash and lovelier hair is almost invariably a man: the Svengali in modern dress, the Trilby (if only she were!), his willing object.

Woman, in short, is consumer first and human being fourth. A wife and mother who stays home all day buys a lot more than a woman who lives alone or who—married or single—has a job. The young girl hell-bent on marriage is the next most susceptible consumer. It is entirely understandable, then, that the potential buyers of detergents, foods, polishes, toothpastes, pills, and housewares are the housewives, and that the sex object spends most of *her* money on cosmetics, hair lotions, soaps, mouthwashes, and soft drinks.

Here we come, of course, to the youngest class of consumers, the swinging teen-agers so beloved by advertisers keen on telling them (and us) that they've "got a lot to live, and Pepsi's got a lot to give." This affords a chance to show a squirming, leaping, jiggling group of beautiful kids having a very loud high on rock and—of all things—soda pop. One of commercial TV's most dubious achievements, in fact, is the reinforcement of the self-adulation characteristic of the young as a group.

As for the aging female citizen, the less shown of her the better. She is useful for ailments, but since she buys very little of anything, not having a husband or any children to feed or house to keep, nor—of course—sex appeal to burnish, society and commercials have little place for her. The same is true, to be sure, of older men, who are handy for Bosses with Bad Breath or Doctors with Remedies. Yet, on the whole, men hold up better than women at any age—in life or on television. Lines on their faces are marks of distinction, while on women they are signatures of decay.

There is no question, in any case, that television commercials (and many of the entertainment programs, notably the soap serials that are part of the selling package) reinforce, like an insistent drill, the assumption that a woman's only valid function is that of wife, mother, and servant of men: the inevitable sequel to her earlier function as sex object and swinger.

At a time when more and more women are at long last learning to reject these assumptions as archaic and demeaning, and to grow into individual human beings with a wide option of lives to live, the sellers of the nation are bent upon reinforcing the ancient pattern. They know only too well that by beaming their message to the Consumer Queen they can justify her existence as the housebound Mrs. America: dumber than dumb, whiter than white.

The conditioning starts very early: with the girl child who wants the skin Ivory soap has reputedly given her mother, with the nine-year-old who brings back a cake of Camay instead of the male deodorant her father wanted. (When she confesses that she bought it so she could be "feminine," her father hugs her, and, with the voice of a child-molester, whispers, "My little girl is growing up on me, huh.") And then, before long, comes the teen-aged bride who "has feelings to feel."

It is the little boys who dream of wings, in an airplane commercial; who grow up (with fewer cavities) into the doers. Their little sisters turn into *Cosmopolitan* girls, who in turn become housewives furious that their neighbors' wash is cleaner than theirs.

There is good reason to suspect that this manic obsession with cleanliness, fostered, quite naturally, by the giant soap and detergent interests, may bear some responsibility for the cultivated sloppiness of so many of the young in their clothing as well as in their chosen hideouts. The compulsive housewife who spends more time washing and vacuuming and polishing her possessions than communicating to, or stimulating her children creates a kind of sterility that the young would instinctively reject. The impeccably tidy home, the impeccably tidy lawn are—in a very real sense—unnatural and confining.

Yet the commercials confront us with broods of happy children, some of whom—believe it or not—notice the new fresh smell their clean, white sweatshirts exhale thanks to Mom's new "softener."

Some major advertisers, for that matter, can even cast a benign eye on the population explosion. In another Biz commercial, the genial Eddie Albert surveys with surprise a long row of dirty clothes heaped before him by a young matron. She answers his natural query by telling him gaily they are the products of her brood of eleven "with one more to come!" she adds as the twelfth turns up. "That's great!" says Mr. Albert, curdling the soul of Planned Parenthood and the future of this planet.

Who are, one cannot help but ask, the writers who manage to combine the sales of products with the selling-out of human dreams and dignity? Who people this cosmos of commercials with dolts and fools and shrews and narcissists? Who know so much about quirks and mannerisms and ailments and so little about life? So much about presumed wants and so little about crying needs?

Can women advertisers so demean their own sex? Or are there no women in positions of decision high enough to see that their real selves stand up?

Do they not know, these extremely clever creators of commercials, what they could do for their audience even while they exploit and entertain them? How they could raise the levels of manners and attitudes while they sell their wares? Or do they really share the worm's-eye view of mass communication that sees, and addresses, only the lowest common denominator?

It can be argued that commercials are taken too seriously, that their function is merely to amuse, engage, and sell, and that they do this brilliantly. If that were all to this wheedling of millions, well and good. But it is not. There are two more fallouts from this chronic sales explosion that cannot be measured but that at least can be expected. One has to do with the continual celebration of youth at the expense of maturity. In commercials only the young have access to beauty, sex, and joy in life. What do older women feel, day after day, when love is the exclusive possession of a teen-age girl with a bobbing mantle of hair? What older man would not covet her in restless impotence?

The constant reminder of what is inaccessible must inevitably produce a subterranean but real discontent, just as the continual sight of things and places beyond reach has eaten deeply into the ghetto soul. If we are constantly presented with what we are not or cannot have, the dislocation deepens, contentment vanishes, and frustration reigns. Even for the substantially secure, there is always a better thing, a better way, to buy. That none of these things makes a better life may be consciously acknowledged, but still the desire lodges in the spirit, nagging and pulling.

This kind of fragmentation works in potent ways above and beyond the mere fact of program interruption, which is much of the time more of a blessing than a curse, especially in those rare instances when the commercial is deft and funny: the soft and subtle sell. Its overall curse, due to the large number of commercials in each hour, is that it reduces the attention span of a people already so conditioned to constant change and distraction that they cannot tolerate continuity in print or on the air.

Specifically, commercial interruption is most damaging during that 10 per cent of programing (a charitable estimate) most important to the mind and spirit of a people: news and public affairs, and drama.

To many (and among these are network news producers), commercials have no place or business during the vital process of informing the public. There is something obscene about a newscaster pausing to introduce a deodorant or shampoo commercial between an airplane crash and a body count. It is more than an interruption; it tends to reduce news to a form of running entertainment, to smudge the edges of reality by treating death or disaster or diplomacy on the same level as household appliances or a new gasoline.

The answer to this would presumably be to lump the commercials before and after the news or public affairs broadcasts—an answer unpalatable, needless to say, to the sponsors who support them.

The same is doubly true of that most unprofitable sector of television, the original play. Essential to any creative composition, whether drama, music or dance, are mood and continuity, both inseparable from form and meaning. They are shattered by the periodic intrusion of commercials, which have become intolerable to the serious artists who have deserted commercial television in droves because the system allows them no real freedom or autonomy. The selling comes first, the creation must accommodate itself. It is the rare and admirable sponsor who restricts or fashions his commercials so as to provide a minimum of intrusion or damaging inappropriateness.

If all these assumptions and imponderables are true, as many suspect, what is the answer or alleviation?

One is in the course of difficult emergence: the establishment of a public television system sufficiently funded so that it can give a maximum number of people an alternate diet of pleasure, enlightenment, and stimulation free from commercial fragmentation. So far, for lack of funds to buy talent and equipment, this effort has been in terms of public attention a distinctly minor operation.

Even if public television should, hopefully, greatly increase its scope and impact, it cannot in the nature of things and through long public conditioning equal the impact and reach the size of audience now tuned to commercial television.

Enormous amounts of time, money, and talent go into commercials. Technically they are often brilliant and innovative, the product not only of the new skills and devices but of imaginative minds. A few of them are both funny and endearing. Who, for instance, will forget the miserable young man with the appalling cold, or the kids taught to use—as an initiation into manhood—a fork instead of a spoon with a certain spaghetti? Among the enlightened sponsors, moreover, are some who manage to combine an image of their corporation and their products with accuracy and restraint.

What has to happen to mass medium advertisers as a whole, and especially on TV, is a totally new approach to their function not only as sellers but as social influencers. They have the same obligation as the broadcast medium itself: not only to entertain but to reflect, not only to reflect but to enlarge public consciousness and human stature.

This may be a tall order, but it is a vital one at a time when Americans have ceased to know who they are and where they are going, and when all the multiple forces acting upon them are daily diminishing their sense of their own value and purpose in life, when social upheaval and social fragmentation have destroyed old patterns, and when survival depends on new ones.

If we continue to see ourselves as the advertisers see us, we have no place to go. Nor, I might add, has commercial broadcasting itself.

The
New
Violence

Joseph Morgenstern

For the better part of two decades, evidence has been accumulating that violence in the mass media can breed aggressive behavior in the mass audience, especially among children. Supporting documents from last month's report to the Surgeon General on "Television and Growing Up: The Impact of Televised Violence" give us the strongest suggestions to date that violent TV programs can have harmful effects on large groups of normal kids. It's unlikely, though, that millions of outraged parents will lower the boom on the broadcasters. Much of the adult audience is on a violence trip of its own at the movies.

Americans love to watch images of violence in the fun house of the mass media. Violence is the best epoxy for holding an audience together between commercials, the very deathblood of such shows as "Mannix," "Gunsmoke," "Cannon," "Hawaii Five-O," "Adam-12," "Cade's County" and "Mod Squad," not to mention all those dumb, undifferentiated Saturday morning cartoons. A recent study by the British Broadcasting Corp. found that American television programs shown in England have twice as many violent incidents as British productions do.

Occasionally an urban riot, campus confrontation or choice assassination will cause the public or Congress to wonder briefly if all this mayhem in the media is such a good thing for the country, after all. The last time the question arose was in 1969, when Sen. John Pastore (Democrat of Rhode Island) sponsored a $1 million study of media violence and its possible relationship to "antisocial behavior among young people." Historically, the networks' position has been that no such relationship has

From *Newsweek.* Copyright Newsweek, Inc., February 14, 1972.

ever been proved. Just to make sure it wouldn't be proved this time, the broadcasters tried to rig the Surgeon General's study in their favor. To a considerable extent they succeeded.

All candidates for membership on the advisory committee that commissioned the research and later summarized it were subject to vetoes by the three commercial networks. CBS declined to exercise any such veto; NBC and ABC had fewer scruples and blackballed seven candidates. The fourth network of 219 noncommercial (and largely nonviolent) stations (PBS) was not consulted. Two of the twelve committee memberships went to incumbent directors of research at NBC and CBS. Three more, went to scholars who had been or still were employed by the networks.

THE LAST WORD

Once the surveys and laboratory experiments were completed, all research data and conclusions were compiled into five large volumes, then summarized by the advisory committee in a 279-page report to the Surgeon General. Whether by intent or ineptitude, the committee misrepresented some of the data, ignored some of it and buried all of it alive in prose that was obviously meant to be unreadable and unread. The five supporting volumes are still being withheld from the public. Thus far, the news media have accepted the committee's summary as the last word on the research. Beneath the misleading headline "TV Violence Held Unharmful to Youth," *The New York Times* story stressed contradictions in the Surgeon General's report and, with incomplete quotations, gave the impression that televised violence leads to increased aggressive behavior only in small groups of youngsters.

In fact, the summary says much more than this, and the supporting data says more than the summary. The summary dismisses as unsubstantiated the catharsis theory—that viewing filmed violence allows pent-up emotions to be released harmlessly. While the summary does say that the most direct effects of media violence may occur among children predisposed to violence, it stresses that this violence-prone subgroup may constitute a "small portion or a substantial portion of the total population of young viewers." And an overview of one of the five volumes of supporting research says, in an italicized conclusion, that "*the present entertainment offerings of the television medium may be contributing, in some measure, to the aggressive behavior of many normal children. Such an effect has now been shown in a wide variety of situations.*"

That conclusion was written by Dr. Robert M. Liebert, a psychologist at the State University of New York at Stony Brook, Long Island. Liebert participated in two of the 23 research studies, has read all 23 and feels strongly that the summary draws inaccurate conclusions from them. "I believe," he says, "that the most reasonable conclusion is that there is a link between televised violence and aggressive behavior for the majority of normal children. The data show no evidence that only a minority is influenced. This is a factual error."

Not all the researchers feel their work was misrepresented, of course, and not all the committee members feel their summary was self-canceling. "Prior to this report," says one of them, Dr. Ithiel de Sola Pool of MIT, "you could not have said that there is a causal relationship between TV violence and aggressive behavior in children. Now we can see that there is a significant causal relationship."

Beyond the baleful light of the box, violence rages in the streets and it's the rage in the movies. Within the past few months a striking new consensus has emerged on movie violence—indeed, on ultra-violence, to borrow a term from the stylish sadists of "A Clockwork Orange." Moviemakers have found ultra-violence ultra-profitable, the mass audience has found it enjoyable and an influential majority of reviewers has found it intellectually attractive and artistically valid.

In the highly praised "A Clockwork Orange," roving bands of dehumanized hoodlums deal out a cool, affectless violence that includes kicking, stomping, gang rape and beating a woman's brains out with a big phallic sculpture. "Straw Dogs" dispenses with the cool and comes to a devastatingly powerful climax of rape, knifing, mutilation, acid-tossing, shooting, beating and burning. Santa Claus tries to crush a fallen kid's rib cage in "The French Connection." A maniac "hippie" in "Dirty Harry" does unspeakable violence to his victims; what the detective hero does to the maniac hippie is no more speakable and equally visible. Roman Polanski's "Macbeth" dispatches its victims with a vividly slit throat, a broadax in the back, a dagger in the forehead, a sword in the groin. When Macbeth himself was beheaded the other day at the Playboy Theater in New York, a matinee audience of high-school students on a field trip screamed in horrified delight as the thane's hands groped for the head that had already split.

'WHAT THE PEOPLE WANT'

If there's any such thing as ultra-sex, it's still largely confined to peep shows, porno houses and X-rated movies that some violence-laden newspapers refuse to advertise out of deference to their readers' sensibilities. But only one movie has ever been rated X for violence—"I Drink Your Blood"—and that rating was changed to an R when cuts were made. All the James Bond pictures carry GP's—suitable for general audiences, with parental guidance advised—even though 007's witty swashbucklings have turned gross and squalid in the new "Diamonds Are Forever." A kiddie version of ultra-violence has even crashed the Radio City Music Hall, which caters mostly to families and young children. The Hall recently played "The Cowboys," a GP rated Western in which John Wayne is slowly shot to death by rustlers, then avenged when a group of children torture one rustler and kill them all.

Does this mean the movie industry's rating system is in a state of collapse? Motion Picture Association of America president Jack Valenti maintains that the ratings are still doing what they're supposed to do, marking certain pictures off limits to children and warning parents that certain other pictures may be unsuitable for children. "I don't think it's the rating system that's in collapse," Valenti says. "It may be that parents just don't care any more." A *Newsweek* survey of theater operators in cities across the nation reveals little or no public dissatisfaction with the ratings or the violence of new movies. "Mores and customs change and movies have become franker," says a manager in Detroit. "Violence is acceptable," says a showman in Chicago. "It's what the people want."

That's no news in itself, of course. Mass audiences have always wanted violence and always gotten it, whether in bear baiting, melodrama, comic books or pro football. Nor is it news that violence, even pornographic violence, is more socially acceptable than sex. In 1949, in a pamphlet called "Love and Death," Gershon Legman wrote: "There is *no* mundane substitute for sex except sadism."

Yet something new did come over media violence in the 1960s. It was the result of an interaction that's always in progress between entertainment and reality. On one side was a convergence of events without parallel in American history—racial strife, assassination, confrontation, the war in Vietnam. On the other side, entertainment stayed in step with the world beyond the studios and gave us the showerbath murder in "Psycho," and the James Bond extravaganzas, with a hero sophisticated enough to lead his audience down hitherto forbidden paths of sex, sadism and stylish decadence. "The Untouchables" flourished on TV, the spaghetti Westerns —made in Spain by Italians—treated American audiences to a level of violence that Hollywood had hardly dared dream of. Roger Corman's "The Wild Angels" rode in on the emerging motorcycle myth. Richard Brooks upped the violence ante in "The Professionals," and Robert Aldrich gave audiences a half-hour high of slaughter in "The Dirty Dozen."

These movies were long on action and short on philosophy, but new attitudes toward violence were beginning to trickle down from literary and scholarly speculations of the day, just as Epicurean and Stoic notions of nature that were popular in Shakespeare's time found dramatic expression in his Edmund and Edgar. This was the decade in which Eichmann was executed, "In Cold Blood" appeared and the English translation of "On Aggression" was published. In the entertainment world it was also the period in which "Bonnie and Clyde" forced a rethinking of the mythology of violence with its daring new notions of criminal behavior and the lyric horror of its climax, and "The Wild Bunch," with another quantum jump in physical intensity, tried to explore the nature of life with the esthetics of death.

PROPHECY OR PARODY

Many critics and moviegoers welcome the new ultra-violence as an extension of such experiments. "Clockwork Orange" is praised as prophecy, or as a dark parody of the present. The horrors of "Macbeth" are seen as historical truths: lords and ladies were close to savagery and killed as savages. Admirers of "Straw Dogs" feel it illuminates the human condition with its vision of violence as a rite of passage in which a man puts himself in touch with his primal emotions—to become, for better or worse, a man.

A few eloquent dissents from this attitude have been advanced in recent weeks. Andrew Sarris, writing in *The Village Voice*, found a facile anti-intellectualism in "A Clockwork Orange," and woeful inadequacies in Kubrick's widely hailed technique. Pauline Kael, in *The New Yorker*, drew analogies between the drug culture's appetite for intense, violent mystery and the mock profundities of "El Topo." Writing about "A Clockwork Orange," Miss Kael condemned the movie's "finally corrupt morality" which betrays Anthony Burgess's novel by making the mod-sadist hero much more human and likable than the contemptible straights he preys on. "How can people go on talking about the dazzling brilliance of movies," her review asked, "and not notice that the directors are sucking up to the thugs in the audience?"

One way they can do it is by following the lead of the old New Criticism in literature, confining themselves to matters of style and structure—cool technicians reviewing the techniques of other cool technicians. Ultimate meaning can be a horrible can of worms, and there's no ethical obligation to deal with it if you believe that violent entertainment has no ultimate effect, apart from instruction or healthy catharsis. There's the rub, though. If the effect of TV violence on children has finally been demonstrated, it's not unreasonable to assume that ultra-violence in the movies has some effect on adults. It's not necessarily the same effect, a heightening of aggressive behavior. But neither do these movies necessarily enlighten their audience in ways that they're supposed to.

A film like "Straw Dogs" may put us in touch with our primal emotions, but that's no great trick—the Nazis did it constantly. It also sets up human existence, on a shaky allegorical level, as a simplistic choice between fighting violence with violence or capitulating to it completely. Where's some provision for the uses of intelligence, or at least craftiness? The film puts us in touch with a machismo that's supposed to be unfashionable in sophisticated circles these days, yet persists in philosophical disguise. A man can only be a true male, according to the movie, when he's won his merit badges in rape, combat and murder. It's as if de Sade had rewritten the worst of Hemingway for a special Nasty Edition of *Playboy*. There's only one possible role for a woman in this macho-violent setting. She's there to be raped, she wants passionately to be raped, she deserves to be raped and raped she most certainly is in "Straw Dogs," "Macbeth" and, of course, in "A Clockwork Orange."

This kind of entertainment is seductive in more ways than one. With its obscurity, macho bravura or both, it puts you promptly on the defensive. You can't be much of a man if you don't dig it, or at least concede its underlying wisdom. Man is base (and woman is baser), say the pundit artists. How true, how true, respond the admiring critics, only too glad to get a secure ride on the hate-humanity bandwagon. "I don't mind saying that I myself was sickened by my own film," says Sam Peckinpah, co-writer and director of "Straw Dogs." "But somewhere in it there is a mirror for everyone." Maybe so, but the mirror is framed in right-wing gilt. It shows the stereotyped liberal intellectual—Dustin Hoffman in simpers and specs —as a cowardly, contemptible nerd who won't take a stand till the barbarians are inside his own house: Neville Chamberlain Meets the New Madmen. "I'm not a Fascist," Peckinpah has been quoted as saying, "but I am something of a totalitarian."

He's a lot more candid than some of his colleagues. Don Siegel likes to be thought of as a tough action director, but the thread of Fascism in his "Dirty Harry" is as strong as the suspension cables on the Golden Gate Bridge. The gallant, ruthless San Francisco detective tries to take a crazed killer out of circulation by fair means or foul, but he's hamstrung by all those dumb rules on arrest that were handed down by a doddering Supreme Court. Polanski takes a simple-minded, totalitarian approach to "Macbeth." The language and poetry seem beyond him, so he uses violence to explain everything. Stanley Kubrick has become a totalitarian of the arts who crushes other people's intricate moral ideas into a pulp of mod decadence.

There's a joke about a fake guru who tells all his disciples that "life is a river." Gurus of the new violence do something of the sort with stylization. Their techniques—slow motion, surreal performances, elegant décor, brilliant editing, fish-eye lenses, repeat frames—seem to comment on the action without saying anything. They lend distance, but they also dehumanize victims in the way that high-fashion photography dehumanizes models, and they create a high-fashion horror that can turn an audience on higher than the real thing. The Vietnamese war could look lovely in slow motion—Skyraiders floating in for the kill like seagulls, fragmentation bombs opening like anemones. But the horror would still be horror, with nothing added but technique. Dancing on a face while singing "Singin' in the Rain" is still dancing on a face. It becomes clear that "Bonnie and

Clyde" was both watershed and quicksand. It used technique within a humanistic design and shocked us awake to violence. Now anti-humanists are using the same technique to lull us into dulcet dreams of death.

ETHICAL CULTURE

Purveyors of the new violence can tell themselves and their critics that they're involved in a program of character building, public service and ethical culture, but a few visits to neighborhood theaters suggest that a large part of the mass audience simply loves the violence as violence. The givens are not always the takens. Kids in the balcony at a recent Times Square showing of "Dirty Harry" were stomping their feet with glee at each shooting or beating. One boy was coming on strong as a munitions expert, giving his girl a run-down on the range and impact of each weapon as it appeared. When the massacres ended and the house lights came up, he breathed a sigh of deep satisfaction and said quietly: "That was nice."

That's the part of the ultra-violence trip that many filmmakers and critics don't like to deal with. At least two sets of signals are operating here, and the confusion between them raises some anguishing questions that no one knows how to answer. Where does an artist's responsibility end? With the truthful depiction of his personal vision, or with its social effects? What are the effects of ultra-violent movies, on the cavemen as well as the sophisticates of the mass audience? Once again we don't know, but it's not enough to say that Shakespeare and Marlowe were violent and civilization still survived. Technology has brought a new amplification effect into play. Never before has so much violence been shown so graphically to so many.

CAUSE AND EFFECT

There's a sense of imminent disaster when you're in an audience that's grooving on ultra-violence, and you're tempted to say that things can't go on this way too much longer. They can, of course, and probably will. Today's ultra-violent films will be tomorrow's "Wednesday Night at the Movies" on TV—with anything sexy cut out, of course. If holograms bring free-standing images into our living room, we may have to shampoo the carpet after each new award-winning blood bath. Violence may also crest, as it has before, and cyclically subside. Something of the sort has happened in the rock world, which lowered its amps and pulled back from the abyss that opened at Altamont.

Whether it crests or not, however, media violence demands to be taken more seriously than it has been in the past. We know now, thanks to the Surgeon General's research, that it helps incite children to aggressive behavior. While we don't know what it does to adults, there's an ominous clue in the public's tolerance of horror in the newscasts from Vietnam. The only way we can possibly tolerate it is by turning off a part of ourselves instead of the TV set. It's very possible that incitement to violent deeds is the false danger for adults, and desensitization the real one. "Dirty Harry" didn't necessarily incite that self-styled weapons expert to buy himself a .44 and cut someone down with it. There's no proof—yet—that such ritualized primitivism turns adults on; not even the poor, the uneducated, the violence-prone, the people who can never get themselves together. The more immediate possibility is that it turns us off, like any other drug, that it freaks us out on make-believe fury, keeps us from doing anything constructive with our aggressions, that it frustrates, demeans and diminishes us.

Two Opinions on Pornography: Censorship vs. Libertarianism

Stanley Kauffmann and Alexander Bickel

STANLEY KAUFFMANN

One pleasant aspect of pornography discussions is that they never end, even within oneself. No set of arguments can be air-tight, and one can always think of points to be added or changed in one's own arguments. But here are some of my present views:

I dislike pornography; and I dislike censorship laws.

I dislike pornography because after the excitements, there comes tedium; and with the tedium comes a sense of imperfection. After sex itself comes no such tedium (languor is something else) and no such basic sense of inappropriateness. Porno excites me because all my neural systems seem to be adequately hooked up, but after the shock of crossing the threshold into that "world" wears off, which doesn't take so long, I begin to think that porno represents an ideal—essentially male—of sexual freedom and power, unrelated to reality as is, or as is desirable. I am an anti-idealist; ideals seem morally and functionally corruptive. I am against this ideal as well.

I dislike censorship laws because they intrude on personal rights. Most laws operate between at least two people: they protect me from you and

The Public Interest, No. 22, Winter 1971. Copyright National Affairs, Inc., 1971.

vice-versa. Laws against pornography, like laws against drinking and drug-taking and suicide, come between me and myself. I object to the state's arrogance.

People want pornography.

This has been true of many cultures, especially for men, in many areas. Porno producers are not philanthropists or missionaries; they're in business because people want what they produce. What right have some of us to tell others that they may not have what they want? (I know some intelligent, cultivated men—and a few such women—who delight in porno.) I disbelieve in the legislation of taste.

DEFENSE AGAINST REPRESSION

The question of theatrical productions like *Oh! Calcutta!* is self-solving. If you want to go, go; if not, don't. The concept of "the dram of eale" is a puritan delusion. Gresham's Law doesn't operate in art. If bad art drove out good, there would not be any good art at all because for centuries there has been more bad art than good.

Most films are now clearly labeled by the ratings system of the Motion Picture Association of America. That system has manifest defects, but I have argued for it—and would still—as the best defense against repression. The X rating is, as is often said, a license for opportunists, but numbers of people want what the opportunists offer and I don't recognize anyone's right to deny it to them. More important, the X rating is a license for the serious film maker who wants to deal with sexual subjects. I'm glad that *Midnight Cowboy* (whatever its faults) was made and widely distributed, something that was difficult anyway and would have been nearly impossible without the protection of the X rating.

DANISH SURVEY

The concept of the state's interest in pornography, possibly related to the Roman concept of the republic of virtue, is gradually being eroded by scientific research. The researches in the Lockhart report, incomplete though they are, support the belief that there is no connection between porno and sexual crime. A Danish study (*New York Times*, Nov. 9, 1970) finds that sex crimes have sharply declined in Denmark—coincidentally?—in the three years since censorship laws have been eased there. The data and conclusions of the British Arts Council report on obscenity laws (full text in the *New Statesman*, August 8, 1969) support a recommendation for repeal of the Obscene Publications Acts. The state surely has a legitimate interest in the moral welfare of the community, but every ground for including porno in that interest is weakening.

The only real legal question is the protection of children. And it is a *question.* I can't define what a child is—six, yes, but sixteen?—and I can't define what "protection" is. I'm simply not convinced that a young person without sexual experience and some maturity of judgment can see pornography as pornography: that is—aside from understanding the acts themselves and understanding the unconventionality (even impossibility) of some of them—can see the relation of porno to experience, as commentary and stimulant and revenge. "Depravity and corruption" are supposed to be considerations, too, though no one seems to know much about them. I have no wish to be blithe about parents' concern for a child (particularly since I have no children), but my guess is that a parent's attitude toward his child's exposure to porno is as much secret embarrassment at revelation of his own fantasies as it is protection of the young.

PROTECTION FOR MINORS

Censorship legislation for minors, however, only moves the semantic and moral problem to a different locus. Two sociologists on the Lockhart commission recommended the abolition of *all* statutory legislation, for young persons as well as adults, on the ground that obscenity and pornography have long proved undefinable. They would rather rely on "informal social controls" and "improvements in sex education and better understanding of human sexual behavior" than on "ambiguous and arbitrarily administered laws."

Nevertheless I confess that, even without scientific data to prove harm, I'm uneasy at the thought of children being exposed to pornography before those "improvements" are realized.

Porno is of two distinct kinds.

I don't mean the difference between porno and erotic art nor the argument that sections of recognized classics—Rabelais, Joyce, etc.—are pornographic. (An argument I cannot accept. A sexual portion of a genuine artwork cannot—in my understanding—be pornographic. The latter means, for me, material devised *only* for sexual stimulation.)

The real difference is between imagined porno—written or drawn or painted—and performed porno, done in actuality or on film or in still photographs. The latter entails the degradation of human beings. It doesn't seem to me to matter that these performing men and women always seem cheerful and busily engaged, or that (reportedly) some of the occupants enjoy it or that some of them perform public sex acts as part of lives that are otherwise quite conventional. Obviously conditionings and rationales can vary widely, but I cannot believe that the use of human beings for these purposes is socially beneficial or morally liberating. On the contrary, I think it socially stultifying and morally warped.

I'm not talking about nudity and simulated intercourse in such plays as *Che!*, which are frequently done quite self-righteously as an attempt to *épater le bourgeois*. I mean (currently available in person and on film in New York and other cities) the public performance of coition, fellatio, cunnilingus, and mutual masturbation—with the coition usually interrupted so that the male ejaculation can be seen.

ACTS OF VINDICTIVENESS

I've been as excited by watching some of those films as a human being ought presumably to be. But essentially those films seem to me acts of vindictiveness by men against women in return for the sexual restrictions and taboos of our society and for the cruelties of women toward men that those restrictions have produced. The vindictiveness is essentially mean-spirited and exploitative. I would hope that the socio-sexual improvements on which the Lockhart sociologists rely may affect performed porno first.

In any event, I think that the lumping-together of all porno—imagined and performed—is a conceptual error. The one-to-one relation of writer and reader is a different matter, in psychic and social senses, from the employment of people to enact fantasies.

Conclusions, *pro tem.*

I am not a swinger. I don't believe in pornography as a healthful reminder of the full genital life amidst a pallid and poky society, or as an extender of consciousness in any beneficial way. These views seem to me phony emancipation—in fact, a negation of the very fullness of life that is ostensibly being affirmed. Much better to concentrate on our silliness about the romanticized restrictions of love and the shortcomings of marriage, on the humiliations of both men and women in our rituals of courtship and bedding and wedding, that make pornography such a popular form of vengeance.

But the legal suppression of pornography seems to me anticivil and anticivilized (because it misses the anticivilizing reasons for porno), and also shows a failure in sense of humor. (If the idea of sex is funny, as it often is, the idea of porno is funniness multiplied.) I'm against censorship laws just as I'm against laws against certain kinds of sexual practice, or against any sexual practice between unmarried people, that still exist in many parts of this country. I want to be able to have porno if I want it. The purely personal opinion that I don't happen to want it very often should not be made the law of the land.

To put it entirely subjectively, I think that one way to cure my uneasiness on the subject of porno is to repeal all the laws restricting it, except possibly the ones forbidding the advertising and sale to minors. The more mature the individual, the more he resents the idea of being forbidden

something that affects him alone; and the more mature individuals there
are, the better the polity.

ALEXANDER BICKEL

The civil libertarian position on obscenity is that if we forget about it, it
will go away. We aren't told to admire the king's beautiful cloak. We are
told not to care whether he has one on or not.

Never mind whether books get girls pregnant, or whether sexy or violent
movies turn men to crime. Assume that they do not, or that, at any rate,
there are plenty of other efficient causes of pregnancy and crime. Assume
further that we must protect privacy; that government, therefore, properly
has no business punishing anyone for amusing himself obscenely in his
home, and must ignore the means by which he may have obtained his
obscene materials, if all it knows is that he uses them at home; assume, in
other words, that the Supreme Court was right in *Stanley v. Georgia*, in
1969, when it held: "Whatever may be the justifications for other statutes
regulating obscenity, we do not think they reach into the privacy of one's
own home. If the First Amendment means anything, it means that a State
has no business telling a man, sitting alone in his house, what books he
may read or what films he may watch."

PROTECTION OF PRIVACY

Take these assumptions, and still you are left with at least one problem of
large proportions. It concerns the tone of the society, the mode, or to use
terms that have perhaps greater currency, the style and quality of life, now
and in the future. A man may be entitled to read an obscene book in his
room, or expose himself indecently there, or masturbate, or flog himself, if
that is possible, or what have you. We should protect his privacy. But if he
demands a right to obtain the books and pictures he wants in the market,
and to foregather in public places—discreet, if you will, but accessible to
all—with others who share his tastes, then to grant him his right is to affect
the world about the rest of us, and to impinge on other privacies. Even
supposing that each of us can, if he wishes, effectively avert the eye and
stop the ear (which, in truth, we cannot), what is commonly read and seen
and heard and done intrudes upon us all, want it or not.

Now, not only books and pictures and speech, but all sorts of behavior
and artifacts—architecture, fashions in clothes and in other aspects of
personal appearance, habits such as smoking and drinking, overt public
homosexuality—all affect the mode and quality of life, all impinge un-
avoidably on the privacy of each of us. Yet each of us cannot but tolerate

The Public Interest, No. 22, Winter 1971. Copyright National Affairs, Inc., 1971.

a very great deal that violates our freedom and privacy in these senses, because the alternative is to let government, acting perhaps in behalf of a majority, control it all; and that is tyranny—massive tyranny, if it works, selective or occasional and random tyranny if, as is more likely, it does not work very well.

So to identify the problem of obscenity truly is to expose its intractability. But to lapse into total permissiveness about obscenity, to equate it with smoking and drinking and the miniskirt, is not the sole option left to us. The problem is no less intractable as it is raised by the physical environment, or by extremities of fashion which are called indecent exposure, or by extremities of behavior, such as boisterous drunkenness or open lovemaking, hetero or homo. Yet the same Supreme Court which during the past decade has decreed virtually unlimited permissiveness with regard to obscenity has not construed the Constitution so as to forbid the placing of legal restraints on architectural designs, for example, or on indecencies of public behavior, and is not likely to do so. Nor is the Court very likely to tell us that fostering heterosexual marriage while not countenancing homosexual unions—which is what the legal order does, of course—is unconstitutional. The reason cannot be that the First Amendment throws special safeguards around speech and other forms of communication, which are relevant to obscenity. That is not even a significant technical point, because the relevant protections are drawn as much from the Due Process Clause of the Fourteenth Amendment as from the First. And in substance, the point is absurd. There is no bright line between communication and conduct. The effect, in the segment of both that we are here considering, is the same. What is *Oh! Calcutta?* Communication or conduct?

OBSCENITY LAWS

Law which attempts to come to grips with the problem of obscenity—or aesthetics in the physical environment, or drinking, or exposure of the body, or drug-taking, or offensive or assaultive speech—is a different kind of instrument, running greater risks and expecting to attain a rather more remote approximation of its ends than the law which forbids murder and theft, or defines the rights and obligations of a property-owner, or governs the relations between General Motors and the United Automobile Workers of America.

Very little of what is called law achieves its ends always or precisely. But much of it tries to, because it is fully confident of the validity of its ends, which it can and does define intelligibly and with some precision. A law attempting to regulate obscenity, however, has to exist in a peculiar tension. It must avoid tyrannical enforcement of supposed majority tastes, while providing visible support for the diffuse private endeavors of an overwhelming majority of people to sustain the style and quality of life minimally congenial to them. This sort of law, even if it is as exact in some of its applications as the statutes proposed by Richard Kuh (in his thoughtful book, *Foolish Figleaves?*) necessarily accepts a certain ambiguity about its ends.

CHANGING LIFE STYLES

It is not meant to wipe all the obscenity it defines off the face of the earth, wherever it finds it. If nothing else, the line drawn in *Stanley v. Georgia* prevents this; on the other side of this line, one would concede, tyranny does raise its head. Moreover, even the mere effort to enforce such a law perfectly, or with the intent to achieve the nearest possible approximation of perfection, as the law against murder is enforced—even just this effort would verge in practice on the tyrannical. And if the life style of large numbers of people changes despite the law, or cannot successfully be affected by it, so that any sort of even-handed enforcement at all, however minimal, is impossible, then any enforcement at all becomes tyrannical, and the law must be abandoned, as we abandoned prohibition of liquor, and ought perhaps to abandon prohibition of marijuana. Again, if such a law, even though vigorously enforced, turns out hardly to touch the activity it forbids, because the motive to engage in it is too strong, albeit only a limited number of people are subject to the irresistible urge, than all the law achieves by making the activity illegal is to place an economic tariff on it, and to cause a "ripple effect" of crime. This, as Professor Herbert L. Packer has pointed out, is the case with laws that punish gambling or the taking of addictive drugs. These laws ought to be repealed and replaced by other forms of regulation that are less productive of undesirable side effects.

The short of it, then, is that its very existence, and occasional but steady enforcement in aggravated cases for the sake of making itself visible, is the real and virtually sole purpose of a law against obscenity. Its role is supportive, tentative, even provisional. It walks a tight-rope, and runs high risks. Every so often in some corner of the country, some idiot finds Chaucer obscene or the lower female leg indecent. For this reason, the federal government itself, as Justice Harlan has long argued, and as Chief Justice Burger agrees, should stay out of the business of censorship altogether, because its idiocies, when they occur, affect the whole country. But the Supreme Court, while exercising procedural oversight, ought to let state and local governments run the risks if they wish. For the stakes are high.

Mass Media
and
Culture

I. Backgrounds and Perspectives

Culture can be defined in several ways. One view of the meaning of culture includes everything that occurs in a society, from its social habits and manners to its religious rites and practices, from its techniques of preparing food or making love to its customs of marriage, family, and work, from its commonplaces of transportation or conversation to its conceptions of time, birth, death, and immediate and ultimate values. This all-encompassing view is generally used from an anthropological orientation. At the other extreme is the more limited interpretation of culture of the aestheticians and critics who refer to the aesthetic, sensory, philosophic, theological, and intellectual patterns and assumptions of a society and its achievements, to the arts, the deep values, the basic attitudes and guidelines a society produces and lives by.

Somewhere between the two, but perhaps closer to a broadly defined aesthetic-intellectual view, is the definition of culture assumed by most of the selections in this book. In them, however, the traditional view of the fine arts and the higher reaches of learning as the repository of culture has been altered to take into account the influential role and contribution of the mass media. The response to the changes in culture produced by the mass media is the burden of this section; it is a response no less varied than the elements of the new culture themselves.

Herbert J. Gans' contribution is one of the longest and most complex in the book. He provides, first of all, a concise and just review of the positions of earlier, generally fearful critics of mass media and mass culture, as exemplified by such writers as Dwight MacDonald and Ernest van den Haag. In his critique of their critique, he arrives at a more sanguine position on the important central issues that they have raised.

Susan Sontag is one of the most articulate spokesman for the values of an evolving mass culture. In defining the ways in which what she calls the new sensibility has bridged the gap between low and high culture, she places particular stress on the sensory aesthetics of contemporary art, its value, and its relationship to the world views of our time.

No one writer has been more influential in redefining our approaches to the media experience than Marshall McLuhan. With some similarities to Susan Sontag's position, McLuhan's belief that "the medium is the message" emphasizes the effect that the *form* of communication produces on human consciousness, both in terms of the structure and workings of that consciousness and of its content. In the selection presented, McLuhan illustrates the processes defined in his general theory by focusing more specifically on the psychological attributes and effects of two kinds of media, which he labels "hot" and "cold."

More than a critique of what he considers the limitations of McLuhan's position, the selection by James W. Carey examines the relationships of McLuhan's ideas to the important theories of Harold Adams Innis. He points up particularly the differences arising from McLuhan's emphasis on changes in patterns of individual consciousness and Innis' contrasting emphasis on social changes. To illustrate Innis' approach, he applies it in a full analysis of one of the most visible effects of media society, the acceleration of differences between generations.

The Critique
of
Mass Culture

Herbert J. Gans

The charges against mass or popular culture have been repeated so frequently and consistently—indeed, many of them can be traced back to the eighteenth century—that it is possible to view them as part of an established ideology or critique.[1] In its contemporary form, that critique has four major themes:

1. *The negative character of popular-culture creation.* Popular culture is undesirable because, unlike high culture, it is mass-produced by profit-minded entrepreneurs solely for the gratification of a paying audience.

2. *The negative effects on high culture.* Popular culture borrows from high culture, thus debasing it, and also lures away many potential creators of high culture, thus depleting its reservoir of talent.

3. *The negative effects on the popular-culture audience.* The consumption of popular-culture content at best produces spurious gratifications, and at worst is emotionally harmful to the audience.

4. *The negative effects on the society.* The wide distribution of popular

From Herbert J. Gans, "Popular Culture in America: Social Problem in a Mass Society or Social Asset in a Pluralist Society?" in *Social Problems: A Modern Approach* edited by Howard S. Becker. Copyright © 1966 by John Wiley & Sons, Inc. Reprinted by permission.

[1] Leo Lowenthal and Marjorie Fiske, "The Debate over Art and Popular Culture in Eighteenth Century England," in Mirra Komarovsky, ed., *Common Frontiers of the Social Sciences.* Glencoe, Ill.: The Free Press, 1957, pp. 33–96.

The principal contemporary statements of the critique are presented in two books: Rosenberg and White, eds., *Mass Culture: The Popular Arts in America.* Glencoe, Ill.: The Free Press, 1957, particularly in articles by Bernard Rosenberg, José Ortega y Gasset, Leo Lowenthal, Dwight MacDonald, Clement Greenberg, T. W. Adorno, Marshall McLuhan, Irving Howe, Ernest van den Haag, Leslie Fiedler, and Melvin Tumin; and Norman Jacobs, ed., *Culture for the Millions.* Princeton, N.J.: Van Nostrand, 1961, particularly the articles by Hannah Arendt, Ernest van den Haag, Oscar Handlin, Randall Jarrell, and Stanley Edgar Hyman. See also T. S. Eliot, *Notes Towards the Definition of Culture.* New York: Harcourt, Brace, 1949; and the works of F. R. Leavis, e.g., F. R. Leavis and Denys Thompson, *Culture and Environment.* London: Chatto and Windus, 1937.

The best empirically based evaluation of the charges against mass culture may be found in Raymond A. Bauer and Alice H. Bauer, "American Mass Society and Mass Media," *Journal of Social Issues,* 16, 3 (1960), pp. 3–66. See also Joseph Klapper, *The Effects of Mass Communication.* New York: The Free Press of Glencoe, 1960; Wilbur Schramm, ed., *The Science of Communication.* New York: Basic Books, 1963; and Edward Shils, "The Mass Society and Its Culture," in Jacobs, ed., op. cit., pp. 1–27, and the sources cited in these references.

culture not only reduces the level of cultural quality—or civilization—of the society, but also encourages totalitarianism by creating a passive audience peculiarly responsive to the techniques of mass persuasion used by demagogues bent on dictatorship. . . .

NEGATIVE EFFECTS ON HIGH CULTURE*   The second theme in the popular-culture critique consists of two charges: that popular culture borrows content from high culture with the consequence of debasing it, and that by economic and prestige incentives popular culture is able to lure away potential high-culture creators, thus impairing the quality of high culture. Ernest van den Haag puts it, "The greatly increased lure of mass markets for both producers and consumers divert potential talent from the creation of art."[2]

Clement Greenberg describes the process of borrowing by mass culture as "using for raw material the debased and academicized simulacra of genuine culture."[3] Dwight MacDonald argues that

> There seems to be a Gresham's law in cultural as well as in monetary circulation; bad stuff drives out the good. . . . It threatens High Culture by its sheer pervasiveness, its brutal overwhelming *quantity*. The upper classes, who begin by using (mass culture) to make money from the crude tastes of the masses and to dominate them politically, end by finding their own culture attacked and even threatened with destruction by the instrument they have thoughtlessly employed.[4]

Van den Haag describes the process:

> Corruption of past high culture by popular culture takes numerous forms, starting with direct adulteration. Bach candied by Stokowski, Bizet coarsened by Rodgers and Hammerstein . . . Freud vulgarized into columns of newspaper correspondence advice (how to be happy though well-adjusted). Corruption also takes the form of mutilation and condensation. . . . works are cut, condensed, simplified and rewritten until all possibilities of unfamiliar or esthetic experience are strained out . . .
> What eagerness for high culture there is in popular culture has abetted the invasion of high culture, with unfortunate effect on the invaded territory. Often the effect on the invaders is unhappy too. In biting into strange fruits they are not equipped to digest, they are in danger of

* Mr. Gans' discussion of themes two and three are included here.
[2] Ernest van den Haag, "A Dissent from the Consensual Society," in Jacobs, ed., *op. cit.*, pp. 53–62, quote at p. 59. See also van den Haag in Rosenberg and White, eds., *op. cit.*, pp. 520–522.
[3] Clement Greenberg, "Avant Garde and Kitsch," in Rosenberg and White, eds., *op. cit.*, pp. 98–107, quote at p. 102.
[4] MacDonald, *op. cit.*, p. 61.

spoiling their appetite for what might actually nourish them. . . . Doubtless they are eager for intellectual and esthetic experience. Yet their quest is not likely to succeed . . . it takes far more than training and formal preparation fully to experience a work of art as meaningful. It takes an environment and a life experience which do not easily grow on the soil of our society.[5]

While both borrowing and the luring away of creators occur, the consequences attributed to both processes strike me as questionable. It is true that popular culture borrows from high culture, but the reverse is also true, for jazz and folk music have been borrowed by high-culture composers. In the past, high culture borrowed only from folk art, especially after the folk had taken up newer versions of it, but as folk art becomes extinct, high culture must borrow from its successor, commercial popular culture. For example, today comic-book illustration has been transformed into pop art. Of course, popular culture borrows much more from high culture than vice versa, but if the high-culture audience were larger, this might not be the case.

When a high-culture product, style, or method is taken over by popular culture, it is altered, but this also happens when popular arts are taken up by the high culture. When something is borrowed from high culture, however, it can no longer be used by high-culture artists because borrowing, having lowered its cultural prestige, would cause it to be rejected by the status-conscious audience for high culture. Popular-culture audiences, on the other hand, are probably pleased by content borrowed from a source of higher status.

To understand properly the charge of debasement, we must distinguish between effects on the creator and effects on the culture as a whole. Undoubtedly, high-culture creators suffer when they see their work changed, but so do popular-culture creators, even though only the former call it debasement. There is no evidence, however, that borrowing has led to a debasement of high culture per se, or of its vitality. The creation of high culture continues even when it is borrowed and changed, and I do not know of any high-culture creator who has stopped working because his previous creations were taken over by popular culture.

The charge that popular culture lures away potential high-culture creators is undoubtedly accurate, at least in some of the arts, where outlets are scarce and working conditions are poor. Young poets must become teachers of jingle writers; concert violinists have to earn their living playing popular music; and currently, fewer young people are preparing themselves for careers as performers of high-culture music than in the past, because opportunities for playing are so few. The performer who cannot

[5] Van den Haag, in Rosenberg and White, eds., op. cit., pp. 524–525, 528.

play undoubtedly suffers, but it still has not been proved that the high-culture creator who earns his living in popular culture is therefore less creative in his high-culture work. This charge can only be tested, however, if he is given a chance to spend all his time on the latter. More important, it is not at all clear that there would be more high culture if the pay scale of popular culture were not so tempting. And not every kind of high-culture creator can work in popular culture. For example, high-culture writers often cannot write for popular audiences, as the failure of famous novelists in Hollywood has repeatedly demonstrated.

Even if popular culture did not lure away potential recruits to high culture, the vitality of high culture would not necessarily be increased. Given the present size of the audience for high-culture music, concert violinists would still have no more opportunity to play, even if popular music did not exist; indeed, they would have to earn a living in nonmusical activities. The genuine issue is not the profitability of popular culture, but the unprofitability of high culture because of the smallness of its audience, so that its creators must be supported by public or private subsidy. This support is already available to many painters and novelists, but it must be extended to poets, musicians, sculptors, and to all creators of high culture who cannot support themselves by their creative work, or who cannot find a place to perform it.

If one looks at high culture from a strictly economic perspective, it may be described as a low-wage industry that loses some of its workers to high-wage competitors and hopes that the rest will be satisfied with the spiritual benefits of low-wage employment. Given the affluence of the rest of society, the spiritual benefits that were once attractive no longer suffice, resulting in a shortage of high-culture creators. This shortage can be reduced only by raising wages, not by reducing the wages of popular culture. Indeed, the effective solution is to tax highly profitable cultural enterprises to subsidize the ones that are unprofitable but socially necessary. Although the television networks now make occasional grants to educational television stations, and book publishers use the profits from best-sellers to subsidize the publication of high-culture books, these efforts, now voluntary, should be made compulsory through legislation.

NEGATIVE EFFECTS ON THE POPULAR-CULTURE AUDIENCE   By far the most serious charge against popular culture is the alleged negative effects it has on its audience. A number of such effects have been postulated: that popular culture is emotionally destructive because it provides spurious gratification, and that it is brutalizing in its emphasis on violence; that it is intellectually destructive because it offers meretricious and escapist content that inhibits ability to cope with reality; and that it is culturally destructive, impairing ability to partake of high culture. For example, MacDonald describes popular culture as "a debased, trivial culture that voids both the deep realities (sex, death, failure, tragedy) and also the simple spontaneous pleasures . . . The masses, debauched by several generations of this sort of thing, in turn come to demand trivial and comfortable cultural products."[6] Irving Howe argues:

> Mass culture is . . . orientated toward a central aspect of industrial society: the depersonalization of the individual . . . It reinforces those emotional attitudes that seem inseparable from existence in modern society—passivity and boredom . . . What is supposed to deflect us from the reduction of our personalities actually reinforces it.[7]

And van den Haag puts it similarly:

> All mass media in the end alienate people from personal experience and though appearing to offset it, intensify their moral isolation from each other, from reality and from themselves. One may turn to the mass media when lonely or bored. But mass media, once they become a habit, impair the capacity for meaningful experience. . . . The habit feeds on itself, establishing a vicious circle as addictions do. . . . Even the most profound of experiences, articulated too often on the same level (by the media), is reduced to a cliché. . . . They lessen people's capacity to experience life itself.[8]

Of these charges, the most important is emotional destructiveness, and much of my discussion will be devoted to it.[9]

Implied in this part of the critique are three assumptions: that the behavior for which popular culture is held responsible actually exists and is widespread; that the content of popular culture contains models of such behavior; and that therefore popular culture is the main cause of it. These assumptions are not supported by the available evidence.[10]

To begin with, there is no evidence that American people can be justly described as brutalized, narcotized, atomized, escapist, or unable to cope with reality. These descriptions are difficult to translate into empirical measures, which is why they can be bandied about effortlessly, but the available community studies and some recent research on the epidemiology of mental illness suggest that the vast majority of people are not

---

[6] MacDonald, op. cit., p. 72.

[7] Irving Howe, "Notes on Mass Culture," in Rosenberg and White, eds., op. cit., pp. 496–503, quote at p. 497.

[8] Van den Haag in Rosenberg and White, eds., op. cit., p. 529.

[9] Complaints about the effects of popular culture content, particularly about violence, have also come from sources quite unrelated to the critics cited here, including especially church and PTA groups. The existence of "too much violence" is also noted by 13 percent of a random sample of viewers studied by Gary Steiner and reported in Steiner, The People Look at Television. New York: Alfred A. Knopf, p. 141. See also Ira O. Glick and Sidney J. Levy, Living with Television. Chicago: Aldine Publishing Company, 1962, Chapter 4.

[10] See the summary of existing studies by Bauer and Bauer, op. cit., especially pp. 31–35.

isolates but members of familial, peer, and community groups.[11] The great amount of mental illness in both urban and rural areas is mostly neuroses and mild character disorders; only a minority suffer from psychoses, the serious mental illnesses implied in the popular culture critique. Serious mental illness does seem to be especially high among the poverty-stricken.[12] This group uses the mass media intensively, but it has been suffering from social and emotional problems caused by poverty for many centuries, long before popular culture was invented, and indeed while the folk art considered healthy by the critics flourished around it.

Although one could therefore reject the charge of negative effects at the outset by showing that the picture of the popular-culture audience is drawn not from reality but from the fantasies and even wishes of the critics, it may still be that the existing mental illness and other negative qualities implied by the charges can be traced to the effects of popular culture. The evidence from a generation of studies on the effects of the mass media suggest that this is not so. The media do not have the simple Pavlovian impact attributed to them, and it is thus impossible to deduce effects from content. Instead, media content is just one of many cultural stimuli people choose, to which they respond, and, more important, that they help to create through the feedback they exert on the popular-culture industries.

Several studies have shown that people choose media content to fit individual and group requirements, rather than adapting their life to what the media prescribe or glorify. They are not isolated individuals hungering for and therefore slavishly accepting what the media offer them, but families, couples, and peer groups who use the media when and if the content is relevant to group goals and needs.[13] Thus the audience cannot be considered a mass.[14] Moreover, people pay much less attention to the media and are much less swayed by its content than the critics, who are highly sensitive to verbal and other symbolic materials, believe. They use the media for diversion and would not think of applying its content to their own

[11] For reviews of the major community studies, see Maurice Stein, *The Eclipse of Community*. Princeton, N.J.: Princeton University Press, 1960; and Harold Wilensky and Charles N. Lebeaux, *Industrial Society and Social Welfare*. New York: Russell Sage Foundation, 1958, Part I. See also Harold Wilensky, "Mass Society and Mass Culture," *American Sociological Review*, 29 (April 1964), pp. 173–197, at p. 177. The major mental health studies are: Leo Srole et al., *Mental Health in the Metropolis*. New York: McGraw-Hill, 1962; Thomas S. Langner and Stanley T. Michael, *Life Stress and Mental Health*. New York: The Free Press of Glencoe, 1963; Dorothea C. Leighton et al., *The Character of Danger* New York: Basic Books, 1963.
[12] August B. Hollingshead and Frederick C. Redlich, *Social Class and Mental Illness*. New York: John Wiley and Sons, 1958; Srole, *op. cit.*, and Langner and Michael, *op. cit.*
[13] Among the principal studies are Matilda Riley and John W. Riley, "A Sociological Approach to Communications Research," *Public Opinion Quarterly*, 15 (Fall 1951), pp. 445–460, and Elihu Katz and Paul Lazarsfeld, *Personal Influence*. Glencoe, Ill.: The Free Press, 1955.
[14] Eliot Freidson, "Communications Research and the Concept of the Mass," *American Sociological Review*, 18 (June 1953), pp. 313–317.

lives.[15] Even adolescents, some of whom are loyal fans of teen-age performers during the period just before puberty, do not model themselves or their choice of dates and spouses on these performers, press agent claims notwithstanding. Finally, content choice is strongly affected by *selective perception*, so that people not only choose content that agrees with their own values but also interpret conflicting content so as to support these values. Thus the prime function of the media is to reinforce already existing behavior and attitudes, rather than to create new ones.[16]

There are, of course, exceptions to such a general finding. People copy dress and other fashions from the media, although those who do so are a tiny percentage of the total audience. People are also known to accept unquestioningly media content on subject matter of little interest to them. Moreover, children are more impressionable than adults and will accept content at face value, although even they become trained in what Freidson calls "adult discount" before they are ten.[17] In addition, some recent experimental studies have shown that mass-media content may have an immediate impact that disappears soon afterward.[18] For example, in the laboratory, movies with aggressive content stimulate the acting out of aggressive impulses among the subjects, but then romantic movies have encouraged balcony necking parties for generations without apparent ill effect. More important, socially marginal and psychopathic personalities may be affected by media content more easily than others.[19] Most important, the mass media may add to the difficulties of the deprived who must watch as outsiders in their own society. Thus a recent community study made in a New York slum concluded that "public communication media and advertising tend to aggravate the effects of poverty. Television, automobiles, holidays such as Christmas, and advertising in general create more serious alienation and psychological damage than is generally assumed."[20]

Finally, all the studies measure conscious effects, and say little or nothing about possible unconscious consequences. Moreover, they deal with short-range impact occurring weeks or months after media exposure, and do not report on the long-range effects of living in a society where media use takes up so much time. There are thus significant omissions in the

[15] For one illustration, see Herbert J. Gans, *The Urban Villagers*. New York: The Free Press of Glencoe, 1962, Chapter 9.

[16] Klapper, *op. cit., passim*. See also Rolf Meyersohn, "Social Research in Television," in Rosenberg and White, eds., *op. cit.*, pp. 245–257.

[17] Eliot Freidson, "Adult Discount; An Aspect of Children's Changing Taste," *Child Development*, 24, 1 (March 1953), pp. 39–49.

[18] L. Berkowitz, R. Corwin, and M. Heironimus, "Film Violence and Subsequent Aggressive Tendencies," *Public Opinion Quarterly*, 27 (Summer 1963), pp. 217–229.

[19] Wilensky, "Mass Society and Mass Culture," *op. cit.*, p. 183.

[20] Sherman Barr, "Poverty on the Lower East Side." New York: Mobilization for Youth, mimeographed, May 1964. The quotation reflects the preliminary nature of the data and is cited here mainly to note a possible effect that deserves systematic study.

available evidence, mainly because subconscious and long-range effects are difficult to study empirically.[21] Nevertheless, if these effects existed—and in the alarming proportions suggested by the mass-culture critique—they should make themselves visible in the society. There is no evidence, however, of a rising tide of violence, crime, or mental illness.[22]

This brief survey of the effects studies permits some evaluation of the charges about mass culture's impact on the audience. As to emotional destructiveness, the only evidence brought forth by the critics is a deduction from content: that since the media content is often violent, it must encourage violence and brutalization in the audience. Of course, the depiction of violence is a frequent theme in the popular arts, but this proves nothing about audience behavior. Undoubtedly violence reinforces pathology among pathological audience members and frightens some children, although an English study showed that the latter were less fearful of the fictional violence that is most often condemned than of more realistic violence in newsreels and naturalistic drama.[23] Moreover, some psychiatrists argue that the vicarious consumption of violence may reduce its expression in behavior. More violence in the popular arts may thus mean less violence among people, although recent experiments that encourage children to be aggressive after having seen a film in which aggressive behavior is prominent suggest that this is not true, at least not in the laboratory.[24] My own feeling is that only when other, more real provocations toward violence are present can mass-media violence affect behavior, and even then the media only influence children and pathological individuals. Further research is unfortunately necessary before it can be determined whether media violence ought to be reduced.

A perhaps more serious charge, with more widespread consequences, is that popular culture provides overly facile, spurious, and misleading gratification of emotional needs, notably through happy endings, false heroics, the appearance of a *deux ex machina* to solve insoluble problems, and stereotypical characterizations, whereas high culture offers genuine gratifi-

---

[21] For a good discussion of subconscious effects and their empirical identification, see Arthur J. Brodbeck, "The Popular Arts as a Socializing Agency," paper presented at the 1955 meetings of the American Psychological Association.

[22] On crime, see Daniel Bell, Chapter 8, "The Myth of Crime Waves," in his *End of Ideology.* Glencoe, Ill.: The Free Press, 1960; on mental illness, see Herbert Goldhamer and Andrew M. Marshall, *Psychosis and Civilization.* Glencoe, Ill.: The Free Press, 1953.

[23] H. Himmelweit, A. Oppenheim, and P. Vance, *Television and the Child.* London: Oxford University Press, 1958. The principal American studies of the effects of the mass media on children are Lotte Bailyn, "Mass Media and Children: A Study of Exposure Habits and Cognitive Effects," *Psychological Monographs,* 73 (1959), pp. 1–48; and W. Schramm, J. Lyle, and E. Parker, *Television in the Lives of Our Children.* Stanford, Calif.: Stanford University Press, 1961. An up-to-date review of all studies of the effects of television on children is to be found in Wilbur Schramm, ed., "The Effects of Television on Children and Adolescents." Paris: UNESCO, Reports and Papers on Mass Communications, No. 43, 1964.

[24] These studies are summarized in Schramm, "The Effects of Television on Children and Adolescents," *op. cit.,* pp. 14–15.

cations through its honest and reality-oriented treatment of individual and social themes. Thus van den Haag has argued that the entire pattern of vicarious emotional release in popular culture is false, that needs for aggression and sexuality are not properly gratified, and that the media offer "substitute gratifications . . . which strengthen internalized hindrance to real and gratifying experience . . . that we are diverted temporarily and in the end perhaps drained—but not gratified."[25] This theory can be discussed as part of a more general charge, that popular culture distorts reality through escapist fiction, meretricious advertising, and superficial news reporting.

Undoubtedly, the content of popular culture can be described and evaluated in this way, but it still permits no conclusion about effects. Van den Haag offers no evidence, for example, that people are drained rather than gratified, or that high culture has the reverse effect, and if so, how. Certainly there are people who fit the mass critique model, living their entire emotional life within and through the mass media, but such people are emotionally disturbed and their use of the media is only a symptom, not a cause, of their difficulties. Conversely, there are also people whose emotional existence is limited to high culture and devoid of human relationships. Although their pathology is no different, it is not considered such and is valued as a testimonial to the desirability of high culture.

Similarly, there are people who use the mass media as guides to problem solving, and who suffer from the false version of reality presented in their entertainment and informational content. Although there are no adequate studies of where people get information used in problem solving, the effects described previously indicate that most people do not take media content at face value; that they use it to provide temporary respite from everyday life, rather than as a guide to it; and that they take material that supports their prior values and predispositions rather than new solutions.[26]

There are also people who are taken in by the puffery and dishonesty of advertising, especially among the most poorly educated, although studies of advertising impact and the complaints of advertising executives show that most people retain little of the ads they see or hear, and misinterpret much of the message. This does not justify dishonest advertising but does cast doubt on the intensity of the effect of advertising on people. Repetitive, hard-sell commercials are equally unjustifiable, especially since they do seem to have a Pavlovian effect on some audience members, at least judging by their effectiveness in raising sales of the products so advertised.

Finally, there is no doubt that popular culture's coverage of national

[25] Van den Haag, op. cit., pp. 533–534.
[26] Herta Herzog, "Motivations and Gratifications of Daily Serial Listeners," in Wilbur Schramm, ed., The Process and Effects of Mass Communications. Urbana: University of Illinois Press, 1955, pp. 50–55.

and world events is quantitatively and qualitatively poor; "human interest," sensationalism and the evasion of controversy are major faults. Even so, all the evidence suggests that the mass media provide more news and controversy than the majority of the audience is willing to accept.[27]

More important, voting studies show that people do not make up their minds about their vote on the basis of mass-media content—or campaign speeches—and that they generally seem to know how to vote their interests, without what intellectuals would consider adequate information.[28] When an issue does not affect them, however, people may accept and vote on the basis of the version that is provided by the mass media. This recourse is especially undesirable when the competing points of view have unequal resources, and the well-financed group is able to obtain publicity for its point of view while the poorly financed group is unable to do so. Here the fault lies less with the mass media than with economic inequities in the society that can be used for political advantage. In fact, the national media usually try to present a "balanced" view of controversial issues by including all points of view in their content and, on television at least, by letting both sides purchase advertising. There is considerably less balance in the content of local media, however. This is also true at the national level of points of view held by small minorities. Nevertheless, the problem is not an effect of popular culture, but a public failure to protect the goals of political democracy in profit-seeking institutions with political communication functions. . . .

One Culture
and the
New Sensibility

Susan Sontag

In the last few years there has been a good deal of discussion of a purported chasm which opened up some two centuries ago, with the advent of the Industrial Revolution, between "two cultures," the literary-

Reprinted with the permission of Farrar, Straus & Giroux, Inc. from *Against Interpretation* by Susan Sontag, copyright © 1965 by Susan Sontag.

[27] Bauer and Bauer, *op. cit.*, p. 53. See also Bernard Cohen, *The Press and Foreign Policy*. Princeton, N.J.: Princeton University Press, 1963.

[28] Paul Lazarsfeld, B. Berelson, and H. Gaudet, *The People's Choice*. New York: Columbia University Press, 1948; and B. Berelson, P. Lazarsfeld, and W. McPhee, *Voting*. Chicago: University of Chicago Press, 1954.

artistic and the scientific. According to this diagnosis, any intelligent and articulate modern person is likely to inhabit one culture to the exclusion of the other. He will be concerned with different documents, different techniques, different problems; he will speak a different language. Most important, the type of effort required for the mastery of these two cultures will differ vastly. For the literary-artistic culture is understood as a general culture. It is addressed to man insofar as he is man; it is culture or, rather, it promotes culture, in the sense of culture defined by Ortega y Gasset: that which a man has in his possession when he has forgotten everything that he has read. The scientific culture, in contrast, is a culture for specialists; it is founded on remembering and is set down in ways that require complete dedication of the effort to comprehend. While the literary-artistic culture aims at internalization, ingestion—in other words, cultivation—the scientific culture aims at accumulation and externalization in complex instruments for problem-solving and specific techniques for mastery.

Though T. S. Eliot derived the chasm between the two cultures from a period more remote in modern history, speaking in a famous essay of a "dissociation of sensibility" which opened up in the 17th century, the connection of the problem with the Industrial Revolution seems well taken. There is a historic antipathy on the part of many literary intellectuals and artists to those changes which characterize modern society— above all, industrialization and those of its effects which everyone has experienced, such as the proliferation of huge impersonal cities and the predominance of the anonymous style of urban life. It has mattered little whether industrialization, the creature of modern "science," is seen on the 19th and early 20th century model, as noisy smoky artificial processes which defile nature and stardardize culture, or on the newer model, the clean automated technology that is coming into being in the second half of the 20th century. The judgment has been mostly the same. Literary men, feeling that the status of humanity itself was being challenged by the new science and the new technology, abhorred and deplored the change. But the literary men, whether one thinks of Emerson and Thoreau and Ruskin in the 19th century, or of 20th century intellectuals who talk of modern society as being in some new way incomprehensible, "alienated," are inevitably on the defensive. They know that the scientific culture, the coming of the machine, cannot be stopped.

The standard response to the problem of "the two cultures"—and the issue long antedates by many decades the crude and philistine statement of the problem by C. P. Snow in a famous lecture some years ago—has been a facile defense of the function of the arts (in terms of an ever vaguer ideology of "humanism") or a premature surrender of the function of the arts to science. By the second response, I am not referring to the philistinism of scientists (and those of their party among artists and philosophers) who dismiss the arts as imprecise, untrue, at best mere toys. I am speaking of serious doubts which have arisen among those who are passionately engaged in the arts. The role of the individual artist, in the business of making unique objects for the purpose of giving pleasure and educating conscience and sensibility, has repeatedly been called into question. Some literary intellectuals and artists have gone so far as to prophesy the ultimate demise of the art-making activity of man. Art, in an automated scientific society, would be unfunctional, useless.

But this conclusion, I should argue, is plainly unwarranted. Indeed, the whole issue seems to me crudely put. For the question of "the two cultures" assumes that science and technology are changing, in motion, while the arts are static, fulfilling some perennial generic human function (consolation? edification? diversion?). Only on the basis of this false assumption would anyone reason that the arts might be in danger of becoming obsolete.

Art does not progress, in the sense that science and technology do. But the arts do develop and change. For instance, in our own time, art is becoming increasingly the terrain of specialists. The most interesting and creative art of our time is *not* open to the generally educated; it demands special effort; it speaks a specialized language. The music of Milton Babbitt and Morton Feldman, the painting of Mark Rothko and Frank Stella, the dance of Merce Cunningham and James Waring demand an education of sensibility whose difficulties and length of apprenticeship are at least comparable to the difficulties of mastering physics or engineering. (Only the novel, among the arts, at least in America, fails to provide similar examples.) The parallel between the abstruseness of contemporary art and that of modern science is too obvious to be missed. Another likeness to the scientific culture is the history-mindedness of contemporary art. The most interesting works of contemporary art are full of references to the history of the medium; so far as they comment on past art, they demand a knowledge of at least the recent past. As Harold Rosenberg has pointed out, contemporary paintings are themselves acts of criticism as much as of creation. The point could be made as well of much recent work in the films, music, the dance, poetry, and (in Europe) literature. Again, a similarity with the style of science—this time, with the accumulative aspect of science—can be discerned.

The conflict between "the two cultures" is in fact an illusion, a temporary phenomenon born of a period of profound and bewildering historical change. What we are witnessing is not so much a conflict of cultures as the creation of a new (potentially unitary) kind of sensibility. This new sensibility is rooted, as it must be, in *our* experience, experiences which are new in the history of humanity—in extreme social and physical mobility; in the crowdedness of the human scene (both people and material commodities multiplying at a dizzying rate); in the availability of new sensations such as speed (physical speed, as in airplane travel; speed of images, as in the cinema); and in the pan-cultural perspective on the arts that is possible through the mass reproduction of art objects.

What we are getting is not the demise of art, but a transformation of the function of art. Art, which arose in human society as a magical-religious operation, and passed over into a technique for depicting and commenting on secular reality, has in our own time arrogated to itself a new function— neither religious, nor serving a secularized religious function, nor merely secular or profane (a notion which breaks down when its opposite, the "religious" or "sacred," becomes obsolescent). Art today is a new kind of instrument, an instrument for modifying consciousness and organizing new modes of sensibility. And the means for practicing art have been radically extended. Indeed, in response to this new function (more felt than clearly articulated), artists have had to become self-conscious aestheticians: continually challenging their means, their materials and methods. Often, the conquest and exploitation of new materials and methods drawn from the world of "non-art"—for example, from industrial technology, from commercial processes and imagery, from purely private and subjective fantasies and dreams—seems to be the principal effort of many artists. Painters no longer feel themselves confined to canvas and paint, but employ hair, photographs, wax, sand, bicycle tires, their own toothbrushes and socks. Musicians have reached beyond the sounds of the traditional instruments to use tampered instruments and (usually on tape) synthetic sounds and industrial noises.

All kinds of conventionally accepted boundaries have thereby been challenged: not just the one between the "scientific" and the "literary-artistic" cultures, or the one between "art" and "non-art"; but also many established distinctions within the world of culture itself—that between form and content, the frivolous and the serious, and (a favorite of literary intellectuals) "high" and "low" culture.

The distinction between "high" and "low" (or "mass" or "popular") culture is based partly on an evaluation of the difference between unique and mass-produced objects. In an era of mass technological reproduction, the work of the serious artist had a special value simply because it was unique, because it bore his personal, individual signature. The works of popular culture (and even films were for a long time included in this category) were seen as having little value because they were manufactured objects, bearing no individual stamp—group concoctions made for an undifferentiated audience. But in the light of contemporary practice in the arts, this distinction appears extremely shallow. Many of the serious works of art of recent decades have a decidedly impersonal character. The work of art is reasserting its existence as "object" (even as manufactured or mass-produced object, drawing on the popular arts) rather than as "individual personal expression."

The exploration of the impersonal (and trans-personal) in contempo-

rary art is the new classicism; at least, a reaction against what is understood as the romantic spirit dominates most of the interesting art of today.
Today's art, with its insistence on coolness, its refusal of what it considers
to be sentimentality, its spirit of exactness, its sense of "research" and
"problems," is closer to the spirit of science than of art in the old-
fashioned sense. Often, the artist's work is only his idea, his concept. This
is a familiar practice in architecture, of course. And one remembers that
painters in the Renaissance often left parts of their canvases to be worked
out by students, and that in the flourishing period of the concerto the
cadenza at the end of the first movement was left to the inventiveness and
discretion of the performing soloist. But similar practices have a different,
more polemical meaning today, in the present post-romantic era of the
arts. When painters such as Joseph Albers, Ellsworth Kelly, and Andy
Warhol assign portions of the work, say, the painting in of the colors
themselves, to a friend or the local gardener; when musicians such as
Stockhausen, John Cage, and Luigi Nono invite collaboration from performers by leaving opportunities for random effects, switching around the
order of the score, and improvisations—they are changing the ground
rules which most of us employ to recognize a work of art. They are saying
what art need not be. At least, not necessarily.

The primary feature of the new sensibility is that its model product is
not the literary work, above all, the novel. A new non-literary culture
exists today, of whose very existence, not to mention significance, most
literary intellectuals are entirely unaware. This new establishment includes
certain painters, sculptors, architects, social planners, film-makers, TV
technicians, neurologists, musicians, electronics engineers, dancers, philosophers and sociologists. (A few poets and prose writers can be included.)
Some of the basic texts for this new cultural alignment are to be found in
the writings of Nietzsche, Wittgenstein, Antonin Artaud, C. S. Sherrington,
Buckminster Fuller, Marshall McLuhan, John Cage, André Breton, Roland Barthes, Claude Lévi-Strauss, Siegfried Gidieon, Norman O. Brown,
and Gyorgy Kepes.

Those who worry about the gap between "the two cultures," and this
means virtually all literary intellectuals in England and America, take for
granted a notion of culture which decidedly needs reexamining. It is the
notion perhaps best expressed by Matthew Arnold (in which the central
cultural act is the making of literature, which is itself understood as the
criticism of culture). Simply ignorant of the vital and enthralling (so
called "avant-garde") developments in the other arts, and blinded by their
personal investment in the perpetuation of the older notion of culture, they
continue to cling to literature as the model for creative statement.

What gives literature its preeminence is its heavy burden of "content,"
both reportage and moral judgment. (This makes it possible for most

English and American literary critics to use literary works mainly as texts, or even pretexts, for social and cultural diagnosis—rather than concentrating on the properties of, say, a given novel or a play, as an art work.) But the model arts of our time are actually those with much less content, and a much cooler mode of moral judgment—like music, films, dance, architecture, painting, sculpture. The practice of these arts—all of which draw profusely, naturally, and without embarrassment, upon science and technology—are the locus of the new sensibility.

The problem of "the two cultures," in short, rests upon an uneducated, uncontemporary grasp of our present cultural situation. It arises from the ignorance of literary intellectuals (and of scientists with a shallow knowledge of the arts, like the scientist-novelist C. P. Snow himself) of a new culture, and its emerging sensibility. In fact, there can be no divorce between science and technology, on the one hand, and art, on the other, any more than there can be a divorce between art and the forms of social life. Works of art, psychological forms, and social forms all reflect each other, and change with each other. But, of course, most people are slow to come to terms with such changes—especially today, when the changes are occurring with an unprecedented rapidity. Marshall McLuhan has described human history as a succession of acts of technological extension of human capacity, each of which works a radical change upon our environment and our ways of thinking, feeling, and valuing. The tendency, he remarks, is to upgrade the old environment into art form (thus Nature became a vessel of aesthetic and spiritual values in the new industrial environment) "while the new conditions are regarded as corrupt and degrading." Typically, it is only certain artists in any given era who "have the resources and temerity to live in immediate contact with the environment of their age . . . That is why they may seem to be 'ahead of their time' . . . More timid people prefer to accept the . . . previous environment's values as the continuing reality of their time. Our natural bias is to accept the new gimmick (automation, say) as a thing that can be accommodated in the old ethical order." Only in the terms of what McLuhan calls the old ethical order does the problem of "the two cultures" appear to be a genuine problem. It is not a problem for most of the creative artists of our time (among whom one could include very few novelists) because most of these artists have broken, whether they know it or not, with the Matthew Arnold notion of culture, finding it historically and humanly obsolescent.

The Matthew Arnold notion of culture defines art as the criticism of life—this being understood as the propounding of moral, social, and political ideas. The new sensibility understands art as the extension of life—this being understood as the representation of (new) modes of vivacity. There is no necessary denial of the role of moral evaluation here. Only the scale has changed; it has become less gross, and what it sacrifices in discursive explicitness it gains in accuracy and subliminal power. For we are what we are able to see (hear, taste, smell, feel) even more powerfully and profoundly than we are what furniture of ideas we have stocked in our heads. Of course, the proponents of "the two cultures" crisis continue to observe a desperate contrast between unintelligible, morally neutral science and technology, on the one hand, and morally committed, human-scale art on the other. But matters are not that simple, and never were. A great work of art is never simply (or even mainly) a vehicle of ideas or of moral sentiments. It is, first of all, an object modifying our consciousness and sensibility, changing the composition, however slightly, of the humus that nourishes all specific ideas and sentiments. Outraged humanists, please note. There is no need for alarm. A work of art does not cease being a moment in the conscience of mankind, when moral conscience is understood as only one of the functions of consciousness.

Sensations, feelings, the abstract forms and styles of sensibility count. It is to these that contemporary art addresses itself. The basic unit for contemporary art is not the idea, but the analysis of and extension of sensations. (Or if it is an "idea," it is about the form of sensibility.) Rilke described the artist as someone who works "toward an extension of the regions of the individual senses"; McLuhan calls artists "experts in sensory awareness." And the most interesting works of contemporary art (one can begin at least as far back as French symbolist poetry) are adventures in sensation, new "sensory mixes." Such art is, in principle, experimental— not out of an elitist disdain for what is accessible to the majority, but precisely in the sense that science is experimental. Such an art is also notably apolitical and undidactic, or, rather, infradidactic.

When Ortega y Gasset wrote his famous essay *The Dehumanization of Art* in the early 1920s, he ascribed the qualities of modern art (such as impersonality, the ban on pathos, hostility to the past, playfulness, willful stylization, absence of ethical and political commitment) to the spirit of youth which he thought dominated our age.[1] In retrospect, it seems this "dehumanization" did not signify the recovery of childlike innocence, but was rather a very adult, knowing response. What other response than anguish, followed by anesthesia and then by wit and the elevating of intelligence over sentiment, is possible as a response to the social disorder and mass atrocities of our time, and—equally important for our sensibilities, but less often remarked on—to the unprecedented change in what rules our environment from the intelligible and visible to that which is only with difficulty intelligible, and is invisible? Art, which I have characterized as an instrument for modifying and educating sensibility and consciousness, now operates in an environment which cannot be grasped by the senses.

---

[1] Ortega remarks, in this essay: "Were art to redeem man, it could do so only by saving him from the seriousness of life and restoring him to an unexpected boyishness."

Buckminister Fuller has written:

> In World War I industry suddenly went from the visible to the invisible base, from the track to the trackless, from the wire to the wireless, from visible structuring to invisible structuring in alloys. The big thing about World War I is that *man went off the sensorial spectrum forever* as the prime criterion of accrediting innovations . . . All major advances since World War I have been in the *infra* and the *ultra*sensorial frequencies of the electromagnetic spectrum. All the important technical affairs of men today are invisible . . . The old masters, who were sensorialists, have unleashed a Pandora's box of non-sensorially controllable phenomena, which they had avoided accrediting up to that time . . . Suddenly they lost their true mastery, because from then on they didn't personally understand what was going on. If you don't understand you cannot master . . . Since World War I, the old masters have been extinct . . .

But, of course, art remains permanently tied to the senses. Just as one cannot float colors in space (a painter needs some sort of surface, like a canvas, however neutral and textureless), one cannot have a work of art that does not impinge upon the human sensorium. But it is important to realize that human sensory awareness has not merely a biology but a specific history, each culture placing a premium on certain senses and inhibiting others. (The same is true for the range of primary human emotions.) Here is where art (among other things) enters, and why the interesting art of our time has such a feeling of anguish and crisis about it, however playful and abstract and ostensibly neutral morally it may appear. Western man may be said to have been undergoing a massive sensory anesthesia (a concomitant of the process that Max Weber calls "bureaucratic rationalization") at least since the Industrial Revolution, with modern art functioning as a kind of shock therapy for both confounding and unclosing our senses.

One important consequence of the new sensibility (with its abandonment of the Matthew Arnold idea of culture) has already been alluded to—namely, that the distinction between "high" and "low" culture seems less and less meaningful. For such a distinction—inseparable from the Matthew Arnold apparatus—simply does not make sense for a creative community of artists and scientists engaged in programming sensations, uninterested in art as a species of moral journalism. Art has always been more than that, anyway.

Another way of characterizing the present cultural situation, in its most creative aspects, would be to speak of a new attitude toward pleasure. In one sense, the new art and the new sensibility take a rather dim view of pleasure. (The great contemporary French composer, Pierre Boulez, entitled an important essay of his twelve years ago, "Against Hedonism in

Music.") The seriousness of modern art precludes pleasure in the familiar sense—the pleasure of a melody that one can hum after leaving the concert hall, of characters in a novel or play whom one can recognize, identify with, and dissect in terms of realistic psychological motives, of a beautiful landscape or a dramatic moment represented on a canvas. If hedonism means sustaining the old ways in which we have found pleasure in art (the old sensory and psychic modalities), then the new art is anti-hedonistic. Having one's sensorium challenged or stretched hurts. The new serious music hurts one's ears, the new painting does not graciously reward one's sight, the new films and the few interesting new prose works do not go down easily. The commonest complaint about the films of Antonioni or the narratives of Beckett or Burroughs is that they are hard to look at or to read, that they are "boring." But the charge of boredom is really hypocritical. There is, in a sense, no such thing as boredom. Boredom is only another name for a certain species of frustration. And the new languages which the interesting art of our time speaks are frustrating to the sensibilities of most educated people.

But the purpose of art is always, ultimately, to give pleasure—though our sensibilities may take time to catch up with the forms of pleasure that art in a given time may offer. And, one can also say that, balancing the ostensible anti-hedonism of serious contemporary art, the modern sensibility is more involved with pleasure in the familiar sense than ever. Because the new sensibility demands less "content" in art, and is more open to the pleasures of "form" and style, it is also less snobbish, less moralistic—in that it does not demand that pleasure in art necessarily be associated with edification. If art is understood as a form of discipline of the feelings and a programming of sensations, then the feeling (or sensation) given off by a Rauschenberg painting might be like that of a song by the Supremes. The brio and elegance of Budd Boetticher's *The Rise and Fall of Legs Diamond* or the singing style of Dionne Warwick can be appreciated as a complex and pleasurable event. They are experienced without condescension.

This last point seems to me worth underscoring. For it is important to understand that the affection which many younger artists and intellectuals feel for the popular arts is not a new philistinism (as has so often been charged) or a species of anti-intellectualism or some kind of abdication from culture. The fact that many of the most serious American painters, for example, are also fans of "the new sound" in popular music is *not* the result of the search for mere diversion or relaxation; it is not, say, like Schoenberg also playing tennis. It reflects a new, more open way of looking at the world and at things in the world, our world. It does not mean the renunciation of all standards: there is plenty of stupid popular music, as well as inferior and pretentious "avant-garde" paintings, films, and music. The point is that there *are* new standards, new standards of beauty and style and taste. The new sensibility is defiantly pluralistic; it is dedicated both to an excruciating seriousness and to fun and wit and nostalgia. It is also extremely history-conscious; and the voracity of its enthusiasms (and of the supercession of these enthusiasms) is very high-speed and hectic. From the vantage point of this new sensibility, the beauty of a machine or of the solution to a mathematical problem, of a painting by Jasper Johns, of a film by Jean-Luc Godard, and of the personalities and music of the Beatles is equally accessible.

Media
Hot and Cold
Marshall McLuhan

"The rise of the waltz," explained Curt Sachs in the *World History of the Dance*, "was a result of that longing for truth, simplicity, closeness to nature, and primitivism, which the last two-thirds of the eighteenth century fulfilled." In the century of jazz we are likely to overlook the emergence of the waltz as a hot and explosive human expression that broke through the formal feudal barriers of courtly and choral dance styles.

There is a basic principle that distinguishes a hot medium like radio from a cool one like the telephone, or a hot medium like the movie from a cool one like TV. A hot medium is one that extends one single sense in "high definition." High definition is the state of being well filled with data. A photograph is, visually, "high definition." A cartoon is "low definition," simply because very little visual information is provided. Telephone is a cool medium, or one of low definition, because the ear is given a meager amount of information. And speech is a cool medium of low definition, because so little is given and so much has to be filled in by the listener. On the other hand, hot media do not leave so much to be filled in or completed by the audience. Hot media are, therefore, low in participation, and cool media are high in participation or completion by the audience. Naturally, therefore, a hot medium like radio has very different effects on the user from a cool medium like the telephone.

A cool medium like hieroglyphic or ideogrammic written characters has

From *Understanding Media: The Extensions of Man* by Marshall McLuhan. Copyright © 1964 by Marshall McLuhan. Used by permission of McGraw-Hill Book Company.

very different effects from the hot and explosive medium of the phonetic alphabet. The alphabet, when pushed to a high degree of abstract visual intensity, became typography. The printed word with its specialist intensity burst the bonds of medieval corporate guilds and monasteries, creating extreme individualistic patterns of enterprise and monopoly. But the typical reversal occurred when extremes of monopoly brought back the corporation, with its impersonal empire over many lives. The hotting-up of the medium of writing to repeatable print intensity led to nationalism and the religious wars of the sixteenth century. The heavy and unwieldy media, such as stone, are time binders. Used for writing, they are very cool indeed, and serve to unify the ages; whereas paper is a hot medium that serves to unify spaces horizontally, both in political and entertainment empires.

Any hot medium allows of less participation than a cool one, as a lecture makes for less participation than a seminar, and a book for less than dialogue. With print many earlier forms were excluded from life and art, and many were given strange new intensity. But our own time is crowded with examples of the principle that the hot form excludes, and the cool one includes. When ballerinas began to dance on their toes a century ago, it was felt that the art of the ballet had acquired a new "spirituality." With this new intensity, male figures were excluded from ballet. The role of women had also become fragmented with the advent of industrial specialism and the explosion of home functions into laundries, bakeries, and hospitals on the periphery of the community. Intensity or high definition engenders specialism and fragmentation in living as in entertainment, which explains why any intense experience must be "forgotten," "censored," and reduced to a very cool state before it can be "learned" or assimilated. The Freudian "censor" is less of a moral function than an indispensable condition of learning. Were we to accept fully and directly every shock to our various structures of awareness, we would soon be nervous wrecks, doing double-takes and pressing panic buttons every minute. The "censor" protects our central system of values, as it does our physical nervous system by simply cooling off the onset of experience a great deal. For many people, this cooling system brings on a lifelong state of psychic *rigor mortis*, or of somnambulism, particularly observable in periods of new technology.

An example of the disruptive impact of a hot technology succeeding a cool one is given by Robert Theobald in *The Rich and the Poor*. When Australian natives were given steel axes by the missionaries, their culture, based on the stone axe, collapsed. The stone axe had not only been scarce but had always been a basic status symbol of male importance. The missionaries provided quantities of sharp steel axes and gave them to women and children. The men had even to borrow these from the women, causing a collapse of male dignity. A tribal and feudal hierarchy of traditional kind collapses quickly when it meets any hot medium of the mechanical, uniform, and repetitive kind. The medium of money or wheel or writing, or any other form of specialist speedup of exchange and information, will serve to fragment a tribal structure. Similarly, a very much greater speedup, such as occurs with electricity, may serve to restore a tribal pattern of intense involvement such as took place with the introduction of radio in Europe, and is now tending to happen as a result of TV in America. Specialist technologies detribalize. The nonspecialist electric technology retribalizes. The process of upset resulting from a new distribution of skills is accompanied by much culture lag in which people feel compelled to look at new situations as if they were old ones, and come up with ideas of "population explosion" in an age of implosion. Newton, in an age of clocks, managed to present the physical universe in the image of a clock. But poets like Blake were far ahead of Newton in their response to the challenge of the clock. Blake spoke of the need to be delivered "from single vision and Newton's sleep," knowing very well that Newton's response to the challenge of the new mechanism was itself merely a mechanical repetition of the challenge. Blake saw Newton and Locke and others as hypnotized Narcissus types quite unable to meet the challenge of mechanism. W. B. Yeats gave the full Blakean version of Newton and Locke in a famous epigram:

> Locke sank into a swoon;
> The garden died;
> God took the spinning jenny
> Out of his side.[1]

Yeats presents Locke, the philosopher of mechanical and lineal associationism, as hypnotized by his own image. The "garden," or unified consciousness, ended. Eighteenth-century man got an extension of himself in the form of the spinning machine that Yeats endows with its full sexual significance. Woman, herself, is thus seen as a technological extension of man's being.

Blake's counterstrategy for his age was to meet mechanism with organic myth. Today, deep in the electric age, organic myth is itself a simple and automatic response capable of mathematical formulation and expression, without any of the imaginative perception of Blake about it. Had he encountered the electric age, Blake would not have met its challenge with a mere repetition of electric form. For myth *is* the instant vision of a complex process that ordinarily extends over a long period. Myth is contraction or implosion of any process, and the instant speed of electricity confers the mythic dimension on ordinary industrial and social action today.

---

[1] Reprinted with permission of The Macmillan Company and A. P. Watt & Son, London, from "Fragments" in *Collected Poems* by William Butler Yeats. Copyright 1933 by The Macmillan Company, renewed 1961 by Bertha Georgie Yeats.

We *live* mythically but continue to think fragmentarily and on single planes.

Scholars today are acutely aware of a discrepancy between their ways of treating subjects and the subject itself. Scriptural scholars of both the Old and New Testaments frequently say that while their treatment must be linear, the subject is not. The subject treats of the relations between God and man, and between God and the world, and of the relations between man and his neighbor—all these subsist together, and act and react upon one another at the same time. The Hebrew and Eastern mode of thought tackles problem and resolution, at the outset of a discussion, in a way typical of oral societies in general. The entire message is then traced and retraced, again and again, on the rounds of a concentric spiral with seeming redundancy. One can stop anywhere after the first few sentences and have the full message, if one is prepared to "dig" it. This kind of plan seems to have inspired Frank Lloyd Wright in designing the Guggenheim Art Gallery on a spiral, concentric basis. It is a redundant form inevitable to the electric age, in which the concentric pattern is imposed by the instant quality, and overlay in depth, of electric speed. But the concentric with its endless intersection of planes is necessary for insight. In fact, it is the technique of insight, and as such is necessary for media study, since no medium had its meaning or existence alone, but only in constant interplay with other media.

The new electric structuring and configuring of life more and more encounters the old lineal and fragmentary procedures and tools of analysis from the mechanical age. More and more we turn from the content of messages to study total effect. Kenneth Boulding put this matter in *The Image* by saying, "The meaning of a message is the change which it produces in the image." Concern with *effect* rather than *meaning* is a basic change of our electric time, for effect involves the total situation, and not a single level of information movement. Strangely, there is recognition of this matter of effect rather than information in the British idea of libel: "The greater the truth, the greater the libel."

The effect of electric technology had at first been anxiety. Now it appears to create boredom. We have been through the three stages of alarm, resistance and exhaustion that occur in every disease or stress of life, whether individual or collective. At least, our exhausted slump after the first encounter with the electric has inclined us to expect new problems. However, backward countries that have experienced little permeation with our own mechanical and specialist culture are much better able to confront and to understand electric technology. Not only have backward and nonindustrial cultures no specialist habits to overcome in their encounter with electromagnetism, but they have still much of their traditional oral culture that has the total, unified "field" character of our new electromagnetism. Our old industrialized areas, having eroded their oral traditions automatically, are in the position of having to rediscover them in order to cope with the electric age.

In terms of the theme of media hot and cold, backward countries are cool, and we are hot. The "city slicker" is hot, and the rustic is cool. But in terms of the reversal of procedures and values in the electric age, the past mechanical time was hot, and we of the TV age are cool. The waltz was a hot, fast mechanical dance suited to the industrial time in its moods of pomp and circumstance. In contrast, the Twist is a cool, involved and chatty form of improvised gesture. The jazz of the period of the hot new media of movie and radio was hot jazz. Yet jazz of itself tends to be a casual dialogue form of dance quite lacking in the repetitive and mechanical forms of the waltz. Cool jazz came in quite naturally after the first impact of radio and movie had been absorbed.

In the special Russian issue of *Life* magazine for September 13, 1963, it is mentioned that in Russian restaurants and night clubs, "though the Charleston is tolerated, the Twist is taboo." All this is to say that a country in the process of industrialization is inclined to regard hot jazz as consistent with its developing programs. The cool and involved form of the Twist, on the other hand, would strike such a culture at once as retrograde and incompatible with its new mechanical stress. The Charleston, with its aspect of a mechanical doll agitated by strings, appears in Russia as an avant-garde form. We, on the other hand, find the *avant-garde* in the cool and the primitive, with its promise of depth involvement and integral expression.

The "hard" sell and the "hot" line become mere comedy in the TV age, and the death of all the salesmen at one stroke of the TV axe has turned the hot American culture into a cool one that is quite unacquainted with itself. America, in fact, would seem to be living through the reverse process that Margaret Mead described in *Time* magazine (September 4, 1954):

There are too many complaints about society having to move too fast to keep up with the machine. There is great advantage in moving fast if you move completely, if social, educational, and recreational changes keep pace. You must change the whole pattern at once and the whole group together— and the people themselves must decide to move.

Margaret Mead is thinking here of change as uniform speed-up of motion or a uniform hotting-up of temperatures in backward societies. We are certainly coming within conceivable range of a world automatically controlled to the point where we could say, "Six hours less radio in Indonesia next week or there will be a great falling off in literary attention." Or, "We can program twenty more hours of TV in South Africa next week to cool down the tribal temperature raised by radio last week." Whole cultures could now be programmed to keep their emotional climate stable in the same way that we have begun to know something about maintaining equilibrium in the commercial economies of the world.

In the merely personal and private sphere we are often reminded of how changes of tone and attitude are demanded of different times and seasons in order to keep situations in hand. British clubmen, for the sake of companionship and amiability, have long excluded the hot topics of religion and politics from mention inside the highly participational club. In the same vein, W. H. Auden wrote, ". . . this season the man of goodwill will wear his heart up his sleeve, not on it . . . the honest manly style is today suited only to Iago" (Introduction to John Betjeman's *Slick But Not Streamlined*). In the Renaissance, as print technology hotted up the social *milieu* to a very high point, the gentleman and the courtier (Hamlet-Mercutio style) adopted, in contrast, the casual and cool nonchalance of the playful and superior being. The Iago allusion of Auden reminds us that Iago was the *alter ego* and assistant of the intensely earnest and very non-nonchalant General Othello. In imitation of the earnest and forthright general, Iago hotted up his own image and wore his heart on his sleeve, until General Othello read him loud and clear as "honest Iago," a man after his own grimly earnest heart.

Throughout *The City in History*, Lewis Mumford favors the cool or casually structured towns over the hot and intensely filled-in cities. The great period of village life and participation still obtained. Then burst forth the full variety of human expression and exploration such as was later impossible in highly developed urban centers. For the highly developed situation is, by definition, low in opportunities of participation, and rigorous in its demands of specialist fragmentation from those who would control it. For example, what is known as "job enlargement" today in business and in management consists in allowing the employee more freedom to discover and define his function. Likewise, in reading a detective story the reader participates as co-author simply because so much has been left out of the narrative. The open-mesh silk stocking is far more sensuous than the smooth nylon, just because the eye must act as hand in filling in and completing the image, exactly as in the mosaic of the TV image.

Douglas Cater in *The Fourth Branch of Government* tells how the men of the Washington press bureaus delighted to complete or fill in the blank of Calvin Coolidge's personality. Because he was so like a mere cartoon, they felt the urge to complete his image for him and his public. It is instructive that the press applied the word "cool" to Cal. In the very sense of a cool medium, Calvin Coolidge was so lacking in any articulation of data in his public image that there was only one word for him. He was real cool. In the hot 1920s, the hot press medium found Cal very cool and rejoiced in his lack of image, since it compelled the participation of the press in filling in an image of him for the public. By contrast, F.D.R. was a hot press agent, himself a rival of the newspaper medium and one who delighted in scoring off the press on the rival hot medium of radio. Quite in contrast, Jack Paar ran a cool show for the cool TV medium, and became a rival for the patrons of the night spots and their allies in the gossip columns. Jack Paar's war with the gossip columnists was a weird example of clash between a hot and cold medium such as had occurred with the "scandal of the rigged TV quiz shows." The rivalry between the hot press and radio media, on one hand, and TV on the other, for the hot ad buck, served to confuse and to overheat the issues in the affair that pointlessly involved Charles Van Doren.

An Associated Press story from Santa Monica, California, August 9, 1962, reported how

> Nearly 100 traffic violators watched a police traffic accident film today to atone for their violations. Two had to be treated for nausea and shock. . . .
> Viewers were offered a $5.00 reduction in fines if they agreed to see the movie, *Signal 30*, made by Ohio State Police.
> It showed twisted wreckage and mangled bodies and recorded the screams of accident victims.

Whether the hot film medium using hot content would cool off the hot drivers is a moot point. But it does concern any understanding of media. The effect of hot media treatment cannot include much empathy or participation at any time. In this connection an insurance ad that featured Dad in an iron lung surrounded by a joyful family group did more to strike terror into the reader than all the warning wisdom in the world. It is a question that arises in connection with capital punishment. Is a severe penalty the best deterrent to serious crime? With regard to the bomb and the cold war, is the threat of massive retaliation the most effective means to peace? Is it not evident in every human situation that is pushed to a point of saturation that some precipitation occurs? When all the available resources and energies have been played up in an organism or in any structure there is some kind of reversal of pattern. The spectacle of brutality used as deterrent can brutalize. Brutality used in sports may humanize under some conditions, at least. But with regard to the bomb and retaliation as deterrent, it is obvious that numbness is the result of any prolonged terror, a fact that was discovered when the fallout shelter program was broached. The price of eternal vigilance is indifference.

Nevertheless, it makes all the difference whether a hot medium is used in a hot or a cool culture. The hot radio medium used in cool or nonliterate cultures has a violent effect, quite unlike its effect, say in England or America, where radio is felt as entertainment. A cool or low literacy culture cannot accept hot media like movies or radio as entertainment.

They are, at least, as radically upsetting for them as the cool TV medium has proved to be for our high literacy world.

And as for the cool war and the hot bomb scare, the cultural strategy that is desperately needed is humor and play. It is play that cools off the hot situations of actual life by miming them. Competitive sports between Russia and the West will hardly serve that purpose of relaxation. Such sports are inflammatory, it is plain. And what we consider entertainment or fun in our media inevitably appears as violent political agitation to a cool culture.

One way to spot the basic difference between hot and cold media uses is to compare and contrast a broadcast of a symphony performance with a broadcast of a symphony rehearsal. Two of the finest shows ever released by the CBC were of Glenn Gould's procedure in recording piano recitals, and Igor Stravinsky's rehearsing the Toronto symphony in some of his new work. A cool medium like TV, when really used, demands this involvement in process. The neat tight package is suited to hot media, like radio and gramophone. Francis Bacon never tired of contrasting hot and cool prose. Writing in "methods" or complete packages, he contrasted with writing in aphorisms, or single observations such as "Revenge is a kind of wild justice." The passive consumer wants packages, but those, he suggested, who are concerned in pursuing knowledge and in seeking causes will resort to aphorisms, just because they are incomplete and require participation in depth.

The principle that distinguishes hot and cold media is perfectly embodied in the folk wisdom: "Men seldom make passes at girls who wear glasses." Glasses intensify the outward-going vision, and fill in the feminine image exceedingly, Marion the Librarian notwithstanding. Dark glasses, on the other hand, create the inscrutable and inaccessible image that invites a great deal of participation and completion.

Again, in a visual and highly literate culture, when we meet a person for the first time his visual appearance dims out the sound of the name, so that in self-defense we add: "How do you spell your name?" Whereas, in an ear culture, the *sound* of a man's name is the overwhelming fact, as Joyce knew when he said in *Finnegans Wake*, "Who gave you that numb?" For the name of a man is a numbing blow from which he never recovers.

Another vantage point from which to test the difference between hot and cold media is the practical joke. The hot literary medium excludes the practical and participant aspect of the joke so completely that Constance Rourke, in her *American Humor*, considers it as no joke at all. To literary people, the practical joke with its total physical involvement is as distasteful as the pun that derails us from the smooth and uniform progress that is typographic order. Indeed, to the literary person who is quite unaware of the intensely abstract nature of the typographic medium, it is the grosser and participant forms of art that seem "hot," and the abstract and intensely literary form that seems "cool." You may perceive, Madam," said Dr. Johnson, with a pugilistic smile, "that I am well-bred to a degree of needless scrupulosity." And Dr. Johnson was right in supposing that "well-bred" had come to mean a white-shirted stress on attire that rivaled the rigor of the printed page. "Comfort" consists in abandoning a visual arrangement in favor of one that permits casual participation of the senses, a state that is excluded when any one sense, but especially the visual sense, is hotted up to the point of dominant command of a situation.

On the other hand, in experiments in which all outer sensation is withdrawn, the subject begins a furious fill-in or completion of senses that is sheer hallucination. So the hotting-up of one sense tends to result in hallucination.

Harold Adams Innis
and
Marshall McLuhan

James W. Carey

There are many similarities between the thought of Harold Innis and that of Marshall McLuhan. Although I do not intend to obscure those similarities, I would like to emphasize, at least in this paper, some significant points of difference. The question I am asking is this: What is absolutely central to Innis' argument and how does it compare with the central notion in McLuhan's work? Although McLuhan has occasionally characterized his work as an extension of Innis', I want to suggest that McLuhan has taken a relatively minor but recurring theme of Innis' work (perhaps only a suggestion) and made it central to his entire argument. Conversely, McLuhan has neglected or ignored the principal argument developed by Innis.

Both Innis and McLuhan agree that historically "the things on which words were written down count more than the words themselves"; that is, the medium is the message. Starting from this proposition, they engage in quite different kinds of intellectual bookkeeping, however, and are seized by quite different kinds of implications.

Both McLuhan and Innis assume the centrality of communication tech-

Reprinted from *The Antioch Review*, Vol. 27, No. 1, by permission of the editors.

nology; where they differ is in the principal kinds of effects they see deriving from this technology. Whereas Innis sees communication technology principally affecting social organization and culture, McLuhan sees its principal effect on sensory organization and thought. McLuhan has much to say about perception and thought but little to say about institutions; Innis says much about institutions and little about perception and thought.

While McLuhan is intellectually linked to Innis, I think he can be more clearly and usefully tied to a line of speculation in sociolinguistics usually referred to as the Sapir-Whorf hypothesis.

The Sapir-Whorf hypothesis proposes that the language a speaker uses has a determining influence on the character of his thought. While it is a truism that men think with and through language, Edward Sapir and Benjamin Lee Whorf proposed that the very structure of reality—if I may use that grandiose and overworked phrase—is presented to individuals through language. When a person acquires a language he not only acquires a way of talking but also a way of seeing, a way of organizing experience, a way of discriminating the real world. Language, so the argument goes, has built into its grammar and lexicon the very structure of perception. Individuals discriminate objects and events in terms of the vocabulary provided by language. Further, individuals derive their sense of time, their patterns of classifications, their categories for persons, their perception of action, in terms of the tenses, the genders, the pronouns, the pluralizations that are possible in their language. This argument, then, largely reduces the structure of perception and thought to the structure of language.

McLuhan adopts the form of argument provided by the Sapir-Whorf hypothesis with two important modifications. First, he adopts a quite unorthodox characterization of the grammar of a language. Second, he extends the "grammatical analysis" to modes of communication such as print and television which are normally not treated as types of languages.

McLuhan does not view the grammar of a medium in terms of the formal properties of language, the parts of speech or morphemes, normally utilized in such an analysis. Instead, he argues that the grammar of a medium derives from the particular mixture of the senses that an individual characteristically uses in the utilization of the medium. For example, language—or better, speech—is the first of the mass media. It is a device for externalizing thought and for fixing and sharing perceptions. As a means of communications, speech elicits a particular orchestration of the sense. While speech is an oral phenomenon and gives rise to "ear-oriented cultures" (cultures in which people more easily believe what they hear than what they see), oral communication synthesizes or brings into play other sensual faculties. For example, in conversation men are aware not only of the sound of words but also of the visual properties of the speaker and the setting of the tactile qualities of various elements of the setting, and even certain olfactory properties of the person and the situation.

These various faculties constitute parallel and simultaneous modes of communication, and thus McLuhan concludes that oral cultures synthesize these various modalities, elicit them all or bring them all into play in a situation utilizing all the sensory apparatus of the person. Oral cultures, then, involve the simultaneous interplay of sight, sound, touch, and smell and thus produce, in McLuhan's view, a depth of involvement in life as the principal communications medium—oral speech—simultaneously activates all the sensory faculties through which men acquire knowledge and share feeling.

However, speech is not the only mass medium, nor must it necessarily be the dominant mass medium. In technologically advanced societies, print, broadcasting, and film can replace speech as the dominant mode through which knowledge and feeling are communicated. In such societies speech does not disappear, but it assumes the characteristics of the dominant medium. For example, in literate communities oral traditions disappear and the content of spoken communication is the written tradition. Speech no longer follows its own laws. Rather it is governed by the laws of the written tradition. This means not only that the "content" of speech is what has previously been written but that the cadence and imagery of everyday speech is the cadence and imagery of writing. In literate communities, men have difficulty believing that the rich, muscular, graphic, almost multidimensional speech of Oscar Lewis' illiterate Mexican peasants was produced by such "culturally deprived" persons. But for McLuhan speech as an oral tradition, simultaneously utilizing many modes of communication, is almost exclusively the province of the illiterate.

McLuhan starts from the biological availability of parallel modes for the production and reception of messages. These modes—sight, touch, sound, and smell—do not exist independently but are interdependent with one another. Thus, to alter the capacity of one of the modes changes the total relations among the senses and thus alters the way in which individuals organize experience and fix perception. All this is clear enough. To remove one sense from a person leads frequently to the strengthening of the discriminatory powers of the other senses and thus to a rearrangement of not only the senses but of the kind of experience a person has. Blindness leads to an increasing reliance on and increasing power of smell and touch as well as hearing as modes of awareness. Loss of hearing particularly increases one's reliance on sight. But, McLuhan argues, the ratios between the senses and the power of the senses is affected by more than physical impairment or, to use his term, amputation. Media of communication also lead to the amputation of the senses. Media of communication also encourage the overreliance on one sense faculty to the impairment or disuse of others. And thus, media of communication impart to persons a particular way of organizing experience and a particular way of knowing and understanding the world in which they travel.

Modes of communication, including speech, are, then, devices for fixing perception and organizing experience. Print, by its technological nature, has built into it a grammar for organizing experience, and its grammar is found in the particular ratio of sensory qualities it elicits in its users. All communications media are, therefore, extensions of man, or, better, are extensions of some mix of the sensory capacities of man. Speech is such an extension and thus the first mass medium. As an extension of man, it casts individuals in a unique, symbiotic relation to the dominant mode of communication in a culture. This symbiosis is not restricted to speech but extends to whatever medium of communication dominates a culture. This extension is by way of projecting certain sensory capacities of the individual. As I have mentioned, speech involves an extension and development of all the senses. Other media, however, are more partial in their appeal to the senses. The exploitation of a particular communications technology fixes particular sensory relations in members of society. By fixing such a relation, it determines a society's world view; that is, it stipulates a characteristic way of organizing experience. It thus determines the forms of knowledge, the structure of perception, and the sensory equipment attuned to absorb reality.

Media of communication, consequently, are vast social metaphors that not only transmit information but determine what is knowledge; that not only orient us to the world but tell us what kind of world exists; that not only excite and delight our sense but, by altering the ratio of sensory equipment that we use, actually change our character. . . .

The most important criticism to make of McLuhan is that much of the argument he wants to make and most of the contemporary phenomena he wants to explain—particularly the conflict between generations—can be more effectively handled within the framework provided by Innis. Furthermore, the utilization of the perspective of Innis opens up, I think, a number of important and researchable questions and puts the argument once more in a historical context.

In this final section let me tentatively attempt to bring Innis' argument up to date; that is, to extend it from the early 1950s, where he left it, into the 1960s. You will remember that Innis argued that Western history began with temporal bias and was ending with spatial bias. I want to suggest that contemporary developments in the electronic media have intensified this spatial bias. Electronic media, particularly with the innovation of satellite broadcasting, increasingly transcend all national boundaries, thereby weakening nationalism or at least tending to undercut the parochial limitations of national identifications. Further, such media are a potent force in generating a more universal, worldwide culture which is urban, secular, and, in Innis' terms, unstable.

Let me put it this way. Among primitive societies and in earlier stages of Western history relatively small discontinuities in space led to vast differences in culture and social organization. Tribal societies separated by a hundred miles could have entirely different forms of economic, political, and religious life and grossly dissimilar systems of expressive symbolism, myth, and ritual. However, within these societies there was a great continuity of culture and social structure over generations. Forms of life changed slowly, of course, and the attitudes, hopes, fears, and aspirations of a boy of fourteen and a man of sixty were remarkably similar. This does not mean there were no conflicts between age groups in such societies. Such conflicts are probably inevitable if only because of biological changes accompanying aging. However, the conflict occurred within a system of shared attitudes and values and within a sytem of mutual dependencies across age groups. Such societies were based on an oral tradition with a strong temporal bias. The continuity of culture was maintained by a shared, collective system of ritual and by the continuity of passage rites marking off the entrance of individuals into various stages of the life cycle. In such a world, then, there were vast differences between societies but relatively little variation between generations within a given society. In Innis' terms, temporal media produce vast continuity in time and great discontinuity in space.

The spatial bias of modern media, initiated by print but radically extended by film and the electronic media, has reversed the relations between time and space. Space in the modern world progressively disappears as a differentiating factor. As space becomes more continuous, regional variations in culture and social structure become ground down. Further, as I have already suggested and as other modern writers have persuasively argued, the rise of a worldwide urban civilization built upon the speed and extensiveness of travel and electronic media have progressively diminished —though they have come nowhere near eliminating—spatial, transnational variation in culture and social structure. It is this fact which has led Claude Lévi-Strauss to re-echo the traditional keen of the anthropologist that primitive societies must be intensively studied now because they are rapidly disappearing.

If in fact the spatial bias of contemporary media does lead to a progressive reduction of regional variation within nations and transnational variation between nations, one must not assume that differences between groups are being obliterated as some mass society theorists characterize the process of homogenization. As Lévi-Strauss has argued, there may be a principle of diversity built into the species or, from our standpoint, built into the organization of man's communication. I am suggesting that the axis of diversity shifts from a spatial or structural dimension to a temporal or generational dimension. If in primitive societies time is continuous and space discontinuous, in modern societies as space becomes continuous, time becomes discontinuous. In what seems like an ironic twist of language, spatially biased media obliterate space while temporally biased media obliterate time. The spatial bias of modern media, which have eliminated many spatial variations in culture and social structure, have simultaneously intensified the differences between generations within the same society. The differences in modern society between a boy of fourteen and a man of sixty—differences in language and values, symbols and meanings—are enormous. It is modern societies that face the problem of generations. It is not only that conflict across age groups continues but there are gross discontinuities between generations in culture and symbols, perhaps best symbolized by the phrase, "Don't trust anyone over thirty."[1] This inversion in the relation of time and space in contemporary society seems to me a logical extension of Innis' argument. The inversion depends on the observation that spatially biased media obliterate space and lead men to live in a non-spatial world. Simultaneously, such media fragment time and make it progressively discontinuous. Temporal media, on the other hand, obliterate time, lead men to live in a non-temporal world, but fragment space.

I think it is important to remember that Innis argued that media possessed a bias or a predisposition toward time or space. He was not arguing for some simple monocausality. Thus, if generations have become an increasingly important axis of diversity, in modern society, the causes include factors other than the media but to which the media are linked in a syndrome. I cannot, of course, attempt to trace out all such factors here, but a couple should be mentioned if only for their suggestive value. The importance of generations and the phenomena of generational discontinuity is linked most directly to the rate of technical change. In traditional societies, societies that change very slowly, the old are likely to be venerated as the repositories of the oral tradition and, consequently, as the storage banks of tribal wisdom. In societies such as ours, where knowledge and technique change very rapidly, the old are not likely to be so venerated. It is the young, the bearers of the new techniques and knowledge, that are likely to have both the power and the prestige. As the transmission of this knowledge is in the educational system, it is in this institution that generational discontinuities are likely to become most apparent. Also, because rapidly changing technical knowledge is difficult to acquire beyond school, the old are likely to be continually threatened by competition from the young and to be subject to fairly early obsolescence, and conflicts between generations bearing different knowledge and different values are likely to become a fact of life in all institutions.

[1] Of course, generational discontinuity is a universal of history. Normally, these discontinuities are explained by the periodic and random shocks to a system caused by relatively unsystematic variables such as wars, depressions, famines, etc. I am suggesting that generational discontinuity no longer depends on these random shocks to the system but that generational discontinuities are now endogenous factors, built into the normal operation of the system and very much "caused" by the bias of contemporary communication.

This conflict is muted and disguised somewhat by the reorganization of the age composition of society. Some 40 per cent of the population is now under twenty, and within the year 50 per cent of the population will be under twenty-five. With the rapid expansion of the economy and institutions such as education, the young overwhelm older generations merely by numbers, and thus the intensity of the conflict is frequently masked by the ease of the political solutions. One thus must not discount the sheer fact of larger numbers in younger generations in heightening our awareness of generational discontinuity. The proportion of youth in the total population is also intensified by the progressive lengthening of adolescence; that is, one is young much longer today than in previous centuries.

Finally, the weakening of tradition caused not only by the media but also by the pace of technical change and progressive dominance of the educational system in the socialization process intensifies, I think, generational discontinuity. I am led to this argument by the belief that structural elements in the society are less able to provide useful and stable identity patterns to youth. Religious, ethnic, regional, and class identifications are weakening, and they are identifications that are *not* temporal in character As religious and ethnic traditions weaken generational identity becomes more important as a means of placing oneself and organizing one's own self-conception. This is true not only in the society at large but also in all subordinate institutions. The importance of generational identity is enhanced by the decline of ritual and passage rites which formerly served as devices for confirming and symbolizing structural identity. In addition, these structural identities simply come into conflict with one another, they counterpoint, and the young are frequently led to reject all past identities and seize upon membership in a generation as the key to understanding what is happening to them. This is a phenomenon Erik Erikson has usefully analyzed under the label the "totalism" of youth.

I am suggesting that generations are becoming more important sources of solidarity than other social groups in spite of Harold Rosenberg's observation that being a member of an age group is the lowest form of solidarity. The spread of a worldwide urban civilization built upon rapid and ephemeral means of communication ultimately means that individuals of the same age in Warsaw, Moscow, Tokyo, and New York sense a membership in a common age group and feel they have more in common with one another than with individuals older and younger within their own societies. This is a phenomenon Innis did not anticipate. When Innis spoke of competition to establish a monopoly of knowledge, he normally was thinking of competition coming from institutions or structural groups: competition from the clergy, politicians, or the middle classes. Similarly, when other scholars have spoken of the role of groups in social change, they have normally thought of structural groups such as the burghers, the aristocracy, or the Jews. The implication of my suggestion is that the bearers of social change are increasingly age groups or generations rather than structural groups. Instead of groups representing individuals of all ages bound together by a common structural characteristic such as religion, race, or occupation, the most important groups of the future will be those of a common age who are structurally variegated. A generational group finds its solidarity in a common age even though some of its members are Catholic, some Jewish, some Protestant, some Northerners, some Southerners, some middle-class, some working-class. If this is correct, then political conflict, to choose just one example, which we have normally thought of in structural terms as conflict between regions, classes, and religions, becomes focused instead around generations. If I correctly interpret the behavior of Robert Kennedy, he is aware of the phenomenon.

Now, unfortunately, things are neither as neat, as simple, or as true as I have painted them in these pages. There are still strong differences within generations. One must speak of generations of musicians and novelists, physicists and sociologists, Northerners and Southerners, Catholics and Jews. Obviously, one has to pay attention to the intersection of structural variables such as class and generational variables or the entire analysis quickly slides into a tautology. But I do think that in modern society generations become more important in all spheres of life. There is a competition to name generations, to symbolize them, to characterize the meaning of a generation. There is a competition within and between generations to choose the culture by which the generation shall be known. Further, there is competition to impose the culture of a generation on the entire society. And this, of course, is what Innis meant by a monopoly of knowledge. It was only a few years ago that David Riesman was suggesting that the media, particularly television, were devices for imposing the culture of the middle class on the entire society. Let me merely suggest that the media, particularly television, are devices by which the culture of youth is imposed on the entire society. In the competition to determine whose culture shall be the official culture and whose values the official norms, the axis of conflict is between generations.

These perhaps overlong notes on the sociology of generations illustrate, I hope, Innis' central point: the principal effect of media technology is on social organization. The capacity of Innis to deal with such phenomena in a reasonably direct and clear way leads me to prefer his characterization of media effects to that of McLuhan. . . .

II. Individual Media

In this section, the examination of individual forms of popular art illustrates further, and more concretely, the psychological and social effects of media, their influences on culture, their embodiment in emotional and aesthetic forms of cultural attitudes and tendencies.

Eugene David Glynn's analysis of the psychological effects television produces in the character of its audience is critical of the current situation, but does glance as well at the potential values inherent in the medium.

The relationship between television and radio is examined by Philip Abrams, who sees the trivialization of experience as the chief problem to be faced and solved in both media.

The two articles on the motion picture take contrasting, but not necessarily conflicting stances. In the first, Alan Casty emphasizes the serious artistic and thematic possibilities of the film, the central role of the director, and the relationship between the film and drama and between the film and the shaping world views of our time. In contrast, Pauline Kael, in examining "movies," emphasizes the role of the actor in effecting the entertainment pleasures of current works as well as embodying current cultural and psychological assumptions.

The unique developments in popular music of the sixties are classified by Robert A. Rosenstone to reveal their close and influential connection to the merging attitudes and values of today's youth.

Television and the American Character: A Psychiatrist Looks at Television

Eugene David Glynn

To consider television as a shaping force on the American character, the attempt must be made to study it so far as possible purely as a form. Content and quality vary in a very great range, and while of great importance in the immediate and particular effects upon the viewer, there is a structure inherent in the very medium of television which must be seen completely in itself. It is this basic form which exerts the greatest influence upon the shaping of character when character is considered as the long-term expectations and responses of a person; automatic, repetitive, more or less conscious. This molding is almost completely outside of the awareness of the viewer. The customary repeated experience of television structures the viewer's whole idea of the world and his relation to it. It is here that permanent responses to television lie; it is here that character is formed, for these attitudes are what the viewer then takes into the rest of his experience.

What attitudes toward the world and what expectations of it does television bring about?

Certain types of adult illness—particularly the depressions, the oral character neuroses, the schizophrenias—and the use they make of television can be most valuable here. Those traits that sick adults now satisfy by television can be presumed to be those traits which children, exposed to television from childhood (infancy, really!), and all through the character forming years, may be expected to develop. Consider these actual clinical examples.

A twenty-five-year-old musician, daughter of an adoring, constantly present, constantly acting mother, quarrels with her parents and gives up her own quite busy professional life. She turns to the television set, and soon is spending ten to twelve hours a day watching it, constantly sitting before it, transfixed, drinking beer or eating ice cream, lost and desperate if the set is turned off. Making a joke one day, she said, "Boy, I don't know what I would do for a mother if that tube ever burned out." This girl, of real intellectual attainment, was completely indifferent as to what

From *Television's Impact on American Culture*, edited by William Y. Elliott. Copyright © 1956. Reprinted by permission of Michigan State University Press.

the programs actually were. A fifty-five-year-old man, hugely obese, all his life close to his three older sisters, who took care of him, becomes depressed after the death of one of them. His only activity for many months is to watch television, looking for interesting programs, but settling for anything. The staff of a hospital for schizophrenic adolescent girls finds that these girls, insatiable in their demands, and yet themselves incapable of sustaining activity, want nothing so much as to be allowed endless hours of television. Without it they are soon noisy, unruly and frequently destructive. Significantly, the only other control of these girls is an adult who constantly directs them or organizes their entertainment for them.

These examples could be multiplied endlessly. They all demonstrate quite clearly the special set of needs television satisfies, needs centering around the wish for someone to care, to nurse, to give comfort and solace. Adults, by their very age and status, can scarcely hope to find someone to take on this role, once their own mothers give it up. These infantile longings can be satisfied only symbolically, and how readily the television set fills in. Warmth, sound, constancy, availability, a steady giving without ever a demand for return, the encouragement to complete passive surrender and envelopment—all this and active fantasy besides. Watching these adults, one is deeply impressed by their acting out with the television set of their unconscious longings to be infants in mother's lap.

These, then, are traits television can so easily satisfy in adults, or foster in children; traits of passivity, receptiveness, being fed, taking in and absorbing what is offered. Activity, self-reliance, and aggression are notably absent. A great deal of activity and aggression may be present, but they are deceptive, for the demands and even rages are not to be doing, but to be getting. Very much energy can be spent, not in constructive accomplishment, but in trying to reestablish or keep a dependent relationship. The image is evident; the relationship clearly established. The musician's joke went to the core, for these are the relationships of a child to its mother; the relationship of a very young child who lives literally on its mother's bounty; her food, her warmth, her knowledge. This is the age described in Freudian psychology as the oral age; the age of intake and being fed, when the mouth is the vital organ in relation to the world. The extensions of this include such things as taking in the sound of others' voices through the ears or of absorbing others' ideas, as can easily be seen. The underlying pattern in whatever symbolic form is worked out will relate it to this oral character orientation: the counting on someone else to supply satisfaction and security rather than oneself. Typical, too, of this character structure are the intensity with which needs are felt, the poor tolerance of frustration and delay, the demand for immediate satisfaction. The television set is easily and agreeably a mother to whom the child readily turns with the same expectations as to her.

These traits, of course, are inherent in all spectator participation, be it sport or art or reading. What is crucially important about television is its ubiquitousness: there is so much television, so early, so steadily; five-year-olds watch television as a matter of course, and, increasingly, so do three-year-olds and even two-year-olds. Television at this age can, in the limited experience of the child, only be seen as a mother-substitute or a mother-extension. These needs of the child should be outgrown, and his relationship to his mother changed. Basically, this growth depends in great part on the mother's attitude toward the child; her encouraging him to greater activity and self-reliance, the lessening of her feeding functions. It is of the greatest importance in character formation that the child can now have these infantile wishes and needs satisfied by the always available television set. Indeed, to continue enjoying television, it becomes necessary these traits remain prominent. The danger is here: the passive dependent oral character traits become fixed. There are endless differences between children playing tag or cops and robbers and watching even the most action-filled Western; even between walking to the movies once a week and just switching on television by reaching out.

Hence, the chief effect of television is passivity and dependence in multiple shapes and forms. The world supplies and the individual feasts. In opposition to the point of view here expressed, the claim is made that aggression is not so much inhibited by television as displaced; that dormant aggressive forces are stimulated in the viewer, and that these forces result in increased activity of many kinds in other spheres. Similarly, television may release many new forces, aggressive or constructive in a direct way. This type of effect, however, depends almost entirely on the content of the particular program. Television might indeed arouse the viewer to extreme activity, but only by the portrayal of specific situations or specific messages. For example, some juvenile delinquency might be shaped by a television crime program, or a tree planting program be inspired. Again, attitudes toward parents, toward husbands and wives, toward social groups, attitudes which could lead to action of a most constructive kind can certainly be caused or influenced by television, but this, however, must always be specifically dependent on the content of the program. Action so aroused does not produce a characterological basis for further activity. The underlying structure, even here, is clear, for the stimulus to action, be it aggressive or sexual, comes from without. Deep characterological attitudes toward parents or family might be shaped, but only by specific propaganda content to programs.

The picture of the American character which emerges has a familiar look, for many students in the field have pointed out that the new American character is one of conformity; the search is for security, not glory, comfort in the group, not individual prominence. The whole present concept of the welfare state illustrates this. Americans today must be much more responsible to their society, much more aware of their group, much more conforming; the nonentrepreneur is rapidly becoming the necessary American character. It must look outside itself constantly for orientation so as to smoothly fit in. Television is simultaneously the result of and the instrument for producing the character needed to live in much of the current American world. To be responsive to and dependent on television, well trained in this, is to be able to live much more easily in our society.

There are other aspects of television's influence. It is used, certainly, in every hospital and in every institution as an extremely effective nonchemical sedative. An interesting parallel has been pointed out recently. It is well-known that fixing on a moving visual stimulus inhibits motor activity. The prime example of this is the situation in hypnosis, and the concentration and stillness of television watchers certainly is reminiscent of the hypnotized. Television-addiction certainly exists, and bears an immediate relation to the drug addicts, those who search for, in pills, what they once found in mother's milk. A forty-four-year-old salesman, a chronic alcoholic, tried to give up liquor. Every night he came home and watched television, "drinking it in" (his words) until he fell asleep before the set. Once off the wagon, he gave up television, too.

How lulling television can be has been wisely observed. Most homes soon give in to the temptation of using television to keep the children quiet and out of mischief. It does this, but in a way much different from playing games.

Marriage after marriage is preserved by keeping it drugged on television; television is used quite consistently to prevent quarreling from breaking out by keeping people apart. This points up a somewhat less obvious side of watching television: its schizoid-fostering aspects. Television seems to be a social activity, an activity performed by many people together. Actually, though, it smothers contact, really inhibiting interpersonal exchange. A group watching television is frequently a group of isolated people, not in real exchange at all. Television viewers are given to solitary pleasures, not the social ones. Children and adolescents frequently revert to thumb-sucking while watching; how much eating and drinking goes on before the set! The complaint is common enough today that social visiting has lost its social, conversational, engaged side.

There are two more important aspects of television to consider: its stimulation and its fantasy. What will be the result of such constant stimulation from such early ages? Will it result in the need for ever increasing stimulation as the response to the old stimulus becomes exhausted? In the early 1940s a radio program which created national interest and caused great excitement was "Take It or Leave It," with its climax of the $64.00 Question. By 1955 television's greatest success had been the $64,000 Question. Discount the monetary inflation of the ten years. What is left is a vivid figure of the acceleration of what it takes to excite. The Lone Ranger served as a radio hero for well over ten years; Davy Crockett, a hero of almost mythic proportions, lasted less than one year. What way can stimulation be continuously increased? As the responses are exhausted, will television move toward increasing violence, as the movies have? Similarly, it is too soon to know what children so massively exposed to sex on television will consider exciting and sex-stimulating as adults. A critical question is raised here: is television ultimately blunting and destructive of sensibility?

Then too, one wonders: Will reality match up to the television fantasies this generation has been nursed on? These children are in a peculiar position; experience is exhausted in advance. There is little they have not seen or done or lived through, and yet this is second-hand experience. When the experience itself comes, it is watered down, for it has already been half lived, but never truly felt. The fate of Emma Bovary may become the common fate. This has always been a "disease" of the literary sensibility and of the romantics, but will this become a mass characteristic?

A word of balance should be put in here. The television generation will not be a completely infantile one, for there are many other forces at work, including the normal growth potentials of the human being. The point here is just to isolate the lines of television's influence. At the same time, equally inherent in its nature, television can be a growth-promoting experience, an enriching force of the most tremendous power.

Horizons have been greatly expanded: millions of people have seen the ballet, have travelled to distant lands, have explored some of the country's best museums; experiences they could never have in their own lifetimes. Television has taken its viewers into the United Nations, into the meetings of Congressional investigating committees. It has led a mass audience into intimate active participation in the political heart of the country in a way never dreamed possible. The range here is without bounds. Television can produce a people wider in knowledge, more alert and aware of the world, prepared to be much more actively interested in the life of their times. Television can be the great destroyer of provincialism. Television can produce a nation of people who really live in the world, not in just their own hamlets. It is here that the great opportunity of educational television lies.

Educational television must be acutely aware of its own nature. By being very conscious of its particular character shaping potential, it can counteract it by extremely careful attention to content. It is always a difficult task for the teacher to liberate his pupil; educational television must remember how many more times difficult it is for it. It must find ways to encourage active audience participation; programs which will not satiate but stimulate its viewers, programs which will leave its audience eager to do and to try. Cooking instruction programs are an example here. Techniques will have to be worked out for educational television for showing, not a baseball game, but how to pitch a curved ball; for sending its audience on nature hunts, into club activity, to the library for books. Being aware of the dependent relationship in its audience, television must look for ways to undo it—the problem of any teacher or parent.

With this orientation, television can overcome the dangers pointed out and find its way to being highly growth-promoting. Otherwise it will find itself degraded into an instrument for the shaping of a group man: dependent, outward seeking, the natural foil of any authoritarianism, be it left or right.

The Nature
of
Radio and Television
Philip Abrams

Unique among the mass media radio and television are given opportunities by time, by the fact that they have the whole day, every day, to dispose of, and that they can break up the day as they please. How do they use these opportunities? We tend to take the existing pattern of programming so much for granted that we do not see the gulf between what could be done in this respect and what actually is done. Time, which might have been used to experiment and innovate, to set contrasting styles and idioms alongside one another and so heighten audience sensibilities, has in fact been used only to reproduce with endless ingenious but minor variations programs built on established formulae of acceptability. With its new lease of time the BBC proposes to fill the night air with "light music"; even the American radio companies are willing to treat the small hours as a time for experiment and for special minority interests. In this country the continuity of broadcasting means that the onslaught on authenticity has become unremitting; there is always something "on"; and the essential nature of what is on is, for almost all of the time, unchanging.

The fact of continuity thus serves to compound the trivializing tendencies of universality. The whole experience of viewing or listening is turned into a glorified version of "Tonight." And the point about a program like "Tonight" is that item follows item too smoothly and rapidly for any one

Excerpt from "Radio and Television" by Philip Abrams, in *Discrimination and Popular Culture*, edited by Denys Thompson. Copyright © 1965. Reprinted by permission of Penguin Books, Ltd.

item to engage the attention or grip the imagination for more than the moment of its passage. Comical items and serious items, the calamitous and the diverting parade before us in unending processions. No pause for thought or differentiation is allowed.

The same is true for broadcasting as a whole. Because something must always be on it is virtually impossible to give different weights to different items. Unless one decides to switch off to think or talk in the split second between items or programs one's chance of absorbing or digesting, let alone criticizing, what one sees or hears is lost. It is a standard feature of the reports of people who have "observed" groups watching television that incipient comment or conversation about a program is quashed as attention is drawn back to whatever next appears on the screen. Discussion gives way to asides and appreciative noises. The effect is of a blurring of edges, an ironing-out of differences of stature and scale between items and programs. Individual programs share the fate of the heroes of Webster's play:

> These wretched eminent things
> Leave no more fame behind 'em, than should one
> Fall in a frost, and leave his print in snow—
> As soon as the sun shines it ever melts
> Both form and matter.

In broadcasting the sun of the next program is always shining. Within ten seconds of a tribute to Bertrand Russell there follows a tribute to Ivor Novello. . . .

And these effects are compounded again by another characteristic of broadcasting, its domesticity. It is this characteristic that makes it virtually impossible for radio and television to escape from the tendencies to trivialization which their universality and continuity encourage and permit. Radio and television are provided in the home. And because they are one does not have to make any conscious act of choice in order to be exposed to them. To see a film one has to decide to go to the pictures (not necessarily to see the film one sees, though). Reading a paper or going to a football match or a pub all involve a relatively deliberate effort; one chooses what to do and what should happen to one. None of this is true for watching or listening. These are activities on which one embarks, typically, unthinkingly; they are so easy to embark on. People can and do switch on in a way that is as routine as the way in which they wash and have tea when they come in. These are activities from which the problem of decision has been removed. "Now," as one man put it, "you don't need to worry how you will spend your time."

Ever present, radio and television provide alternatives, not just to other activities, but to the whole problem of thinking what to do. One BBC survey found that the more an individual watched television the less likely he was to describe himself as "choosey" rather than "not choosey" about the programs he watched. And this is not very surprising. Because television is so easily available it is given functions which have nothing to do with conscious choice or cultural discrimination. For people who watch a lot it is not just what they watch but the fact of watching that is important. There seems to be a direct progression in this respect from the "choosey" ten per cent at one end to the ten per cent of "addicts" at the other extreme for whom watching and listening have become rewarding activities in their own right regardless of what is seen or heard. Most people are not in either of these groups of course and do discriminate to a greater or lesser degree. But the domesticity of broadcasting, combining with its universality and continuity, opens a primrose path along which the audience has an open invitation to be led toward addiction.

In one particular way the domesticity of broadcasting furthers the decline of choosiness. Because programs are so easily and constantly available one thing that most members of the audience are likely to ask of the media sooner or later is that they provide a certain minimum of wholly undemanding distraction. Radio and television are asked to do things which other, nondomestic, discontinuous, selective media cannot—to allow listeners and viewers to relax, to provide just the sort of "cushion against reality" that Raymond Williams describes, to create an agreeable background for passing and wasting time. Because they are domestic these media are expected to be unexacting, to provide relief from routine and effort. Nor do I see how this demand, even if we call it a demand for "escape," can be said to be unreasonable or improper. The quality and pace of modern work make it difficult to censure the use of broadcasting for light relief. Broadcasting, in short, through its special character, acquires strictly nonaesthetic, social, and psychological functions which other media do not have (or do not have to nearly the same extent). R. H. S. Crossman, indeed, goes so far as to speak of a "right to triviality." Certainly, a nonstop supply of programs making rigorous demands on the judgment, attention, and imagination would deny to most viewers and listeners an important and proper use of the media. . . .

At the same time, one cannot lead taste if one has no sense of direction; one cannot raise standards unless one will allow that some things are better than others and some worse. And what has happened with these media is that the public service image of their own role has made broadcasters so afraid of imposing that they do seem to have lost all sense of direction. In its place they have set up a largely spurious public service ideal of impartiality. Other mass media may have the wrong values; one's first impression of radio and television is that they have no values. The press and cinema may glamorize the shoddy and they may have false, even vicious, priorities. But at least they have priorities; they do patently select and editorialize; some things are headlined and some ignored; if a newspaper felt like flaying the government's defense policy it would do so; it is sensible to talk about the "character" of these media. Radio and television, on the contrary, have no editors, they do not take stands, they do not admit to having conscious and consistent principles of selection—except perhaps the worst of all possible principles, the principle of "news value." The Pilkington Committee had a hard time getting the controllers of these media to admit that they ever chose or planned anything. What the broadcasters offered the Committee were the ideas of neutrality, balance, and the mirroring of society. . . .

Arguments about giving the public what it wants are the over-arching claims in terms of which all the trivializing tendencies of the media are drawn together and collectively justified. Like the belief in impartiality the appeal to what the public wants is spurious through and through. Just as something has to be selected and something rejected whether the selecting is done consciously or not, so the highly centralized structure of broadcasting means that judgments are constantly being made about the nature of audience wants and that in practice the only test of these supposed wants is audience size. And I would suggest that to defend programs that are more "acceptable" than "authentic" on the ground that such programs have huge audiences and that these huge audiences show that such programs are what the public "wants" is to ignore the real relationship that exists between the broadcaster and his public and to make nonsense of the idea of a want.

Gilbert Seldes, in one of his essays on the mass media, tells a story of a cinema proprietor in Nigeria who owned, and showed, only two films, *King Kong*, and *The Mark of Zorro*. Three days a week he packed the house with one of these; on the other three he did the same with the other; on Sunday as a surefire double feature he showed them both. This went on for years. The story epitomizes the relationship between communicator and public in the mass media. This enterprising man had fastened on to a *general* demand for entertainment; this he had met in a somewhat specific way; and he had gone on to work up an audience for the specific form of entertainment he was able to provide; finally, since he monopolized the means of entertainment in that region, he had contrived to "prevent an audience for any other sort of entertainment from coming into existence."

The sorts of demands people actually make are diffuse and unspecific. If one asks what "want" a particular program is meeting one very rarely finds that the want is one that could be met *only* by the program in question. Rather, general wants, for amusement, background, excitement, are met in the particular ways the broadcasters find most convenient. The relationship between communicator and public is a manipulative one with the initiative firmly on the side of the communicator. When television provides a glut of Westerns the public selects Westerns as its favorite type of program; when the companies switch to providing hospital dramas the public discovers a want for these. A series of recent studies has shown with growing clarity how far, as Dr. Himmelweit puts it, "taste is the product of the producer, rather than television entertainment the response of the producer to the public's taste." Or as Gilbert Seldes writes:

Demand is generalized and diffuse—for entertainment, for thrills, for vicarious sadness, for laughs; it can be satisfied by programs of different types and different qualities; and only after these programs have been offered is there any demand (specifically) for them. Supply comes first in this business and creates its own demand.

The nature and working logic of these media tend, in short, "to create those conditions in which the wants that can be most easily satisfied by the communicator take precedence over others." And what this means in practice is that tendencies to trivialization are built into almost everything that the media do. This is the easy and convenient way to operate; to some extent even the unavoidable way.

Trivialization is, at heart, a simple failure to treat the subject one is handling, whatever it may be, with the respect it deserves. A program, as the Pilkington Committee point out in what is perhaps their most important single argument, is not trivial because its matter is light or unimportant; it is trivial if its matter is devalued in the process of communication:

Triviality resides in the way the subject matter is approached and the manner in which it is presented. A trivial approach can consist in a failure to respect the potentialities of the subject matter no matter what it be, or in a too ready reliance on well-tried themes, or in a habit of conforming to established patterns or in a reluctance to be imaginatively adventurous . . . in a failure to take full and disciplined advantage of the artistic and technical facilities which are relevant to a particular subject, or in an excessive interest in smart packaging at the expense of the contents of the package, or in a reliance on gimmicks so as to give a spurious interest to a program at the cost of its imaginative integrity, or in too great a dependence on hackneyed devices for creating suspense or raising a laugh or evoking tears.

I have quoted this passage at length for it provides the best brief statement I know of the nature of the problem that is built into the organization of television and radio in this country and of the sorts of tests we ought to apply to broadcast material. . . .

The New Style
in Film and Drama

Alan Casty

Despite undeniable differences of technology and psychology, the contemporary film and drama do share a set of common assumptions and conventions involving techniques, themes, aesthetics, and even epistemology, since they rise from a basic likeness in ways of attempting to know reality and ways of giving it form. Both have taken a decided turn toward something beyond the assumptions and conventions of traditional realism—a turn that was initiated in the drama, and without lasting effect on the film in its earlier stages, but one that has now been accelerated by the film, and with reciprocating effects on the current drama. Because of these affinities, what has been going on in the contemporary film can best be understood and appreciated by focusing on its connections to the drama, not by following the prevailing critical assumption of a distinct divorce between the two.

The way in which the authority of conventional realism has been challenged and at least partially overturned in the film has been shaped by the basic sensory fact of motion pictures: The tangible immediacy, the impact, the psychological reality of the film image. No other medium evokes images of reality so strongly. Whatever is shown becomes real for the audience. And so most of the attempts by film directors to break loose from the trap of literal, surface, limited realism—whether physical, social, or psychological—have continued to use the realism of the film image. The essence of the new style of film-making is how to use the concrete, tangible details of acts, appearances, possessions, surroundings, movement, looks, to convey a complexity that goes beyond this surface of phenomena, to get beyond (in Ionesco's phrase) "the kind of realism that no longer captures reality."

The assumptions and methods of these attempts have much in common with those of contemporary playwrights; whereas the earlier forms of non- or anti-realism in the drama, particularly Expressionism, had only a passing and glancing impact on the film. The German film of the Twenties, as Siegfried Kracauer has thoroughly described in *From Caligari to Hitler* (albeit with sociological interpretations that are debatable), was the most

From *The Midwest Quarterly*, 11 (January 1970), 209–227. By permission of *The Midwest Quarterly*.

strongly influenced; but by the end of the decade even its uneven efforts at the "outward projection of psychological events" and the "transformation of material objects into emotional ornaments" had ceased. It might be noted that the greatest residue in the films of the Thirties was in the comedy. There were the fantasies of Rene Clair, the Marx Brothers lunacies that were constantly turning the figurative into the literal (mention of the college "seal" in *Horsefeathers* results immediately in a physical seal), that were constantly breaking up the manners and conventions of the superego with the explosive, liberated antics of the id—at dances, trials, custom inspections, classes, meetings, traffic jams, football games, or marriages. There were the projective ballets of Chaplin, eating the old shoe, down to the shoe laces, in *The Gold Rush*, while the old cabin teeters in an archetypal nightmare anxiety; being stuffed with food by the machine in *Modern Times*, while made a prisoner by the straps that are a part of the machine. In musical comedies too there were Expressionistic leftovers, especially in the dreamlike, constructivist numbers of Busby Berkeley, with their large masses moving in unison, their human patterns of violins, gears, flower petals.

But in the main the movies stayed with the traditions of the realism of the late nineteenth and early twentieth century melodrama, as in the Zola-like compendium of degradation and the naturalistic exaggerations of Von Stroheim's *Greed*. In the thirties this realism was reshaped by the conventions of the dominant social realism of the stage of that period and produced what were the basic conventions and aesthetics of the movies until the fifties.

The reasons behind the turn to something beyond this realism are much the same in both films and drama. Science itself, the prime shaper of the realistic assumptions and their categories, has contributed to their dissolution. Not only has it not produced a total, vital set of faiths to replace those it had left obsolete, its formulations themselves have taken us beyond viewing physical reality as a neat, completely classifiable and perceivable monolith. The new mechanics, for example, allows for randomness, insists that our very examination of data must alter these data and thus forever make them, in final terms, unknowable. Psychology, too, in its examination of human consciousness, perception, knowledge, memory, has irrevocably altered our ideas of any objective relationship of man and reality.

Science has also had a part in the impact that recent history has had upon our assumptions about reality, our attitudes toward our existence. None of the arts has *not* responded to the technology of peace—the repetitions and reductions of mechanization—and the technology of war—the horrors of death camps, fire bombings, atomic bombings, ultimate weaponry.

Of the philosophies that have, in turn, provided responses to the facts of modern life, none has had a greater impact on artists than the varied breeds of Existentialism and Phenomenology. In their basic premises can be found most of the assumptions that have produced the contemporary film and drama.

Our dramatic arts have become the weathervanes of the principles of Subjectivity. That life is a random set of separate experiences, with no continuing essence; that it is perceived by a single consciousness at a single moment; that these limits of subjectivity produce the burden and the terror of absurd meaninglessness; that they also produce the complementary possibility and joy of imaginatively creating meaning—all this is the tenor and vehicle of much of what we regularly view. As are the usual corollaries: Isolation and the struggle for connections; the limits of the rational and the significance, even value, of the irrational; the ambiguity, the flux, the contradictoriness of things-as-they-are out there and the elusive nature of identity, motivations, perception within.

But beyond these premises, and the situations and themes they produce, the attitudes and methods of phenomenology have spread through our culture until they have become commonplace. The attitude of a film director toward the reality of the images he creates has its model in the attitude of the phenomenologist toward the reality of the images he creates with his mind. Like the phenomenologist, the director recognizes that his images, for all their seeming realism, are an incomplete suggestion, an arbitrary if necessary reduction of a reality that cannot be fixed, contained, categorized. But like the phenomenologist, the director believes it necessary (in Husserl's phrase) "to place the world in brackets," to reduce existence arbitrarily and artificially to patterns of visible and tangible phenomena if anything is going to be understood and said about it—even though that existence is beyond being captured in such phenomena and thus can only be imperfectly, fleetingly grasped. This awareness of the limitations of the director's own tools—his images of reality—has produced the dominant style of the film today.

This style has gone beyond literal, representational realism, but has only infrequently ventured into the world of phantasy or fully grotesque Expressionism. Rather, the style tends to use the devices of surface realism of the film but to reapply them with the kind of indirection we find in the dominant strain of theatricalism in the drama today. Without necessarily resorting to the Pirandellian fusion and confusion of play and reality, this theatricalism—in both film and drama—no longer aims at the consuming illusion that suspends all disbelief. Instead, it insists on a constant subversion of the illusion of reality, insists on its devices as theatrical devices; and yet in parading and flaunting this insistence it finds a form for the current assumption about the tentativeness of all perceptions of reality, theatrical or otherwise.

The devices of dislocation and discontinuity in the film have many parallels in the contemporary drama, but are particularly consonant with the alienation theories of Bertold Brecht. The films of Jean Luc Godard are probably the clearest embodiment of this Brechtian theatricalism. Godard has that blend of rationalism and emotionalism that one finds in Brecht, the blend that produces scenes of dramatic intensity yet maintains an intellectualizing distance. This distancing, this breaking up of the audience's immersion in, and too-easy identification with, the "reality" of the play-acting, is Godard's way of shattering the conventional responses of the audience and getting them to see past the stereotypes of perception that they create and the stereotypes of art that he must use.

Brecht had hoped to achieve this refreshment of reality with alienation effects. In his notes to the play *The Roundhead and the Peakheads* he commented, "Certain events of the play—by means of inscriptions, interpolations of music and noise, and the technique of the actor—should be elevated (alienated) out of the realm of the ordinary, natural, or expected. . . ." In his essay "New Technique of Acting," he provided one of his clearest explanations of the reasons for this alienation. "For a man to see his mother as the wife of a man an A-Effect is necessary; it occurs, for example, if he acquires a step-father. If a person sees his teacher oppressed by a bailiff, an A-Effect arises; the teacher is torn out of a context in which he appears big, and transferred into a context in which he appears small. We make something natural incomprehensible in a certain way, but only in order to make it all the more comprehensible afterwards. In order for something known to be *perceived* (italics added) it must cease to be ordinary; one must break with the habitual notion that the thing in question requires no elucidation."

Brecht's particular devices for wrenching our consciousness to perceive reality more freshly are but one aspect of the general process of abstraction that has been the basis of modern art. As Wilhelm Worringer showed in his landmark study of 1908, *Abstraction and Empathy: A Contribution to the Study of Style*, empathy (and thus immersion, identification, illusion) rises from ease and security and results in representationalism; however, "the urge to abstraction is the outcome of a greater inner unrest inspired in man by the Phenomena of the outside world." In the face of the intractable nature of these phenomena the artist through abstraction seeks "to wrest the object of the world out of its natural context," and in so doing gain some new hold on it.

The elliptical style of the recent film is one of these attempts to wrest the objects of the world out of their natural, and habitual, contexts—both real and artistically conventional. The rapid cutting breaks up the commonplace patterns of the expected movie scene; scenes start late, at their crises, without the traditional establishing shots; they end early or late, without the traditional signals of climax. Transitional relationships are left more ambiguous, less signaled, both in terms of time and of cause and effect.

This impulse toward discontinuity is carried by Godard, among others, into the separate Vignettes, the *stationem*, of the Expressionist theater, and in his work is reinforced often with distinctly Brechtian devices. In one direction, as in the handful of set scenes in *Contempt* and the three major sequences of *A Married Woman*, Godard breaks up the normal sequenced pattern of a long scene's flow, breaks it into varied series of separate shots, of parts of people, or of rooms, or of furniture, or even of the contents of a magazine, so that one has to see these expected ordinary situations and relationships more freshly, in the fragmented re-creation that, in Brecht's terms, seems to make things incomprehensible only to make them finally more comprehensible. In another direction, he sets up a series of Brecht-like vignettes, as in *Vivre Sa Vie* and *Masculine Feminine*. Each has its sub-title, its philosophic discussion (either in the scene or voiced offscreen by a narrator), and its visual pattern. In *Vivre Sa Vie* these establish many variations on the theme of the objectifying of the girl, by herself and by others. In one we see the girl's back only through a long conversation with her husband; in another we see her back nude, being touched by the hand of a client, after she has become a prostitute; in her crucial conversation with her pimp, our view of her face is blocked throughout by his head and shoulders. In *Masculine Feminine*, the scenes are stages, variations of the confusions of the emotions of the boy and girl, who want to love (beyond both the commercial and idealistic cliches of their time: Godard calls them "the children of Marx and Coca Cola") but do not exactly know how. Each scene presents a confusing mixture of emotions and actions; the transitions between are undefined. Most involve static, undynamic interchanges rather than full dramatic confrontations; there are many variations of question and answer sessions, from a public opinion poll to the groping attempt at understanding that takes place in a public toilet, while the girl fixes her hair, as she habitually does. All the patterns of movie-watching are shattered, for this is the way the boy and the girl experience their lives: Discontinuous, elliptical, without complete dramatization in neat, clearcut actions.

The mixing of moods and emotions in these scenes introduces another, separately definable characteristic of the new style, and that is the same kind of complex, ambiguous tones and moods that we find in the contemporary theatre, particularly in the Theater of the Absurd. Ionesco has said, in discussing the attempts of Antonin Artaud to revitalize the varied languages of the drama, that the goal of culture generally, and of the drama specifically, is "to reestablish contact with the absolute, or as I should prefer to call it, with multiple reality." This quest for the simultaneously many-dimensional nature of reality, for the consistent contradictoriness of human nature, has led to an art of counterpoint and paradox. In it language is used and abused, language and action clash and coalesce; the trivial and the significant are counterpointed, the simple and the subtle, the consistent and the inconsistent, the comic and the tragic, the brutal and the amusing, the pitiable and the awesome. This theater is the fulfillment of the call of Guillaume Apollinaire, one of its earliest advocates, who believed that "to bring forth life itself and all its truth," "the theater should not be an imitation of reality;" but, rather, it should be "modern, simple, rapid, with the shortcuts and enlargements that are needed to shock the spectator."

In a typical scene of Godard's *Masculine Feminine*, we shift from the undefined anger of the young boy and girl to the bizarre comedy of another girl's selling him a feel of her breasts while they stand in a photography booth, then to the poignance of the boy's making a record in the next booth in a futile effort to communicate with his girl, and then to the sudden terror of his being stalked with a knife by a man he had watched playing a bowling game, and finally to the abrupt shock of the man turning the knife into his own guts.

The films of Francois Truffaut are full of these counterpoints and juxtapositions, whether with the hard irony of the story of the romantic intellectual who is more bourgeois than he admits in *The Soft Skin* or the awed whimsy of *Jules and Jim*. In the ending of *Shoot the Piano Player*, Truffaut builds the comic gangster hunt (that had opened the film and continued sporadically throughout) to a parodic chase climax of ludicrous gangster inefficiency, only to subvert it with the sudden horror of the gratuitous, accidental shooting of the heroine, and to subvert that thematically absurd horror with a final shot of beauty, pure, plastic, formal beauty, in counterpoint to the meaning of the composition: the girl's body gracefully sliding through the snow and then coming to rest, her head lovely, her hair luxuriant, couched and framed in the billowing white snow. At the close of *Jules and Jim*, Truffaut undercuts Catherine's perverse, driven, foolish and noble destruction of herself and Jim with a sight gag: the camera pulls back and we watch the tiny antique car, so reminiscent of its counterparts in many silent comedies, gracefully and ridiculously racing off the opened bridge into the water.

This general ambiguity of tone and mood, in addition, often runs parallel to another kind of ambiguity, that of character. In his *Little Organon for the Theater*, Brecht asked, "Where is the living man himself, the inimitable one, the one who is not quite the equivalent of his counterparts?" And in conversation at this same time (1948) with a colleague, Max Wekworth, he stressed the need to maintain in the theater "the vital multiplicity, the innumerable shadings, the all moving unrest of contradictions and absurdities." He hoped to encompass the "self-contradictoriness" of the "concrete" with his dialectic, the opposed pairs of Shen Te and Shui Ta in *The*

Good Woman of Setzuan, Puntilla drunk and Puntilla sober, or the fragmented oppositions within the title characters in *Mother Courage* or *Galileo.* In one way or another, much of the modern theater has attempted to encompass the elusiveness of human character—the inner contradictions of traits, the tentativeness and confusion of motivations, the precariousness of identity and the often abrupt changes of personality that result, the intangibility of cause and effect.

The use of the surface phenomena of life—human and non-human—to suggest the intangible states of character beyond these phenomena is one of the key features of the work of Michaelangelo Antonioni. (Erving Goffman's *The Presentation of the Self in Everyday Life* analyzes the concrete evidences of the inner life in a way that is strikingly parallel to the use of these devices in the film.) In Antonioni's work the enigmatic ennui, the deadened register of feelings, the tenuousness of cause and effect in the motivations of the characters are constantly evoked by the "objective correlatives" of the facticity of the details of rooms and buildings, streets and countrysides, shapes, pictures, interrelationships of bodies, and in his last films, by colors. With this kind of indirection, to cite just one example, he uses the size, the furnishings, the colors of the tiny bedroom in the shack on the pier in *Red Desert* and the interrelationships of the bodies of the people, and of their looks and movements, as they lie on the bed talking and reading, to suggest the bound-up, restricted state of their emotions and the distortions of their yearnings for release.

Truffaut's Catherine of *Jules and Jim* is an example of the distance the movies have come from the schematically, carefully defined characterizations of the traditional film. She is not the good girl who is really bad, nor the bad girl who is really good. She is alive, vital, gay, spontaneous, free and elusive; and yet she is so trapped, unhappy, yearning, destructive. And she remains so to the end.

This multiplicity of personality is allied with the dislocation of the traditional cause and effect sequences of motivation, the conventional movie movement of event A producing character change or action A. These parallel ambiguities are illustrated in Allen Resnais' *Muriel,* which interweaves personality complexity with the tenuousness of motivations, both in the past and the present. The direction of change can be seen in movies that focus on psychological problems. In the traditional framework and devices of *David and Lisa,* specific actions and events produce, in turn, specific psychological responses of improvement or regression, all neatly and logically schematized. Whereas in Robert Rossen's *Lilith* (which was not given its due in America, though highly praised in France) the precarious ambiguity of the line between sanity and insanity, love and power, joy and cruelty, help and destruction, is conveyed in terms of a much more subtle and discontinuous relationship of causes and effects. In a similar manner, the complex interrelationship of the patient and nurse in Ingmar

Bergman's *Persona* and the tormented confusions of consciousness within each character are moored to cause and effect (the finding of the letter produces responses in the nurse which lead to the attempt to hurt the patient with the broken glass, which in turn leads to further responses), but they are not fully determined and explained by such causal sequences. The responses overflow such boundaries, overlap schematic classifications.

The Bergman film includes a sequence of three scenes in which the subjective emotional states of the nurse are projected in concrete visual terms. This externalization of inner states, this making literal and concrete the metaphors of consciousness, is another central characteristic of the new film. And it has been the major contribution of Expressionism to the drama of our time. From the station dramas and dream plays of Strindberg on, from the surrealistic works of Apollinaire, Jarry, and Artaud, through the Theater of the Absurd, much of the exaggeration and distortion, the physical grotesquerie, the acceleration and confusion of time sequences and causal sequences, has been part of the attempt to make visible and audible the workings of subjective consciousness. In this revelation of the truths of subjectivity the words, actions, symbolic properties, even the characters of the drama serve two functions. They can be the dream-like embodiments, the projections, of the intangible inner states of consciousness; or they can truly be external reality, but external reality reshaped, and even misshaped by subjective perception.

The recent film has used realistic images for both of these functions. Of the current directors Federico Fellini has taken these devices furthest in the direction of surrealist Expressionism—in *8½* and *Juliet of the Spirits*. In *8½* the crisis in the professional and personal lives of the film director Anselmi is conveyed through five aspects of his consciousness. We see his dreams; his memories, generally distorted into grotesque fantasy; current imaginative fantasies; real external scenes distorted into fantasy; and real external scenes left relatively conventional. In all cases the distortions are a concretizing and externalizing of his inner tensions and emotional states: the inhibiting and repressive force of the Catholic Church is, for example, conveyed in a memory that distorts the faculty of a Catholic school into a group of cruel, cold hermaphrodites and is also conveyed in a real scene in which the Catholic Bishop in a steam room is turned into a grotesque, the steam room situation into an inquisition in hell.

In *8½* the different modes of externalizing consciousness are kept distinct and distinguishable. In *Juliet of the Spirits* Fellini goes a step further. Here the boundaries are blurred; memories, fantasies, distortions of reality, projections into reality of inner tensions, all are interchangeable, and are carried, as well, to greater lengths of surrealistic distortion and exaggeration. The sexy next-door neighbor of the middle-aged woman in crisis is distorted by the subjective perception of the woman, but becomes as well a fantasy projection of the woman's ambivalent tensions over her own sexuality. The neighbor's party undergoes an acceleration of distortion and association as it ambiguously proceeds and simulatneously also becomes the external projection of the ambiguous sexual yearnings and fears of the heroine.

This focus on consciousness is effected by quite different means in the films of Antonioni. As the theme as well as the imagery of *Blow-up* indicate, he is concerned with the paradoxes of reality and the role played by subjective consciousness in creating or re-creating that reality. In his earlier films, which were not so directly addressed to this theme, his objective correlatives for the emotional states of his characters did have this element of projective subjectivity as well. That is, the external correlatives often took their emotional coloration from the projected state of the characters, where organized and shaped by subjective perception. In *L'Avventura* what could be seen as a lovely white and modern village nestled in the beautiful hills is shaped into the embodiment of the isolation and deadness of the characters; in *The Eclipse* a series of flag poles, which have no particular conventional association, are shaped into the correlative of the threat of phallic, aggressive, selfish masculinity upon the girl. Antonioni's most daring use of realistic, undistorted external objects for projection of inner states occurs at the end of *The Eclipse*. Here the commonplace objects of a street corner at which the protagonists had previously met are presented in a long montage: the objects of a construction site, a park and sprinklers, a bus stop, people alighting from the bus, the street lights, which become the final closeup, eclipsing all else in the emptiness of light. The montage shapes a final mood of sadness and loss, an unarticulated final state of alienation, the failure of connection of the central characters who are not even seen.

Antonioni's projections maintain the realistic base; Fellini's soar into the fantastic. While the recent film generally has not gone as far as the drama in the direction of the fantastic, the grotesque, the mythic, this phase of the artistic processes of abstraction has, in varying ways, also become a part of the new film style. The use of mythic forms and mythic figures by Ingmar Bergman represents the most comprehensive adaptation of this element of dramatic abstraction.

In many of his films, Bergman has constructed the kind of paradoxical allegories—replete with Figures, personifications of philosophic or psychological attitudes or projections of inner states—that have been so prevalent in the modern drama since Strindberg's first station drama, *To Damascus*. But whereas in the drama these allegories and Figures have moved toward simplification, abstraction out of textural contexts, condensation, exaggeration into caricature, in Bergman's films the textural contexts have generally been maintained. Employing the basic fact of film technique, he has filled in the abstract allegorical roles with the realistic phenomena of human character and concrete situations. The result is the kind of parable —one thinks of Kafka's use of matter of fact contextual detail—that, to some degree, does produce illusion, immersion, identification.

Even in an earlier, generally realistic film like *The Naked Night*, Bergman opened with a self-contained ten-minute mythic sequence that served as a parable for the torments of love in the rest of the film: in the sequence a clown's wife strays and displays herself before some soldiers at a beach, and the aging clown, pathetically yet nobly, must carry her naked body past his tormentors and up a long hill, a humanly flawed Christ bearing his cross up Calvary. In *The Seventh Seal, the Magician, The Virgin Spring* Bergman filled traditional mythic settings and forms with realistic details. In *The Silence*—with its symbolic hotel setting and symbolic failures of communication, its exaggerated personifications of varieties of destructive self-love and lust, its grotesques—he has come closest to the forms so common in the drama. Yet even here the outlines are filled in, the texture made tangible and concrete with realistic details that produce an immediate, and strong, sensory response: a woman's armpit, a breast, a buttock, a thigh, the facial expressions and the breathing patterns of orgasm or of pain or of imminent death, the positions, movements, and the sounds of the act of sex (not love) in the seat of a theater, in the bed of a hotel room.

In *Persona*, Bergman has explicitly dramatized his awareness of the limitations of the realistic film image. The film, both in technique and theme, is an attempt to get beyond the surface of the face (the mask, the persona, the "seeming") to the tangible reality beyond (the self, the anima, the "being"). Its bizarre opening montage (parts of which are repeated through the film)—with its cross-section of stock film images, its burning of the film, its closing image of a boy reaching to get beyond the giant face in the film frame—is Bergman's ironic acknowledgment of the raw materials he must use, but can imaginatively refresh and revivify by such means as the projection of inner states that he employs at the climax of the film.

The Bergman work, then, is typical of the major movement in the aesthetics of the contemporary film, a movement that runs parallel to that in the drama. For in both film and drama the dominant style has moved toward making the intangible visual and concrete—from what Cocteau called "poetry in the theater" to "poetry of the theater." It has moved toward capitalizing on and exploiting its own devices of theatricalism, rather than hiding them beneath a surface of complete illusion. It has recognized the limits of its own kind of perceptions and its forms for embodying them. And in all of this, it has sought to find a form for our contemporary root assumptions about the ambiguities of reality and the subjectivity of our attempts to know its truths.

Notes on New Actors,
New Movies
Pauline Kael

Frank Capra destroyed Gary Cooper's early sex appeal when he made him childish as Mr. Deeds; Cooper, once devastatingly lean and charming, the man Tallulah and Marlene had swooned over, began to act like an old woman and went on to a long sexless career—fumbling, homey, mealy-mouthed. Can this process be reversed? It's easy to see why Richard Benjamin has been working so much. He's a gifted light romantic comedian (on the order of Robert Montgomery in the thirties), and he's physically well suited to the urban Jewish heroes who dominated American fiction for over a decade and have now moved onto the screen. Benjamin is good at miming frustration and wild fantasies, and he's giggly and boyishly apologetic in a way, that probably pleases men, because it reminds them of their adolescent silliness, but he doesn't quite appeal to women. What's missing seems to be that little bit of male Fascism that makes an actor like Robert Redford or Jack Nicholson dangerous and hence attractive. Benjamin needs some sexual menace, some threat; without that there's no romantic charge to his presence. There's a distinctive nervous emotionalism in his voice (there is in Deborah Kerr's, too); one isn't quite sure how to react to it, because, although his sensitivity is sometimes rich (like Miss Kerr's), it's also on the borderline of weakness. He uses his voice for tricky comic effects: he cackles when one least expects it, or lets the sound break on a word, as if his voice were still changing. (That's a borderline device, too, although Melvyn Douglas always got by with it—but only within limits. Douglas was a leading man, never a star.) When Benjamin slips into nasality—even when it's for humor—there's the danger that he'll slide down into the Arnold Stang range and be sexually hopeless. Can Benjamin get by in the movies without that bit of coarseness or aggression which seems so essential to sex appeal? Fredric March did, but I can't think of many others. And now there's a new question: Can Benjamin get by if he *develops* sex appeal?

Richard Benjamin has, of course, been in demand for some roles just *because* he can project lack of confidence and suggest sexual inadequacy; he can impersonate the new movie stereotype of the American male as perennial adolescent. The Tony Perkins boyish juveniles of the late fifties

Reprinted by permission; © 1971 The New Yorker Magazine, Inc.

are now exposed, like Art Garfunkel in "Carnal Knowledge," in terms of their failure to become men. The new trend is to show the women as abused, deprived, and depersonalized, and an actor with sexual assurance wouldn't function right in these movies, because then there might seem to be something the matter with the woman if she wasn't having a good time. In "Diary of a Mad Housewife," the mopey heroine is meant to be superior to her tormentors; she's given a nagging social-climbing fool of a husband (Benjamin), and her selfish lover is played by Frank Langella, the new chief contender for the acting-in-a-mirror (or Herman Hesse) award. The period coming up may not be the best period for actors who project sexual competence. In Paula Fox's fine novel "Desperate Characters," the husband is civilized and fastidious, a rather elegant man, who deeply loves his wife; in the movie version, the director, Frank Gilroy, cast an actor best known for his mad Nazi in "The Producers," and so the reason for the woman's isolation becomes largely the brutish man she is married to, who at one point in the movie is so sexually excited by the vandalism of their home that he is moved to rape her.

Though directors become fairly knowledgeable about the chemistry of performers, even the greatest directors are not always in control of the effects the performers produce. I was offended for Bibi Andersson in Ingmar Bergman's "The Touch" when Elliott Gould, playing a lout, but also playing loutishly, was nuzzling her—offended that she should have to be touched by him. Gould's performance threw me out of the framework of the movie, since what was happening on the screen made me react for the actress, and not in terms of the role she was playing. Most of the women I know felt Gould's touching Bibi Andersson as a physical affront to her and recoiled in the same kinesthetic, empathic way that I did. Some men have said they felt it, too, and were embarrassed for the women they were with. At "Waterloo," the audience broke into laughter when Rod Steiger, as Napoleon, spoke his first line, simply because he was so unmistakably Rod Steiger. Second-generation actors and actresses may throw us out of the movie because of a line reading or a camera angle that recalls their parents. Peter Fonda can't move or talk without creating an echo chamber, and he looks as if somehow, on the set of "The Grapes of Wrath," John Carradine and Henry Fonda had mated.

In "Doc," Stacy Keach presents so obdurate a face that you feel he has to consider when to let a flicker of expression through. Those who fight easy expressiveness may be actors of integrity, but they're likely to be repellent screen actors. In movies, one can accept nonactors and mediocrities, one can accept stone-faced dummies, but deliberately masked, intellectualized acting—acting by a theory—is intolerable. Keach doesn't offer himself to the camera; he fights it, and in so doing he limits the meaning of his roles and sharply limits our pleasures. Such pleasures may have as much to do with what we see in an actor as in what he consciously projects. We care more for a trace of personality than for all of Keach's serious intentions. If Richard Benjamin is too lightweight, and maybe even too *loose*, Keach turns himself into a heavyweight and is much too tight. He's so determined to give us the constricted performance he has worked out that he gives us less than most Hollywood bums do just by not caring.

Dustin Hoffman has become such a culture hero that one hesitates to point out that he's more relaxed and likable on TV talk shows than when he's acting. In his screen roles, he hasn't yet found the gift of moving into a part and then just going with it. I love to watch him, because he's intelligent and he has extraordinary drive and he takes us by surprise, but he isn't an intuitive actor, and we're aware of how cleverly he's playing the part. To some degree, his rapport with the audience is based on our awareness of his cleverness, and our rooting for him, but then when his dexterity fails, and he's open-mouthed—and Hoffman, like Richard Benjamin, is nasal—we have nothing to fall back on. When his role isn't funny, he's usually helplessly tense; you can see him wishing he had something to *play*.

Though the dream of movies as a great popular art slips further and further away as the audience grows smaller and smaller, still, every year there are a handful of really good movies and others that reveal social changes, and almost always, even in bad films, one can count on some good performances. That's probably what holds the remaining audience together: actors like Dustin Hoffman and Richard Benjamin are fun to watch. There aren't any rules about movies—except maybe the fluky ones, such as that it's impossible to get a college atmosphere on film that feels authentic, and that pictures set in ancient Egypt are always ridiculous— but one might say with some confidence that feature filmmakers who don't care about actors and acting may have some sporadic luck but they're not likely to make movies for long, because nobody is going to go to their pictures. The promising American directors are not those who try to give us a sensory overload (we get enough overload without getting it at the movies) but directors, such as Robert Altman, Paul Mazursky, Jack Nicholson, Irvin Kershner, John Korty, Woody Allen, Brian De Palma, and Tom Laughlin, who are trying to find new ways for the performers to connect with the audience. They use quick-witted performers—often those trained in cabaret theatre, who can enter into the moviemaking in a different spirit from the actors who just learn their lines.

In the past two decades, male movie actors have carried the pictures, not only without much help from women but often without much help from the scripts and the directors. Still, they have had a rough time trying to keep some pride in themselves as actors. Every time we pick up the paper, another top-box-office actor informs us that he wants to become a director in order to do something "creative": Paul Newman, George C. Scott, Jack Lemmon, and even John Wayne and Clint Eastwood—though perhaps in their cases for other reasons. Maybe just a change? (The actresses don't want to direct, they want to write books—but that's another story.) Men—and not only American men—have always had hangups about acting; heterosexual men, in particular, tend to feel that acting is not a fit occupation, and that it doesn't fully use their abilities. One famous male star said in conversation, "I just can't say lines anymore"—meaning, I suppose, among other things, that he'd grown up. Yet few of the men stars risk more difficult roles or attempt new styles of acting, in which they might grow up as actors. The stars prefer to become directors, usually to turn out more of the same kind of movies that make actors feel like fools.

But movie acting has been loosening up, and it could be turning into a profession for smarter, more intuitive people. Some of the most inventive performances have been in flops—like the performances of Peter Bonerz, the hero of the neglected film "Funnyman," and Barry Primus, the hero of "Been Down So Long It Looks Up to Me," and William Tepper, the hero of "Drive, He Said"—and so they aren't talked about. But these put-on artists are part of a new and already taken-for-granted style of screen acting, which affects how we look at star-commodity performances. It's now difficult for us to accept the established stars in contemporary settings. We've lived for years with stars who didn't know what to do with a laugh line. (Has anyone seen Charlton Heston, for example, trying to play comedy?)

George Segal, who is probably the best light comedian in American movies, bridges the styles of the romantic screen stars, such as Cary Grant and Paul Newman, and the hip, loose, put-on comedy style of the sixties. He seems to be one of the few actors to find their challenge in acting, and he gives his roles solidity and some human weight—the way Spencer Tracy did but without Tracy's boring pugnacity. He's kept working for seven years, as if the old studio system were still intact, and he gets better all the time—maybe because he's never quite made it to the top box-office brackets, so he isn't image-conscious, like the million-dollar-a-picture men, whose films become high-risk corporate enterprises. Last year, he did the failed artist in "Loving," the self-deceiving book clerk in "The Owl and the Pussycat," and the frustrated lawyer in "Where's Poppa?," and now he has tried, and brought off, the prodigiously difficult role of a hipster junkie in the Czech director Ivan Passer's new film—and his first to be made in this country—"Born to Win."

Movies are so porous a mixture of intentions and accidents that when cultures are crossed the resonances may become confused. Dubbing is the most egregious example, but the resonances can go more subtly wrong, as when the locale of a story is changed, or when the director is a foreigner. In Miloš Forman's first American picture, "Taking Off," the suburban Americans looked Czech to me and seemed to be living in the thirties, and

I got a little sleepy, the way I sometimes do at Czech films, in which the rhythm of life seems too mild, too pokey. I didn't have that problem with "Born to Win;" Passer's sense of America is very sharp, and the rhythm of the picture, edited by Ralph Rosenblum, who was once a jazz musician, is active, volatile. You feel your senses are being quickened as you watch. The only way Passer reveals his foreignness is in the innocent, idealistic sincerity with which this slice-of-life film appears to be made, and in the tactful intelligence with which he spares us needles in the arm. He doesn't try to turn the audience on; it's clear that he wants to show us this junkie's soul, not his habit.

"Born to Win," from a screenplay by David Scott Milton, was shot under the much better title "Scraping Bottom;" I assume that the title was changed to con audiences into thinking they were going to see an upbeat movie. But it isn't that the movie is downbeat that works against it commercially—it's that it's downbeat in a way that isn't glamorous. J, the junkie, isn't mutinous, isn't anti-establishment. J isn't even chasing freedom. The movie doesn't make him a romantic loser (which is the path to box-office success). It's like those other stories of driven men who destroy themselves—usually prizefighters, as in "Requiem for a Heavyweight," or gangsters. Anyone can see that "Born to Win" isn't totally successful. It's the best of the addict movies, yet, like the others, it has no place to go but the too familiar down. Junkies don't get cured in contemporary movies—they don't even want to be cured—so we know everyone is doomed. And the explanations never suffice: we come out still puzzled as to why people do it to themselves. Maybe the best clue to J's character is his line "I'm a very boring guy when I'm straight." But though, in all probability, nobody will come out of "Born to Win" fully satisfied, I don't think anybody will regret having gone to see it, either.

Segal gives the most imaginatively complete performance in an American movie since Jane Fonda in "Klute." His J, the city rat, is a smarter version of Dustin Hoffman's Ratso—not pathetic and not a simpleton. You know J isn't going to get away with anything, yet this stoolie—the lowest of the low, and not because of stupidity but because of an addict's moral vacuity and indifference—holds you. J doesn't know or care that New York City is under siege. At the bottom, things don't change that much. Yet the bottom can also be funny in a different way from any other place (as Samuel Beckett recognized), because of the insane freedom of total losers. Words come easily to this smart, funny hipster, who seems essentially harmless and yet manages to wreck everyone who gets close to him. He has an anguished but ironic and knowing face; the transitions of mood are so fast they seem never to have gone through the brain. The glee and the horror are rolled up together; he's like Harry Ritz in agony, yet he has a sense of the ridiculous that includes whatever he's doing. Like many good movie actors, Segal can be very quiet, very still; he seems able to incorporate a character and then let it come out easily, naturally—as if it had always been there in him. But he has never before attempted such a quick-silver character: J is a comedian in pain yet so shallow he forgets his own pain, a man with absolutely no sense of tomorrow or of yesterday—an absurd man seen not in the abstract setting of an absurdist play but in the lower depths of New York City.

If an actor has any screen presence at all, his ego usually shows: you know he thinks well of himself. (When he pushes his luck, we call it conceit.) For a while in the thirties, juvenile leads did the passive-vulnerable bit, like some of the ingénues, but that was when there were strong women to overpower them—Garbo swooping down over them and exposing her throat, and Hepburn playing tomboy to fey young men—and it doesn't work anymore. Even a juvenile like Ryan O'Neal comes on cocky-vulnerable, and when you see a non-egocentric performer, like Timothy Bottoms in "The Last Picture Show," you know that he requires a director to bring him out—that, like the European actors who often fail over here, he doesn't have the strength of the actors who bust through no matter what. Richard Benjamin's comic persona is based on his self-confidence as an *actor*. George Segal has this cockiness, Spencer Tracy carried it to monotonous extremes, Gable wore it as his crown. It's what gives Warren Beatty his comic edge—he uses it ironically; so did Burt Lancaster and Kirk Douglas. A dull actor like Rock Hudson lacks it, and so does Gregory Peck—competent but always a little boring, a leading man disguised as a star. It's a quality that is usually described unflatteringly in women, though the only recently arrived woman star, Barbra Streisand, has got it, and I doubt if a new woman star could come up without it.

Robert Mitchum has that assurance in such huge amounts that he seems almost a lawless actor. He does it all out of himself. He doesn't use the tricks and stratagems of clever, trained actors. Mitchum is *sui generis*. There have been other good movie actors who invented for themselves without falling back on stage techniques—Joel McCrea, for one, a talented romantic comedian who became a fine, quiet, and much underrated actor. But there's no other powerhouse like Mitchum. This great bullfrog with the puffy eyes and the gut that becomes an honorary chest has been in movies for almost thirty years, and he's still so strong a masculine presence that he knocks younger men off the screen. His strength seems to come precisely from his avoidance of conventional acting, from his dependence on himself; his whole style is a put-on, in the sense that it's based on our shared understanding that he's a man acting in material conceived for puppets. He can barrel his way through, as he does in the new "Going Home," even when the role isn't worth playing. The script, an original by Lawrence B. Marcus, is about a man who kills his wife, with their child as witness (this opening scene is bloody powerful); when he is paroled from prison thirteen years later, the obsessed boy, full of fear and hate for his father, comes to visit him. I'm sure the script looked good on paper; like the scripts—also originals—that Alan Sharp wrote for "The Hired Hand" and "The Last Run," this Marcus script has a literate, "gritty" surface and a symmetrical structure. The trouble with these scripts is that they achieve their classicism too easily: there's nothing *under* them; they have the paper thinness of TV drama. In "Going Home," the ominous atmosphere (Will the son do something terrible? Will the father kill the son?) is simply for its own sake; there isn't enough revelation to justify keeping us so tense. The lurid big sequences (a rape in a room full of crowing gamecocks; an Expressionistic party and fight in the old family home, now a restaurant called the Inferno) are beyond redemption, but the director, Herbert B. Leonard, has done an impressive professional job; the small towns and seashore trailer-camp locations have an authentic and lovely melancholy, and are not presented condescendingly. Still, "Going Home" is an empty suspense film that exploits its star for a fake humanity. Mitchum is forced to overdraw on himself.

The Times They Are A-Changin':
The Music of Protest

Robert A. Rosenstone

At the beginning of the 1960s, nobody took popular music very seriously. Adults only knew that rock n' roll, which had flooded the airwaves in the 1950s, had a strong beat and was terribly loud; it was generally believed that teen-agers alone had thick enough eardrums, or insensitive enough souls, to enjoy it. Certainly, no critics thought of a popular star like the writhing Elvis Presley as being in any way a serious artist. Such a teen-age idol was simply considered a manifestation of a subculture that the young happily and inevitably outgrew—and, any parent would have added, the sooner the better.

In recent years this view of popular music has drastically changed. Some parents may still wonder about the "noise" that their children listen to, but important segments of American society have come to recognize popular

From *The Annals* by permission of The American Academy of Political and Social Science and the author.

musicians as artists saying serious things.[1] An indication of this change can be seen in magazine attitudes. In 1964, the *Saturday Evening Post* derided the Beatles—recognized giants of modern popular music—as "corny," and *Reporter* claimed: "They have debased Rock 'n Roll to its ultimate absurdity." Three years later the *Saturday Review* solemnly discussed a new Beatles record as a "highly ironic declaration of disaffection" with modern society, while in 1968 *Life* devoted a whole, laudatory section to "The New Rock," calling it music "that challenges the joys and ills of the . . . world."[2] Even in the intellectual community, popular music has found warm friends. Such sober journals as *The Listener, Columbia University Forum, New American Review*, and *Commentary* have sympathetically surveyed aspects of the "pop" scene, while *The New York Review of Books*—a kind of house organ for American academia—composer Ned Rorem has declared that, at their best, the Beatles "compare with those composers from great eras of song: Monteverdi, Schumann, Poulenc."[3]

The reasons for such changes in attitude are not difficult to find: there is no doubt that popular music has become more complex, and at the same time more serious, than it ever was before. Musically, it has broken down some of the old forms in which it was for a long time straitjacketed. With a wide-ranging eclecticism, popular music has adapted to itself a bewildering variety of musical traditions and instruments, from the classic Indian sitar to the most recent electronic synthesizers favored by composers of "serious" concert music.

As the music has been revolutionized, so has the subject matter of the songs. In preceding decades, popular music was almost exclusively about love, and, in the words of poet Thomas Gunn, "a very limited kind [of love], constituting a sort of fag-end of the Petrarchan tradition."[4] The

---

[1] The definition of "popular music" being used in this article is a broad one. It encompasses a multitude of styles, including folk, folk-rock, acid-rock, hard-rock, and blues, to give just a few names being used in the musical world today. It does so because the old musical classifications have been totally smashed and the forms now overlap in a way that makes meaningful distinction between them impossible. Though not every group or song referred to will have been popular in the sense of selling a million records, all of them are part of a broad, variegated scene termed "pop." Some of the groups, like Buffalo Springfield, Strawberry Alarm Clock, or the Byrds, have sold millions of records. Others, like the Fugs or Mothers of Invention, have never had a real hit, though they are played on radio stations allied to the "underground." Still, such groups do sell respectable numbers of records and do perform regularly at teen-age concerts.

[2] *Saturday Evening Post*, Vol. 237, March 21, 1964, p. 30; *Reporter*, Vol. 30, Feb. 27, 1964, p. 18; *Saturday Review*, Vol. 50 (August 19, 1967), p. 18; *Life*, Vol. 64 (June 28, 1968), p. 51.

[3] "The Music of the Beatles," *New York Review of Books* (January 15, 1968), pp. 23–27. See also "The New Music," *The Listener*, Vol. 78 (August 3, 1967), pp. 129–130; *Columbia University Forum* (Fall 1967), pp. 16–22; *New American Review*, Vol. 1 (April 1968), pp. 118–139; Ellen Willis, "The Sound of Bob Dylan," *Commentary*, Vol. 44 (November 1967), pp. 71–80. Many of these articles deal with English as well as American popular groups, and, in fact, the music of the two countries cannot, in any meaningful sense, be separated. This article will only survey American musical groups, though a look at English music would reveal the prevalence of the themes explored here.

[4] "The New Music," p. 129.

stories told in song were largely about lovers yearning for one another in some vaguely unreal world where nobody ever seemed to work or get married. All this changed in the 1960s. Suddenly, popular music began to deal with civil rights demonstrations and drug experiences, with interracial dating and war and explicit sexual encounters, with, in short, the real world in which people live. For perhaps the first time, popular songs became relevant to the lives of the teen-age audience that largely constitutes the record-buying public. The success of some of these works prompted others to be written, and from the second half of the decade on there was a full efflorescence of such topical songs; written by young people for their peers. These works may be grouped under the label of "protest" songs, for taken together, they provide a wide-ranging critique of American life. Listening to them, one can get a full-blown picture of the antipathy that the young song writers have toward many American institutions.

Serious concerns entered popular music early in the 1960s, when a great revival of folk singing spread out from college campuses, engulfed the mass media, and created a wave of new "pop" stars, the best known of whom was Joan Baez. Yet, though the concerns of these folk songs were often serious, they were hardly contemporary. Popular were numbers about organizing unions, which might date from the 1930s or the late nineteenth century, or about the trials of escaping Negro slaves, or celebrating the cause of the defeated Republicans in the Spanish Civil War. Occasionally there was something like "Talking A-Bomb Blues," but this was the rare exception rather than the rule.[5]

A change of focus came when performers began to write their own songs, rather than relying on the traditional folk repertoire. Chief among them, and destined to become the best known, was Bob Dylan. Consciously modeling himself on that wandering minstrel of the 1930s, Woody Guthrie, Dylan began by writing songs that often had little to do with the contemporary environment. Rather, his early ballads like "Masters of War" echoed the leftist concerns and rhetoric of an earlier era. Yet, simultaneously, Dylan was writing songs like "Blowin' In the Wind," "A Hard Rain's A-Gonna Fall," and "The Times They Are A-Changin'," which dealt with civil rights, nuclear war, and the changing world of youth that parents and educators were not prepared to understand. Acclaimed as the best of protest-song-writers, Dylan in mid-decade shifted gears, and in the song "My Back Pages," he denounced his former moral fervor. In an ironic chorus claiming that he was much younger than he had been, Dylan specifically made social problems the worry of sober, serious, older men; presumably, youths had more important things than injustice to think

[5] *Time*, Vol. 80 Nov. 23, 1962, pp. 54–60, gives a brief survey of the folk revival.

about. After that, any social comment by Dylan came encapsulated in a series of surrealistic images; for the most part, he escaped into worlds of aestheticism, psychedelic drugs, and personal love relationships. Apparently attempting to come to grips in art with his own personality, Dylan was content to forget about the problems of other men.[6]

The development of Dylan is important not only because he is the leading song writer, but also because it parallels the concerns of popular music in recent years. Starting out with traditional liberal positions on war, discrimination, segregation, and exploitation, song writers have turned increasingly to descriptions of the private worlds of drugs, sexual experience, and personal freedom. Though social concerns have never entirely faded, the private realm has been increasingly seen as the only one in which people can lead meaningful lives. Today the realms of social protest and private indulgence exist side by side in the popular music, with the latter perceived as the only viable alternative to the world described in the former songs. . . .[7]

YOUTH AS VICTIM

Throughout the decade, young people have often been at odds with established authority, and, repeatedly, songs picture youth in the role of victim. Sometimes the victimization is mental, as when the Mothers of Invention complain of outworn thought patterns and say that children are "victims of lies" which their parents believe.[8] On a much simpler level, Sonny Bono voices his annoyance that older people laugh at the clothes he wears, and he wonders why they enjoy "makin' fun" of him.[9] Now, Bono could musically shrug off the laughs as the price of freedom; but other songs document occasions when Establishment disapproval turned into physical oppression. Thus, Canned Heat tells of being arrested in Denver because the police did not want any "long hairs around."[10] The Buffalo Springfield, in a hit record, describe gun-bearing police rounding up teen-agers on Sunset Strip.[11] On the same theme, Dylan ironically shows that adults arbitrarily oppose just about all activities of youths, saying that they should "look out" no matter what they are doing.[12] More bitter is the Mothers' description of police killing large numbers of hippies, which is then justified on the grounds that because they looked "weird" it "served

---

6 Willis, "The Sound of Dylan," gives a good analysis of his work.
7 It must be pointed out that, in spite of the large amount of social criticism, most songs today are still about love.
8 We're Only in It for the Money (Verve, 65045).
9 "Laugh at Me," Five West Cotillion, BMI.
10 "My Crime," Boogie (Liberty, 7541).
11 "For What It's Worth."
12 "Subterranean Homesick Blues," Bob Dylan's Greatest Hits (Columbia, KCS 9463).

them right."[13] A fictional incident when the song was written, the Mothers were clearly prescient in believing Americans capable of shooting down those who engage in deviant behavior.

Though the songs echo the oppression that youngsters have felt, they do not ignore the problems that all humans face in a mass society. Writer Tom Paxton knows that it is not easy to keep one's life from being forced into a predetermined mold. In "Mr. Blue" he has a Big-Brotherlike narrator telling the title character, a kind of Everyman, that he is always under surveillance, and that he will never be able to indulge himself in his precious dreams of freedom from society. This is because society needs him to fill a slot, no matter what his personal desires. And Mr. Blue had better learn to love that slot, or "we'll break you."[14] Though no other writer made the message so explicit, a similar fear of being forced into an unwelcome slot underlies many songs of the period:

The society of slotted people is an empty one, partly described as "TV dinner by the pool."[15] It is one in which people have been robbed of their humanity, receiving in return the "transient treasures" of wealth and the useless gadgets of a technological age. One of these is television, referred to simply as "that rotten box," or, in a more sinister image, as an "electronic shrine." This image of men worshipping gadgets recurs. In the nightmare vision of a McLuhanesque world—where the medium is the message—Simon and Garfunkle sing of men so busy bowing and praying to a "neon god" that they cannot understand or touch one another. Indeed, here electronics seem to hinder the process of communication rather than facilitate it. People talk and hear but never understand, as the "sounds of silence" fill the world.[16] Such lack of communication contributes to the indifference with which men can view the life and death of a neighbor, as in Simon's "A Most Peculiar Man."[17] It also creates the climate of fear which causes people to kill a stranger for no reason other than his unknown origins in Strawberry Alarm Clock's "They Saw the Fat One Coming."[18]

Alienated from his fellows, fearful and alone, modern man has also despoiled the natural world in which he lives, has in Joni Mitchell's words, paved paradise to "put up a parking lot."[19] With anguish in his voice, Jim Morrison of the Doors asks "What have they done to the earth?" and then angrily answers that his "fair sister" has been ravished and plundered.[20] In a lighter tone but with no less serious intent, the Lewis and Clark Expedi-

[13] *We're Only in It for the Money.*
[14] "Mr. Blue," *Clear Light* (Elektra, 74011).
[15] Mothers of Invention, "Brown Shoes Don't Make It," *Absolutely Free* (Verve, 65013).
[16] "Sounds of Silence," *Sounds of Silence* (Columbia, CS 9269).
[17] *Sounds of Silence.*
[18] *Wake Up . . . It's Tomorrow* (Uni., 73025).
[19] "Big Yellow Taxi," *Ladies of the Canyon* (Reprise, RS 6376).
[20] "When the Music's Over," *Strange Days* (Elektra, 74014).

tion describes the way man has cut himself off from nature in the great outdoors, where chains and fences keep him from the flowers and trees. With a final ironic thrust, they add that there's no reason to touch the flowers because they are "plastic anyway."[21]

This brings up a fear that haunts a number of recent songs, the worry that the technological age has created so many artificial things that nothing natural remains. Concerned with authenticity, the songsters are afraid that man himself is becoming an artifact, or in their favorite word, "plastic." Thus, the Jefferson Airplane sings about a "Plastic Fantastic Lover," while the Iron Butterfly warns a girl to stay away from people "made of plastic."[22] The image recurs most frequently in the works of the Mothers of Invention. In one song, they depict the country as being run by a plastic Congress and President.[23] Then, in "Plastic People" they start with complaints about a girl friend who uses "plastic goo" on her face, go on to a picture of teen-agers on the Sunset Strip—who are probably their fans—as being "plastic," too, and finally turn on their listeners and advise them to check themselves, for "you think we're talking about someone else."[24] Such a vision is frightening, for if the audience is plastic, perhaps the Mothers, themselves, are made of the same phony material. And if the whole world is plastic, who can be sure of his own authenticity?

LOVE RELATIONSHIPS

Toward the end of "Plastic People," the Mothers say that "true love" cannot be "a product of plasticity." This brings up the greatest horror, that in a "plastic" society like the United States, love relationships are impossible. For the young song writers, American love is viewed as warped and twisted. Nothing about Establishment society frightens them more than its attitudes towards sex. Tim Buckley is typical in singing that older Americans are "Afraid to trust in their bodies."[25] Others give graphic portraits of deviant behavior. The Fugs tell of a "Dirty Old Man" hanging around high school playgrounds; the Velvet Underground portray a masochist; and the Mothers depict a middle-aged man lusting after his own thirteen-year-old daughter.[26] The fullest indictment of modern love is made by the United States of America, which devotes almost an entire album to the subject. Here, in a twisted portrait of "pleasure and pain," is a world of loveless marriages, homosexual relationships in men's rooms, venomous attractions, and overt sadism—all masked by a middle-class, suburban

21 "Chain Around the Flowers," *The Lewis and Clark Expedition* (Colgems, COS 105).
22 *Surrealistic Pillow* (Victor, LSP 3766) "Stamped Ideas," *Heavy* (Atco, S 33–227).
23 "Uncle Bernie's Farm," *Absolutely Free.*
24 "Plastic People," *Absolutely Free.*
25 "Goodbye and Hello," *Goodbye and Hello* (Elektra, 7318).
26 *The Fugs,* "Venus in Furs," *The Velvet Underground and Nico* (Verve, 6–5008); "Brown Shoes Don't Make It," *Absolutely Free.*

world in which people consider "morality" important. To show that natural relationships are possible elsewhere, the group sings one tender love
lyric; interestingly, it is the lament of a Cuban girl for the dead Ché
Guevara.[27]

The fact that bourgeois America has warped attitudes towards sex and
love is bad enough; the songsters are more worried that such attitudes will
infect their own generation. Thus, the Collectors decry the fact that man-
woman relationships are too often seen as some kind of contest, with a
victor and vanquished and in which violence is more acceptable than
tenderness.[28] Perhaps because most of the singers are men, criticisms of
female sexual attitudes abound. The Mothers are disgusted with the American woman, who lies in bed gritting her teeth, while the Sopwith Camel
objects to the traditional kind of purity by singing that they don't want
their women "wrapped up in cellophane."[29] This is because such a
woman will bring you down with her "talking about sin."[30] All the musicians would prefer the girl about whom Moby Grape sings who is "super-
powered, deflowered," and over eighteen.[31]

Living in a "plastic" world where honest human relationships are impossible, the song writers might be expected to wrap themselves in a mood
of musical despair. But they are young—and often making plenty of
money—and such an attitude is foreign to them. Musically, they are hopeful because, as the title of the Dylan song indicates, "The Times They Are
A-Changin'." Without describing the changes, Dylan clearly threatens the
older generation, as he tells critics, parents, and presumably anyone over
thirty, to start swimming or they will drown in the rising flood-waters of
social change.[32]

In another work, Dylan exploits the same theme. Here is a portrait of a
presumably normal, educated man, faced with a series of bizarre situations, who is made to feel like a freak because he does not understand
what is going on. The chorus is the young generation's comment to all
adults, as it mocks "Mr. Jones" for not understanding what is happening
all around him.[33]

The changes going on are, not surprisingly, associated with the carefree,
joyful experiences of youth. As Jefferson Airplane sings, "It's a wild time"
one in which people are busy "changing faces."[34] The most full-blown
description of the changing world is Tim Buckley's "Goodbye and Hello,"

27 *The United States of America* (Columbia, CS 9614).
28 "What Love," *The Collectors* (Warner Bros.-Seven Arts, WS 1746).
29 *We're Only in It for the Money*; "Cellophane Woman," *The Sopwith Camel* (Kama
Sutra, KLPS 8060).
30 "Cellophane Woman."
31 "Motorcycle Irene," *Wow* (Columbia, CS 9613).
32 *Bob Dylan's Greatest Hits*.
33 "Ballad of a Thin Man/Mr. Jones," *Highway 61 Revisited* (Columbia, CS 9189).
Though this song has obvious homosexual overtones, it also stands as youth's criticism of
the older generation.
34 "Wild Tyme (H)," *After Bathing at Baxter's* (Victor, LSO-1511).

a lengthy and explicit portrait of what the youth hope is happening. Throughout the song the author contrasts two kinds of people and their environments. On the one hand are the "antique people"—godless and sexless—of an individual civilization, living in dark dungeons, working hard, worshipping technology and money, sacrificing their sons to placate "vaudeville" generals, and blinding themselves to the fact that their "masquerade towers" are "riddled by widening cracks." Opposed to them are the "new children," interested in flowers, streams, and the beauty of the sky, who wish to take off their clothes to dance and sing and love one another. What's more, the "antique people are fading away"; in fact, they are already wearing "death masks."[35]

Buckley's vision of the new world that is coming is obviously that of a kind of idyllic Eden before the fall, a world in which men will be free to romp and play and indulge their natural desires for love. It is a pagan world, the antithesis of the Christian ideal that would postpone fulfillment to some afterlife. Elsewhere, Buckley explicitly condemns that part of Christianity which saves pleasure for an afterlife. Similarly, the Doors' Jim Morrison wants to cancel his "subscription to the resurrection," and then shrieks for a whole generation: "We want the world and we want it now."[36]

HOW TO LIVE

Though the times may be changing, the songsters are well aware that—despite their brave words and demands—there is plenty of strength left in the old social order. Obviously, they can see the war continuing, Negro demands not being met, and the continuing hostility of society toward their long hair, music; sexual behavior, and experimentation with drugs. Faced with these facts, the musicians have occasionally toyed with the idea of violent revolution. Some, like the Band, see it as an inevitable great storm "coming through" the country. Others wish to force the issue. The Doors, claiming "we've got the numbers," call on people to get their guns, for "the time has come," while Jefferson Airplane echoes the same plea in asking for volunteers to change the world.[37]

Yet most musicians have not believed revolution feasible, and more typically they have dealt with the problem of how to live decently within the framework of the old society. Here they tend toward the world of private experience mentioned earlier in connection with Dylan. Many of their songs are almost programs for youth's behavior in a world perceived as being unlivable.

[35] "Goodbye and Hello," written by Tim Buckley, *Goodbye and Hello.*
[36] "Pleasant Street," written by Tim Buckley, "When the Music's Over," *Strange Days.*
[37] "Look Out, Cleveland," *The Band* (Capitol, STAO–132); "Five to One," *Waiting for the Sun* (Elektra, EKS 74024); "Tell all the People," *The Soft Parade* (Elektra, EKS 75005).

The first element is to forget about the repressive society out there. As Sopwith Camel says, "Stamp out reality . . ." before it stamps you out.[38] Then it is imperative to forget about trying to understand the outside world rationally. In a typical anti-intellectual stance, the Byrds describe such attempts as "scientific delirium madness."[39] Others combine a similar attitude with a strong measure of *carpe diem.* Spirit derides people who are "always asking" for "the reason" when they should be enjoying life, while H. P. Lovecraft admits that the bird is on the wing and states, "You need not know why."[40] What is important is that the moment be seized and life lived to the fullest. As Simon and Garfunkel say, one has to make the "moment last," and this is done best by those who open themselves fully to the pleasures of the world.[41]

The most frequent theme of the song writers is the call to freedom, the total freedom of the individual to "do his own thing." Peanut Butter Conspiracy carries this so far as to hope for a life that can be lived "free of time."[42] Circus Maximus and the Byrds—despite the fact that they are young men—long to recapture some lost freedom that they knew as children.[43] Such freedom can be almost solipsistic; Jimi Hendrix claims that even if the sun did not rise and the mountains fell into the sea, he would not care because he has his "own world to live through."[44] But for others, it can lead to brotherhood. H. P. Lovecraft asks all to "try and love one another right now."[45]

A desire for freedom is certainly nothing new. Neither is the attempt to find freedom far from smoggy cities in the rural world of nature that Dylan celebrated in his 1970 album *New Morning* and that Joni Mitchell depicts in "Woodstock." What is different in the songs is the conviction that freedom should be used by the individual in an extensive exploration of his own internal world. Central to the vision of the song writers is the idea that the mind must be opened and expanded if the truths of life are to be perceived. Thus, the importance of external reality is subordinated to that of a psychological, even a metaphysical, realm. The most extensive treatment of this subject is by the Amboy Dukes, who devote half of a long-playing record to it. Their theme is stated quite simply: mankind would be happy if only people took the time "to journey to the center of the mind."[46] Like any mystical trip, what happens when one reaches the

38 "Saga of the Low Down Let Down," *The Sopwith Camel.*
39 "Fifth Dimension," *Fifth Dimension.*
40 "Topanga Window," *Spirit* (Ode, 212 44004); "Let's Get Together," *H. P. Lovecraft* (Phillips, 600–252).
41 "Feeling Groovy," *Sounds of Silence.*
42 "Time Is After You," *West Coast Love-In* (Vault, LP 113).
43 "Lost Sea Shanty," Circus Maximus (Vanguard, 79260); "Going Back," *The Notorious Byrd Brothers.*
44 "If 6 Was 9," *Axis* (Reprise, S 6281).
45 "Let's Get Together," *H. P. Lovecraft.*
46 "Journey to the Center of the Mind," *Journey to the Center of the Mind* (Mainstream, S 6112).

center of the mind is not easy to describe. Perhaps the best attempt is by the Iron Butterfly, who claims that an unconscious power will be released, flooding the individual with sensations and fusing him with a freedom of thought that will allow him to "see every thing." At this point, man will be blessed with the almost supernatural power of knowing "all."[47]

Such a journey is, of course, difficult to make. But youth has discovered a short cut to the mind's center, through the use of hallucinogenic drugs. Indeed, such journeys are almost inconceivable without hallucinogens, and the so-called "head songs" about drug experiences are the most prevalent of works that can be classified as "protest."[48] In this area, the songs carefully distinguish between "mind-expanding," nonaddictive marijuana and LSD, and hard, addictive drugs which destroy the body. Thus, the Velvet Underground and Love both tell of the dangers of heroin, while Canned Heat warns of methedrine use and the Fugs describe the problems of cocaine.[49] But none of the groups hesitate to recommend "grass" and "acid" trips as a prime way of opening oneself to the pleasures and beauties of the universe. As the Byrds claim in a typical "head song," drugs can free the individual from the narrow boundaries of the mundane world, allowing him to open his heart to the quiet joy and eternal love which pervade the whole universe.[50] Others find the reality of the drug experience more real than the day-to-day world, and some even hope for the possibility of staying "high" permanently. More frequently is the claim that "trips" are of lasting benefit because they improve the quality of life of an individual even after he "comes down."[51] The Peanut Butter Conspiracy, claiming that "everyone has a bomb" in his mind, even dreams of some day turning the whole world on with drugs, thus solving mankind's plaguing problems by making the earth a loving place.[52] An extreme desire, perhaps, but one that would find much support among other youths. . . .

[47] "Unconscious Power," *Heavy*.
[48] There are so many "head songs" that listing them would be an impossibly long task. Some of the most popular protest songs of the decade have been such works. They include Jefferson Airplane, "White Rabbit," *Surrealistic Pillow*; the Doors, "Light My Fire," *The Doors* (Elektra EKS 74007); Strawberry Alarm Clock, "Incense and Peppermints," *Incense and Peppermints*; and the Byrds, "Eight Miles High," *Fifth Dimension*.
[49] "Heroin," *Velvet Underground*; "Signed D. C.," *Love* (Elektra, 74001); "Amphetamine Annie," *Boggie*; "Coming Down," *The Fugs*.
[50] "Fifth Dimension," *Fifth Dimension*.
[51] See Country Joe and the Fish, "Bass Strings," *Electric Music for the Mind and Body*; or United States of America, "Coming Down," *United States of America*.
[52] "Living, Loving Life," *Great Conspiracy*.

III. Critiques
and
Cases

The criticism of individual works, artists, and creators can take many forms which go beyond the usual kind of content summary and snap value judgments of many newspaper and magazine reviewers. The selections in this section illustrate several of these forms.

Peter Michelson's piece defines what he considers the central, shaping personality of two popular magazines—*Playboy* and *Cosmopolitan*—and then draws critical implications from the kind of reductive, commercialized sexuality of that personality. The aptness of his parallel between the two magazines has been more recently accentuated by the appearance in *Cosmopolitan* of the first nude male center-fold photograph, the playboy of the month.

The *Time* article goes on to indicate how the stereotyped images of men and women shaped by *Playboy* and *Cosmopolitan* have been affected by recent developments in the women's liberation movement.

In his approach to a number of the basic genres of television, Richard Carpenter conjectures imaginatively about some of the indirect fulfillments of psychological and cultural expectations supplied by the regular repetition of genre patterns.

Using material from a symposium and interviews, Jean Carey Bond summarizes a cross-section of black responses to the images of black life currently projected on television; she places these specific examples in the broader context of the problems and possibilities present in the media's role in increasing understanding between blacks and whites.

Leonard Gross' piece on the successful comic bigotry of Archie Bunker is more topical and reportorial. Nonetheless, using interviews with the chief figures involved in *All in the Family* and details from specific programs, Gross raises a number of key issues about television's treatment of controversial topics and the functions and effects of comedy.

Three essays on contemporary films present variations on evaluating and interpreting individual works in the light of broader contexts. Charles C. Hampton sees the four movies under discussion as revealing a major, and valuable, shift in audience expectations about film genres. Stephen Farber not only explicates what he finds successful and valuable in the films he discusses, but also places them in a meaningful pattern that links current filmmaking and current psychological attitudes. William S. Pechter adeptly argues the differences between two controversial films—differences which in turn are used to argue differences between the films' directors and their individualized bodies of work and differences between ways of approaching violence on the screen.

In interpreting the work and deaths of Janis Joplin and Jimi Hendrix (as well as the work of Jim Morrison, whose death, however, is not mentioned), Mary Josephson derives a fascinating and meaningful connection between their public performances and their private drives. In turn, she places that connection within the wider perspective of tendencies within the field of rock music.

The Pleasures of Commodity,
or How to Make the World Safe for Pornography:
Playboy and *Cosmopolitan*

Peter Michelson

Playboy magazine, perhaps more than any other single pop culture phenomenon, has managed to change sex from a dirty joke into "entertainment served up with humor, sophistication, and spice," to purloin a phrase from its original apology. *Playboy* has been a paradigmatic force in making the world safe for pornography because it has always been careful to use sex for "higher" ends—essentially for the establishment of its fundamental image, the well-heeled Playboy who can and should afford his monthly Playmate. From its beginnings *Playboy* projected the image of a latter day (executive *né* business) man of mode; again from the credo of its first issue, "We like our apartment. We enjoy mixing up cocktails and an hors d'oeuvre or two, putting a little mood music on the phonograph, and inviting in a female acquaintance for a quiet discussion on Picasso, Nietzsche, jazz, sex." The audience was intended to be, as it has proved to be, "young men-on-the-move" (another *Playboy* PR phrase). It was intended to be and has become a magazine for the young executive, and, more inclusively, for the hopeful fantasies of aspiring pre-executives. But, more than anything else, it is a monumental pop celebration of commodity.

Playboy has grown, in fifteen years, from the twice-hocked furniture of its founder Hugh Hefner's apartment to a $54 million "empire," as we are told in the 1968 financial report from *Playboy*; and we are reminded by Hefner—president of the enterprise—that, being a private corporation, *Playboy* is not required to make a public financial statement. He does it, presumably therefore, because he *wants* to. And if there is any question about *Playboy's* most important product, one need only check its own public relations brochures. The introductory paragraph of one, the cover of which shows the new Playboy Building backed up by Chicago's Gold Coast, goes thus:

Reprinted from *The Antioch Review*, Vol. 29, No. 1, by permission of the editors. From *The Aesthetics of Pornography* by Peter Michelson. New York; Herder and Herder, Inc., 1971. By permission of Herder and Herder, Inc.

Topped with the world's largest aviation beacon, the Playboy Building at 919 North Michigan Avenue in Chicago is today the headquarters of one of the brightest lights in the world of entertainment for men—Playboy. A landmark since its construction, the building, formerly called the Palmolive Building, is a fitting symbol for a magazine and subsidiary enterprises which have witnessed lightning success during the past decade.

One might note here that after *Playboy* moved out of its old Ohio Street buildings it took the United States Post Office and the Museum of Contemporary Art to fill its "shoes."

But profit is really the simplest and even most predictable of *Playboy's* achievements. More complex and more culturally significant is the cause of that awful success—*Playboy's* adroit use of sex. So adroit has it been, in fact, that one has the uncomfortable feeling that Pamela, our old flame, has not done with us yet. One feels, in the image of the Playboy, that Pamela's Squire has been mightily domesticated (and calling domesticity "urbanity" or "sophistication" doesn't relieve the anxiety). Yet again from the original credo: "Most of today's 'magazines for men' spend all their time out-of-doors—thrashing through thorny thickets or splashing about in fast flowing streams. We'll be out there too, occasionally, but we don't mind telling you in advance—we plan on spending most of our time inside. We like our apartment." Etc. The rest we've already seen. And not the Playboy's broadest, knowingest wink, not even a desperate psychedelic discussion of Picasso, Nietzsche, jazz, *and* sex all at the same time can dissuade us that Pamela hasn't stuffed that velvet smoking jacket and silk scarf with the carcass of her long tamed Squire, put a high-ball in his hand, a cigarette holder in his teeth, an impressionistic nude on his paneled den wall, and called him PLAYBOY. At last Pamela and the Squire are on equal terms (a fact which *Cosmopolitan* magazine has recently recognized much to its own advantage), and Pamela, our vital parts firmly in her grip, demands, "and now Monsieur your wallet." Hemingway warned us, but we wouldn't listen.

The first thing, then, that *Playboy* has done by equating sex with profit is to sublimate it from its fearful psychic depths to the heights of that "fitting symbol formerly called the Palmolive Building." And, by being made into capital, sex has been psychologically neutralized. It has become a contemporary (and historical) community standard: it is proved profitable and therefore socially redeeming. Concomitant, of course, with *Playboy's* showing cause for sex has been its cleaning up of the image of sex. Attributing the observation to a Kinsey Institute authority, Nat Lehrman, a senior editor of the magazine, says that *Playboy* has raised sex to respectability, made it fit matter for coffee conversation (along, remember, with Picasso, Nietzsche, and jazz). This is probably true, but in the beginning *Playboy* had some difficulty getting launched into the antiseptic sex imagery which is its latter-day hallmark.

SEX IN THE STONE AGE

The early foldouts, called "Playboy's Eyeful" then, were standard low-grade skin pictures. Nor did they have the now-familiar personality sketch accompanying them. It took three years for the Playmate image to find the girl-next-door quality that now has currency. *Playboy* legend has it that one Janet Pilgrim, a circulation secretary whose name is still on the masthead, went to Hefner requesting a new typewriter. He told her she'd have to pose nude for it, *à la* Lady Godiva. She did, and the Playmate image was born—bright eyed, bushy (I beg your pardon?) tailed, and clean, clean, clean. Up to this time (about 1955), as one editor acknowledges, the magazine was obliged to use either "hookers" or professional models for its foldouts and the image was, excepting perhaps the celebrated Marilyn Monroe calendar nudes featured in the first issue, more sleazy than piquant. And, though Jack Kessie, *Playboy's* managing editor, claims that the sublimated *Playboy* Image we can now perceive was planned from the magazine's inception, sleaziness pretty much describes its character for at least the first four or five issues. Such photographic features, for example, as "Strip Quiz," a Paris *bistro* strip routine, or Beaux Arts Ball, a portfolio of prurient snapshots, or illustrations of criminal assault, indicate something of the imagistic tone of the first three issues. The fourth issue, though, presented two marvellously prophetic features. One is called "Sex Sells a Shirt," and simply shows a girl taking off her clothes, including of course her shirt. The text, in its banal way, discusses sex and merchandising for a few column inches. It intends to say nothing, and it does. But this nevertheless is the first public presentation of the profit formula on which *Playboy* was to ride to fiscal glory. The other feature is billed as a pictorial history of surgery, and it is essentially a vehicle for naked ladies pictured in the context of medical history. Sex, thus, is both a delight and an instruction, satisfying not only classical poetics but, more importantly, providing the proper scholarly elevation for so base a subject. This kind of augmentation was also to become an editorial staple of the magazine's success formula.

Today's Playmate, through which the *Playboy* Image is projected, is the scrupulously antiseptic incarnation of almost virginal contemporary community standards, an occasional lapse into prostitution notwithstanding. And she even has sufficient social redemption potential to be rented out to colleges over football weekends. At which, to show her healthy respect for the Working Man (or Labor or The People or the Dollar—as you prefer), she will charge overtime for conversation above and beyond an eight hour day. (This really happens!) Playmates, lest their title be misleading, do not indulge idle pleasure for its own sake; the meter on these puritanic taxi-dancers is always running. And well it might, for Nathanael West to the contrary, a clean young girl is always worth more than a clean old man—especially on a college football weekend at an all-male college.

Especially too when one notes that *Playboy's* notion of its editorial "responsibility" is to serve, according to managing editor Jack Kessie, as a guidebook to the good life for the young, university-educated man. The vocabulary *Playboy* editors use to describe their magazine and its goals reads like Dr. Johnson's own lexicon of aesthetic terms: Balance, Proportion, Taste, Elegance, Imagination, Wit, etc. And it is easily acknowledged that *Playboy* is the most balanced, tasteful, elegant, imaginative, and witty skin book in the business. (By "skin book" I don't of course mean *skin* at all, but rather skin sublimated to *capital*. In which sense one understands that *Playboy* is the more honestly pornographic analogue of *Fortune* magazine. Though it is less honest, and therefore more obscene, than the *Evergreen Review*. So much for the periodical scheme of things.) Of all the terms in the *Playboy* vocabulary, "taste" is perhaps the most significant. "We present sex," says Kessie, "in proportion to its over-all degree of importance in man's life." This is true, but it's not the whole truth. In modesty, Kessie ignores the fact that, in making sex a respectable thing and in demonstrating its commodity quotient, *Playboy* expanded the popular horizons for sex's over-all degree of importance in man's life. What he means by *Playboy's* tastefulness is that *visually* there is no more sex showing than there should be.

This is elaborated in Kessie's notion of *Playboy's* editorial contribution to the culture. *Playboy* was, he says, the first to assert not only nudity and sex, but also something else—a rounded view of the good life. He points out, for instance, that if *Playboy* "advocates materialism, so do we advocate other things—civil rights for example." And what, after all, is the end of Taste (not to mention Balance, Proportion, Imagination, and Wit) if not to give a rounded view of the good life? The *Playboy* editors are tastefully aware that "too much" of anything—such as civil rights activism, or an eyeful of genitals—is bad for standards, of both business and taste. Thus the Playmate has breasts with glamorized nipples, a groin without pubic hair, vagina, or urinary tract, and a backside without anus. She has feminine shape without female, or for that matter even human, function. She is not made for coitus or procreation or motherhood. She has body without consequence. So when it comes to nakedness (absolute nudity) as distinguished from nudity ("tasteful" nudity, guess whose taste: yes, Pamela's), the "cleanliness" of sex is threatened, and so, therefore, is business: "Our standard has been taste," Kessie says, "and of course there is the risk of legal action. We like to think of ourselves as trend setters, but here we have, for business and other reasons, to wait for society to know its own mind." So, despite the PR assurance that "It was Hefner's unorthodox belief (a belief he still holds today) that editing a magazine should be a personal matter, that the primary criteria for choosing content should be the editor's own taste and judgment rather than the preferences of a preconceived audience," there *is* in fact a preconceived audience—the young, university-educated man—and the taste of the *Playboy* editors has long since been determined by the sublime cultural marriage of commodity and morality. And *Playboy*, one of the massive offspring of that union, has as much as any other cultural product reaffirmed that its parents are indeed one flesh.

The effect of sentimentalizing materialism, i.e. of giving it the moral value of an ideal, is to transform the natural world into a pop art toy which exists for the Playboy's *well-earned* amusement. After all, he brings home the fatback. (Nor can we, in honesty, be condescending to the *Playboy* Image, for it metaphors all of us, the whole consumer culture on which our egos, economics, and politics depend.) Therefore, all things are seen in the context of *Playboy's* peculiar ethos of amusement. Women, particularly, are *objets d'art*, created for the Playboy fantasy by the photographer's air brush art and in the Image of *Playboy* by the sketch writer's Playmate-as-home-town-girl fictions. The mere idea of his Playmate menstruating, not to mention the disgusting *fact* of it, is enough to make the Playboy impotent. The Playmate is the Playboy's Beatrice. She does not function, she *is*. Like Shakespeare's Cleopatra, age cannot wither nor custom stale her infinite variety; like Keats' still unravished bride of quietness, she is forever warm and still to be enjoyed, forever panting and young, far above the stinking breath of human passion, and with *her* we avoid after-sex hangover, that "heart high-sorrowful and cloy'd/ burning forehead, and a parching tongue." The Playmate is not an object of sex. She is an object of art, low art to be sure, but art nonetheless. And who put her on that pedestal and on the mantlepiece of our den? Pamela, we smell a rat.

Playboy's pornography consists in its transformation of women—i.e. female human beings—into Playmates and Bunnies, i.e. into erotic art objects designed to titillate the sexual sense and then sublimate it into spending money (in the Playboy Clubs hopefully), or into fantasizing about spending money (in *Playboy* magazine). The greenback dollar, in the *Playboy* ethos (and the *Playboy* ethos is fundamentally the capitalistic ethos) is the sublimated analogue of sperm. Money and the making of it is the masculine symbol in this cultural climate. Spending it therefore is the masculine privilege. It is no accident that the verb *spend* is a common pornographic metaphor for male orgasm. And since, in a capitalistic democracy, money can buy everything, women are, as they have really always been, commodity; and all commodity is available to him who has the power to take it. Thus the power to buy becomes, in the capitalistic ethos, the sign of sexual power. So the world is sexualized, and sex is commercialized, and we have a pornographic image of the world—an idealized, socially lionized, metaphor of prostitution as a way of life. And that, traditionally, is what pornography is—the literature of and about whores and whoring.

But then this process is rather subtle, and one is seldom conscious of himself as the Playboy. Nor does one think of his woman as a whore. And so long as he has Playmates, Bunnies, and their analogues the movie sex stars (who of late have been knocking one another's knockers for the chance to be nude on *Playboy's* pages) he needn't think of her—if he thinks of her at all, his mind being filled with more enticing fantasies—as such, or as property. She may continue in her time-honored rhetorical role of the sometimes dull, sometimes bright but always slightly irrelevant companion. So it is a curiously lonely bed that Pamela after all has made and in which she must lie. But she is not through yet. Having established her ethos, she labors now to imprint her personality. She has before her, therefore, the task of creating a feminine pornography.

Feminine pornography requires a fantasy structure in which women are invited, as women, to be sexually excited. For the socially redemptive pornography we have been considering this means an alteration of the sex-profit nexus. Theoretically it needs a shift from money and expenditures as an exclusively masculine symbology. Imagistically it involves a transition from the *Playboy* cultural mode to that of the Career Girl. The basic model, still of course, is that of *Playboy*. The emphasis is merely reversed—from male cultural potency to female cultural potency. The woman's magazine most perspicacious in recognizing the *Playboy* mode and in exploiting it for its own audience and purposes is the new *Cosmopolitan*. *Cosmopolitan* has only recently tapped in to the pornographic tradition we have been considering. And coming from its own imperial stock, the Hearst syndicate, it is not a pornographic empire builder but is merely capitalizing on the female potential of the ethos *Playboy* has by this time stabilized. And though *Cosmopolitan* has its own cultural significance as a feminist pornographic voice, it isn't consequently as historically instructive or important as *Playboy*.

It emerged from the maze of what William Iverson, in a marvelously witty series of *Playboy* articles—"The Pious Pornographers" (1957 and 1964)—called "the bizarre bulletins on glands, guilt, grief, gynecology, and intercourse which are the peculiar specialty of some of America's most widely read sex books—the women's magazines." His general thesis is that women's magazines offer sentimentalized sexual voyeurism which takes the form of a "sick, sad sex approach to the problem of getting a [man to drop his pants] [or a woman to lift her skirts], so that a million odd women [can] get a few vicarious kicks from 'playing doctor.'" Here is part of what Iverson calls a "sampler" of prurient ladies' home preoccupations:

'That inverted nipple *seems better than it was*' the doctor told Evelyn Ayres after he had concluded his usual examination. 'Have you been pulling it out gently several times, morning and night, the way Mary Ann showed you?'

'Yes, Doctor . . .'

'I believe I told you that there is a difference of medical opinion as to the best method of toughening the nipples . . .'

'. . . Your uterus is small and firm. . . . Your breasts show no signs of pregnancy engorgement . . .'

. . . This was an atavistic dream of a man and a woman alone in a Garden of Eden, perfumed, flecked with butterflies. A red petal fell from the African tulip tree . . .

'Oh, Bill,' she whispered, half-choking. . . . Then he kissed her. Her lips were like orchids—crumpled, soft, cool, moist. They clung to his. Her arms were around his neck . . .

The range of frequency in intercourse for couples 25 to 35 is great. A few have intercourse as often as 20 to 30 times a month; others only twice a month. For the majority, the average is 2 or 3 times a week . . .

'If he has his way, it would be every night. It isn't that I'm a frigid wife, for I am not. Once a week (which is my preference) I respond readily . . .'

Q. *What about the forceful technique of making love? Do you think that women prefer it?*

A. *Sometimes. Many couples think that variation in sex simply means a different position. Variation can also mean a different psychological attitude. If a man surprises his wife, spontaneously, on a Sunday afternoon, or in a different room of the house, aggressively taking her, this type of approach can make their relationship enormously more erotic . . .*

'He said I was cold, and I said he was oversexed. Once he even wanted to make love at lunchtime!'

'Of course it's awfully hard not to. You both want to so much. Sure, Jim used to get fresh with me now and then, but I'd always handle it by saying 'Look at the television' or something. But once I thought Oh, why not? . . .'

'The hymen is a thin little membrane, Phyllis, stretched across the lower end of the vagina . . .'

'Am I afraid to use mine?' I said.

'No,' George said, 'like I say, you're naturally lascivious. You use your pelvis. . . .'

I did a little bump.

'But I wouldn't go too far,' George said. I could feel from his neck that he was beginning to color.

'Why do men want sex to be like a burlesque show? Why can't they realize that it is a solemn thing?'

'. . . And . . . well, one night I drank a can of beer in the car with him,

*and it happened again . . . I just couldn't help it. After all, girls want it
just as much as boys do, don't they?'*

The summing up, where Iverson recalls,

> the curious saga of Evelyn Ayres, troubled heroine of another stirring
> episode of 'Tell Me, Doctor,' the Ladies Home Journal's long-playing
> feature on clinical sex and gynecological horrors. Years of familiarity with
> its format of fear, disaster and medical salvation had led me to think of
> this everexpanding anthology of female malfunctions as a kind of crypto-
> prurient Memoirs of a Woman of Misery, in which Evelyn Ayres now starred
> as the anxiety-fraught Fanny Hill of Breast Feeding.

For Iverson's real complaint, *Playboy*'s complaint, is not that the
women's magazines are *pornographic* (he and *Playboy* know all about
that, although such language makes them nervous, being bad for business), it is that they are *obscene*. Nor is his objection to their piety (i.e.
sentimentality); he and *Playboy* know all about that too, as we have seen.
The problem is that these magazines undermine the Playmate image.
Think of the Playmate. Imagine her with inverted nipples! Or menstruating! Or, worst still, imagine her being sexually unsatisfied *after* a bout
with the prodigiously phallic Playboy! Smearing her neuroses, obstetrics
and gynecology all over the hard-earned sanctuary of his den. Not only
that, as if it weren't enough, they also undermine the *Playboy* image.
Iverson's citation of the following rebuke of vestigial "19th Century Puri-
tanism" is revealing in this regard:

> All shapes and varieties of marital anguish were laid squarely at the door of
> the clumsy husband. It was the man, the marriage manuals unanimously
> declared, who was responsible for success in sex, and equally responsible
> for its failure. For the enlightened readers of the manuals, making love
> became a kind of challenge . . .
> Frequently couples spent so much time worrying about whether their
> technique was right, whether their climaxes occurred simultaneously as the
> book said they should, whether the wife really had an orgasm, that they
> lost all the meaning of marital intercourse, not to mention the pleasure . . .
> 'Pleasure' was a word that the ladies' books had seldom mentioned in
> connection with sex, and T. F. James' reference to it came as a welcome
> surprise.

Iverson argues, though with more clever outrage than analytical energy,
for a "recognition of the need for greater sexual responsibility in women . . .
(to) reduce the impossible number of restrictions . . . imposed upon the
sexual deportment of the American male." The *Playboy* spokesman is

annoyed that women, too, want some fun but aren't getting it and are imposing their frustrations on his fantasies. Women, alas, want to *feel* something down there and, alack and alas, they want to feel it more often than men want to make them feel it. *Playboy* may or may not acknowledge the problem. That isn't clear either from Iverson's articles or from *Playboy* generally. What is clear, however, is that *if* there is a problem it is a problem for *women*, so *Playboy* lays it discreetly at their door and strides manfully off to a rendevous with mood music on the hi-fi and a quiet discussion of Picasso, Nietzsche, jazz, and (still undaunted) sex.

Perhaps *Cosmopolitan* got the message, for five months after Iverson's articles had been concluded it appointed Helen Gurley Brown (author of the best-selling *Sex and the Single Girl*) as its editor. *Time*, in March of 1965 (the same month Miss Brown was appointed *Cosmopolitan's* editor), noted the magazine's transition from a "rather bland" character into a female counterpart of *Playboy*. And in July of 1966 *Newsweek* observed that Helen Gurley Brown had sexed *Cosmopolitan* up, especially in terms of its advertising and the identification of its audience. So *Cosmopolitan's* press noted the terms of its new formula very quickly. *Cosmopolitan*, or more likely the Hearst hierarchy, had recognized how *Playboy* was making the world safe for pornography, and it very neatly cut itself in on the sex-profit nexus. It took women out of the home, away from children, housework and such like dowdiness, and put them into careers. It imagistically counterpointed the Playboy with the Cosmopolitan Girl. This advertisement copy defines her, accompanied by the usual photograph of a sleek and sexy career girl: "A girl can do almost anything she wants to, don't you agree. She can tan instead of burn, look sexy but also look like a lady, have a job that PAYS because she's smart and still stay fascinating to men. I've done all these things and thank goodness there's one magazine that seems to understand me—the girl who wants everything out of life. I guess you could say I'm that Cosmopolitan Girl." It also counterpointed its editorial image with that of *Playboy*. If Hugh Hefner, complete with smoking jacket, pipe, hi-fi mood music, girls, quiet conversation on, etc., is the *Playboy* incarnate, so is Helen Gurley Brown the complete woman and therefore the Cosmopolitan Girl's ideal tutor.

Cosmopolitan is not through with neurosis, obstetrics, and gynecology, but they are no longer occasions for morbidity. It fosters the fantasy that every woman can be taught what she doesn't know or be artificially augmented with what nature hasn't awarded her. A sampler of titles alone gives a fair idea of *Cosmopolitan's* vast pornographic curriculum: Why I Wear my False Eyelashes to Bed; How to Make Your Figure More Perfect; What Keeps Some Girls from Getting Married and What to Do About It; How to Turn a Man On; Spectacular Beauties Reveal Their Special Tricks; Get Him to Marry You with this Revolutionary New Method; How to Make $100,000 Before You're 35 (Without a Man), and so on into infinity. There is also of course a good deal of voyeuristic entertainment (and mayhap instruction) in such features as, The Men Surrounding Jacqueline Kennedy—and the One Who's Winning Her (they pick wrong); One Young Wife's Shocking Marriage, or When a Young, Pretty Girl Discovers She's Married a Homosexual (which subject, incidentally, *Playboy* won't touch); Jim Brown is Coming on *Strong* and *Big*, and with that pun twister, we may desist. *Time*, in February of 1968, accused *Cosmopolitan* of exploiting every sexual anxiety and every sexual fantasy of "the 18 to 34 year old single women who are not knock-outs, who are unsure of themselves, who are searching for a man." This is probably true, though there is no reason to put a lid on at the age of 34. Voyeurism is for all seasons, and sexes too, for that matter.

But, if one can provide instruction while celebrating commodity, as both *Playboy* and *Cosmopolitan* do, then one has not only an acceptable but even a socially redemptive license for pornographic fun. The trick, quite simply, is to make it slick. The Cosmopolitan Girl may not be so slick or affluent as the Playboy, but then she is fifteen or so years younger, and it really does seem difficult to sublimate gynecological messiness into profitable status than it does to do so with crudely simple phallic power. Bathispheres will never capture our imagination so well as space rockets, and the idea of a concave skyscraper with a miner's beam at its bottom just won't do. Nor is the Cosmopolitan Girl so intellectually pretentious as her Playboy friend. Miss Brown disclaims intellectual ambitions for her magazine. "We don't want very many cosmic pieces—about space, the war on poverty, civil rights, etc., but will leave those to more serious general magazines." But *Playboy* too made similar disclaimers at the beginning: "Affairs of state will be out of our province. We don't expect to solve any world problems or prove any great moral truths." So if the Cosmopolitan Girl has not yet devised let alone published a philosophy, she does at least read the poetry of Dorothy Parker, which the Playboy has never done. And the future lies, after all, securely ahead. Standing on the troubled shores of our land, looking neither too far out nor too deep in, haunch by hip these twin colossi, guarding the divine grace of capital, are beacons to the world that, with "taste" and a little Yankee ingenuity, all is safe for pornography.

Cosmopolitan and Playboy: Cupcake v. Sweet Tooth

Time

It seems only yesterday that Helen Gurley Brown told *Cosmopolitan* readers: "You've got to make yourself more cupcakeable all the time so that you're a better cupcake to be gobbled up." Meanwhile Hugh Hefner was giving *Playboy* readers lessons on how to lick off the frosting without actually paying for that cake. Like silent partners, Brown and Hefner— Miss Cupcake and Mr. Sweet Tooth—shared the profits of the sexual revolution* while remaining happily oblivious to the militant feminism that arrived in its wake.

What has happened to *Cosmopolitan* since Women Liberationists let Mrs. Brown know that a cupcake must learn to bite back? What has happened to *Playboy* since Gloria Steinem told Hefner, "A woman reading *Playboy* feels a little like a Jew reading a Nazi manual"?

LIB LIP SERVICE

Desperate if not deep signs of change are becoming visible. Now in its 19th year, *Playboy* is maintaining its posture of dauntless virility while try-ing to be less of a male chauvinist pig about it. Recently "The Playboy Adviser"—Hefner's answer to "Dear Abby"—piously rebuked a reader who asked if *Playboy* would help him persuade his wife to give up her career. "To deprive her of a chance to feel valuable to herself and society above and beyond the roles of wife and mother would be not only selfish but cruel," the "Adviser" preached in the gassy rhetoric once reserved ex-clusively for *Playboy* philosophy. At the same time, the "Adviser" managed to hint that a woman "engaged in work that is meaningful to her" might well become a more pleasing Bunny in bed.

"The Playboy Forum," the magazine's letters column, also does con-spicuous Lib lip service, especially on the issue of legalized abortion, though the guffaws of pregnancy jokes continue to echo from other pages. But other questions seem to trouble *Playboy* readers—and the editor who

Reprinted by permission from *Time*, The Weekly Newsmagazine; © 1972 Time, Inc.
* 1971 circulation. Cosmopolitan, 1,475,487; Playboy, 6,400,573.

selects which letters to print—far more. How much does one tip a black-jack dealer? What is malmsey wine? How does a fellow get—and get rid of—the crabs? Why do Japanese girls think American men smell bad? (Answer: carnivorous Americans eat ten times as much meat as Japanese and their odors prove it.)

A curious datedness hangs over *Playboy*. The props never change—the stereo wailing, the fake gun collection framed in place on the wall, the satin sheets on the bed. One poor swinger who failed to keep up with his status symbols had to have the editor explain to him why there are so few convertibles on the market. Girls are still called chicks, and the cartoons are often 1930s vintage—elderly lechers chasing gamboling nymphs around the old yacht. *Playboy* fiction often features the best names— Vladimir Nabokov, Graham Greene—though not too often their best work. *Playboy* interviews, alertly conducted with subjects worth talking to—Saul Alinsky, Charles Evers—are the magazine's quality product. But they seem to belong to another world: the real one. *Playboy*, alas, has become the voice of sexist Middle America, and Hefner its Archie Bunker. When *Playboy* ventures into the '70s, it is with tokenism—a modest amount of pubic hair on his Playmate and four-letter words in his prose.

BALLOON LESSON

For *Cosmopolitan* readers, "Oh, horseradish!" is about as far as strong language goes. And Mrs. Brown is just getting around to her own center-folds. Germaine (*The Female Eunuch*) Greer's estranged husband will be the first *Cosmo* boy in April's British edition. For the American edition, Burt Reynolds is the anticipated playmate.

The articles still bear those titles that sound like bad 19th century novels. Example: "How an Unpretty Girl Copes and Conquers." Cope and conquer as she might, the *Cosmo* girl is still treated like an idiot who can survive only if everything is spelled out for her and then *underlined*. If she is fat, she must scribble notes to herself: "I who wish to lose weight and am a self-confessed nibbler, do hereby promise to keep the above rules." Nothing is taken for granted. If her man is out of town, she is instructed to send him a balloon with "I love you" written on it—and *Cosmopolitan* explains just how: "Write when the balloon is inflated, mail *deflated*." Even if the reader is a mother and a divorcee, she must be reminded to *lock that bedroom door* lest her stray children wander in while she is funning with a gentleman caller. Unbelievably simple questions receive unbelievably simple answers. Question: "If a girl likes both men and women, what is she?" Answer: "Bisexual." Though the lesbian has thus been more or less identified, the nymphomaniac still gets circumlocuted as "a girl who's the opposite of frigid."

PURITAN STRUGGLES

"The One-Night Affair" is accepted, even defended, as nothing shameful. But the sophistication pours out in the melted-marshmallow style of Faith Baldwin: "You're lying face-to-face—two pairs of brown eyes, greeting. Hello. You both smile, remembering last night," etc., etc.

Despite all the contradictions of a formula in transition, there is evidence that *Cosmo* may be adapting more successfully than *Playboy*. The going *Cosmo* philosophy remains: "Every girl needs a supportive man." But the nuance is important: the new emphasis is on "supportive." "He loved me," an erstwhile cupcake goes on to complain, "but he didn't love me enough, or perhaps in the right way, to help me build the kind of life that I would find liberating."

Can *Playboy* guy liberate *Cosmo* gal or vice versa? Puritan swingers, struggling dutifully for their orgasms as if doing homework for a self-improvement course, they do seem a couple with much in common. But the *Zeitgeist* that has failed to move *Playboy* much is beginning to shake *Cosmopolitan*. Dangerous words like "self-expression" and "self-fulfillment" are starting to appear. The *Cosmo* girl is still drawing a straight chalk line down her full-length mirror to check her posture. But does she want her shoulders back for marching down the aisle or marching in a protest demonstration? The answer is no longer clear. And that's the way the new cupcake crumbles.

Ritual, Aesthetics, and TV

Richard Carpenter

Coupling aesthetics and television in a morganatic marriage with ritual as officiating priest may appear to be a mere attempt at sensationalism, designed only to catch the attention of jaded audiences at conferences. TV is apparently the very antithesis of aesthetic, a wasteland no less dreary than T. S. Eliot's, as a steady diet of a week or so of programs watched indiscriminately should prove to almost any aesthetician or literary critic. The same old fare shows up night after night: cowboys, detectives, spies,

From *Journal of Popular Culture* (Fall 1969), p. 251. By permission of *Journal of Popular Culture*.

and the husbands and wives (or their surrogates) of situation comedy appearing in fifty seven variations of the basic characters and plots, with never any real difference to disconcert the expectations of the experienced viewer. Each "new" season brings along only further variations, so that the cowboys show up in modern Africa and the detectives in wheelchairs, while the father becomes a bachelor surrogate, with the mother's place taken by a rotund and bearded butler. But there is, of course, nothing actually new, or even mildly surprising at all.

Yet it seems to me that I can more or less unsensationally sneak aesthetics in TV's back door for a surreptitious courtship, with the help of a comment from D. W. Prall and some observations from Marshall McLuhan. Prall once said we may think quite legitimately about those things that are aesthetically unsatisfactory in discussing what might be aesthetically satisfying, a remark I take to mean that the field of aesthetics includes the dull and dreary as well as the ugly and messy, which of course is often part of the aesthetic experience. Dull and dreary may simply be excesses of valuable aesthetic qualities, while the work that is characterized by them lacks other qualities necessary for a satisfying experience. The cliché-ridden TV show is, from this point of view, not so much an aesthetic nonentity as an aesthetic failure, and may be considered in that light. Of this we shall have more to say later.

That grand shaman of the media, Professor McLuhan, is helpful in his usual provocative though wrong-headed way by providing some concepts of broad applicability to the present scene. He tells us that we are living in a partly revitalized "tribal" culture and that our steadily shrinking world is reaching the status of a "global village," where we are as conscious of events on the other side of the world as the primitive is of events on the other side of the compound. Despite my feeling that this monolithic approach blurs over important distinctions and that there is an enormous difference between knowing in a tribal, holistic way that Grun Tu Molani has broken his spear and knowing that we have lost three F-111's over Hanoi, Professor McLuhan's insights may assist in understanding the place of TV, the most ubiquitous of the performing arts, in contemporary life.

TV, McLuhan says, is the primary means by which tribalization is taking place because it alters sense ratios from the exclusively visual orientation of the world of print to the richer auditory-tactile, visual world of the tube. While this is perhaps stretching things a bit, it does seem undeniable that TV has changed habits and given people different ways of perceiving. Constant exposure to the combined picture and sound of the TV screen cannot help but stimulate certain perceptual processes, as it may impoverish others.

In addition to altering sense ratios, TV has supplanted many ritual activities common to the American family until recently, from Monopoly to picnics, and may be in the process of supplanting more. Communal enterprises have not faded away completely under the baleful glare of the tube, but time once spent in performing a variety of more or less ritualized acts is now devoted to earnest watching of favorite programs. Now, no aspect of tribal life is more pervasive and important than its rituals. From making a pot to celebrating the rite of passage of the children into adulthood, from preparing for the hunt to inaugurating a new chief, the tribe functions by means of ritual, from the relatively simple to the extremely complex. Without ritual, tribal life could not exist; it seems fair to assume that if we are indeed returning to tribalization the primary instrument in that process should be heavily ritualized.

From this perspective TV's sameness is more understandable. A most important characteristic of any ritual is that it be performed always in exactly the same way: variation is contrary to the whole idea of controlling processes or participating in rites by observing systematic regularities. TV, of course, labors under the delusion that it is supposed to offer some originality along with the familiar formulas, so that it is less than efficacious as pure ritual. But it has discovered that too much originality loses audience, directly contrary to what might be expected if the primary appeal of the programs was to our delight in what is different. And as a consequence, writers, producers, and actors are properly wary of straying too far afield. Far-out programs appeal only to the small fringe of the intelligentsia, the minute proportion of the public who watch educational channels. Ritualized quiz shows, comedy hours, and the perennial encounter of the hero with the forces of evil are always "safer"—that is, they appeal more steadily to more people.

Specific rituals are not only to be conducted in the same way; rituals in general exemplify but few patterns. In an authentic tribal culture they celebrate such things as the journey from one state of being to another, the relationship of the living generations with the ancestors, the encounter with and overcoming of evil, the creation of the world, the return of fertility to the land. In any case they celebrate the values of the culture, and we might expect that TV would do the same thing in a neo-tribal world.

A look at any one week's offerings of programs indicates that this is so, although the values of contemporary culture are both more fragmented and more hidden than those of a primitive tribe. But the giveaway show, for example—which has occasioned so much speculation as to its appeal, since the viewers are not getting the riches—quite blatantly exemplifies the ideal of getting something for nothing, a basic value in an acquisitive society. (Without too much pummeling it can also be made to give up its archetypal pattern of the search for treasure, if one wants to look for such universal paradigms.) The giveaway shows are also as repetitious in their format, that is to say, they are as ritualistic, as any programs on the air. Although there are attempts to make the games have some variety, getting the dough is the thing, so that the celebration of materialism comes through loud and clear.

Most comedy shows are built around domestic situations and may be seen as ritualistically celebrating the values of family life, filled as it is with fundamental fidelity and good will despite the silliness of husbands and the strains that develop from conflicts with relatives, bosses, and rivals. The simple fact that family life in America does not fit this picture at all is simply more evidence that the programs are concerned with what the audience values than with what it actually has.

In terms of both number of shows and popularity, however, the cowboys, the detectives, the soldiers, and the spies—the heroes, in short—have the edge. And since they celebrate the conquest over evil within a highly ritualistic context, they are the most important indicators of the peculiar aesthetic function of TV in our culture. The pattern they exemplify, despite the different milieus in which it appears, is familiar enough to readers of Joseph Campbell and Lord Raglan, a truncated but nonetheless accurate duplication of the classic hero-tale. Whether he is a town marshall in Dodge City, a warden in command of a group of convicts released for commando duty, or a secret agent leading a trained crew of experts in an impossible mission, the hero is assigned his duty by higher authority, undertakes it skillfully though at great risk to himself and his followers, contends with the powers of evil in their most dynamic form, and by the end of the program has succeeded in overcoming them and restoring peace and harmony to the community, just as did Odysseus and Theseus before him.

Such a pattern, repeated night after night in dozens of versions all portraying the same basic theme, implies that the TV audience derives satisfaction from a ritual formalization of ingrained feelings that the evil in the world can be overcome by men working together under the guidance of a leader. The overwhelming complexities of individual and social problems are thus simplified and brought within a manageable compass. The actualities of war, crime, and social malaise, too baffling and disturbing to contemplate imaginatively, can be both grasped and solved vicariously through the nightly ritual of the TV hero. The tribal values—leadership with teamwork, courageous effort under stress, willingness to sacrifice for a higher good, and faith in a stable future once wickedness has been defeated (a form of eschatological optimism)—are affirmed nearly every time *Gunsmoke, Garrison's Guerillas, The Invaders, Mission Impossible, The Big Valley, Ironside,* or *Bonanza* appears in full living color in the darkened family room.

But I have perhaps lingered too long with ritual, who was merely to officiate at this dubious marriage of aesthetics and TV: it is high time we took a look at the bridegroom to see whether or not it can be estimated what his relations with his blowsy-looking spouse are and what they might be made to be. First, we probably should consider the aesthetic nature of rituals in general. In authentic tribal cultures, even simple rituals such as those that are part of building a hut or shaping a dugout canoe have a good deal of aesthetic quality: the activities are rhythmic, coordinated, graceful; they often partake of the qualities of the dance, are often accompanied by specific dances and nearly universally by music; the hut or canoe is richly decorated with designs and colors; the entire process has well-defined stages that give it a dramatic development leading to the climax of the celebration that completes the task.

More solemn and significant rituals, especially those concerned with the periodic rites of the community—planting, puberty ceremonies, funerals—have the same qualities of the simple rituals but are more formalized, aesthetically richer, more detached from practicality. Oriented around the fundamental values of the society, they are complex symbolic means of giving form to the communal imagination, the most complete and exact manifestation of the total tribal spirit. In the words of Susanne Langer: "A rite regularly performed is the constant reiteration of sentiments toward 'first and last things'; it is not a free expression of emotions, but a disciplined rehearsal of 'right attitudes.' " Although they are much *more* than aesthetic they are certainly that also since they body forth in gesture, song, dance, and design the inner world of the community.

Despite this rich texture, however, tribal rituals are strictly limited in their aesthetic appeal. They are, of course, completely repetitive: once you have seen a puberty rite for a particular tribe you have seen them all, for innovation creeps in only by accident and over long periods of time. Tribal rituals are usually undertaken in dead seriousness; although some involving clowning and a good deal of fun, as a rule they are too important to be taken lightly. And this in turn means that they necessarily lack urbanity, irony, lightness. A ritual seen from the inside is life and truth conducted according to certain patterns laid down by superior powers; it is only from the view of an outside spectator that it becomes primarily aesthetic. The aesthetic quality probably comes from the nearly universal tendency to make valued objects and acts as attractive as possible; it is an accompaniment, an efflorescence of the aesthetic spirit, rather than a prime motive in ritual. There is little or no room for individual improvisation or improvement; originality is not tolerated, much less encouraged. The participant in a tribal ritual who would add his own little variation is there, of course, but only because that is the way performers are, not because it is the thing to do. And finally, there is the accompanying aesthetic limitation of only a few generalized patterns into which all the other aspects must fit; rituals are occupied with this, that, or the other facet of communal interest, not with as wide a variety as the human imagination can invent.

Oddly enough (perhaps because I planned it that way, but I hope not), these limitations are very much those of TV: repetitiveness, lack of invention, lack of irony, lack of individuality and originality, a few generalized patterns that squeeze nearly all others out. For instance, *Mission Impossi-*

ble, one of the more successful spy programs, differs only in one detail from all the others—its team that accomplishes the impossible tasks is composed of technical specialists rather than simply two or three adepts with fists and guns, and its plans are made to utilize the skills of these specialists. Once this has been settled, the rest follows automatically: the leader gets the assignment; he briefs his team; they appear on the scene where they are to operate; they function like a well-lubricated computer; despite implications that something will go amiss they brilliantly succeed and save the kidnapped statesman, the treasure, or eliminate the villain, usually by a kind of hoisting with his own petard. Program after program follows this format, with the ingenuity confined to details, where it can be ingenious indeed but only to the viewer whose sophistication reaches to that rather low level.

Mission Impossible, like most TV hero rituals, is uniformly deadpan. No matter how farfetched the situation, it is approached with the solemnity of a sacred ritual even to the point of an utter lack of demonstrable personal emotion on the part of the team members. Its aesthetic quality is thus very low, but what there is comes from that same solemnity, the feeling that the confrontation with evil is a serious business. Interestingly enough, audiences seem to participate strongly in this feeling, for *Mission Impossible* fans are extremely loyal, even slightly obsessed. Only an emergency will cause them to miss their ritualistic encounter with, and triumph over, wickedness on Sunday night.

The popular program that followed *Mission Impossible* on Mondays—*I Spy*—is instructively more aesthetic, because its ritual nature, while still evident, is enlivened with a good deal of variety, in setting, situation, and character. The two heroes have weaknesses, and find themselves often in situations where ethical decisions must be made between their duty and their human desires. The confrontation with evil is sometimes ambiguous, and their approach to it filled with irony. In addition they are themselves ironists, whose humor comes to the fore under dangerous conditions. One would not want to go so far as to claim that there is a very high quality of aesthetic experience in this program, but the rumor that it has lost audience appeal and will soon go off the air indicates that it has gained originality and variety at the expense of ritual, so that audiences who find their greatest pleasure in TV tribalization are turning to purer forms where repetition, rhythm, recognizable and clearcut exponents of good and evil, and equally clearcut dramatic success at the end of the ritual are not confused for them by ambiguity and irony.

Quite probably they are turning to one of the many Westerns that limpidly demonstrate the more elemental celebration of our values. The Western is, of course, the principal American myth, with the cowboy truly our hero with a thousand faces. Myth, in turn, is the enactment of ritual, the dramatic form that ritual takes. It is not surprising, then, that the

Western finds it most profitable to stick with the traditional patterns and avoid too substantive deviations from them. Cowboys who ride in trucks instead of on horses, or cowboys who are soldiers, or cowboys transported from their native territory into Africa are quite conceivable, but cowardly or sophisticated cowboys are much harder to swallow. They may work in teams or as members of a family, with a patriarch or matriarch at the head, but they become professional gunslingers or wealthy entrepreneurs only rarely and on special occasions, not as part of the pattern. In order to preserve the essential outlines of the myth the hero must be basically honest, brave, devoted, and successful as a hero, even if not in material terms; and the opposition must be basically dishonest, scheming, sadistic if not cowardly, easily tempted, and losers. Although fiction could easily encompass a cowboy hero who ironically happened to be brave when he intended to be cowardly—like Henry Fleming—and a villain who had some excellent qualities, the TV Western eschews such complications except on rare occasions.

The Western does, however, have one significant aesthetic quality that may be part of its appeal: distance. Unlike most other types of popular programs it takes place in a formalized setting of the past, in a region that is nearly as much a product of the imagination as Tolkien's Middle Earth. No real cowboys ever dressed or talked like those on the living-room screen, nor did they spend the greater part of their time in homespun conversation with wise old medicine men or prospectors or in friendly, platonic chitchat with virtuous blonde fancy-house madams. The entire ambience is a fantasy, but one that memorializes attitudes that hordes of Americans must find perennially satisfying, more so than those of the other types of rituals on the air, for the Western is the most durable and popular of programs. At this writing there were fourteen regular shows, not to mention the old movies with John Wayne or Ronald Reagan heading them off at the pass. Other types of programs struggle valiantly for something different to say, while *Bonanza, The Big Valley, High Chaparral, Gunsmoke*, and *The Guns of Will Sonnett* go on forever.

The dreary sameness of the Western, like that of the spy program, the domestic comedy or problem show, the quiz, the variety, the detective program is, as Prall helped us to note before, not an utter absence of the aesthetic but rather the result of two complementary errors in using potentially satisfying aesthetic material. The first of these is the inability to see most TV shows as inescapably affording the satisfactions of ritual to the audience and the concomitant inability to use the kind of aesthetic enrichment appropriate to ritual. And the second is the attempt to graft on to an essentially ritualistic medium the aesthetic values, even at the most primitive level, of variety, tension, surprise, complexity, ambiguity, and so on, values more appropriate to individualistic than to communal art forms. If the Western, for example, could face up to the fact that it is as ritualistic as the classical ballet, it could provide some of the satisfactions of the ballet. It is not too hard to think of Marcel Marceau or Charlie Chaplin giving us a totally satisfying ritualized Western, as ridiculous as this might seem on the surface. Undoubtedly such a departure would lose the greater part of the audience, but it would indicate a logical direction in which the TV program could develop aesthetically.

The problem here is somewhat the same problem as that which comes from trying to individuate the medium: it is too frequent, too ubiquitous. One ballet western a week might be conceivable, but fourteen is completely beyond credibility. At the same time, no performing art can hope to be directed toward the values of very large masses of people and be highly original and innovative in any real sense. The appeal to communal values, to tribal sensibility, means large simple, general patterns with only superficial engraftment of innovations, in surface not in substance.

From this perspective the fault with TV as a performing art lies not in the stifling influence of commercialism so much as in the very nature of the medium itself. Primarily tribal and ritualistic, it cannot hope to satisfy the demand for originality and variety that is so valued an aspect of modern art forms; suffering from the effects of over-exposure it cannot achieve the aesthetic richness, as limited as that is, of authentic tribal rituals. The only ways in which it escapes these limitations are through an occasional "special," which usually, however, breaks completely with the characteristic tendencies of the medium; and in the great communal rituals such as the funeral of President Kennedy, which are aesthetic *a fortiori* and cannot really be compared with the function of TV as a performing art. TV, in short, cannot be rehabilitated as a mass medium by eliminating commercial influences; it has aesthetic quality but at the necessarily low level of tension that accompanies the attenuation of its force.

Although the prospect is hardly encouraging, realism rather than despair is called for. To heighten the aesthetic quality of TV as a whole is impossible, but certain improvements are quite feasible. Against the background of mass production the networks could if they wished present occasional programs, more frequent than the present "specials," of ritual material enriched in various ways—by music, dance, varied patterns, visual effects, irony, and humor. The possibilities are limitless; the models for this kind of enrichment are to be found in innumerable tribal rituals. Or on the other hand, it would be possible to have special performances calling on the talents of individual artists in the dance, the plastic arts, music, the cinema, literature where true innovation and originality would be the center of interest rather than ritual values. A program, not *on* Picasso, but *by* Picasso, not *on* John Cage, but *by* John Cage could do very much for TV as an aesthetic medium. Admittedly, commercialism rears its ugly head in this connection, but if Xerox or American Can wants to water the television wasteland, here is a good opportunity for them to do so. If they do not so choose, all the rest of us can do is observe the drab married life of aesthetics and TV, while whispering to each other "If only they would listen to us."

Flip Wilson,
The Mod Squad,
Mission Impossible:
Is This What It's
Really Like to Be Black?
by Jean Carey Bond

For most of us, legends of the American way of life have been an early part of our development. Our schools and parents taught us that America was democratic, law-abiding, just, a champion of the rights of the oppressed and a "melting pot"—a harmonious blend of many ethnic and religious elements. Today, however, the melting-pot concept is regarded with some suspicion by almost everyone.

The civil rights movement of the '60s showed many of us that the melting-pot theory merely camouflaged an insidious reality—that the United States views itself as a *white* country.

Evidence of the nation's failure to deal with the needs of its nonwhite citizens is all about us: in the unpaved streets of East St. Louis; in the eyes of Puerto Rican children whose special educational needs go untended; in death-haunted pueblos; in the empty pockets of migrant farm workers and of Cesar Chavez's battle-scarred laborers.

I think the proof is everywhere but is most damning in the communications industry.

How do members of America's largest minority feel about the way they are portrayed by television, radio, newspapers and magazines? *Redbook* asked 13 Black women to discuss this and related questions at a symposium. The symposium members and other women I later interviewed included teachers, students, welfare recipients, a writer, an editor, working mothers and mothers who do not hold outside jobs.

Symposium panelists quickly established the theme that was to dominate our discussion—that the character, culture and tastes of Afro-Americans

Reprinted courtesy *Redbook* Magazine, copyright © 1972 The McCall Publishing Company.

were either systematically ignored or tampered with by the media. And television, because it is the most influential and aggressive medium, was judged to be the major culprit.

The attitudes of the symposium participants toward television were marked by neither acceptance nor resignation. Both they and the women who were interviewed turned out to be highly selective in their own viewing habits; even when they are eager to be entertained, their antennae are out to pick up the offensive reference, the "jive" concept, the preposterous situation. Their remarks clearly indicated that despite the industry's recent gestures toward portraying the Black experience, the gap between what is true about Blacks and what television broadcasts about Blacks has not narrowed.

On the whole, the women agreed, television's Blacks either are depicted as eagerly seeking the good white life or are integrated into shows in token fashion as rather distinctive pieces of scenery. They felt that both representations discredited their own ethnic individuality.

Many women pointed out that the Black TV presence is constantly being neutralized by the ridiculous contexts in which it is placed. Essentially we are asked to disregard Greg Morris' racial identity on *Mission Impossible* and encouraged to view him as simply another pretty face among the superefficient, CIA-type *Mission* agents. The token Black member of the cast of *Land of the Giants* was considered equally ludicrous.

Clarence Darrow Williams III, who plays the Black member of *Mod Squad*, a pseudo-hippie trio operating as an undercover police unit, is generally regarded as projecting a negative Black image. (As one student remarked, "Does God love a police informant?") Similarly Don Mitchell, of *Ironsides*, is considered something of a fink, overdisdainful of his checkered ghetto past. And Diahann Carroll's highly touted but now defunct network show *Julia*, a comedy-drama about the widowed mother of a small boy, was roundly condemned as an insultingly unreal slice of Black life.

One counselor in a self-help program put it this way: "Julia is no different from the characters in the Black films Hollywood made for segregated movie houses during the 1930s and '40s. In both, acting and situations are caricatures of the middle-class, upward-mobile, white world. Producers and writers haven't changed. They're still contriving a picture of Black life based on white manners, values and experiences." A Vassar student agreed. "Julia," she said, "is the Metrecal Aunt Jemima—released from the pancake box and transferred to the video box, live and in color."

Panel members felt that *Julia* illustrates the fact that the entertainment industry has traded extremes. They have gone from presenting the old, minstrel-like stereotype to cosmetizing or "whitening" the Black personality and life-style in order to make them palatable to the only audience whose taste dictates programing policy—the white audience. It is assumed that non-Black audiences would find a realistically drawn Black character distasteful—that a "Julia" who wore an Afro, whose activities were set among the life and people of a typical Black community, who had a *living*, strong Black husband or boy friend, would alienate white audiences.

But Blacks are not fooled or appeased by the new stereotypes. We know, as the poet and political activist Imamu Amiri Baraka (Leroi Jones) has said, "We are not imitation Mozarts—we are original James Browns." Brown's innovative and distinctive rhythm-and-blues stylings as a singer-composer illustrate for many Blacks a creativity that arises solely from the Black experience.

Another student on the panel observed that white television writers could not be expected to rise above these offenses "because for them, Blacks are an unknown community."

Yet as many panelists noted, Black writers who could show the Black community with true perception are largely excluded from the creative (as well as the technical) sector of television.

Symposium members singled out two programs as exceptions to the general TV rule. *Room 222*, in contrast to the plastic Julia and the cardboard Blacks of the adventure programs, won general approval as a comparatively realistic portrayal of Black students and teachers in an urban, integrated high school. The magazine editor among our panelists found the show "refreshing."

"I think the Black life-style is shown in the way the kids act—particularly 'Jason,' a student whose moods are measured by his eyes, his hands, his smile—most of all, his walk," she said. "If you're Black and you went to a public high school, you know what Jason is all about." Other women described the series as "intelligent," "thought-provoking" and " a pleasant change from the usual television bag of fake people and situations."

Sesame Street, the award-winning program for preschoolers produced by the Children's Television Workshop, received high praise too. One college counselor, expecting her first child, candidly acknowledged her membership in the *Sesame Street* audience. "There are so few quality shows on TV," she said, "that I catch as catch can." The program's successful fusing of Black patterns of speech, family life, food preferences and history into its format was attributed by panel members to the presence on the *Sesame Street* production staff of Blacks in creative and management positions.

Other children's programs, such as the Saturday-morning cartoon blitz, met with little approval. Some panelists said they did not permit their children to watch the war cartoons and the more obnoxious of the Saturday shows—including the Our Gang comedies, in which a Black child is cast in a classically stereotyped role. But many parents have chosen not to censor or restrict their children's viewing, and several mothers admitted they used television as an aid to baby sitting.

One stenographer said with some annoyance that her four-year-old seemed more affected by the child-oriented commercials than anything else. Another mother volunteered her counterstrategy: "There's a rule in our house. We don't buy toys that are advertised on TV." She explains to her children that TV toys often are poorly made and fall apart soon after they are purchased. This strategy seems to reflect a tendency of mothers not to ban television completely, but instead to emphasize values within the home that will counterbalance possible negative influences.

Symposium members expressed mixed feelings when they considered Black comedian Flip Wilson, who, according to television critic John Leonard, writing in *Life* Magazine, "has taken the threat out of Blackness." A high-school teacher agreed. She described his antics and humor as a "safe" ethnic phenomenon, "hence his popularity with whites." She added: "Sometimes I'm uncomfortable with his over-all image, but almost everything he does I find irresistibly funny."

Flip's detractors have answered this familiar claim by remarking, "Sure, the man is funny. But Amos and Andy were funny." "Geraldine," the female creation Flip made famous, has been the object of especially heated discussion. Many find his impersonation derogatory to Black women. They interpret his transvestite image as a dramatization of the Black woman stereotype—domineering, castrating, a male in female clothing. Ironically, according to the actor himself this is the very thing he was trying to avoid. In *Ebony* Magazine, Wilson said, "I wanted to relate to women, but I didn't want to knock them. I wanted to make my character the heroine of the story."

One mother, while generally agreeing that many television characterizations were objectionable, insisted on the importance of Black images on the home screen in whatever capacity. "Remember," she said, "a generation ago Black kids didn't see anything that looked like them on the box." A 26-year-old artist conceded this point but warned nevertheless: "These shows aren't harmless. They're sugar-coated stink bombs."

The symposium members were unanimous in feeling that television propagandizes everyone, Black and non-Black, serving as a kind of Voice of Madison Avenue America—programing all of us for whiter washes, larger homes, antiseptic and odorless bodies and acquisitive natures meant for the consumption of products. And, one panelist pointed out, white people in the adventure series and situation comedies are unrealistically shown too.

"It's true whites don't treat themselves much better than they treat us— but anyway we must demand a change," said one college instructor. "After all, we have more to lose than whites. For Black children to accept and emulate television's Black undercover agents, spies and female impersonators at this stage of our development is self-hating and defeatist. I think we should be demanding something relevant—something that speaks to Black people and doesn't just perpetuate a white value system. Black writers, writing out of the many levels of the Black experience, should take part in program production."

Turning their attention to the more information-oriented programs, panel members enthusiastically endorsed *Black Journal*, the Public Broadcasting Service's weekly program, and *Like It Is*, a local New York City show geared to the Black and Puerto Rican communities. "*Black Journal*," said one secretary, "is seeking not simply to entertain but to inform and educate. Program content is largely in the hands of Blacks."

Panelists felt that white control is responsible for the "low educational value" of much of Black-oriented programing and thought that this criticism was particularly true of radio. One woman's angry reaction to radio's programing was heartily endorsed by other panel members. "Black and Spanish-speaking radio stations as a rule are exploitative," she said. "They're guilty of the too-frequent and too-fast commercial sell, the constant bombardment of music, the unceasing jive patter—in short, the utter lack of substance. These stations must be made accountable to the needs of their listeners."

A free-lance writer cited an article in 1970 by Fred Ferreti in the *Columbia Journalism Review*. "Of some 310 stations that program for Blacks, all but 16 are white-owned," Ferreti wrote. "Most are 'soul radio' stations devoid of news and public affairs." As an indication of what is missing from Black-oriented programing in both radio and television, he quoted William Wright, a community organizer, who challenged the licensing of a TV station in Washington, D.C.:

"Do we need *24 hours* of James Brown? No, we don't. If we're going to talk about freedom and self-determination, we need to hear our Black heroes performing in other art forms. We need to talk about drug addiction, about slum landlords, about jobs, about education. But the white man gives us 24 hours of 'soul' because it pads his already stuffed pockets and keeps Black people ignorant."

Radio and television broadcasting requires not only capital but also licenses from the Federal Communications Commission—a lily-white agency (and all efforts to have Blacks appointed to the commission have failed so far) that until recently did not even question the transfer or renewal of licenses.

When asked in a separate interview what kinds of programs she would wish to see if a Black-owned television channel existed in the New York area, a medical secretary rattled off a string of program ideas that included shows for the elderly and political-discussion hours for housewives. For children she suggested shows that focused on African history ("to strengthen our kids' sense of identity").

In another interview a welfare mother emphasized the need for a Black-owned TV network that would devote its schedules almost exclusively to education. "Ignorant people are like open sores," she said. "They just fester and get worse." She stressed the importance of adult-education programs broadcast in some of the "prime-time" slots. Such programing would constitute a radical change for commercial television.

Charles Hobson, producer of the award-winning, Black-oriented television show *Like It Is*, thinks cable television offers the best opportunity for Blacks to penetrate the communications industry. Interestingly enough, the first full-time independent cable-cast channel in the United States, San Diego Cable Television (SDC), is owned by a Black man, Chuck Johnson, who started it in 1970. Johnson also is general manager of XEBG, a Black-oriented radio station in San Diego, as well as founder of the Black Video Syndication Network, which provides taped programs for television stations.

Although his early efforts to keep his cable TV channel afloat met with operating difficulties, today SDC is so successful that Johnson plans to open four new cable stations in July in the San Diego area, gearing programs to the Black and Chicano neighborhoods as well as to the center-city community at large. Johnson's enterprise has enabled him to hire large numbers of Blacks in television's technical sector. Such jobs have been largely unavailable to Blacks because of discriminatory union practices.

Panelists observed that wider Black ownership of broadcast facilities would help release Black actors and actresses from the many compromising roles now offered them, roles that for economic reasons they can't always reject. At the same time, the development of Black writing and other talents might be stimulated.

Similarly, Black control would provide domestic exposure for Black jazz artists whose cultural contributions are recognized and acclaimed in every country but the United States. Many receive little or no play on "white-oriented" radio stations or on those Black stations run by whites. Because radio exposure dictates record sales and domestic recognition, the industry keeps many a Black musical giant in an economic bind.

The dissatisfaction expressed by the women regarding television and radio was less acute when they discussed the "print" media. Black publications are havens for Black points of view. Ferreti said in his article in the *Columbia Journalism Review:* ". . . the Black press, for all its problems, always has been owned largely by Blacks. Because its main commodity is news and features, it has to provide at least minimal reporting and comment on community concerns; develop Black management talent; and not only respond somewhat to the Black community but at times provide critical leadership."

Our panelists and the women I interviewed reported that they read white newspapers and magazines as well as a number of Black publications regularly, including the national magazines *Jet* and *Ebony*. They look to these publications for a kind of "spiritual sustenance," as one panelist said, and they depend on them for information about events in the Black community.

Muhammed Speaks, the nationally circulated newspaper of the Nation of Islam, was praised by several panelists as an invaluable source of Pan-African news and general news analysis—coverage that runs counter to the social and political orientation of the white press. Said one mother: *"Muhammed Speaks* tells it like it really is. And for the most part, the quality of the writing is first-rate. The paper exposes facts that the white press suppresses and helps you to find out and understand what's *really* going on."

What can be done about changing the way television and radio present Blacks? One effective approach is to let people who broadcast and sponsor television and radio shows know how you feel and what you would like to see. Whether you are white or Black, there is much to gain by seeing that the Black point of view, Black life, becomes a regular part of everyone's life. Mutual acceptance of each other will do us more good than anyone's melting into someone else's pot.

Big, Bigger, Bigot
Leonard Gross

Under normal circumstances, the chances are one in four that you watched television make history last night. It happened—or should have happened—on *All in the Family. Fade in:* Mike and Gloria are alone in Archie Bunker's living room. Mike, studying for exams, is distressed. Gloria is bewildered. Her efforts to soothe him only anger him more. Despairing, she retreats to the kitchen, where she confesses to her mother, Edith, that in recent weeks Mike has been unable to perform in bed.

With Edith's approval ("It's probably something that's going around"), Gloria calls the family doctor. He assures her that impotence is often caused by anxiety, and that it disappears as soon as the cause of the anxiety—in this case, Mike's exams—disappears.

A week later, Mike passes his last exam. Gloria persuades her parents to disappear for the evening. Edith prepares to visit a sick friend, Archie,

From the *Los Angeles Times,* November 21, 1971. Copyright © 1971 by Leonard Gross. Reprinted by permission of The Sterling Lord Agency, Inc.

grumbling, goes off to Kelsey's saloon—where, to his father-in-law's chagrin, Mike appears with a new anxiety: now that his excuse is gone, what if he *still* can't perform?

Enter Henry Jefferson, Archie's black neighbor. Archie solicits advice. "I got this friend of mine who's run into some, what you call, connubile difficulties," Archie explains. "Now, Jefferson, it's a well known fact that youse people . . . when it comes to members of the opposite sex there . . . you're champeens." Archie wonders if it's something in their soul food. After being coaxed by Archie ("We're neighbors and practically friends, ain't we?") Jefferson reveals the secret of black sexual prowess: "Hog jowls." But beware of side effects, he warns. "You start in with them jowls, you might develop a sudden craving to shine shoes."

It remains for Gloria to employ a simpler home remedy. Alone with Mike, she massages his neck to ease his tension. One look, one kiss, and Michael is cured. *Fade out.*

As this article is written, the only certainty about the November 20th episode of *All in the Family* is that 35 million Americans—roughly one-fourth the television audience—would watch it. The thought of a prime-time, half-hour comedy whose plot pivots on a fit of the sexual poops was too much for the program practices division of CBS. Its chief, William Tankersley, had ruled that the show could not be aired, and the creator-producer of the series, Norman Lear, had stated, "It will be on or I will be gone."

However the dispute was resolved—and if you watched the show, you'll know by now—its outcome is likely to affect not only a property rich to both network and producers, but what you will and won't see on television for years to come.

"*All in the Family* has bent our heads," says Alan Wagner, CBS vice-president for program development. "There are things we're doing now that we never did before."

In less than a year, a series that began life hidden between two Tuesday night movies has vaulted into the number one slot at CBS and earned a reputation as the most controversial show on television. Its central character, a lower-middle class, white Protestant bigot, is so closely monitored that even his choice of derogations has provoked a national debate.

Archie is more than a characterization; he is a social weapon. For better or worse, *All in the Family* stands today as television's first comic morality play. As such, it offers one pip of a signal that we have moved to ground never before occupied in terms of how we think and feel about ourselves. That is some big load for a situation comedy, so let's take it from the top.

Lear is a wiry man with a long history of pugnacity and a fighter's appreciation for daring. Both qualities figured prominently in the birth of the show, which required four years, three pilots and two networks to mature. It was not until the night before the show was to appear that Lear could telephone his wife Frances and say, with assurance, "We're on."

The trouble then, as now, was with the program practices division of CBS, which had demanded a number of deletions in the first script. Lear refused to make them.

"We held, on the theory that we had to get all wet," he recalls. "If we could get all wet together, and we didn't drown, they could trust me. If I gave in, they'd be after me every week. My point would not have been proved, and I could expect further requests for deletions in following weeks." With satisfaction, he adds: "America did the rest."

What America did was validate Lear's prediction that the show would either be off the air in a few weeks, or be a smash. By the end of its first season, *All in the Family* was first in the Nielsen ratings, and there it was again when the current season began.

What made Archie Bunker America's favorite bigot?

"The show works, above and beyond everything else, because it's funny," one veteran of the business suggests. "It's the funniest show on television."

One reason for that is Lear's audacious decision to create a character for television out of authentic cloth. A second reason is the show's snap-finger timing, for which credit goes to director John Rich. Reason three is a superior cast, led by Carroll O'Connor.

"Carroll is like God," says Sally Struthers, who plays Archie's daughter, Gloria. "He gives Archie that first breath of life." Says Rich: "You couldn't write it the way he does it. You start to improve the scene and out comes gold."

One of the earliest episodes in the series concerned Archie's attempt to prosecute a dubious accident damage claim. To represent him, he decides on a firm of Jewish attorneys in the conviction that Jews are "shrewder." But because Archie lives in a non-Jewish neighborhood, the firm sends him the house Gentile. Archie's frustration burst from O'Connor during rehearsal with this spontaneous line: "You go back where you came from and send me a Jew!"

During rehearsals for the play about Mike's impotence, O'Connor, groping for a delicate explanation to Archie's neighbor, Jefferson, blurted, "He's stuck in neutral, you know what I mean?"

The deeper reason why Archie has become such a favorite is a good bit more solemn and complex. It involves what O'Connor calls the laughter of recognition. If Archie makes us laugh, he also does what any character must do who aspires to be significant. He tells us about ourselves. *All in the Family* employs farce and satire to achieve the same result. Listen to O'Connor:

"I've given Archie a New York characterization, but people like Archie live all over the country. They are the bulk, I think, of the white American Protestant, lower middle class. They are conservative, perhaps without understanding quite why they are. Many of them have what I call 'the fine people rationale'—that is, they feel the fine people are conservative and therefore conservatism is the cause to follow. It puts them closer to the top, they feel. And since success is part of our national religion, that's the heaven we aspire to on earth.

"Some bias goes with any viewpoint," O'Connor continues. "The liberals are biased, Communists are biased and the conservatives are biased, too. You're biased in favor of what you want. If you're influenced too strongly by that success dream—which is really the culmination of material security and all that goes with it—then you become angry at things that seem to get in the way.

"Archie feels that he is preyed upon. He thinks that the black people are victimizing him, and the poor people are victimizing him. He thinks that a welfare society gnaws away at his vitals.

"And then, of course, he has this almost inborn racism. He learned it at his mother's knee. He learned that the white race is superior to the other races, and that belief was reinforced by other things he was told all through the process of his maturation.

"I'd encountered Archie Bunker over and over again, through life. He was the milkman," says O'Connor, "the man who came to fix the drains on the house, to do gardening; he delivered the cleaning; he was the conductor on the trolley car. He was a man who always had plenty of advice to give kids a man who would always say, 'Stick around. Maybe you'll learn something.'

"The American dream and the American reality combined to make Archie. The American dream gave him his horizon—an unattainable horizon, as far as he's concerned—and it gave him the reality, a restricted life."

Somewhere in the memory of every Jewish boy sits an apocryphal grandmother who darns quietly while her children argue and finally, meekly, interjects a single question that is thunderous with clarity: "Is it good for the Jews?"

The question is pertinent here. Is Archie Bunker good for the Jews *and* the blacks *and* the ethnic groups his bigotry maligns? Is he, in sum, good for America?

Many Americans think not. The most notable critic thus far is Laura Z. Hobson, the author of *Gentleman's Agreement*, a watershed novel-turned-movie of 24 years ago about anti-Semitism. In a long *New York Times* article several weeks ago, she charged that *All in the Family* had sabotaged the battle for tolerance by creating a "lovable bigot."

Archie, she said, does not evince enough bigotry. He uses words that shock but don't offend: for example, "Hebe" and "spade." Your true bigot, she argued, says "kike" and "nigger." "How about showing the real thing for awhile, before accepting any more praise for honest shows and honest laughter?" Mrs. Hobson taunted.

Mrs. Hobson's argument may have been overpopulated with straw men, but she raised a respectable point. Should children, in particular, be taught that "they're not wanted in certain neighborhoods, that there's something that makes people laugh at them and look down on them and call them names? To teach children that it's quite all right to go around saying spade and Hebe and coon and spic—for, of course, kids always imitate what they see on TV—seems to me pretty cruel."

Certainly, a bigoted viewer might take a measure of comfort from the show. When Archie asks whether there aren't any laws for hard-working white Anglo-Saxons, he is articulating a sentiment shared by many Americans. It is precisely because he's authentic that he creates attention; to be authentic, he must incorporate contradictions—one being that, bigot though he is, he is nonetheless enjoyable.

"How do you manage to make a bigot lovable?" a young lady in the audience asked *All in the Family*'s producer, Lear, before a screening a few months ago.

"Why do *you* think he's lovable?" Lear inquired.

"Because he reminds me of my father," the young lady replied.

There are reasons why he does. Archie is modeled in part on Lear's own father, whose neck veins used to swell when he would command his wife to "stifle," who called his son a "meathead, dead from the neck up." But Archie is by now a combination of other fathers Lear has encountered.

Over the months, the characterization has been enriched by contributions from the members of the company, especially the senior members. "Carroll and Norman and I have a great advantage because we remember," says Jean Stapleton, the deftly vaporous Edith of the series. "My parents laugh and laugh at Archie," says one cast member. "Five minutes later they're saying the same thing, but they don't get the connection."

"Archie's not a monster," says O'Connor. "With all his racism, he'd never burn a cross on anybody's lawn." If Archie were an all-out villain, he wouldn't be believable—which means he wouldn't be laughed at, which means he wouldn't be watched.

"Archie has his good points," says Rob Reiner, who plays Mike. "He's just ignorant, that's all." And that really is the point the critics seem to have missed.

Archie *always* loses. "Mike is always the one who is making sense," Lear wrote in his rebuttal to Mrs. Hobson. "Archie, at best, will work out some kind of convoluted logic to make a point. But it's always foolish. Totally foolish."

In one episode, Archie explains to his family how Jews will change their last names, but retain their first names as a kind of code by which they recognize one another. *"Morris* Smith," he offers. *"Sol* Nelson. *Izzy* Watson."

"Abe Lincoln," Mike replies caustically.

The audience laughs at Archie—and then roars when wife Edith remarks, "I didn't know Lincoln was Jewish."

"In every stand Archie takes, we try to show him as wrong," Reiner says. "He's always lousing himself up at the end." That point could hardly be lost, even on children. As for bigots, director John Rich declares: "If the wrong people have to have a hero, what better hero than Archie Bunker?"

Blacks, on balance, seem to agree—among them Michael Evans, the fledgling actor who plays Lionel Jefferson with surprising assurance.

Andrea Rich, the director's wife, who teaches a course in communications at UCLA to a predominantly black class, says, "I think the Jews weren't sure it was good for the Jews, but the blacks were sure it was good for the blacks. For the first time, they feel a white Anglo-Saxon is presented as he really is."

Sammy Davis, Jr. now concludes his nightclub act with a 10-minute speech about *All in the Family,* and has asked Lear to write in a part for him, which Davis says he will play for free. Lear is constantly approached by blacks who want to express their pleasure. Adds O'Connor: "I have never met a black person who hasn't said, 'That show is the most, that show is the greatest, that show breaks me up.' "

But if, as some critics contend, appreciation of this sort is really disguised hostility, is *that* a good feeling to smoke out? Or does it further inflame our emotions?

If there is a bit of the bigot in all of us, then the show may inevitably do good. The basis of all humor is that you laugh *at* someone. If you laugh *at* someone you can't laugh *with* him. Laughing at Archie, for feeling as he does, does something to the man who laughs.

"Is it good for a person to see an honest picture of himself?" O'Connor asks. "When I see a bad candid photograph of myself, I say, 'Oh my God, do I look like that?' If a person sees Archie as an honest reflection of his own seamy side, hopefully he'll do something about it."

The guiding premise of *All in the Family* is that there is nothing in a strong democracy that can't be talked about. "If it's a word, it can be said; if it's an idea, it can be expressed," Lear told a studio audience. "The kids say, 'Let it all hang out,' and that's the way we feel." The audience responded with applause.

That kind of openness may be all very normal for kids, but it does not come so easily for members of minorities. Still, whether *All in the Family* is good for America's minorities is no longer an adequate point. What the program says about the *state* of these groups must also be considered: they just may be in the kind of shape they have never been in before.

Twenty years ago, Jews were in flight. There was a hemorrhage of Jewish loyalty. Jewish university students declined to answer questions about religious affiliation. Assimilation was the watchword.

Lear was raised an Orthodox Jew. In Hartford, Connecticut, he conducted high holiday services for children. But from the moment he left the shelter of his community, other forces intruded. His black hair and moustache gave him a chameleon's powers.

"When I was with Jimmy Gorman, nobody thought I was anything but Irish—but I didn't trouble to correct them," Lear recalls. One night, dining in the home of an Italian friend, he was addressed in Italian by a member of the family. "Aren't you Italian?" the man inquired when Lear failed to respond. "I said, 'No. I'm Jewish'—and it didn't come out easy," Lear remembers. "My orientation from a number of experiences was that it wasn't easy to be Jewish—and sometimes wasn't popular."

By his own admission, Lear was not secure enough in his own identity to have done the show 20 years ago. What changed him? "The emergence of Israel," he says. "Identification with the struggle of blacks made me stronger in my self-identity. I think the overwhelming nature of the problems made me want to help. You can't do that until you feel oneness with yourself."

Twenty years ago, black consciousness simply did not exist. Today, blacks are experiencing a painful confirmation of self. Twenty years ago, ethnic groups were crawling into the woodwork. Today, public opinion polls show that ethnic pride is at an all-time high.

What this means is that it's okay, at last, to be different. If so, we really are approaching new ground in America, where we can kid the pants off our bigots and publicly examine previously unmentionable contemporary issues.

"Audiences are more mature than people tended to give them credit for," CBS' Wagner acknowledges. O'Connor emphatically agrees, saying: "I think Archie would have been accepted 10 years ago, 15 years ago. I agree with Oscar Wilde who said that art doesn't imitate life, life imitates art. In other words, art doesn't proceed from some life force that is happening in the community. Art occurs, and life responds to art. This could have happened long ago, and I see no reason why it couldn't have been accepted long ago."

Which means that if Mike's problem didn't get resolved last night, it will before very long.

Four Movies That Play for Keeps

Charles C. Hampton, Jr.

Pauline Kael, in an article comparing *Bonnie and Clyde* to the long string of tough-and-violent black humor films from *Dr. Strangelove* to *Point Blank*, explains why ". . . *Bonnie and Clyde*, an entertaining movie that has some feeling in it, upsets people . . . Maybe it's because *Bonnie and Clyde*, by making us care about the robber lovers, has put the sting back into death." What follows is an attempt to examine the strategy by which this sting is produced and to point out its use in other recent films— films which have a reputation for being the "best" (i.e., somehow corresponding to the strange sensibility of our time) in recent years: *Elvira Madigan, Blow Up, Easy Rider, Butch Cassidy and the Sundance Kid*.

Every movie-goer knows that he attends a film for the fulfillment of expectation, but what he perhaps only dimly knows is that beyond the obvious desire to "see a flick" or to experience a sad or comic movie to match his mood, there is a specific sequential emotional workout (or specific filmic structual sequence) which the movie leads him to expect in its opening moments ("oh, good a Joan Crawford") and which it, traditionally, subsequently fulfills. In the structure of the film these similarities from one film to another allow us to speak of movie genres (western, gangster films, horror movies), and for the movie-goer they allow a certain familiarity, an at-homeness, which in turn allows him to relax and to apprehend the film at the proper depth of feeling in the certainty that he will not be either startled or bored more than he wants. For in fulfilling the function of relaxing the audience, the film must not relax it too much: it must go along the old track of the genre but be in some respects different. Otherwise the audience is bored ("Oh, it's just like her last one"). Conversely, if the film is so different from its predecessors as to "leave its audience behind" (*Last Year at Marienbad*, perhaps, at least for audiences trained by Hollywood films) it does this because the genre expectation of the audience is frustrated, it can find no traditional emotional foothold, no way of getting into the film, and is again bored. So each new

Copyright © 1970 Film Comment Publishing Corporation. Printed with permission from *Film Comment*, Vol. 6, No. 3 (Fall 1970).

film must be different but not too different; and it is this slow change from film to film that allows us to speak of history of the film, audience education, the maturing of a given genre (westerns), and which, hopefully allows movies to keep pace with the emotional needs of a changing audience in changing times.

Now, this is not to say that those films which are too much the same or too much different don't have their audiences; there are those who find enjoyment in sameness (Warhol) and in apparent chaos (*Marienbad*), and this may be so because their view of the world (and hence their emotions) sees the world as totally the same or as chaotic. In this case the emotional foothold comes not from the recognition of a familiar emotional pattern, the film genre, but from the recognition of the structural equivalent of an emotional state in life: the ill-made play matches an ill-made world.

But for the everyday movie-goer, the response to the frustration of genre expectation is simply boredom without recognition or enjoyment. His hold on the patterns of his emotions, like his hold on the patterns of his life, is too rutted, too solid, too rooted in the patterns of the past for him to recognize genre deviations of such magnitude as any thing but boring chaos. Unless, of course, there is something in his daily life experience ("these troubled times") which, as in the case of the art movie devotees, forces on him a recognition of the correspondence of the film's chaos to his own. This moment of recognition is bound to be painful: when a structural film sequence is emotionally apprehended as being broken and further that this breaking is emotionally "right" (recognition of life emotional pattern) it means the old life pattern and its corresponding film genre are wrong. We have consciously known for a long time that we can't *live* like a John Wayne film, but we had thought it was *all right* to *feel* that way—but not since *Butch Cassidy*.

Structurally, we are of course only speaking here of variety (the film must be the same but slightly different) in another sense. Instead of variety in the smaller segments of film structure (costume, number of outlaws, setting, how many gunfights) we have now to do with larger elements. The old emotional verity now reads: Boy gets girl, boy loses girl, boy and girl are killed by somebody we don't even KNOW. The fracturing of expectation in one level of form makes us aware of another layer beyond it: a recognition that there are emotional and life truths as yet undreamed of in our philosophies, that is in our emotional and corresponding film genres. We may turn away from this recognition by means of the device of boredom (Sontag: only another word for frustration), but not if in jumping from film reality back to life reality we find the same spectre there in our own life.

Something like this painful recognition of a life threat which we would rather not look at and which is brought on by the fracturing of genre expectation is behind, I feel, the effect of putting back the sting into the deaths (and violence) of *Bonnie and Clyde*. The genre of this film is usually identified by movie critics (Kael included) as that of the gangster film; indeed, there have been several previous filmings of the same story within that genre. But I would submit that that appelation fits only in retrospect; that except for minor elements of detail the genre expectation which the movie evokes for most of its length is not gangster but pastoral: the expectation that the innocent and playful young persons presented to us will be protected by their innocence; that they may learn from their misadventures but not suffer for them, that violence may be threatened but never real. Like Jack Lemmon in *The Apartment*, bumbling will be instructional, even funny, but never lead to maiming and death. The pastoral genre expectation is set up, followed and then broken; *Peter Pan* is revealed to have been dominated by the rules of *Public Enemy*. The movie sets up a spirit of play and then plays for keeps.

The audience is keyed into the pastoral genre expectation in the main by two major elements in *Bonnie and Clyde*: character and style of action. In the gangster genre our empathy with the lead character is mitigated by his nature as a professional: he knows he is outside of society, knows that it will kill him if it can; is watchful; and handles himself in every situation with this knowledge as well as with an expertness that comes of having faced the situation many times before. Bogart or Cagney knows what he is doing, is aware of all possibilities and consequences: as a professional his fight with the law is fair since their power is matched by his knowledge and awareness. Both are serious, both know the rules and their respective roles (roles in both the professional sense and in the genre expectation sense). But both Bonnie and Clyde appear as innocent children beside these gangsters: they show off for one another; they enjoy what they do too much (and we realize that they *don't* realize the consequences), they want fame not money, in every situation they are *trying out* the situation (once they have mastered the techniques of bank robbery or car theft we no longer see these sequences). Above all they are just having fun: their victims are not threatened but swashbuckled. The humorous details of escape sequences, from parking problems in front of a bank to carrying a kitchen spatula in a dash from the police, mark their adventures as the tentative, surface, unserious, this-is-the-first-time, improvisational playing at adult roles by children. In this context Clyde's impotence and Bonnie's bumbling attempts to remedy it can be seen not as the spurious side plot that most critics label it but as the sexlessness of Peter Pan and Wendy; and the arrival of sexuality for Bonnie and Clyde corresponds with the crashing arrival of the retributive adult world of law and order.

As strategy toward audience this pastoral beginning fools the audience into too deep an empathy with the characters, and it is this depth of feeling which makes the violence so telling, puts the sting back in death. If we had recognized from the beginning that the film would end as do all gangster films (if it had set up a gangster genre expectation) then we would have withheld some of our feeling and instead have substituted admiration for daring and professionalism. For from the beginning of all dramatic structures the empathy evoked by characters has always been divided into that which is recognition of humanness, and that which is admiration for daring. In Greek tragedy we feel for the chorus or the suffering victim but are chary of lending sympathy to Oedipus. Our admiration of his daring is a sign that we must withhold some feeling—we know what daring leads to.

Bonnie and Clyde's style of action is not role-limited professionalism, but playfulness: the tentative trying out of any situation for the fun of it. The result is that we apprehend every scene with empathy and enjoyment (we feel with the characters) and at the same time with a certain dread that they don't know what they're doing. Clyde's gun (as oversized as any Charlie Brown might play with) is used in the farmhouse sequence in exactly the way that any body might use it: for breaking windows. But before this resolution we have the frightening feeling that he doesn't know what to do with it, that that child is in an unknown situation, that like a child he might do anything: kill the farmer or his family. The gun is real, loaded, and he doesn't know what could happen. Kael rightly points out that it is Beatty's slowness of timing that throws us here: we read it as the hesitance of the innocent amateur in an unknown situation.

When the world of law begins to close in (when the pastoral genre is shattered by the gangster genre) it occurs in the form of the Texas Ranger, who appears in the still-pastoral world of the gang as too serious, too much a villain. The Ranger won't play. Like any child, Clyde throws a tantrum: the scene ends with his screaming "I got you, I got you!" at the Ranger.

From this point onward the pastoral fun is gone, money becomes important; sexuality arrives on the scene; the action of constant flight is forced on the characters by the law which we and they apprehend as alien, too harsh in the light of their past actions: they were only playing; the law is playing for keeps.

The final shot of the film, the slow motion dance of death, is moving and grotesquely beautiful because it is a loss of beauty—the beauty, freedom, playfulness of childhood. Mr. Darling has shot Peter Pan for kidnapping his children, and this is right (gangster genre) because that is just what Peter did do. But it is also wrong because within the context of pastoral kidnapping is only a game (as when Captain Hook captures the boys and Wendy). This ambivalence (life and death, right and wrong, grotesque and beautiful) is captured in the final shot (fast death and slow motion) in exactly the same way that it is evoked by the stop frames of life in death, vitality in stasis which end *Elvira Madigan* and *Butch Cassidy and the Sundance Kid*, by the sudden vanishing of David Hemmings into the child world of the invisible tennis ball at the end of *Blow Up*, and, in a more traditional manner, by the aerial backing shot of the burning motorcycle which ends *Easy Rider*. Each is death, but each evokes the beauty, vitality, playfulness of childhood-pastoral. Our ambivalent feelings toward these endings are the result of the juxtaposition and subsequent breaking of mutually incompatible genre expectations.

In order for the audience to apprehend such breaking of genre expectation as anything except chaos, it is necessary that this apparent nonsequenter have a life emotion parallel. The appeal of these films is largely to the young and one need not go far to discover a parallel in the playful and exuberant hip life style and the crushing repression which the forces of conformity have visited upon it. And while the idea that society will punish you for who you are rather than what you have done may be no surprise to American minority groups, it does come as an emotional surprise to middleclass white young people. The subsequent feeling of unjust, reasonless hounding by the forces of society is an exact parallel to that evoked by the genre change in *Bonnie and Clyde*: just playing and playing for keeps.

But the shock of the film is also felt by those on the other side of the generation gap; indeed it is from these people that the loudest protests at the film's violence have been heard. The fact that bang-for-bang and blood-for-blood *Bonnie and Clyde* is left far behind by many Hollywood films indicates that such objections can be viewed not as analysis but as symptom: the sting has indeed been put back in death. For the Silent Majority has also suffered its own form of repression at the hands of society's forces. Its self image too is of a playful, innocent childlike character who suddenly finds that the world is playing for keeps. He is the inheritor of the tradition of the boisterous, smiling, fast-shooting, wheeling and dealing, always-kidding gun that won the west, and has found suddenly that whether the subject is capitalism, or ecology, or racism or war he is the villain and the whole world blames him for its ills. The happy-go-lucky American, his actions limited only by a full-speed-ahead-and-the-devil-take-the-hindmost-what-ever-the-traffic-will-bear has found that it bears a good deal less than it used to, and the loss is not simply in limited action and enforced responsibilities but in the loss of life style and thus in surety of identity.

Such a feeling is the emotional and identity loss provoked by an era of rapid change whose new requirements in act and responsibility are bound to be felt as prohibitive simply because they are new, unaccustomed; and this is true whether one's sympathies lie with the world of law or of childhood: the emphasis lies on their mutual *incompatibility,* as though the two genres existed in separate dimensions. In the transition, both worlds seem unreal: the law is arbitrary, a cause and effect mechanism which exists apart from felt reality; and childhood seems recklessly careless, oriented only in present time, egoistic. It is this double vision of contemporary transitional society that is evoked so clearly by the central metaphor of *Blow Up*, a detective genre film that breaks (or rather degenerates) into a disconnected series of montage events as a cause-and-effect sequence expectation is evoked, strained, confounded, dissolved. The world of law here is symbolized by physical law: the eye of the camera is compared to the emotional eye of the protagonist. The sequence of photographic blowups to which the title of the film points lead us not toward greater clarity of vision but to the startling discovery that the subject of the photograph disappears as we get closer and breaks up into the grain of the photographic negative. In exact parallel the body in the park also disappears when examined too closely, as does the heroine, and finally as does the protagonist himself. This last disappearance also takes place in a photographic medium, the movie itself, and, by giving us the ultimate in human identity loss in terms of both content and medium playfulness (the invisible tennis ball and the cinematic trick of image disappearance) holds both the worlds of law and childhood in mutually incompatible juxtaposition. And the effect is not simply chaos but disquieting truthfulness.

Like *Blow Up*, *Elvira Madigan* depends upon the audience's latent sense of the truth of excessive and retributive necessity to overcome the common sense, cause-and-effect genre expectation evoked in its beginning. We are no strangers to romance, nor to romances which end in death, but by means of its sheer beauty and by hypnotically exclusive focus on the romantic couple this film seeks to convince us that retribution lies not in the law or the wicked prince or the jealous woman, father or brother, but in the incompatibility of love and simple work: stated badly this film insists that if you really love you will really starve to death.

Such an assertion is patent nonsense from the practical point of view, but the movie is able to push for the emotional acceptance of it by the audience since the felt repressive pressure of our transitional era tends to make a difference of kind out of a difference of degree: playfulness is seen as incompatible with work, present oriented love or freedom as unable to cope with the future oriented practicalities of work and money in the cause and effect world. This effect of separate dimensions makes it unnecessary for the retributive agent to be personified in this film; it is enough that these people love, for then they cannot attempt work (Elvira's abortive attempt to earn money by dancing) without threatening their love. It is the simple fact of loving that brings them to the threshold of starvation and finally to suicide.

In *Easy Rider* also this incompatibility of two genres tends to make the two worlds (here the straight and head worlds) mythically polarized: the straights are mindless barbarians; the heads exist in innocent Eden (the commune) or in a realm in which sex-cum-acid takes on the dimensions of religious communion. To be of one world and to attempt to traffic in the other is to court disaster. It is not the moral questionability of the transaction in smack which brings on the final disaster, but the dealing in money, the major idol of the straight world: it is the money that makes our heroes visible by financing both the journey and their trappings. Better to disappear as in *Blow Up*; be in the world but not of it. To have money is to be of the straight world, the cash nexus is the door which brings these characters into the world of the straights and under its retribution. "We blew it," refers to the characters' inability to exist in both worlds: the incompatibility of life styles and genre seen in *Bonnie and Clyde, Blow Up* and *Elvira Madigan*.

Butch Cassidy and the Sundance Kid continues the same theme but with the addition of an historical metaphor: the train and the bicycle appear as premonitions of the mechanical cause-and-effect efficiency which will in the end destroy the playful life of the protagonists. In this film the genre deviation of *Blow Up* is played backwards as the child-like western genre is replaced by the machine-like efficiency of the posse that behave like modern detectives and by the numerical superiority and regimentation of the Bolivian army. The use of sepia tone still photographs at the beginning and end of this film (like the snapshots that background the titles in *Bonnie and Clyde*) evoke the aura of a world irretrievably lost in the past, a childhood of the race now overcome by modern efficiency.

All of these films have in their sequence begun to create a genre of their own, a genre of genre deviation, which has its own expectations and repeated motifs. In each of these films it is the need for money which brings about the protagonists' visibility in the retributive world and eventually their downfall. (*Blow Up* is the exception since the transition is reversed; the horror is not at the retribution of the practical world but at the unconcerned playfulness of the child world.) In each also there is a journey, a freedom of motion which makes the child life style possible, and which ironically takes place by means of the vehicles created by the mechanical world: the cars, motorcycles and steamships. Even the camera in *Blow Up* offers an insight which leads to the destruction of its own mechanical nature. This metaphor points to the life irony that while our mechanical world has created the means by which to free us it has made us unable to be free since we too have been mechanized.

This new genre differs from the old genres which it holds in mutual juxtaposition and mutual incompatibility. As pastoral it shows innocence in a new perspective of awkwardness and practical need: these lost boys must eat, have clothes, fall down and die. As gangster or detective story realism, we see the characters surrounded by the sympathetic effects of childhood, feel with them to a greater extent, suffer as they suffer. The sting is put back into death.

Easy Pieces

Stephen Farber

The success of *Five Easy Pieces* in America has been one encouraging sign for American movies in an otherwise depressing time. In 1969 the surprising popularity of unconventional, 'downbeat' movies like *Midnight Cowboy, Alice's Restaurant, They Shoot Horses, Don't They?* and, particularly, *Easy Rider* seemed to represent the beginning of a vital new phase in the development of the American film. Younger film-makers were given unusual freedom to create personal projects dealing frankly with contemporary social problems. But most everything went wrong in 1970. On the one hand, many film-makers tried a little too self-consciously to make 'youth movies', bringing only the most superficial understanding to highly-charged subjects like campus rebellion and revolutionary politics. And the audience recognised the superficiality; almost all of these films were commercial failures. Other film-makers became infatuated with their freedom and blinded by the new star-status of the movie director, and turned to indulgent 'personal films' that often seemed so private as to be impenetrable. 1970 began with promises of a renaissance in American films, but by the end of the year the industry was in the middle of a new slump, and there was little to be optimistic about. By far the most successful pictures of the year were two corpses from an earlier era of movie-making—*Airport* and *Love Story*.

Only *Five Easy Pieces*, written by Adrien Joyce and directed by Bob Rafelson, fulfills the promise of the 1969 films. Like *Easy Rider, Five Easy Pieces* is a 'road' picture, the loosely structured, rough, lyrical picaresque adventures of a contemporary American drifter. It is an independently produced film, unorthodox in both theme and style, as *Easy Rider* was; but it is also a more mature and honest work, a critique of some of the unacknowledged assumptions of *Easy Rider*. (Since many of the same people worked on both films, I don't think it is going too far to see *Five Easy Pieces* as a deliberate comment on the earlier film's evasions.)

The quietness of *Five Easy Pieces* comes as something of a surprise. In the last few years American films have been growing steadily harsher in their denunciations of the failures of contemporary American society. By early 1970, in films like *Easy Rider, Midnight Cowboy, Medium Cool,*

From *Sight and Sound* Magazine. By permission of The British Film Institute, London.

Tell Them Willie Boy Is Here, They Shoot Horses, Don't They? Joe, and
WUSA, the accusations against America had reached an extremely fever-
ish, hysterical pitch. *Easy Rider* was the archetypal paranoid anti-American film. It began by invoking some enduring myths—the freedom of the
open road, the magical power of the unpolluted land, the journey away
from civilisation as a regenerative experience containing the secret of life.
But when the free-living heroes reached the end of the road, they came up
against the true virulence of contemporary American civilisation, and were
slaughtered by men who could not tolerate their unconventionality. The
interesting thing about *Easy Rider* was its sentimentality about American
frontier myths; the film never questioned the myths themselves—which
desperately *need* questioning—but instead turned its anger against the
Southern bigots who, in forgetting their nation's heritage, betrayed a once
noble dream.

Another film released at about the same time, Francis Ford Coppola's
The Rain People, tried for a much more penetrating and comprehensive
examination of the failure of the myths; as a result, while *Easy Rider* was
breaking box-office records, *The Rain People* died quietly and disap-
peared. They began at almost the same point. *The Rain People*, like *Easy
Rider*, concerned a journey away from civilisation, into the open spaces of
middle America—a woman trying to escape the growing oppressiveness of
her suburban married life by breaking free and running, looking for an
answer to her frustrations on the road. But unlike *Easy Rider*, Coppola's
film asked us to see that the search for freedom might conceal an evasion
of responsibility. The heroine of *The Rain People* was running from an
honest confrontation with herself when she headed for the open road.
Though this was a modest, unselfconscious film, it was moving toward a
more radical reconsideration of American society than could be found in
the shriller anti-American films; it meant to point up the inadequacy, the
hollowness of even our most cherished ideals.

Five Easy Pieces extends these criticisms of American myths in a more
thoughtful and coherent way. The character played by Jack Nicholson in
Easy Rider, a smalltown liberal lawyer, felt an exuberant sense of liberation travelling with his motorcycle buddies; he was murdered by Southern
rednecks bitterly envious of his freedom. Shortly before his death, trying to
analyse the hatred he had encountered, he said, 'This used to be a hell of a
good country. I don't know what happened to it . . . People talk about
individual freedom, but when they see a really free individual, it scares
them.' The character played (brilliantly) by Nicholson in *Five Easy Pieces*
still believes in the mystique of the open road, but something more disturbing has gone wrong. This time there are no rednecks to prevent him from
realising his dream; he moves from place to place casually, picking up and
leaving whenever he feels like it, travelling free and easy, always uncom-
mitted. But he seems lost, and his life seems empty. At first, to be sure, his

rootlessness has a certain charm; we are taken by his vitality and direct-
ness, his openness to experience, the relish with which he plays at a variety
of roles. But the irony of his situation is striking: this time, in his desperate search for freedom, the drifter has *turned into* a redneck.

Five Easy Pieces looks for some of the psychological reasons for the
hero's rootlessness, tries to 'place' it in very specific autobiographical
terms, and so provides a more rounded, dispassionate understanding of the
American drifter than a more sentimental film 'ballad' like *Easy Rider*.
Bobby Dupea comes from a family of distinguished musicians who live on
a lovely estate on an island in Puget Sound; but he finds their provinciality
suffocating, and he has run from their withering gentility. When the film
opens, he is living almost a defiant caricature of his past life—working as
an oil rigger, living with a dumb, sluttish waitress, hanging around cheap
cafés and bowling alleys. But the caricature becomes indisguishable
from its target. Bobby knows that the ignorant poor are as provincial and
complacent as the cultured rich. He is looking for an honest, direct life-
style that will shatter the polite pretences of the world in which he has
been bred, but his 'honesty' becomes another lie, a new kind of mask, a
way of closing out the insecurities that haunt him. Even his sexual direct-
ness, which he sees as a rebellious challenge to the intellectual aridity of
his family's world, can be an evasion. After a low-key scene of a painful,
dispiriting meeting between Bobby and his sister, Rafelson cuts boldly to a
startling scene of Bobby engaging in some very vigorous lovemaking with
a casual pickup. The transition economically and effectively implies the
defensiveness of Bobby's sexual intensity.

Bobby *uses* his alienation, his rootlessness, his 'freedom' as a way of
getting himself out of difficult situations. When things begin to turn sour,
or when the emotional ties become too complicated, he can always say, 'I
don't belong here,' and move on. His alienation is only an excuse to evade
the responsibilities of relationships with other people. After Bobby has
admitted that he is thinking of leaving his girl-friend Rayette, though she is
pregnant, his oil-rigger friend begins a homely, self-righteous sermon about
a man's responsibility to a woman. Bobby blows up, sneering, 'I don't
know why I'm sitting here listening to some cracker asshole give me advice.' Because he remains an outsider to every world he travels through, he
can mock the pieties that the people who *are* involved take more seriously.
Although the film expects us to share Bobby's scepticism toward clichés, it
does not ignore the moral appraisals that he scoffs at so cavalierly. We can
see that Rayette is utterly dependent on him, and that he has encouraged
her quite recklessly, without any concern about what she may suffer whenever he decides to move on.

For Bobby's carelessness—towards himself as well as toward others—is
an inevitable price of his liberation. In a rare moment of self-awareness, he
sums up a few years of his life to his father: 'I move around a lot, not

because I'm looking for anything, but to get away from things that go bad if I stay. Auspicious beginnings . . .' In *Easy Rider*, as in the classic American myths that it reworks, drifting is a poetic experience, and the drifter's life is enriched by all his hard travelling. In *Five Easy Pieces* Bobby's drifting prevents him from confronting who he is, and stunts his life. On his return home in the second half of the film, he becomes deeply attracted to his brother's fiancée Catherine, a lovely, withdrawn pianist. But after a brief affair, she rejects him, judging him harshly and directly: 'Where would it lead? A man with no love for himself, no respect for himself, no love for friends, family, work, *anything*—how can he ask for love from someone else?' The life that she has chosen for herself—retreating to what Bobby calls a 'rest home' of music and gentility—may be excessively safe and provincial, but her honesty with herself, her willingness to accept realistic limitations, provide a gauge against which we have to measure Bobby. She knows who she is, and he does not.

Bobby's rebellion against his family is empty and misguided—his emotional ties to his past are still strong, and in attempting to make an absolute break, he simplifies his own nature, ignores the ambivalence of his responses, and cuts himself off from the gentleness and sensitivity he might draw on. His carelessness means that he must lose Catherine, and the film convinces us that he has lost something valuable. His future, 'free' though it may be, seems doomed to contain no grace, no beauty, no love. The scenes between Bobby and Catherine are quiet and unobtrusive, but they establish a possibility that Bobby's rootless way of life inevitably sacrifices. In all of these scenes with Bobby's family, Rafelson works with great delicacy and close attention to detail, and he achieves an almost Chekhovian sense of melancholy and pathos; his is a distinctive directorial talent.

Perhaps the young audiences that have made *Five Easy Pieces* a success in America read the film as another celebration of the heroic free spirit in revolt against a repressive, enervated society. They do applaud Bobby's irreverence, even in the falsest scene in the film—the cocktail party at which he savagely attacks the intellectual pretensions of his brother's guests. But if young people blindly identify with Bobby as one more abused, put-upon victim of materialism, they are misreading the film. *Five Easy Pieces* is remarkable for its scepticism and understated complexity; it is also remarkable for the perception and precision with which it delineates an *individual* character, who is idiosyncratic enough to resist anyone's theories of social malaise.

The end of the film is bleak; frightened of the prospects ahead of him, Bobby leaves Rayette and picks up and runs again, on a spur-of-the-moment decision riding off with a truck driver who is heading for Alaska, the last American frontier. Shivering in the truck in the very last scene, Bobby mumbles 'I'm fine, I'm fine,' but his face is like a frightened child's; we cannot hold out much hope for his future. Even so, the film as a whole does not seem cynical or masochistic. Unlike *Easy Rider* or *Midnight Cowboy, Five Easy Pieces* is not content simply to wallow in a self-satisfied paranoid fantasy of an America gone mad: its interest in questioning myths is an interest in re-creating life. Rafelson's serious attempt to imagine alternatives to Bobby's empty existence, though not entirely satisfactory, represents a concern about the quality of personal life that may presage a gentler, more open and explorative mood in American films.

Already one can observe similarly inchoate tendencies toward revaluation of social and personal myths in several more awkward and confused American films. Like the hero of *Five Easy Pieces,* the hero of *Adam at 6 a.m.,* a young semantics professor, finds his intellectual middle class world stifling, and he leaves Los Angeles to journey back to his family home in rural Missouri, hoping to refresh his life by spending a summer with simpler people. Gradually he realises that their life is as false and empty as the one he has tried to escape, and that there is no answer to his dissatisfaction on the open road. The point of the Charles Eastman-Sidney Furie film *Little Fauss and Big Halsy* has been badly obscured by some last-minute changes in structure; but Eastman's original intention was to undercut the tendency to idealise the free-wheeling, free-loving motorcycle hero played by Robert Redford. The film meant to trace the moral awakening of the once idolatrous Little Fauss (Michael J. Pollard), as he came to realise the irresponsibility and callousness implicit in the swaggering style of his hero Big Halsy. Some of this moral concern can still be seen in the film, although its focus has been blurred.

In *I Walk the Line* John Frankenheimer tries to question American myths by casting Gregory Peck in another version of the archetypal role which made him a star—the simple, upright smalltown sheriff—and then having Peck play *against* type. During the film Peck's confident sense of virtue is shattered when he falls desperately in love with a cunning moonshiner's daughter, and begins to lie and even break the law for her. Although he is disoriented by this change in his life's moral pattern, he is brave enough to want to leave his past behind and run off with her; but ironically, it is she who is too closely tied to her family to imagine such a radical break. Paul Mazursky's *Alex in Wonderland* concerns a film director fresh from the success of a first film, trying to keep his private life in control in spite of tremendous external pressures. All of these films have very serious flaws, and *Adam at 6 a.m.* and *Alex in Wonderland* are almost complete failures, but they are interesting as a group because of their examination of people trying to absorb changes in their lives, reassessing and repudiating cultural myths as they work to refashion personal identity.

These are the same qualities that distinguish Arthur Penn's evocative *Little Big Man.* This film does not at first seem comparable to the others, for it is an ambitious, expensive historical epic. But in spite of the great events that it covers, from before the Civil War to the Battle of Little Big Horn, and the historical figures who swirl through it—General Custer, Wild Bill Hickok and Buffalo Bill—its strongest impulse is a gentle nostalgia for ordinary life. Unlike *Five Easy Pieces, Little Big Man* treats large social questions—the settlement of the West, the relationship of white man to Indian—but, like Rafelson's film, it shows an unusual interest in the quality of *individual* life, the search for personal identity even in the midst of social cataclysms.

Some critics have taken the social message as the dominant one, and have read the film simply as one more portentous sermon on white American racism. But although this is certainly part of its meaning, and although the massacre sequences are the dramatic high points, the true significance of the film is to be found elsewhere, in the rich mosaic of *undramatic* moments that surround these peaks of social outrage. In fact, in the very first scene Penn and writer Calder Willingham warn the liberal audience to be wary of political generalisations. The 121-year-old survivor of Little Big Horn, Jack Crabb (Dustin Hoffman), is being interviewed by a rodent-like oral historian about the culture of the plains Indians. The researcher talks very glibly about 'genocide', and sees Crabb as no more than a crude racial stereotype, a white man who must have helped to exterminate the red man. The story that Jack tells may seem, at moments, to document the charge of genocide, but by mocking the researcher's attempt to summarise Jack's life with fashionable liberal slogans, Penn clearly is alerting us to look at Jack Crabb's past in a more complex way. Penn refuses to see Jack's life as merely an illustration of a cause, an example to be used in some dispassionate historian's theory. *Little Big Man* insists that a man's life is irreducible, and that it has a significance which eludes and transcends any simple sociological labels.

Actually, all of Penn's films concern an individual searching for a sense of identity, testing himself against cultural myths as he attempts to define who he is. Jack Crabb's search involves a phenomenal number of transitional stages; he tries on identities like new suits of clothes—at various moments in his life he is a religious fanatic, a swindler, an Indian scout, a mule-skinner, a gunfighter, a drunk, and a hermit. The great national heroes portrayed in the film provide him with models (for example, when he first looks up at General Custer, he sees only a burst of sunlight), but the progress of the film is a series of disillusionments. Role after role proves false and hypocritical. A white boy raised by the Cheyenne, then recaptured by whites, and moving back and forth between Indian and white society throughout most of the film, Jack is an outsider to both worlds; like the hero of *Five Easy Pieces*, he belongs nowhere. But it is the Indians, and especially the old chief whom he calls Grandfather, who offer the only measure of permanence in his life. And yet, ironically, he is obsessed with the urge to make something of himself in white society; he is not willing to accept the simpler identity—'Little Big Man'—that he has among the Indians.

Jack Crabb is a drifter, an adventurer in the classic American mould, but at times he seems like a chameleon; he is so malleable that even his character changes in response to his environment and the people around him. The simplicity and gentleness he has among the Indians give way to awkwardness, aggressiveness, and deceitfulness whenever he returns to white society and moves among the poseurs and the madmen. (The variations in Dustin Hoffman's performance express Jack's rather frightening adaptability; in the scenes with his white wife, or Custer, or the lascivious preacher's wife played by Faye Dunaway, Hoffman is often deliberately mannered, arch and artificial, while in the scenes with Old Lodge Skins he plays with surprising understatement and dignity. This is easily his best performance to date.) Jack is seduced by the ideals of his society and he tries for heroic action, but he can never bring it off. Even when he tries to kill Custer, he bungles it, and is painfully humiliated because of his ineptitude. Though he is resolutely ordinary, he does not see that his ordinariness conceals a quiet moral strength; he is by nature incapable of violence, and although he is enough of a victim of American myths to regard this instinctive gentleness as cowardice, we see it as his greatest quality. In the same way, Jack spends years emulating the heroes of American society, searching for a career that will bring him respectability, fame and fortune. He does not see that in Indian society, where he is simply a 'human being' without a career or an honorific social role to play, his life has a 'centre' that it otherwise lacks. Like Bobby Dupea, he runs away from what he is in pursuit of self-defeating dreams; his restlessness is an evasion, and he matures only when he realises that he can settle down.

Jack's life is a chaotic mosaic of irregular, undramatic pieces. Only one scene in the film—the killing of his Indian wife—is conceived in extraordinary terms, as a high tragic climax, a searing vision of annihilation; and it is beautifully filmed and edited, the details frozen and abstracted to suggest the one transcendent moment in Jack's life. But it is interesting that this climax comes not at the end of the film, but only about two-thirds of the way through. Penn insists on following it with anti-climaxes—more ragged, picaresque adventures as a drunk and a hermit, an abortive suicide attempt, and Jack's final return to the Indians after the Battle of Little Big Horn. Penn, like Rafelson, wants to explore notions of personal maturity and self-definition, and *Little Big Man*, like *Five Easy Pieces*, shows respect for the quirks of individual life; it is almost a tribute to the eccentricities of human experience.

Movies mirror the times, and it is not surprising that many American films in the Nixon era are once again celebrating wholesomeness and apathy, retreating from a realistic appraisal of social evils to safe romantic fantasies. Films like *Five Easy Pieces* and, in a different way, *Little Big Man*, suggest one positive aspect of this withdrawal from society. These films represent a turning inward, a concern with self-knowledge; they both reflect and criticise contemporary experimentation in the area of personal relationships, the questioning of traditional conceptions of identity. Their interest in reassessing American myths, but with tentativeness and compassion instead of anger, and their success in creating complex unheroic characters, are welcome new qualities in American movies.

Peckinpah and Kubrick:
Fire and Ice

William S. Pechter

"Of directors to have emerged in the American film during the 1950's, Stanley Kubrick seems to me the most interesting."

A week before I saw *A Clockwork Orange*, I saw *2001: A Space Odyssey* for the second time. I had liked it the first time I saw it, and I liked it now; the experience of seeing it again providing no large revelations but only a reminder of those things which I'd been aware of before. The idea of the film's being a non-narrative work seemed perhaps even less tenable than it had before—the narrative is, to be sure, an attenuated one, broken up by leisurely, non-narrative intervals, but the main action falls firmly into place as a coherent story, and is easily paraphrasable as such, despite the absence of a single protagonist to link the parts. Perhaps it seemed a bit clearer to me than it had before that the character of the work divides roughly at the point of the film's intermission: part one, chiefly a comic capsule history of an incorrigibly banal mankind's technological progress (man discovers weapons, eats at Howard Johnson's and watches wrestling on TV in outer space, copes with "zero gravity toilets," etc., while computers declare in interviews that they "enjoy working with people"), climaxing, in effect, with the scientists posing for pictures in front of the "intelligent" slab they have discovered like fishermen with their trophy; part two, chiefly the melodrama of machines which have become like men turning against men who have become like machines, climaxing in the astronaut's dismantling of the computer. About what follows, I have my strongest reservations: the "light show" is pedestrian, and the concluding sequence of the astronaut in the Louis XV suite suffers, I think, not from obscurity

Reprinted from *Commentary*, by permission. Copyright © 1972 by the American Jewish Committee.

but rather from an excess of clarity in conveying Arthur C. Clarke's message of man's rebirth through the benign guidance of extraterrestrial intelligence. Yet such fatuity notwithstanding, this final sequence of the film is realized by Kubrick in a succession of images which truly astonish in their surreal strangeness and beauty; and, indeed, with its wit, it is the film's visual beauty (the light show excepted) which seems to me its most secure achievement. For all his intellectual distrust of them, Kubrick does love his machines as aesthetic objects, and no other film I know has dwelled with such obsessive fascination on the painterly and scultural detail of flashing light-panels and mesmerically sliding doors—or made so oddly lulling a spectacle of them.

Given my liking for *2001*, as well as my much greater admiration for *The Killing* and admiration also for *Paths of Glory* and for things in Kubrick's other films, it seemed to me more than likely that I would want to write about his latest work, and not premature to draft, before seeing it, the first sentence of a review: "Of directors to have emerged in the American film during the 1950's, Stanley Kubrick seems to me the most interesting." I've now seen *A Clockwork Orange*, and have been staring dumbly at that sentence ever since, as if waiting for it to rewrite itself, or at least move protestingly across the page. For, if, there is one thing *A Clockwork Orange* is not, it is "interesting"—striking, perhaps; even brilliant, though in a way I find specious and repellent; but not interesting. And if there is another thing the film is not, it is, all the ballyhoo in the mass media to the contrary, the embodiment of its maker's "startling vision."

One could, I think, say much the same of Anthony Burgess's thin, anecdotal fantasy of an imminent future from which Kubrick's film has been adapted. Neither *1984* nor *Brave New World* may be a great novel, but the fantasized futures of Orwell and Huxley take root in one's imagination because they connect with the realities of a recognizable present and are extensions of them; their projections are founded in urgent ideas, and usable in one's thinking these ideas through further (thus the observation that Orwell's book has made the actual materialization of what he describes less likely, a consequence one can't imagine ever ascribing to the Burgess). For all the greater closeness of its writing to us in time, *A Clockwork Orange* posits a future (in which a soulless socialist state reconditions its violent criminals into virtuous automatons) whose elements seem both more tangential to our present exigencies and less convincing as an extrapolation from them than do those of the futures of Orwell and Huxley; while the ideas that prop the Burgess novel up consist of little more than a few pages (43 and 96 in the Ballantine reprint edition) of platitudinous conjecture (put, to be sure, in the mouths of characters who can't be identified with the author) on the primacy of selfhood and dubious goodness of those unable to choose evil.

Still, if there is a "vision" in Kubrick's film, it is the novel's, and, even if the novel's vision of the future seems finally less its imaginative moving force than something manufactured to serve the author's distaste for the present, the book has at least what the film does not: a center. This center, in the novel, is the voice of its narrator; not so much the invented slang in which Alex, the teen-age hoodlum, speaks to us, as the cold nihilism with which he perceives his narrow but vivid world. (The language itself, a compound of adopted Russian and sub-Joycean wordplay, can seem mainly an irritating impediment to one's reading at first, though the fact of finding oneself finally proficient in it is really part of the book's amusement.) Some of Alex's narration remains in the film, but, with the loss of its concentration in a sustained, controlling voice, the paucity of the work's narrative invention is rather cruelly exposed, and none of the director's pyrotechnics—the slow and fast motion, hand-held camerawork, distorting lenses, phosphorescent color—will really substitute for it. And they are directorial pyrotechnics rather than directorial technique—which, however brilliant, finally is about something more than this film's anthology of photographic chic. Even before *A Clockwork Orange*, the notion of Kubrick as a technical genius did not really stand scrutiny; there is, I think, some justice in Gilberto Perez-Guillermo's characterization of *2001* as the work of a Stroheim in outer space; yet, if that film's technical triumph seemed to be less a director's than an art director's, there was at least a director's art to be seen both in the film's wit and beauty.

But *A Clockwork Orange* only marks the further progress of Stanley Kubrick's art into that of interior decoration; and, with its shapelessness, limp rhythms, clumsy rear-projection (the scene of a joyride in a stolen car), it is not only lame technically (compare it with *Alphaville*, Godard's vision of a proximate future, to see of what the difference between dull literalness and innovative genius in film-making consists), but deficient even in those things in which one might expect a show of Kubrick's characteristic strengths—of wit and originality. (And though Kubrick has never been better than an erratic director of actors, no other film of his from *The Killing* on has placed such weight on a performance as badly misguided as Malcolm McDowell's leering, smirking, swaggering Alex.) Watching an ape (that one knows to be an actor in ape's costume) contemplate a bone and discover its use as a weapon while *Also Sprach Zarathustra* swells on the soundtrack in a section entitled "The Dawn of Man" in *2001* was funny because it ironically mocked its own pomposity; the speeded-up orgy to the accompaniment of the *William Tell* overture in *A Clockwork Orange* is no more than bad varsity-show humor, as is just about all the other slapstick deviation from Burgess—the stage faggot probation officer drinking from a glass containing Alex's mother's false teeth, Alex falling face first into a plate of spaghetti, etc. And the other instances in which the book has been smartened or tarted up seem equally misconceived—Alex being given a pet snake, the feeble "black comedy" of

Alex doing a soft-shoe rendition of "Singin' in the Rain" while preparing to rape one of his victims, the transformation of a wretched old woman whom Alex murders into the bitchy proprietress of a "health farm," surrounded by erotic artworks including a huge phallic sculpture with which he bashes her. (There seems to be a streak of puritanical meting out of punishment in this last touch, as in Kubrick's having the teeny-boppers whom Alex lures to his apartment introduced sucking phallic popsicles, as though the assaults on these victims were somehow invited by their impropriety.) Having no great attachment to the novel, I'd be a hypocrite to take the film to task just for departing from the book, if it weren't that all the departures are for the worse. (To be fair to Kubrick, it seems clear that he admires the novel, and Burgess himself has expressed approval of the film of it.) Even the omission of a single word can constitute a betrayal. In the film, Alex, restored by the government for politically expedient reasons to his former brutality, exultantly declares, "I was cured!" as the music blares triumphantly on the soundtrack and gives way to a reprise of "Singin' in the Rain" as performed by Gene Kelly. In the novel, noting the return of his familiar murderous desires, Alex simply remarks, "I was cured all right," in that tone of casual but total contempt which never wavers.

Yet, even had there been no novel with which to compare it and had *A Clockwork Orange* been a better film than it is, what would it mean to speak of the "vision" of a director who, only one film before, was soliciting wisdom from the heavens? Even at its best, Kubrick's work seems less the product of a vision than of a temperament, an idiosyncratically misanthropic temperament as capable of finding expression in tandem with the "vision" of Arthur C. Clarke as of Burgess. When the material is as attuned to the temperament as it is in *The Killing*, the result is what, I think, is still Kubrick's best film; *Paths of Glory* may be more skillfully put together, but it suffers from its simplistic demonology and its sentimental ending. But the films that follow are about as uneven in their quality as those of a director who claims serious consideration can be, with frequently little more than their misanthropy and photographic preoccupations to mark them as the work of the same film-maker. Yet what is most distressing about *A Clockwork Orange* is not that it is as sophomoric in its misanthropic humor as *Dr. Strangelove* (which at least had Peter Sellers at his goonish best as the mad doctor), but that the misanthropy has now become merely another aspect of the decor—more chic—to be offered to the photographer; and it is this, and not the misanthropy itself, which makes *A Clockwork Orange* so peculiarly repellent. The "vision" of *A Clockwork Orange* is really quite tame compared with that of a *Yojimbo* or *Viridiana* (which both happen also to be incomparably more funny). But when, in *Viridiana*, we watch a beggars' orgy and attempted rape while the "Hallelujah Chorus" of the *Messiah* is heard, the effect is black but bracing because the feeling behind it has such strength of conviction. When, in *A Clockwork Orange*, we watch the "stylized" and "balletic" sequence (the adjectives are Malcolm McDowell's) of two rival teen-age gangs clashing violently in an abandoned theater while the soundtrack plays the *Thieving Magpie* overture, the effect is repellent not because of an intensity of feeling but just because there is no feeling at all—only the desire to be clever and photogenic.

Even at his best, Kubrick is ice; Sam Peckinpah is fire. Before seeing *Straw Dogs*, I could have described Peckinpah as the most exciting director to have appeared in the American film since the 40's, and his new work only confirms me in that judgment. Like his earlier *The Wild Bunch, Straw Dogs* is a violent work, and, like *A Clockwork Orange*, it is about violence. But the violence of *Straw Dogs* isn't "stylized" and "balletic" as it is in the Kubrick film, nor does one stand coolly and antiseptically aloof from it. Rather it closes like a trap around one until, at the end, one finds oneself grabbed by the throat and plunged inescapably into the sweaty, bloody, palpable thick of it.

The protagonist of the film is a young American mathematics professor on a leave to write a book, and recently arrived to spend the time in an English country town where his British wife had once lived with her family. From the start, despite the pastoral surroundings, things are not right, both between the mathematician and his wife, and around them, in the town, where everyone seems to be intensely aware of the stranger's presence among them, and preternaturally informed of his comings and goings. The young men who work at repairing the farmhouse he has rented on the outskirts of the town barely disguise their resentment of him as an affluent outsider and of his wife's having left the town, or their sexual interest in her (with whom one of them once had an affair); and the wife, excluded by her husband's work and attracted to the cruder, more aggressive masculinity of her former lover, encourages the men's attentions. The wife mocks her husband only half-playfully; she had lived in the farmhouse with her family, and, when the husband asks if a certain chair was her father's, she gibes, "Every chair's my daddy's chair"; and she accuses him of attempting to hide, in his work and at this secluded place, from commitment and from the violent turmoil of the country he has left behind. But the town seems to be only a microcosm of that country, and violence or the threat of violence everywhere around them: in the bellicose old man starting fights in the town pub, the man on the street slapping his simpleton brother; even a boy's slamming against the mathematician's parked car as he runs past seems an expression of scarcely veiled and unfathomable hostility.

That hostility bares its face when the wife's cat is discovered hanged in their closet; put there by one of the workers, the wife insists, "to prove to you they can get into your bedroom." But though his wife prods him to take action against the men, he says nothing, and even agrees, in an act of bravado, to join them in a bird shoot. He does, and while he is duped into waiting for them in the woods, the wife's former lover returns to the farmhouse and rapes the wife (who first invites him in and finally gives herself to him responsively); then another of the men appears, with his shotgun, and, despite the protest of the unarmed former lover, a much more real and ugly rape ensues. The next day, the mathematician, incensed at his humiliation by the men during the hunting party, fires them, unaware of what has happened to his wife, who tells him nothing but only taunts him for his "cowardice." Then, on the evening of a "church social" at which the town's population congregates, all the strands come together. Niles, the simpleton, leaves with a young girl, the niece of the pub-brawler, who flirts with him after flirting unsuccessfully with the mathematician, and the demented man accidentally kills her. Hunted by the old man and the four workmen, he is struck by the car of the mathematician, who takes him to the farmhouse to which the others soon track him. They demand that Niles be turned over to them, but the mathematician refuses, and the men attempt to force their way inside. The town magistrate appears and tries to restore order, but he is killed by a half-accidental blast from the old man's shotgun. And then all hell breaks loose. When it is over, the house is a shambles, though successfully defended, and the old man and four workers have been horrifyingly slaughtered.

These are the bare bones of the film's action, but such an account of them gives almost no sense of the undercurrents and tensions which wrack the work: of the subtle malevolence of old men's watchful eyes in the town, the foul cauldron of animosities that boils among the men loitering at the pub, the intricate web of goading and provocation in which everyone finally is entangled. Above all, is the insistent linkage of violence with sex (and of sexual with territorial relations). The wife taunts the husband about his lack of the workmen's kind of masculinity, while provoking them by exposing her breasts at the window; the workmen in the pub tease the old man for being past it sexually, while the old man is tigerishly protective of his sluttish niece in a way that suggests his own fantasies of her ravishment. When the men actually go after the simpleton, they are not even aware that the girl is dead, but they hardly need this further incitement to violence, so soon does the violence that has been seething everywhere establish its own momentum. And suddenly what had seemed to be one thing becomes quite another. The wife, sickened now by the prospect of more violence after her rape, begs her husband to give Niles to the men, but he refuses, and, when one of them asks why he is taking responsibility for Niles, replies not (as might seem most compelling) that the hurt man was struck by his car, but: "This is my house." And one sees that this is, for him, his second chance to confront the men who have humiliated him; his second chance, in effect, to save his cat; and, though he is properly dismayed by his wife's willingness to turn Niles over to their attackers, that is not really what his stand is about at all. "This is where I live. This is me," he says, turning furiously even on his wife when she is reluctant to aid him. "I will not allow violence against this house."

And the terrible irony of this is not just that, unknown to him, violence has already been committed against his house, but that it is nothing compared with the violence which follows. And, further, that, somewhere during the course of that prolonged and horrendous violence, one becomes aware, as one watches him take to his task as though possessed, that he actually *enjoys* what he is doing. "Why don't you entertain Niles?" he says to his wife, winking lasciviously, when she refuses to help him, at one point dragging her by her hair just as one of the rapists had earlier. When the violence subsides, the old man's foot blown off, two others shot full blast, a fourth bludgeoned with a poker and the fifth mangled in a trap, the mathematician rights a fallen chair, and says to himself in incredulous exultation, "Jesus, I got 'em all!" (Though, in fact, it is the wife's ex-lover who has killed one of them, the second rapist, who surprises the wife upstairs, and attempts to rape her again. She calls for help—not her husband's but her lover's name—and so he, too, has his second chance to prove himself heroic in her eyes.) At the end, the mathematician drives Niles back to the town. "I don't know my way home," Niles tells him. "That's OK," his benefactor replies, his face breaking into a sickeningly knowing smile. "I don't either."

Yet even to give this much of an account of the film's features is to leave it at bare bones insofar as one fails also to suggest its film-making mastery and extraordinary beauty. No other American director now working (with the exception of Hitchcock when he feels like it), and perhaps no other who has worked since the advent of sound (with the exception of Capra at his best), edits film with Peckinpah's brilliance and precision, and the climactic section in particular, as ugly in subject matter as a work of art can be, is paradoxically beautiful as well in the command of dynamics and rhythms and the sheer stunning virtuosity with which this passage of film, of images in motion, is pieced together. *Straw Dogs* is like *The Wild Bunch* in its embodiment of this paradox, and surpasses the earlier film, I think, in the way the isolation of the violence by slow motion here magnifies it without any aesthetic softening; for really, of course, Peckinpah's film is no less stylized than Kubrick's—it's just that the style of *Straw Dogs* isn't preening and effete. And *Straw Dogs* is like Peckinpah's other films, too, in the way the actors—here Dustin Hoffman—are both used for what they bring to their roles as types and allowed to develop performances which, at least in Hoffman's case, draw deeper on their individual resources than anything they have done before. But, curiously, the film I am also put in mind of by *Straw Dogs* is *The Birds*—because of Peckinpah's technical mastery, in part, but also by both films' sense of gathering dread, and by the way the characters and spectators of both too late find themselves ensnared. *Straw Dogs* is less spacious and visually dazzling than *The Wild Bunch*; a darker, more brooding work in both mood and visual style; and probably I could say I enjoy it less than I do the earlier film. And the beginning is, I think, really somewhat too looming and deliberate in its oppressive sense of ubiquitous peril. But the later film is finally, if anything, even more complex and amazing in the way it forces one to an agitated confrontation with one's own emotional involvement in the violence it depicts. Nor does Peckinpah evade complicity with the spectator in this;[1] surely, whatever his conscious attitudes toward the violence of his films, no one can stage scenes of violence with the kind of controlled frenzy Peckinpah brings to them without being susceptible to the frenzy despite his controlling it; without, in some sense, enjoying what he does. And it is this investment of himself and attempted exorcism of his devils in his work, perhaps even more than his film-making genius, that makes Peckinpah at once so hard to take and so impossible to turn away from. Kubrick coldly lectures us that we are living in a hell of our own making. Peckinpah writhes in the flames with us, burning.

Joplin and Hendrix: A Note on the Rhetoric of Death

Mary Josephson

ROCK music, with its chains of influence and styles, its periods and innovations, concurrently developed its own version of the higher criticism, which, in its grim anal disquisitions, is the puritan reflex of rock's abandon. That rock should have been so closely accompanied by this scrupulous jailer, locking its wildness into formal prisons, is not the least of its many contradictions. But then everything about rock, from its utopian fervor to its expressionist crescendo around 1968, is slippery and elusive. To emphasize one aspect is to summon up its opposite by default. So the imposition of cerebral schema on what, to most people, was un-

From *Art in America* (September–October 1971) by permission of the author and *Art in America*.

1 It is perhaps relevant to note here the source of the film's title in Lao-tse: "Heaven and earth are ruthless, and treat the myriad creatures as straw dogs. The sage is ruthless, and treats the people as straw dogs."

differentiated noise, makes one aware of the sexual denominator to rock's heroic cycle from love to desperation—and now final amiability. The sexual theme is of course freighted with contradictions for which sexual donnés were simply a handy vehicle. It manifests itself clearly in the way rock stars present themselves.

The Beatles' charisma, on their first appearances, was classified with that of Sinatra; they were the undifferentiated locus of sub-teen dreams, and the polymorphous purity of these radiant guttersnipes emancipated everyone from the dirty world. Their willingness to be loved was a little at odds with the pulsations of their music; indeed their amiable presences finally stimulated a reflex hysteria that stood in for the transcendence they were once permitted to summon through their sound.

From the Beatles on, many performers breached the sub-teen psyche with frank sexual innuendo. Mick Jagger's famished and lascivious energy promoted a release very different from the Beatles' pellucid high. Jagger exhausted his audience by releasing ravenous passions and then abruptly transcending them (and vice versa), so that the two states blurred into each other. Audiences felt he might do *anything*. His importance, here, however is his introduction of the sexual theme. More than any of the others Jagger seems to have understood that sex contains both the possibility of transcendence and its frustration, and that to force the first was to court the second. Jagger's protean changes—from male to female, from saint to demon, from mystical union to contempt—allowed him numerous points of exit from the loaded sexual theme, which he most frequently used to reflect, but not to profoundly engage, his volatile energies. His epicene persona protected him from the sexual engagement which pushed others into desperation and obsolescence.

Particularly Jim Morrison. For any history of rock music must mark a pause at that moment in Miami when Morrison, seeking to regenerate his failing liaison with the audience, hung out his penis. Morrison, like Jagger, had used the sexual route to couple with his audience—indeed his music became the background to this. His rapid cresting and fall was annotated all along the way by sexual gestures and burlesque, of which this limp exposure was the last, and the last possible, for it displaced the symbolic and suggestive with the real thing—an act of diminishing literalism no stripper would have been guilty of. With this act Morrison not only illustrated an impotence to consummate a dream, but the degradation of the male rock singer by the lusts he released and exploited. Performers who have lost touch with themselves (and their audience—it's the same thing) are forced into parody in a destructive attempt to prolong their careers; and Morrison had placed all his nuts in this one basket. Similarly the Plaster Casters, those demented Girl Guides, stamped their imprimatur on performers by reproducing their erect phalluses—an act both celebratory and contemptuous, reflecting the single-mindedness with which groupies hunt the star into bed (and human dimension), thus licensing the projection on him of their own self-contempt. This is exactly the mechanism which woman's liberation has identified as a male prerogative.

As single-mindedly as Morrison, Joplin and Hendrix directed their performances through the sexual channel. With this difference: where Morrison had worked at seducing the audience, Joplin and Hendrix seemed to have forgotten it. Watching them perform, one was drawn into their narcissism, which, as the concert went on, became increasingly magnetic. The more Joplin and Hendrix eliminated the distance between themselves and their music, the more the music choreographed their bodies in spastic tics that sometimes made it look as if they were generating their own strobe light. It was very far away from Jagger's razor-sharp muggings; for they had accepted the invitation he had always left open: to make sex a lingua franca for everything—love, communication, drugs, utopia and angst—bringing into play all the threats of impotence and the promises of transcendence implicit in its use. Joplin and Hendrix were expressionist performers with the usual necessity to maintain a head of emotional pressure against the stylizing that repetition of emotion imposes. They suffered—particularly Joplin, the more original talent—from the most crippling contradiction of their moment: the necessity to sing of the New Jerusalem at the very moment it was being pulled out from under them. Their lyrics shunt between love-peace and a bestial vision. Hendrix was tormented by the dream of the lion and the lamb, evil and good, lying down together, and his self-image climbed to godly heights before plummeting down again.

He exploited the myth of the black man's potency and the white man's fear—which Presley had neatly put together and, after initial rejection, made acceptable (an important moment in the history of popular music in that it made the minority ethos available to white performers and a new audience available to the black). Hendrix' phantom comes and explicit jerks of the guitar had conviction insofar as they fused rock music with its sexual undertow; but there was the great disadvantage that the two couldn't be unfused again, even when he hit on the idea of achieving a climax by beating his guitar to death, and ritualizing each performance with the certainty of this release. It was, like Morrison's gesture, an admission of impotence, but done with conviction and style. Ultimately it fixed his talents in an area incapable of bearing for long rock's savage epiphanies.

Joplin's formidable personality was rooted in deeper ground—that of the blues singer as scapegoat. Her viragolike blendings of po' white trash with a veneer of blonde movie-queen glamor placed her dishevelment between reality and fantasy, despair and hope. Her generation's appropriation of the Negro style and voice salted this a bit further. Joplin was a mess, as Judy Garland was a mess; both made an appeal for sympathy by public hysteria, but both had a ballsy core that refused aid even when inviting it. The move from her raw early style to her final appearances, when it looked as if an invisible stranger was up there trying to strangle her, had the requisites for tragedy—the audience's voraciousness, the subversion of great gifts and the hint of darker energies about to be released. The latter increased as she was forced, by her expressionist and sexual bias, to play the tough babe.

By making a public sexuality intrinsic to their styles, both Joplin and Hendrix forced on sex the full burden of rock's dilemmas. In attempting to maintain the sense of emergency necessary to release their gifts, they blocked their gifts' fulfillment. For a while that impotence could be discharged by violence, even if the violence had to be exercised mostly on themselves. But here one must make a distinction necessary in rock performing—the dissociation of the music from the rhetoric of a public presence that bespoke a certain life-style, the destructive imperatives of which began, particularly in Joplin's case, to be shadowed by its orgiastic climax—death. In both cases there is a transfer of the rhetoric of rock sexuality to a tragic dimension, which to fulfill itself needed its lethal resolution.

Yet in their last work, Joplin and Hendrix, responsive to the less urgent mood around them, had lessened their expressionist intensity and brought it into line with the quieter mood of 1970. But the personas hurtled on, giving the two deaths (from drugs) the *possibility* of mythic stature. Which, between their deaths and now, has not been fulfilled. For while the music is more amiable, there is a harder mood around, one less generous in giving legendary status to the young, gifted and dead. The quasi-tragedy of Joplin and Hendrix partly resides in the fact that their sexual postures could be authenticated only by doing violence to their music; and their lifestyles could be vindicated only by doing violence to their deaths. For their deaths remain desperately artificial, and lack the rhetorical conviction that ignites the imagination. They traverse a too-familiar route—the burned-out performer, with the remaining incandescence alighting on his memory.

Nothing brings this home more than the example of a smooth and easy post-Joplin and Hendrix performer, Elton John, who turns sexual rhetoric into happy parody. Sometimes he wears a light-bulb codpiece which accompanies his beat with its pulsations. It is a cutely elegaic lighthouse marking the darker waters where Joplin and Hendrix went down.

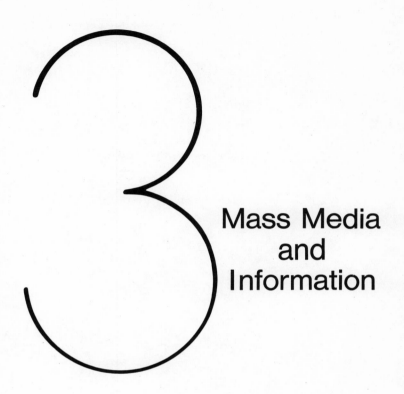

Mass Media
and
Information

I. Backgrounds and Perspectives

The mass media affect more than our cultural and emotional lives. The pictures of the world retained in our minds (and the ideas and opinions we have about those pictures) are the result of more than personal experience. They are also formed by what might be called audience experience. Even in our personal worlds, the data of our experience are often present in random, fluctuating forms; it may take the patterns we have read or heard or seen in the media to shape this data into patterns of our own— patterns which may be valid or distorting. In the public worlds—science, economics, law, government, diplomacy, war, education, even sports—the effect of the media is even stronger. For within this context, it is the media that supply both the information and the patterns that give this data meaning for us. We are members of the mass audience while witnessing events, reports of events, discussion about events, and discussion about the reports of events.

The selections in Part 3 are concerned with the reporting of this public world and the perceptions of it and opinions about it that are shaped by the media, whether through intentional persuasion or not.

In this section, C. Wright Mills provides some basic definitions and interpretations of the processes involved in the media's influence on public opinion.

In a complementary piece, Theodore Peterson is interested in defining and advocating an approach to the media that takes into account as fully as possible the nature of the processes of conveying information and opinion. It is a theory that goes beyond the concept of freedom of the press to that of the responsibility of the press to society—a concept extremely difficult to incorporate in press performance.

Mass Media
and
Public Opinion

C. Wright Mills

So, the history of the idea of public opinion has gone through the classic democratic and the totalitarian phase. Today, a third phase is emerging in American intellectual circles. With it we arrive at a sort of synthesis, the whole dialectics of which has taken three stages:

(i) Two centuries ago, before mass media as we know them today, it was thought that in a democracy the public of public opinion consisted only of small groups of people talking among themselves, electing spokesmen for their groups, who in turn talked among themselves. Problems occurred and were discussed until a public opinion was formed as to its popularly correct solution.

(ii) Then, in all industrialized countries, the mass media arose and grew to be large-scale in their coverage. When these were taken over by totalitarian parties and states, the idea arose among some students that the public of public opinion was merely the audience of these media, and public opinion merely the result of an impressment upon isolated individuals of the communications carried by radio and newspapers or movies which uphold the institutions of authority.

(iii) Today in the United States, a synthesis of these two stages of thought is coming about: both mass media and person-to-person discussion are important in changing public opinion. It is a question of which is the more important in different areas of opinion, at different times, and of just how the two, as forces causing opinion change, sometimes work together, and sometimes clash.

The American public is neither a sandheap of individuals each making up his own mind, nor a regimented mass manipulated by monopolized media of communication. The American public is a complex, informal network of persons and small groups interchanging, on all occupational and class levels, opinions and information, and variously exposed to the different types of mass media and their varying contents. There are many influ-

From *Power, Politics, and People: The Collected Essays of C. Wright Mills,* edited by Irving Louis Horowitz. Copyright © 1963 by The Estate of C. Wright Mills. Reprinted by permission of Oxford University Press, Inc.

ences at work upon those publics and masses and within them, and there are many resistances and counter-forces to these various influences. But today it is still the case that the most effective and immediate context of changing opinion is people talking informally with people. "All conversation," Ralph Waldo Emerson once wrote, "is a magnetic experiment." . . .

It was clear from the beginning that two broad sets of influences were at work in public opinion change: (1) the media of mass communication and (2) person-to-person discussion.

(i) One school, reflecting the second stage in our understanding of public opinion, believed that the newspapers and radio, magazines and movies were now so powerful and influential that they would be found to be the chief cause of changes of opinion. This school pointed out that 60 percent of the people go to at least one movie a month, 25 percent to four or more; that 50 per cent listen to the radio on an average week-day between one and three hours, and another 25 per cent listen three or more hours; that 60 per cent read at least one magazine regularly; and so on. The typical American is part of the audience for one or another of these mass media for several hours every day. With such wide coverage it seems only natural that the mass media would exert a great influence on opinion change.

(ii) The other school of thought admitted this, but they pointed out that after all not all people were very much exposed to the mass media, and moreover, that most people certainly spend more time talking with others than they do listening to radio or reading magazines. How do we know, they asked, that the mass media are *effective* in changing opinion. We should not forget what we said at the beginning: although most newspapers, for instance, are for the Republican party, most voters have for sometime voted for the Democratic party. However, they pointed out, the various mass media differ on many topics—despite the increased monopoly in newspapers, radio and movies, there is still considerable competition of ideas and opinions between the different radio commentators and magazine writers. One radio commentator is very much for President Truman's views, another is very much against them and says so to a million radio listeners a day.

Now, one thing that is well known about communication habits is that people of one or the other opinion tend to select the mass media with which they generally agree. Insofar as they can, Democratic party members listen to Democratic radio commentators, and Republican party members read Republican newspaper editorials. This self-selection of audiences means that the chief influence of the mass media is not really to *form* or to *change* opinion but to *reinforce* a line of opinion already held, or at least already well known.

Yet, here, in our sample were people who *did* change their opinions about various topics between our first and our second interview. Therefore there must be other influences than the mass media at work in these changes. There must, in fact, be some news of resistance to the contents of the mass media.

There were other arguments for the greater influence of mass media, and other arguments for the greater influence of person-to-person discussion. But nobody knew for sure. You can only know for sure if you get your own facts together and study them carefully. Well, that is what we had done in the Decatur study. Which of these schools of thought turned out to be correct?

So far as our study goes, the second is more nearly correct than the first: in the last analysis, it is people talking with people, more than people listening to, or reading, or looking at, the mass media that really causes opinions to change. Of course, the mass media do have an influence; in fact, we were able in this study to measure the relative influences of mass media versus talking to other people in changes of opinion. In every topical area of opinion that we studied, the personal conversations weighed a great deal heavier and more effectively than the mass media in the opinion change.

Now, it is an old sociological rule, supported by many statistics, that social position exerts an influence on opinion, and this despite what goes on in the mass media and despite what opinions are held by those in upper positions of power. In spite of the attempt of those handling the formal means of communication to manage opinion, there exist many counter-opinions especially among the middle and lower classes.

These tokens of resistance to media or counter symbols, do not themselves depend upon any formal media. In fact, they go precisely against the media, operating to guide the further exposure to the media and to refract and even reject its messages.

Now, it might seem, as both liberal and Marxian theory holds, that a rational understanding of their position would lead individuals to reflection, and hence to opinions rationally commensurate with their position. Yet from what we know of false consciousness, this is not the typical way social position comes to influence opinion. It is not by reflection and argument that opinions are adapted to interests, or at least that is not a major way. We also know that "interests" select the media contents to which people are exposed; and different opinions and slants are perpetuated and reinforced by this self-selection. Yet there are many opinions held that have never been carried by any formal media. So neither interests nor reflection fully explains class differences in opinion.

No doubt to some extent counter-opinions rest upon personal experience and deprivations, but for them to effect opinion they must be generalized at least on a rudimentary level; this work is done, and the counter-opinions sustained, by informal face-to-face publics, which thus act as a sort of legal underground to the formal communications system.

We have come to expect people in lower economic levels to hold different opinions, to vote somewhat differently, and to feel about local matters in a different way than do those on top. Underlying this fact is the further fact that in the American community there is a certain autonomy of opinion formation and change, a certain independence from those in charge of the key institutions of the political economy.

The range of social contact available to the individual is limited by his class and social position, and thus he is exposed to only one or two circles of opinion within his stratum. It is upon what is said and believed in these circles that his opinions feed. Such person-to-person influences, within delimited social contexts, form and sustain opinion. In every area of conduct and opinion, these pressures of social consensus, these minute daily influences of personal contact are at work.

Let us examine more systematically the available means of resistance to the mass media, from the standpoint of an individual on the receiving end. How can the single individual resist their media? or, what in his situation enables him to resist them?

(i) So long as the media are not completely monopolized, he can play one off against another; he can compare them. The more competition there is among the media, the more resistance the individual is able to command. But do people play one media content off against another? (a) We know that people select media which carry those contents with which they already agree. There is that kind of selection from prior opinion. Very few seem to search out counter-statements from alternative media offerings. Given radio programs and magazines and newspapers often get a rather consistent public; then they reinforce their messages in the minds of this public. (b) This idea of playing one medium off against another assumes that the media have varying contents; it assumes genuine competition. Although this is not always true, variations in media content do provide the individual with a leverage by which to resist media persuasions. Regardless of what the local paper says about Decatur labor, the radio commentator in talking about Detroit labor can provide food for the individual's opposition to the paper. Nevertheless the trend of mass communications is on the whole against its use.

(ii) The individual can compare what is said on the media with his own personal experience and direct knowledge of events. This would seem a good democratic and pragmatic way of resisting or rejecting or reinterpreting media. But two things must be recognized: (a) Obviously the individual cannot experience all the events and happenings that are discussed and displayed on the media. He only has experience of an infinite fraction of them. That is quite obvious in the case of international and national and even local political events; but we have evidence that in the field of consumer opinion, where direct experience with the objects discussed is readily available that such direct experience plays very little role in changes of opinion. (b) At any rate, even if he has direct experience, it is not primary, not raw, not really direct. It is mediated and organized in stereotypes. It takes very long and skillful training to so uproot an individual that he sees things freshly, in an unstereotyped manner. One might suppose, for instance, that if all the people went through a depression they would all "experience it," and in terms of this experience, that they could all debunk or reject or at least refract the media. But the experience of such a structural shift has to be organized, to be interpreted, if it is to count. The kind of experience that might serve as a basis for resistance to mass media is not experience of raw events, but experience of meanings. The fleck of interpretation must be there in the experience if we are to use the word seriously. Experience is socially organized; the capacity for it, socially implanted. Often the individual doesn't trust his own experience until it is confirmed by others or by the media. Canons of acceptability, standards of reality, are not gained by direct experience; for direct exposure to be accepted, it must not disturb beliefs that the individual already holds; and, it must relieve or justify the feelings that often lie in the back of his mind as key features of ideological predisposition.

(iii) There is a third kind of resistance operation: individuals may gain points of resistance against the mass media by the comparison of experience and of opinions among themselves. These discussions of the primary public are at once the spearhead and the master context against which resistances may develop. They give the individual support; they feed his assurance for his criticism. The undercover network of informal communication in the primary public may select and reflect, debunk or sanction what is said in the formal media. And everybody who talks with anybody is part of this network.

But it is reasonable to suppose that certain types of people having certain social positions and relations with others may be more important than others in channeling the flow of talk and mediating and shifting the impact of the formal media. The existence of these opinion leaders is one major reason why the flow of influence may go on within and between the structures of power, why opinion is not subject to its overweening dominance. For they rally those who by their informal discussions manufacture opinion. They are the radiant points, the foci of the primary public. This primary public is a resistor of media and the pressure upon the individual: at the same time it protects, it constantly molds. If there is any socially organized intelligence which is free to answer back and to give support to those who might answer back, it must somehow be this primary public.

No centralized agency of power effectively controls the informal discussions which go on among people in various sections and classes of the city. The network of discussion and the flow of influence which move through the streets and over the fences of the city are not formally organized by any centralized power. The ebb and flow of influence go on within the framework of power, with its organizational infiltrates and its control of communication agencies. But the informal flow of opinion is still autonomous and cannot be said to be weak. From the standpoint of the manipulator, as from that of the resisting individual, the primary public is crucial.

But the primary public is a complicated affair. The people who make it up are, in the end, different individuals. Everyone knows, for example, that some individuals regardless of their class or social position, talk more than others, and that some talk to more people than do others. Also some people's expressions of opinion are listened to more and are more respected than others'. These common sense facts lead us to the idea that among the various publics, there may be "opinion leaders"—people who influence others more than others influence them.

We wanted to spot such opinion leaders among the people in our study. Now, we had asked every one we interviewed a set of questions like these: has anyone recently asked your advice about any political matter? Do you think, in general, that you are asked your opinion more or less frequently than other people you know? And so on. The answers to several such questions, scattered through the interview, were combined into an index, and with this index we were able to spot the people who were opinion leaders. Then we began to study these opinion leaders in order to see how they differed from those who were not opinion leaders.

One thing we found out that we think is important to understanding how American public opinion changes is that opinion leaders are more exposed to the mass media of communication of all sorts than are the opinion followers. They listen more to various radio programs, and read more magazines, and so on. What seems to happen is that these opinion leaders pick up opinions from the mass media and pass them on to other people in face-to-face conversation. But that is by no means the end of the story.

You remember that people tend to select the radio programs and editorials and magazine articles with which they already generally agree. There is thus a self-selection of the audiences for these various media and their competing contents, which means that the media reinforce existing opinions more than they cause changes of opinions. Now, opinion leaders are no different than other members of the media's audience in this respect.

But listening or reading differs from talking with others in two very crucial respects: (1) you can turn off the radio, put down the magazine; if you don't like what it says, you can select another program or another magazine. But you can't do that so easily when you're talking with other people, or when you overhear them at your place of work or in a neighborhood store; very often you have to listen, at least for a while, even if you don't agree. There is less self-selection according to already agreed-to lines of opinion in personal conversation than there is in media exposure. (2) Formal media also differ from personal talk in that you can't answer back the media so easily as you can answer back another person with whom you are talking. You can, of course, write a letter to a magazine or call up a radio station on the telephone, but not so readily and not with the immediate result as you can tell another person you don't agree with what he says and why. There is a give and take about private conversation that just can't exist in mass media communication.

Now these two differences mean that even though opinion leaders—those unofficial concentration points of informal influence—are more exposed to media and try to pass on these opinions to others, these others are in contact with other opinion leaders who in turn are exposed to other selected programs and articles. So it is just here in the give-and-take of persons talking with persons, brought about by counter-influence, that differences and clashes of opinion occur. And it is in these conversations, more than in any other way, that opinions are actually changed.

So the media are influential, directly, and indirectly through opinion leaders there is a clash of opinion occurring in conversations between different opinion leaders and between all the people who are in contact with different opinion leaders and different media offerings. For in these conversations, these informal and unofficial relationships of persons talking with persons, public opinion is most effectively formed and changed. . . .

Social Responsibility: Theory and Practice

Theodore Peterson

The professional attitudes that a reporter for the Buffalo *Courier-Express* and the writer for *Pravda* hold toward their craft have been shaped in part, whether they realize it or not, by the assumptions of their societies. So are their public's expectations of the functions of the press. For the ideas that any society holds about what the press should be and do arise from the way in which that society has answered certain basic questions: What is the nature of man? What is the ideal relationship between man and the state? What is the nature of truth?

Both our theory of the press and our theory of democratic government

© Copyright, 1966, Gerry Gross.

rest upon the answers we have come up with to those questions. We have taken our answers from a number of theorists of the seventeeth and eighteenth centuries whose ideas added up to the libertarian philosophy.

Behind this philosophy was the Newtonian idea that the universe is a vast perpetual motion machine, going on timelessly according to certain laws of nature. The Creator had set man down into this rationally planned universe and then withdrawn. But man could work out his own salvation because his Creator had given him reason. Applying that reason, man could discover the timeless laws of nature which govern the universe and bring his institutions into harmony with them. By so doing, he could build the good society.

All men, those early thinkers also believed, are born with certain natural rights. To enjoy those rights to their fullest, men formed goverments, their badge of lost innocence. Before men first got together to establish governments, the libertarians thought, men lived free and equal in a state of nature. In such circumstances, they held their rights precariously; there was ever the danger that the strong bullies among them might take away their liberty and their property. So men by common consent formed governments to protect their property and to make sure that their natural rights were not curtailed.

The best way the government could assure men of their rights was by leaving the individual as free as possible. Hence, according to the libertarians, the best government was that which governed least. If the government betrayed the liberties of the people or failed to protect private property, the whole deal was off; government was at an end, and the people had the right and duty to establish order anew.

Those early libertarians, who had long seen church or state hoard truth as its monopoly, argued that truth does not derive from any temporal authority, but from man's intellect. Man can find truth by using reason; he is not to be directed or led to it. By feeding his free mind from the open marketplace of ideas, man can discover the all-embracing truths which unify the universe and everything in it.

The libertarians, then, had their answers to the basic questions mentioned earlier. What is the nature of man? Man is a perfectible creature of reason, born free, who wishes to know truth and be governed by it. What is the ideal relationship between man and the state? The state should interfere as little as possible in the affairs of its citizens. What is the nature of truth? Truth is the key to understanding the laws of nature and the good society. It is not the proud possession of the few, but the property of all men if they will but use their reason to find it.

From those same answers came our traditional libertarian theory of the press. Under it the press was to have only wide and scattered boundaries to its freedom—laws against obscenity and libel, mild laws against sedition. Virtually everything the press carried served the cause of truth. If what it carried was false, men would reject it; if what it carried was true, men would accept it. More often, of course, man would find some truth amidst falsehood, some falsehood amidst truth. But as long as he had free access to all information and ideas, he would eventually find the truth he sought. The system carried its own built-in correctives against those who would lie and distort and suppress. For although some men might find it profitable to lie, other men might find it profitable to expose them. And over all was that most powerful safeguard of all—men's rationality.

For several reasons, the libertarians held no truck with censorship before publication. For one thing, censorship violates man's natural right of free expression. For another thing, censorship provides those in power the means to retain their power and to deprive citizens of their freedom. For still another thing, it might temporarily hinder the quest for truth by weighting the balance in favor of one cause or another. Moreover, censorship implies a fear of ideas—a fear unwarranted, given man's rationality and his desire to know the truth.

Libel laws, however, were acceptable. On the one hand, they protect the individual from unjustified defamation. On the other hand, they allow the press to make its contribution to the marketplace of ideas even if it later must answer for indiscretions.

Traditional libertarian theory gave the press arguments for justifying the publication of almost anything it wished. Any interference was an interference with its natural right of free expression and with the search for truth. Furthermore, the theory provided the press with a rationalization for giving the public what it wants. What seems more in accord with the libertarian tradition than the often-made remark that readers vote with their coins every time the editor brings out a new edition?

Over the years, as libertarian theory evolved, theorists and practitioners alike ascribed six social functions to the press. Most of these functions have firm roots in theory, although the last one or two were merely grafted on:

1. *Enlightening the public.* The press should be a major source of the information which man needs to form his own opinions and should keep him in touch with the opinions and ideas of others.

2. *Servicing the political system.* Under a system of popular government, citizens should know how the business of government is conducted on their behalf. They should be aware of the important problems and issues. The press is an important means of providing them with the information and ideas they need.

3. *Safeguarding personal liberties.* The press should keep a close watch on government, that ever-dangerous foe of freedom, and sound the alarm whenever the citizens' rights are infringed.

4. *Making a profit.* The press, to be free, should be beholden to no single individual or group. Hence it should earn its way in the marketplace.

5. *Providing entertainment.* Almost from its beginning, the press has entertained as well as edified. Few persons have questioned entertainment as a legitimate function, although some have been disturbed by what they regard as the emphasis given it.

6. *Servicing the economic system.* Through advertising, the press can contribute to a dynamic and expanding economy by bringing together the buyers and sellers of goods and services. It can also serve the economy by carrying much of the information on which the decisions of business are based. . . .

Meanwhile, however, some newspapermen were preaching a different kind of journalism. In the mid-nineteenth century, there were such men as Horace Greeley, who thought that the newspaper should ignore the trivialities of the penny press and the political bondage of the partisan press. The newspaper should not be politically neutral, but neither should it owe allegiance to any political party or faction. Rather it should furnish political leadership by setting the public good above duty to party. At mid-century, too, there were men such as Henry Raymond of the New York *Times*, who thought that the newspaper should be free of party but not of principle, that it should give the readers the broadest possible editorial coverage, and that it should actively promote the community welfare. Later in the century there were men such as William Rockhill Nelson of the Kansas City *Star*, who saw the newspaper as an aggressive force for civic betterment.

In all of this there were traces of a growing sense of social responsibility, for the publishers were acknowledging that a newspaper had some duty to the public.

In the new century, the professions of public responsibility became more numerous and more explicit. In 1904 Joseph Pulitzer, that noble old lion, blind and no longer stalking the pulp-paper jungle, took nearly forty pages of the *North American Review* to defend his proposal for the creation of a college of journalism. But his article was more than a plea that education for journalism be given academic sanctity. It was his call that the press should put public duty above duty to the counting-room. "Commercialism," he said, "has a legitimate place in a newspaper, namely, in the business office. . . . But commercialism, which is proper in the business office, becomes a degradation and a danger when it invades the editorial rooms. Once let the publisher come to regard the press as exclusively a commercial business and there is an end of its moral power." He had a clear idea of the sort of men needed to staff the nation's press. They were to be courageous and moral men who would resign rather than sacrifice their principles to any business interest, men who, if they could not keep a newspaper from degrading itself, at least would not be a party to the degradation. They were to give the newspaper its ideals; and, as Pulitzer put it, "without high ethical ideals a newspaper not only is stripped of its splendid possibilities for public service, but may become a positive danger to the community."

Let me mention just two twentieth-century developments which strike me as underscoring the point that American publishers have come to hold a different attitude toward press freedom than formerly.

One was the voluntary adoption of media codes as standards of performance—the Canons of Journalism of the ASNE in 1923, the production code of the movie industry in 1930, the radio bradcasters' code in 1937, and the television code in 1952. By the very fact of adopting those codes, the media have linked freedom with responsibility. True, those codes may have little binding force. One may argue that their standards are inadequate. Some of them probably were inaugurated to forestall government intervention. Grant all of that; yet every one of the codes explicitly acknowledges the media's duty to perform in the public interest, however variously that interest is defined.

Moreover, apart from the Canons of journalism, those codes reflect a break with traditional libertarian theory in other ways. Three of them—those for movies, radio and television—regard man not as the creature of reason that libertarian theory saw him, but as essentially immature and susceptible to moral corruption. Hence ethical performance for those media seems to consist less in informing than in promoting public morals.

Second is the relatively recent campaign to gain access to information because of "the public's right to know." Social responsibility is implicit in that campaign, in which the press pictures itself as an organ of the people, working to gain access on their behalf. In another significant respect the campaign departs from traditional theory, which was basically negative. Libertarians assumed that, granted freedom, some people would talk, some would listen. But traditional theory, being negative, provided no lever for prying open the lips of persons who would not talk, since it was inconceivable that they would not. Indeed, it is hard to read into our negative Constitutional guarantee of free speech—"Congress shall make no law"—any means for forcing the mute to speak.

Publishers today, then, seem to agree with Grove Patterson, who in 1955 defined the social responsibilities of the American newspaper (the term was his own) as making certain that the people shall know; providing interpretation; including views representative of the people as a whole, not just those of special interests; and raising standards of American journalism.

Editors and publishers are not the only ones with a hand in fashioning the social responsibility theory. In its most complete and coherent form, the theory has been stated in several books issued in the mid-1940s by the Commission on Freedom of the Press headed by Robert M. Hutchins. The Commission's basic report said little that has not been said before or since by publishers themselves, although they might not agree with all of the logical extensions of the Commission's ideas.

Few newsmen would really disagree with the Commission's requirement of the press: to provide "a truthful, comprehensive, and intelligent account of the day's events in a context which gives them meaning"; to serve as "a forum for the exchange of comment and criticism"; to give "a representative picture of the constituent groups in society"; to help in "the presentation and clarification of the goals and values of society"; and to provide "full access to the day's intelligence." In fact, Grove Patterson in the talk just mentioned gave those as the social responsibilities of the press, although he expressed them somewhat differently.

Practitioners even seem to agree with social responsibility theory in some of its philosophical breaks with libertarian theory, among them these:

1. The negative freedom of libertarian theory is inadequate to modern society. (The attempts of the press to gain free access to information reflect this view.)

2. Freedom carries with it responsibility. (The various media codes of performance reflect this view.)

3. Man is not a wholly rational creature; he is not so much irrational as lethargic, and his reluctance to use his reason makes him ready prey for special pleaders. (The various media codes except the Canons also reflect this view. And so does the great bulk of advertising that all of the media carry.)

So far social responsibility is still more theory than practice. But it is by no means all theory: In a good many places, it has spilled into practice. . . .

From all that I have said so far, we should see that the press today is operating not only in a different environment from that of a century ago, but also under a different conception of freedom. The final shape that social responsibility theory will take is still to be evolved and remains in large measure up to the press itself. Reviewing the history of the past century, newsmen may feel either helpless or complacent—helpless because press performance has been determined to large degree by the nature of the system, which itself has been shaped by social, economic and cultural forces outside of their direct control; complacent because they have had an important part in shaping social responsibility theory. They should feel neither. On the one hand, while the nature of the system in part governs the performance of the press, men still have a good deal to say about the nature of the system; on the other hand, social responsibility is still more theory than fact, and newsmen still have much work to do in molding its future form.

One of the greatest deeds that the press could perform, I think, is helping its readers to accept an idea that the press has already accepted—

that responsibility goes with freedom. If the press links responsibility with freedom to publish, then should not the reader link responsibility with freedom to read and listen? In short, does the citizen in a democratic society have the right to be misinformed, ill-informed or uninformed? The press has begun to see its own responsibilities, but it has done precious little to make readers see theirs.

Before it can, the press must get rid of its curious notion, shared by the public, that what it sells is a commodity like detergents, depilatories and dog biscuits. There is a vast difference between the products of the AP and the A & P, and newsmen really know there is, even if they and the public sometimes talk as if there isn't. Consumer choice is one of the blessings of the supermarket, and if a customer wants to stock his wire pushcart with pretzels and beer instead of proteins, milk and leafy green vegetables, his dietary eccentricities are no concern of the merchant. But the diet of the reader is of concern to editor and publisher. They should be far less quick than at present to keep their shelves of beer and pretzels filled with a superabundance of items, because that is where the traffic is, and far more prone to move their nourishing foods.

When the issue is survival, the citizen, however he may grumble, accepts certain obligations such as bearing arms or producing them. Even for the smooth operation of a peacetime democratic society, the citizen accepts certain duties which he may not like, such as serving on juries and paying taxes. When the issue is both survival and the smooth functioning of a democratic society, the citizen certainly should be as obliged to be informed as the press is to inform him. He has the duty to study the facts, unsettling as they may be; weigh ideas which do not necessarily match his own, disturbing as that may be; and put his basic assumptions up for challenge, impossible as that may seem. The press is accepting only half of its responsibility if it does not help him to realize that he must.

Since the uncomplicated time of Ben Day, editors have been justifying whatever they have found profitable on the grounds that the readers want it. All too often, some of them have rationalized part of their content on the shaky grounds of public interest. Editors may say that in their heavy coverage of crime and trivia they are simply reporting the seamier and brighter sides of society, something readers have a right to know. They may say that in running pictures of mangled corpses in crumpled cars their civic-minded intent is to reduce highway fatalities (although I have seen no evidence that fear is a deterrent to those bent on getting killed). And presumably they would say that in informing their readers of the every bowel movement of an ailing President they were practicing reporting in depth. What God lets happen they are proud to publish in the public interest, although it is amazing how many things God lets happen that they overlook.

In all of this there is a big difference, I submit, between public interest and public curiosity. If the intent behind much of what the press carries is really public interest, then there seems something wrong, not so much with the subjects themselves as with the editorial approach.

Social responsibility theory puts strong faith in the conscience of every newsman. It expects him, in following it, to do duty not only to himself but to society as well. On his everyday assignments, he cannot dodge an ethical decision on the grounds that the boss, not he, edits the paper; for that is a little as if Polly Adler's piano player should say that what goes on in the other rooms of the establishment doesn't concern him, that his dedication is to Bach.

II. Individual Media

Each of the pieces in this section deals separately with the workings, problems, and trends of one of the four main conveyors of information and opinions.

Christopher Driver's consideration of the functions of the newspaper and the audience needs it fulfills draws some helpful implications from the information and opinion encounter of audience and newspaper; it also relates this direct public information function to other intellectual and emotional needs that the newspaper caters to.

The veteran media interpreter Roland L. Wolseley in his piece examines current trends and problems in the periodical press and relates them to the basic functions and contributions of magazines to society.

Harry J. Skornia, as seems rather typical among interpreters of television news coverage, is far more critical of the current performance of TV news and special events programs. His classification of his complaints into a series of cogently defined trouble spots is useful as a starting point for any approach, positive or negative, to the news on television.

Radio commentator Edward P. Morgan speaks from personal experience of the present dilemmas facing radio generally, and news coverage in particular, but reaffirms nonetheless the great potential this medium is still capable of fulfilling.

Why Newspapers Have Readers

Christopher Driver

From the consumer's point of view, four main functions of a newspaper can be isolated. It structures people's time; it orders their experience; it provides detailed, up-to-date, accurate, and accessible market information; and it satisfies in some degree the human appetite for novelty (which is not to be confused with news).

After twenty years' addiction to newspapers and ten years' direct involvement in them, I feel that the time-structuring aspect of newspaper-reading is the one most apt to be neglected by journalists themselves. Obliged to read several newspapers as soon as they are published (though I do know one journalist who always reads two-year-old newspapers on his way to work and finds that time is a splendid selector), they do not easily enter imaginatively into the circumstances and preoccupations of their readers. The men whose business it is to advertise newspapers know better: hence those ads, humiliating to journalists, which try to sell one London evening rather than the other not by content but by size and shape. Journalists only consider their readers in accepting, more willingly than dons or politicians, the discipline of making themselves comprehensible, relevant, and short. Thus, Arthur Christiansen used to ask *Express* men to write for "the man in a back street in Derby," and it was good advice. Any newspaper, however serious, values highly the man on the staff who can put himself where the reader sits, who knows instinctively when it is necessary to explain or amplify and when a running story is its own explanation.

But even sympathetic identification of this kind may not be enough without an understanding of the role which the process of newspaper-reading plays in the customers' lives. Newspaper-reading, I believe, is essentially a pastime, as defined by Dr. Eric Berne in his *Games People Play* (1966):

a series of semi-ritualistic, simple complementary transactions arranged round a single field of material, whose primary object is to structure an interval of time.

Excerpts from "Why Newspapers Have Readers" by Christopher Driver, by permission of the author and *Encounter*.

Dr. Berne was of course referring to inter-personal transactions—the basic good-morning-how-are-you's of social intercourse. Newspaper-reading, by contrast, is perhaps more often used as a device for avoiding social intercourse. But the ritualistic, habit-forming element remains. English people read an extraordinary number of newspapers, and are extraordinarily loyal to their own. The *News Chronicle*, in the years when it was succumbing to managerial sclerosis, was barely competitive, but it was much mourned on its demise. The *Guardian*'s recent difficulties evoked numerous offers from readers to buy two copies a day instead of one. (How could one explain to them that if they liked to send us the money, that would be fine, but that printing an extra copy, thanks to the industry's Erewhonish economics, got us almost nowhere?) The reason for this loyalty is that a man reading his morning paper in a tube is conducting a daily ritual transaction with a corporate personality whom he may well find more congenial than either the wife he has just left at the breakfast table or the colleague he is about to greet in the office. For the wife herself, trapped in her suburban box, the newspaper may be the sole adult personality whom she encounters during her working day. It provides—I quote an actual testimony—"ever-renewed, never-fulfilled hope of finding that morning the dress, the idea, the book, the recipe which will dispel, for that day at least, all sense of personal inadequacy. . . ."

It is therefore very important that the perusal of the newspaper should structure the right interval of time; not too little, not too much. This reflection saves me from what would otherwise be professional resentment when people complain in times of advertising stringency that their paper is "thin" and that there's "nothing in it." If it is well edited, a paper is often more compact and readable at 12 pages than at 24. But that is no good if it structures the wrong amount of time. In the leisurely, automated future every day might begin to feel like half an hour at the hairdresser's with only the Saturday edition of the *Sun*. This situation is pressed to the point of nightmare in David Campton's play *Little Brother, Little Sister*, which depicts a boy and a girl and the old family cook living in a deep shelter years after the nuclear holocaust, with only a page from the vanished *Daily Express* to serve as Bible, encyclopaedia, and householder's vade-mecum.

Lord Thomson's newspaper-manufacturing policy, first with the *Sunday Times* and now with the *Times*, rests on the psychological assumption that the danger of surfeit is too remote to care about, at least when you are the market-leader. Certainly the appetite grows by what it feeds on, and one of the current danger signals for daily newspapermen is the sight of fellow passengers in the tube still ploughing through the Sunday review sections on Tuesday morning. For those British papers which have little chance of ever tapping really rich advertising markets, the main hope must be that the threshold of resistance to a huge weight of advertisements, pushed apart by tediously padded-out editorial, is lower here than in America.

(The Sunday edition of the *New York Times*, weighing about three pounds, is made to be thrown away almost unread. A single copy, incidentally, uses enough newsprint to supply the present consumption of an average African for twenty-five years.)

It is equally important that the newspaper should stimulate the reader without actually outraging him. People vary in the extent to which they are prepared to be contradicted by their newspapers, and newspapers vary in their willingness to risk such contradiction. Newspapers have the advantage over television in that they are expected to provide a corporate point of view, pungently expressed, but for sound psychological reasons they generally reflect rather than mould the unspoken opinions of their readers. The purpose of the ritual transaction between the newspaper reader and his chosen partner is mutual stroking rather than cuffing. The reader uses it to locate himself in a particular sub-group of society, holding an identifiable social ethos. (Hence the use which sociologists are able to make of newspaper-readership as a class denominator.)

This brings me to the second function of a newspaper, which is to order our experience, and through our own, the experience of the tribe. As Marshall McLuhan remarks in *Understanding Media* (1964), "The first item in the press to which all men turn is the one which they already know about," whether it is a football match, a concert, or a mining disaster. This is true even—or perhaps especially—when the reader is convinced before he turns the page that the account of the event in which he has been involved will be inaccurate or hostile. It is true even when people have not themselves directly experienced the event in question, but only lived through it vicariously on television the night before. It is fortunate indeed for newspapers that this is so. Television has changed, though not enough, the style in which events already known to the public are recapped and amplified for newspaper readers in the morning. "Depth analysis" has become more fashionable, and there has been one more trivialising change. Between television and radio shutdown and the time in the early hours when the final editions of popular papers go to press, almost any remotely newsworthy event is given disproportionate prominence because it restores to these newspapers their vanishing function of telling the reader something he does not know. (The *Times* news team, we are told, will be "making their maximum effort from 9 p.m. in the evening until the small hours of the next morning.") When everything that happened after the last editions of the evening papers was hidden from the public until the morning, comparative news values could (at least in theory) be a little saner.

However, television has hardly changed at all the actual criteria by which an event is adjudged worthy of newspaper notice. One recalls two moments in the last three or four years when people in Britain felt tied to their television sets by a news event: the assassination of President Kennedy and the engulfing of the Aberfan school. The same people's appetite for newspapers was magnified by their viewing. This pattern is repeated in far less momentous happenings, and this is why a national paper's news editor is generally indifferent when beaten to a story by radio or television, to which all his readers will have had access, but furious if beaten by a rival newspaper, which the vast majority of his readers will never pick up. The reason, says McLuhan, is central to any understanding of media: "Experience translated into a new medium liberally bestows a delightful playback of earlier awareness." It occurs to me that the preaching of evangelical revivals was based on this insight. You were converted, and then through another medium—the pulpit, or the congregational hymn—you heard over again what it was like to be converted.

Naturally, the newspaper does more than simply feed back in an agreeable way a man's own direct or vicarious experience. Other people have had other experiences, and out of the ruthless, highly wasteful process of selection that takes place in every newspaper office there emerges a pattern which appeals precisely because it is a pattern, a triumph of the human mind over anarchy. Each individual experience has been incorporated like a tile into a mosaic whose final shape some individual editor or small group has already partially visualised. A person's choice of newspaper will depend not only on his preference for words or pictures but on the degree of patterning which his mind and personality are capable of absorbing and retaining. To the *Express*, everything comes as a surprise, a present from the inexhaustible galaxy of random happenings. The excitement of the *Express* on its good days stems very largely from its ability to mirror the way its readers themselves experience events as unpredictable in onset, inexplicable except through an identifiable person's fault or virtue, and once past forgotten. The strength of the *Times* or the *Telegraph*, on the other hand, lies largely in their ability to find room for the day's small, unobtrusive contribution to a long-running story that from time to time will burst on to the front pages. This practice reduces the apparent randomness of the world's events, and satisfies the educated, conservative reader's longing to find order in his universe.

It has also been noted by both McLuhan and Daniel Boorstin that newspapers, by the inquiries they make and much more by the very technology they employ, create the communal experience which they exist to describe. Both writers quote the "announcement to readers" in the first American newspaper, Benjamin Harris' *Publick Occurrences Both Foreign and Domestick*, published in Boston on 25 September 1690. Faithfully reflecting the 17th-century Puritan view of Providence, the journal was "to be furnished once a month (or if any Glut of Occurrences happen, oftener). . . ." Since then, Professor Boorstin comments, "We need not be theologians to see that we shifted responsiblity for making the world interesting from God to the newspaperman." "Today's press-agent," says McLuhan, "regards the newspaper . . . as a painter does his palette and tubes of pigment; from the endless resources of available events, an endless variety of managed mosaic effects can be attained." (Boorstin less charitably calls these effects "Pseudo-events.") It seems a pity that in England native commentators—like Mr. Raymond Williams in his book on *Communications* (1966)—were so slow in advancing beyond such obvious aspects of newspapers as the proportionate space which they devote to different types of news and features.[1] Newspapermen are always quarrelling among each other about these proportions, but academic critics of the press would serve the consumer's interest better by evolving techniques for source and form criticism of newspapers, and by enabling ordinary people to calculate which story is a pure discovery, which a pure public-relations gambit, and which an adroit piece of news-management by a politician or businessman or civil servant with a much better story to hide than the one he has chosen to tell.

However, it is only fair to take into account, as Boorstin and McLuhan do, the technological factors which compel us to order our communal experience in these roundabout, apparently shady, ways. It is not essentially the consumer, but the technology, that is insatiably hungry for round-the-clock space-filling in newspapers, television, and radio. I irritated Sir William Haley, in a group discussion the other day, by suggesting that the dominant motive in every newspaperman's mind was nothing more spiritual than the compulsion to "feed the machine." If I had not thought I was right before, the *Times'* new business section would have convinced me of it. But as nature abhors a vacuum, so does radio abhor silence and a newspaper an unfilled column. The consumer's interest is quite different. At the same discussion Mr. John Lawrence described visiting a pre-electric Aegean island where time had so imprecise a meaning that anything before lunch—whether soon after dawn or just before noon—happened in "τό πρω." He then returned to London to help organise B.B.C. broadcasts to this island and others like it, knowing that the simple act of broadcasting at a stated hour information which the inhabitants wanted to hear would quite quickly alter their whole pace and concept of existence—a concept which, had they had the option, they might well have liked to preserve. By a development of the same process, the wire-service reporter, serving thousands of different media in different cities or continents with different publishing times, knows that his "story" is never complete. He has to make it look new at each stage for each customer. He has to proceed—as preachers used to be advised to proceed—by saying first what is going to be said; then reporting what has been said (making something, if possible, out of the difference between the expectation and the event); and then stimulating, often quite artificially, some "reaction" from a third party to what was actually said. These infinite regressions, says McLuhan,

---

[1] See also Raymond Williams' essay in *Your Sunday Paper*, edited by Richard Hoggart (*ABC* Television and University of London Press, 6s.).

are the result of electric speed, which in diplomacy "causes the decisions to be announced before they are made in order to ascertain the varying responses that might occur when such decisions actually are made." Indeed, publicity in newspapers—which old Foreign Office hands still find rather distasteful and unprofitable—has in one sense become a substitute for the secret diplomacy which our new sense of human contiguity makes so difficult to operate successfully. The real "open diplomacy" would be conducted person-to-person on television, with global satellite relays; but we have not yet evolved the tribal leaders who could cope with a *panchayat* of this kind; instead, they are reduced to sending each other delphic signals via newspaper columns.

I named the third function of a newspaper as "the provision of detailed, up-to-date, accurate, and accessible market information." Without more technical knowledge than I possess it would be absurd to enlarge on this side of my trade, but it is from this area that the death sentence on newspapers, as a product of a particular epoch of civilisation, will sooner or later be pronounced. British newspapers began as gazettes and advertising sheets before they acquired anything that we would now recognise as an editorial personality, and it is obvious that the press could not survive in its present form if there emerged an alternative means of easy universal access to such diverse daily items of information as the Classified Ads and the Stock Market quotations. Television has eaten some way into the reservoir of display advertising—the iconographic jam on a text newspaper's bread. But it cannot match the newspaper for masses of detailed material, and the chance of reference back to a missed item.

It is clear that newspapers are entering a period of industrial change whose effects will be more far-reaching than the invention of the rotary printing press. Industrial relations permitting, papers should be able by the end of the century not only to print electronically in a dozen different centres simultaneously, but also to abandon printing in the conventional sense. The completed newspapers could drop from a television-like machine at the local newsagent's or even at home if the machine were adaptable to enough other domestic functions to be economic. The cumbrous, expensive, monopolistic and therefore anti-libertarian procedure for manufacturing a product on a large scale and distributing it by courtesy of the railways and W. H. Smith would then have been successfully by-passed, and at first sight it seems that if a "minority" newspaper like my own can survive until technical changes like these begin to work in its favour, civilisation may yet beat Lord Thomson. But progress may yet beat us both, for it is doubtful whether the end product would be much like a newspaper as the school of Northcliffe understood the word. In the computer, the newspaper as a medium of information has another and perhaps more serious rival than television. Once information can be stored, automatically up-dated, and instantly retrieved at the turn of a bedside dial, it becomes unnecessary to buy and peruse a newspaper, in which nine-tenths of the "hard" information is of no interest to a given individual looking for a particular job or stockprice. Once it becomes possible to pre-select the kinds of information—whether editorial or advertising—that you actually want new every morning, the market for a "mosaic" product of wide general appeal will surely shrink.

Newspapers, I argued earlier, can be thought of as corporate personalities able to structure a man's time as agreeably as any of his other acquaintances, but they were able to develop to this point because they had a particular economic usefulness and took a particular technical form. The question for modern newspapers is whether or not they have in their evolution created a demand for them that is self-perpetuating. If this is so, it will be because newspaper-reading has become an aspect of leisure rather than work—in short, because newspapers have become "mere" entertainment.[2]

This entertainment is, of course, dependent on the fourth task which newspapers perform for their readers: that is, daily satisfaction of the human appetite for novelty. This appetite should not be confused with an appetite for news, in the old newspaperman's sense of "a Glut of Occurrences." So many professional myths surround the purveying of what newspapers call news that it is hard for someone involved in the business to see the distinction clearly. In the myth, "news" is a spontaneous event which comes as a surprise to the reader. But modern news, as we have seen, is less and less spontaneous. "Man bites dog" is far more interesting—to a newspaper—if the man is already (in Boorstin's phrase) "well known for his well known-ness." Nor is newspaper news very often a genuine surprise, for by the time it is read it is already known to some or all readers, either through the electric media or through the previous week's controlled news leaks.

From the consumer's side, too, the distinction between novelty and news needs to be drawn. Most people cannot bear very much novelty. The apostle Paul, a conservative Jew by upbringing, realised that the people of Athens were unusual in always wanting "to hear or do some new thing." In a modern society, whose economic health depends on frequent, compulsory, and often unwelcome innovation, the consumption of "news" has for millions become a substitute for, even a protection from, the experience of novelty at the level of personal thought and action. There is in fact a pornography of news which—as *Time* magazine (and, later, Mr. Clive Irving) discovered—exerts almost as strong a pull on the reader as pornography of the traditional Fleet Street sort. The currently fashionable staple of this pornography is a bout between two or more public personalities. The outcome is known in advance. The bout is described in exhaus-

---

[2] "Newspaper reading . . . has all the earmarks of play," says William Stephenson in *The Play Theory of Mass Communication*. University of Chicago Press, 1967.

tive detail, relished for its own sake rather than for its (assumed) fidelity to what actually occurred. It ends, for the reader, in psychic release, conveyed through the twin illusions of participation and omniscience. It is democracy adapted for masturbation.

Does this, then, mean that newspapers, as a medium of social exchange, are entering a dying phase? Not necessarily. Shifts of function are endemic to media. Fifty years ago, problems were stated by the newspapers—by campaigning reporters like W. T. Stead—and solved at booklength by the diligence of people like the Webbs. Today television is beginning to be the problem-stating medium, and because it demands instant replies, newspapers have to devote energy to solving these problems rather than to uncovering new ones (which when uncovered, are anyway instantly picked up and given real popular immediacy by television).

The public fuss earlier this year over the television programme *Cathy Come Home* is a good example of the new balance of power as it works in practice. The documentary play said nothing that a reasonably attentive reader of the serious liberal-left press did not already know. But this apart, it had an impact very similar to the combination of Florence Nightingale and William Howard Russell—social reformer and wire correspondent— in the Crimea. McLuhan's comment on that episode is very apposite:

> The electric gives powerful voices to the weak and suffering, and sweeps aside the bureaucratic specialisms and job descriptions of the mind tied to a manual of instructions. The "human interest" dimension is simply that of immediacy of participation in the experience of others that occurs with instant information. People become instant, too, in their response of pity or of fury when they must share the common extension of the central nervous system with the whole of mankind.

Newspapers will only remain indispensable in the future as long as they realise that their bread-and-butter function will be to tidy up, amplify, and canalise these instant human responses; doing for media more immediate than themselves the job which books did (and still do) for newspapers. Naturally, "Gluts of Occurrences" will continue to occur, sometimes in a form which lends itself much better to typographic than to televisual treatment. Confidential documents will still be obtained and published, to the embarrassment of governments. But the genuine novelty at which serious newspaper journalism aims will gradually become more and more a question of perceiving and communicating connections between known facts, rather than of uncovering new information. (The difference between a good and a bad newspaper library is worth at least half a dozen reporters.)

This process will not be complete until television has learnt how to report and present events as easily, ruthlessly, and unfussily as the newspaper operation now does. This in turn depends partly on structural reforms in broadcasting organisations, partly on technical developments like miniaturisation of camera equipment. But the direction is clear, and in a few years' time, it will be no reproach to a newspaper that it is "a daily magazine."

The American Periodical Press and Its Impact

Roland L. Wolseley

While this article was being written the world of the periodical press in the U.S.A. was the maker of front-page news. One of the country's oldest and most famous magazines, *The Saturday Evening Post*, died of malnutrition, i.e., of lack of advertising revenue. At its death, almost its 150th birthday anniversary, it had more than three million subscribers and newsstand buyers; a few months before it had in excess of six million, but half the subscription list was dropped in an economy move that was unsuccessful.

Too much circulation is a disease from which a number of American magazines have suffered in the past two decades. On the surface it appears to be a paradoxical situation. Generally speaking, in all print journalism it has for years been the rule that the higher the circulation the higher the advertising rate and consequently the greater the income. This formula still is followed, by and large. But an enormously expensive magazine to manufacture and distribute by the millions of copies each week (in recent years every other week), as was the *Post* and as were such other giants of circulation that succumbed at mid-century (*Collier's, Coronet, American,* and *Woman's Home Companion* were among them) must enlarge the formula to include 'if costs of production and distribution are kept in ratio'.

Once, too, magazines and newspapers could take for granted that if they offered an advertiser the readers he wanted they could count on him to buy the space to reach those readers. But today there is a new type of competitor: broadcasting, and particularly television. It can tell an advertiser that he can reach the mass of the people through television sets, of which in the

From *Gazette*, 1969, 15, No. 1, p. 1. By permission of *Gazette* and the author.

U.S. there now are more in use than there are motor cars or telephones. Since television's arrival as an advertising competitor, two decades ago, magazines of mass circulation have had problems.

All this about the failure of widely-known American magazines may leave the impression that the periodical press is in an unhealthy state. But this conclusion has no basis in fact. On the contrary, the health of this industry as a whole is sound. The animal kingdom was not destroyed, centuries ago, when the dinosaurs, and almost all other huge animals, died out. Similarly, some of the giant magazines have not been able to adjust to new competition, new tastes, new climates of opinion, and a changing economic order. But there are at least 20,000 periodicals in the U.S.A., and the handful of huge-circulation publications is only a small, if widely-publicized, minority.

To understand the American periodical press and its impact it is necessary to see it whole. Only a few generalizations can be made about the entire industry, for it is in many segments. In fact, neither the industry itself nor the public at which it is aimed agrees on what that industry includes. To most Americans the word *magazine* (the term *periodical* is not much used) connotes a publication, weekly or monthly, intended either for all persons, as is *The Reader's Digest*, or for a large portion of the population, as is *McCall's* or *Ladies' Home Journal*, both multi-million circulation periodicals for women. And many persons employed in this consumer or general area of magazinedom take the same narrow view. In fact, the most widely used reports and studies of the industry usually cover only the consumer books (in the jargon of the publishing business a magazine often is called a *book*, to the utter confusion of outsiders), as if the thousands of small periodicals did not count. This situation came about, of course, because the bulk of the dollar investment in advertising space is in the consumer area: these magazines have been the big money makers. Actually, the majority of the consumer magazines do not have large circulations despite their broad content.

Just what kind of publication the others are considered by the owners of the consumer magazines is not clear. Those others exist, just the same, and are far greater numerically and in the long run have a different and perhaps greater impact.

Depending upon how you count them, the consumer magazines may number as few as three and as many as 900. Perhaps *The Reader's Digest*, with 27,000,000 circulation, is the only true American consumer magazine left. The figure 900 is reached by including those that attempt to reach a wide public. The majority have small circulation and little advertising. They print trivia. They include sensational, sexy adventure magazines for boys and men, various fan publications for the worshippers of cinema idols, sports stars, and other entertainers; various collections of thin articles about hobbies, and numerous attempts to catch the teen-agers' coins with magazines telling the girls how to apply cosmetics and the boys how to become a professional football player.

The remaining 19,100 are for the most part the actual core of the magazine press. That figure, in round numbers, includes about 10,000 known as industrial periodicals but more commonly called house organs or company magazines, and are ignored by the entrepreneurs in the business because they do not accept advertising and are given to readers, who are employees of a company, its customers, its dealers, or its prospects. Also, in the 19,100 are 2,500 business magazines, that is, commercially-published periodicals catering to the business world and ranging from the austere *Fortune*, published by Time Inc., to the highly specialized *Roads and Streets*, issued by the Reuben H. Donnelley Corp., which has 17 others equally specialized. And it also includes about 400 published by associations, embracing the *National Geographic* and the *Journal of the American Medical Association*, two of the most profitable enterprises in the business.

To these can be added about 1,500 that deal with religion, 300 magazines of education at different levels, 200 about labor, and the remaining thousands that are devoted to such subjects as science, specialized sports, all of the arts, and various juvenilia.

In America, it appears, if three or more people get together their first act is to form a committee and their second is to launch a publication; generally it is a magazine.

The periodical press in the U.S. therefore is overwhelmingly composed of specialized journals. Yet those who trace the press's current fortunes insist upon judging it by the fate of a minority of large periodicals hardly typical of the entire industry.

The situation is made even more complicated by the realization by some of the larger publishing companies that issue consumer magazines that the specialized field is a less risky one and that a mixture of operations is desirable. Cowles Communications, Inc., for example, is a widely diversified firm that issues several mass magazines (including *Look* and *Family Circle*, with 7,750,000 and 6,000,000 circulation, respectively) but also has a clutch of business periodicals which it calls 'Magazines for Industry'; these include *Candy Marketer, Food & Drug Packaging, Bottling Industry* and nine others. Another large firm, Condé Nast, is best known for its popular *Vogue, Mademoiselle,* and *Glamour.* But only insiders realize that it also issues *Analog,* a science fiction periodical, and *House and Garden,* whose function is obvious from its title. Similarly, the Hearst firm, one of the ancients of American magazine journalism, has *Good Housekeeping* as well as *Motor* and *American Druggist,* among others, in its group of more than a dozen.

The picture of the industry must include certain trends. One relates to advertising. In each of the past four years the gross income from advertising has exceeded one billion dollars. Year by year the intake was higher. Actually it is more, for those who do the adding include mainly the consumer magazines. But at the same time the number of pages of advertising sold has decreased, the decline in 1968 from 1967 amounting to 2 per cent, for example. There has been some question about the soundness of an industry where such a situation exists. But it is a debatable situation and of concern, perhaps, largely to businessmen who insist on quantity, who measure success by numbers: number of subscribers, number of readers, number of advertisers, numbers of pages of it sold, and numbers of dollars brought in. They are so fascinated by numbers that they neglect quality and fail to see the danger of the numbers game, as did *The Saturday Evening Post* and several other magazines, before it is too late. Within the bitterly competitive consumer magazine business however, the worry about losses in amounts of advertising sold is justified, if for no other reason than that buyers of general advertising space tend to place their orders with periodicals already swollen with copy. They give little thought to any obligation to support a publication that may be in temporary distress so as to keep competition alive, if not a voice heard. In other words, the successful publication becomes still more successful and its rivals are killed off by advertisers who flock to the leader.

The worshippers of numbers stand in strong contrast to one of the great American editors, Frederick Lewis Allen, who was at the helm of *Harper's*, for many years a leading serious magazine. Writing in his magazine in 1950, Allen said: 'Our circulation . . . is a practically microscopic figure when set alongside the circulations of the monster slicks and digests. But it includes so many people who write, speak, teach, edit, manage, and govern that we may perhaps be permitted to remind you that the ignition system is a very small part of an automobile.'

The American periodical press is an industry which is fundamentally sound so long as printed communication is vital and has not been replaced by electronic means of communication. It also is a highly segmented and diversified industry. Few generalizations therefore can be made about its impact as a whole. Easier to point out are the effects of the various types of periodicals. The main obstacle to a clear, broad answer is that tools or techniques for the measurement of effect or influence still are rudimentary. Some progress has been made in noting the effect of single elements that can be isolated: certain advertisements or specific articles, for example, but little reliably beyond that. Some studies have been made which indicate effects within the segments, however, and these can be put on the record for what they may be worth.

The impact of the American periodical press also has been technological and social. The large, mass-circulation magazines have influenced the smaller magazines, which in many instances seek to imitate their appearance and to emulate the high quality of their printing, layout, and make-up. They also have influenced magazines around the world. Europe, for example, is given to publishing magazines resembling *Life* and *Look*, and almost no heavily industrialized country is without its imitator of *Time* (*The Link* in India, *Elseviers* in the Netherlands, *Tiempo* in Mexico, *Der Spiegel* in Germany, and *L'Express* in France, for example).

The social effect has to do with the discharge or failure to discharge its social responsibilities. These responsibilities the magazine press shares with all communications media, printed or electronic. They include the obligation, in a political democracy such as is the U.S.A., to provide the people with a fair presentation of facts, with honestly held opinions, and with truthful advertising. All but the subsidized periodicals hold—or seek to hold—to these goals within a certain framework; that of the business order, the private initiative, profit-making system.

As business institutions, commercial magazines, consumer and specialized alike, have influenced the progress of the business world by stimulating the desires for products and services on the part of readers through advertising and editorial content. This result has in turn affected the living standards of readers, influencing their decisions about how they dress, what they eat, and how they use their spare time. The enormous consumption of cosmetics by American girls and women is in part due to the years of commodity advertising in magazines for those readers. The sale of motor cars is heavily influenced by the advertising and special editorial content about new models.

What might be considered the official concept of the influence of the general magazines has come from the Magazine Advertising Bureau of the U.S.A. Placed first among general effects is the shaping of public opinion. 'The national magazine does not have the spot news function of either the newspaper or the radio,' MAB said. 'But being edited with deliberation, it is read with equal deliberation, and therefore has the unique ability to form a *mature* public opinion, nationally.' It also is a reflector of American life or what the owners think is American life. Said the MAB: 'Life is not the daily headlines of the newspaper, nor is it the artificial dramatics thrown out daily, hourly by radio. The solid values of the lives of millions of American families are reported by the national magazine, unsensationally but vividly and accurately, in articles and fiction, in pictures and illustrations.' The contrast with television, even sharper, might have been added.

James Playsted Wood, a magazine official and writer of several books on periodicals, reminds us that the magazine is read more persistently than any other medium, is less perishable, and is read attentively. It provokes results, receives reactions. Much magazine material later goes into books and motion pictures; reprints are made.

'The character of a given magazine limits its audience,' he says, 'thus, to some extent, the spread of its influence, its educational force, its persuasion to belief, and possibility to individual or social action.'

Wood properly qualifies his generalization by using the word *given*. The effects of the comic magazines are unlike those of the literary, and within the specialized magazine world the effects of one technical journal only in a superficial way resemble those of another.

Led by *The Reader's Digest*, condensed material and pocket-size magazines have stimulated popularized reading by the middle-class public, have spread certain social positions and attitudes, and have increased demand for short, quickly-read publications. The digest made the portable magazine among the most popular of those published, one of them being of world influence.

With magazines of seven and eight million circulation setting the pace, the women's group, with which may be associated the service and shelter books (*Woman's Day* representing service, with its many recipes, and *Better Homes*, the shelter group) has been principally responsible for influence wielded by advertising departments on homes and families of the middle class. They have to some extent standardized housekeeping tools, widened the variety of cookery, introduced or popularized certain habits, such as more frequent bathing and shaving, use of deodorants, and hair coloring, and called attention to books, motion pictures, and art works, considerably broadening their effect. Not a minor result has been the introduction of fictional stereotypes; most heroes and heroines of fiction in women's magazines seldom are realistic, although there is a trend away from that in a few. Consumer magazines try to exert influence through their advertising and editorial policies. *Esquire* in 1968, after the assassinations of Dr. Martin Luther King Jr. and Senator Robert F. Kennedy, adopted a policy of accepting no gun advertising of any kind. This decision came after a campaign against gun advertising launched by *Advertising Age*, a business weekly. *McCall's*, with a circulation of more than eight million, on the day of Senator Kennedy's assassination, stopped its presses and inserted a two-page editorial calling on its women readers to support stronger guncontrol legislation, help stop excessive violence on broadcasting programs and in films, boycott certain toys, and follow other policies.

The confession magazine, more and more an imitator of the slick ones in content, has had a changing influence. In its early days it played a psychological role: it offered spiritual release for uneducated or immature readers (whether adults or adolescents) enabling them to experience adventures of the more daring and unorthodox without personal risks. Now, except for a surviving group offering stories of sex adventures and crime detection, it is achieving on its own economic level a standardization in reader habits and practices similar to the women's slicks.

The circulation and advertising leaders among men's magazines have turned away to some extent from tales of wartime bravery to tales of bedroom exploits, holding as admirable man's sexual domination of women and gratification of his dreams of wealth, power, and comfort. They encourage their readers to a hedonistic philosophy of life and to be primarily patrons of entertainment.

The religious magazines, less given than they once were to regularizing moral concepts, now are influencing their readers to apply their religious principles to social concerns as well as to personal conduct. Some have helped bring social movements into existence, such as the civil rights groups, and mustered support for social legislation in various areas of human activity: conscientious objection to war, better housing, and employment opportunities for minorities, for example.

American literary magazines have started movements, erected critical standards, and founded schools of criticism, introduced new writers, maintained the following of older ones, and provided an outlet for work not marketable to the public through general or consumer periodicals.

Magazines for juveniles have had definite effects, since their readers are in formative years. A youngster's heroes once were provided almost solely by books and magazines; today radio, television, cinema, and recordings also have strong influence, perhaps stronger. The religious juvenile publications have built concepts of right and wrong in human conduct and of individual responsibility at home and in the church or temple. They have aroused loyalties. The secular juveniles in more recent times have been simplified versions of magazines for grown-ups. Their effect has been at once to create little adults and to encourage youthful independence and also standardization of mores among adolescents. The comics have appealed to childish imaginations so effectively, and with so much questionable content, that they have been treated as social phenomena to be studied as seriously as are educational practices.

The effects of specialized magazines are vertical rather than horizontal. A clothing publication or a food magazine affects the profession, industry, business, or other group it serves by conveying news created by the group, evaluating trends within, providing an outlet for ideas, and stimulating business through advertising. Business periodicals have taken dramatic stands to correct what they consider evils. The company magazine (house organ, as often dubbed) has established itself as a bulwark or dam against ideas that its publishers deem undesirable or has helped to stimulate business.

These influences and effects have not escaped criticism. The adverse critics say that the magazines, particularly the consumer type, are too much inclined to give the public what it wants, they deprive the public of the fullest knowledge of facts and ideas; through advertising content they stimulate desires for possessions that cannot be gratified by the average reader's income. Nor is that all the criticism. The critics go on to say that the periodicals present only conventional or ultra-conservative viewpoints, that they evade their duty to provide leadership in solving social problems, that they are time-wasting, distracting the reader from more valuable uses of his leisure, and that they knuckle in to advertisers.

The favorable critics, on the other hand, counter that magazines have helped produce the high standard of living in the U.S.A. through their advertising content, have helped to stimulate mass consumption of goods and, thereby, mass production; have therefore contributed toward the lowering of the cost of living; that they have merchandised, as one proponent has put it, new ideas; and that they have played a part of importance in every national crisis, whether it be flood, war, depression or recovery from such disasters.

As with so many arguments, this collection is not a clear case for either pro or con. To begin with, most critics of either side are talking exclusively about the consumer magazine, and, as usual, overlooking all the rest, which as we know are in the U.S.A. fifty times as numerous, and in some instances just as influential. Accepting the consumer scope, some parts of each set of criticisms may be accepted as true.

A business society such as that of the U.S.A. prevents the majority of the magazines, consumer or specialized, from fulfilling the role of the institution wholly devoted to the welfare of society as are, for example, the church, school, and the professions of medicine and nursing. It is left for the periodical press to play a part short of full devotion to the common-weal.

Television and the News: Some Trouble Spots
Harry J. Skornia

. . . The redefinition or mis-definition of news which television has unwittingly imposed upon the nation, as a result of its many unique and unsuspected powers as a visual medium in which action and motion attract most powerfully, is one of the least clearly perceived effects of television. The criteria of news significance which have emerged have changed greatly

From *Television and the News: A Critical Appraisal* by Harry J. Skornia. Palo Alto, Calif.: Pacific Books, Publishers, 1968, pp. 32–47. Used with permission of the publisher.

from pre-television days. Some of these criteria, and non-news practices resulting from them, deserve separate identification:

1. Emphasis on the superficial. On October 12, 1960, Russian Premier Khrushchev addressed the United Nations. He banged the podium with his shoe to punctuate what he said. This punctuation was reported by the news media. How many Americans can recall what he said, or what was being debated at the time? How well did television, which showed this scene several times, report the dramatic effect that what Khrushchev *said* (on the subject of colonialism) had on the representatives of new African nations? Before the days of television, would newspapers, too, have magnified this shoe-thumping to such a point that it displaced what Khrushchev *said*, or would pre-television reporters not have had different reportorial standards for reporting this event? While most American correspondents, under the pressure of television competition, were reporting only Khrushchev's shoe-thumping, African and Asian delegates, who in a few years would not even remember whether Khrushchev wore shoes or not, would recall what he *said* about how communism meant more rice, milk, steel, electricity, and education. As long as shoe-thumping makes more news than the pronouncements it punctuates, as it does so generally on television under present conditions, history will continue to take Americans by surprise again and again.

U.S. networks have often boasted of their programs on the Near East, Korea, and other parts of the world. We would hope such programs may increase more in quality than in quantity. For in many instances, such as ABC's program on Korea a month before students rebelled against President Rhee, no suggestion of the latent and explosive omens of things to come was provided. Visual aspects of Korea, a strange troubled land, were reported with little depth. In what respect such programs are greatly useful for genuine understanding, excellent as they may be in production standards, is not clear. Certainly they still have far to go. The same was true of ABC and CBS programs on the Middle East, which seemed to see little danger of trouble only a few weeks before violence burst forth. The scenery, parades, and mug shots were splendid. But substance was thin. Are such superficial reports, which lull rather than awaken or warn, not more a disservice than a national public service?

Perhaps the most urgent danger concerning the foreign news situation is that while Americans are ill served, they *believe* they are well-informed. For this is what they are told. Network and trade association "studies" every few months "prove" how well-informed television keeps its viewers. TV management and public relations departments, particularly, promote this view. But it is contrary to the warnings of the newsmen themselves who know better. Walter Cronkite, among others, has said that if, as surveys show, 55 per cent of the American people get most of their news from TV, then

> . . . fifty-five per cent of the public is inadequately informed. . . . It is impossible by the spoken word to communicate all the information that the individual citizen needs. . . . We are charged with a responsibility which in all honesty and candor we cannot discharge. . . . We do such a slick job that we have deluded the public into thinking they get all they need to know from us.

The temptation to glance at a problem, comment briefly on it, and consider that "coverage," leaves much to be desired. Problems cannot be grasped when given such brief review. The impression that they have been covered is conducive not to action but to smugness or passivity on the part of American viewers. More seriously, since an adequate analysis of cause and background would take too much time by management standards, the news is usually simplified by finding scapegoats for events. The fact that the delinquent may have been partially created by slums, unemployment, poor schools or no schools, racial or religious persecution, or drunken parents is assumed to be of no interest. A news service characterized by these types of blindness, exclusions, discontinuities, astigmatisms and by such superficial coverage, however visually exciting or entertaining, does not provide adequate news.

2. Editorial avoidance of anti-sponsor, anti-business orientation. Distinguished journalists like Eric Sevareid, Gunnar Back, Howard K. Smith, and the late Edward R. Murrow have repeatedly pointed out that the conditions under which they must work give a one-dimensional view of news, and give the lie the same prominence as the truth. What is needed is analysis, and the time to explain and discuss. But most networks forbid such analysis or allow too little time for it. There is, of course, much disguised editorializing on behalf of business, sponsors, and commercial values. One commentator has said that analysis is acceptable to the extent that it agrees with the viewpoint of television managers and sponsors. When it differs from what they want, it is called editorializing and is banned.

The peculiar and intimate nature of the electronic media and the way in which news and non-news are intermingled, make non-news as well as news programs editorial. Many so-called institutional advertising programs provide examples of non-news, but editorial, uses of television.

The very selection and balance of programs generally, of course, reflect a kind of editorial judgment. Commercials, with their loaded words and psychological implications, are editorial in effect. The way announcers speak, as well as the words they utter, constitutes editorial comment. Pictures selected, and those rejected, depend on editorial judgment. . . .

3. Firstness and recency as news criteria. Among the principal criteria of news which have come to predominate in a television age is that of being first—of scooping the competition. By these standards, "fast news is better news." Recency comes to have a value of its own. In this system of values the second phase of a crisis in a given country is likely never to be heard because "something new" or totally different and unrelated has happened more recently somewhere else. Continuity and relevance are replaced by other values. Emphasis on firstness results in both discontinuity and lack of planning or coherence in news handling and understanding.

In his address to the International Conference of Journalists in 1964, referred to earlier, the U.S. representative, Robert Manning, noted:

> . . . the all too-common phenomenon of important developments being "authoritatively" reported and analysed for a curious public and officialdom before the developments have emerged from their cocoons and sat in the daylight long enough even to be properly classified. . . .

> . . . more interest in what is *going* to happen than what in fact *has* happened. . . .

Commenting on the problem raised by Manning, Jerome Aumente observed: "The rush and superficial fullness of news reporting (which) leaves the modern man with hardly time to notice the day's vital developments before a new flood of fragments overwhelms him the next day. . . .

4. Preoccupation with gadgetry and celebrities. In his Elmer Davis Memorial Lecture February 15, 1966, David Brinkley urged an end to the "star" system for news reporters. Several passages from this address are admirable statements of television's problems as a news medium:

> Journalism, well-practiced, requires time for reading, thought, reflection and study. It requires time to get about, to see, to listen, to talk to people, and then to reflect on what has been said and heard.

> It cannot successfully be combined with the time-consuming, taxing and fatiguing trappings of the star system.

> It may be that Huntley and Cronkite and I and a few others are the last of a type. . . . The world and the news of it grow more complex. . . . And the time when one man can give it to them is coming to an end. . . . Television's ancestor, the movies, promoted stars because they were selling

romance and sex and adventure. . . . Television . . . ought to be developing an identity of its own, a coherence, a clear sense of itself and its place. Not what stars it can offer, but what it itself is. . . .

When it does . . . it will have its own institutional, or corporate, status of integrity and stability, free of the artifice of show business. And it will then have grown up.

Meanwhile, however, the star system goes on, and emphasis on celebrities rather than historically significant events is preserved.

As might be expected in a medium which is admittedly show business, as Brinkley and other newsmen have ruefully noted, there is a heavy preoccupation with gadgetry. This view of TV and radio news leads to the use of a wide range of sound effects, whistles, echo chambers, space sounds, vibrations, buzz saws, oscillators, predictions, alleged exclusives, recordings of news tickers, opinions of ignorant celebrities and members of the public on the most specialized subjects, and other similar habits. Trained by such practices, television viewers, it appears, have come to judge newscasts by excitement and other *entertainment* standards, rather than by substantive news criteria. The impression which foreign visitors receive of what is considered "news" on American television or radio has been criticized often, as noted earlier in this chapter.

E. B. White, in his classic story, "The Crack of Doom," recreates a typical network coverage of a hospitalized scientist. Coverage is achieved by placing reporters at various places in the hospital while others are in planes, diving at and passing by the hospital window behind which he lies. A heroic newsman is killed when his plane crashes. This calls for other planes to cover the crash, as a simple story is escalated by broadcast practices and is blown up out of proportion.

With control of newsmen, procedures, and policy in the hands of the kind of individuals who are likely to label as "good show" the type of coverage E. B. White describes, we come very close to what might be termed Hollywood news standards, instead of journalism. In such an environment, it is not too surprising that the falling of government or tragedies in which millions may be involved, are left unreported if Frank Sinatra decides to take a swing at someone, or take a young bride, or if Elizabeth Taylor and Richard Burton appear in any conspicuous public spot. Television and radio news media then cease to report news; they become tools for the indulgence of the public in the entertainment sense.

In a speech to the American Society of Newspaper Editors a few years ago, the late Adlai Stevenson recalled a period of great crisis for the United States. Khrushchev was in India; Mikoyan was in Cuba; the French had just exploded an atomic bomb; the United States had just discovered the missile gap. What was most of the "news" on TV about? Baseball;

Jack Paar's flight to Hong Kong; the family problems of several Holly-wood stars; and political accusations and counter-accusations of American politicians. Is preoccupation with show business and celebrity values not a dangerous practice for a news medium?

5. Quantity and expense as criteria of excellence. Since the superiors of most news directors are not journalists, the effectiveness of the news job being done by television and radio is usually "proved" by quoting quanti-tative criteria which are their stock in trade: costs, ratings, number of personnel engaged, number of pieces or tons of equipment used, what a "great show" it was, how much income the networks sacrificed, value of time "given," and so on. Quoting how many millions of dollars coverage cost, or how many hundreds of people are used, however, is not necessar-ily a valid way to measure television's news effectiveness. Sometimes a single man speaking simply may communicate more than the most expen-sive documentary or team production. Few great reporting successes, in fact, are traceable to the efforts of crowds of so-called newsmen. Most, instead, are the results of the efforts of single fine journalists, left free to do their jobs without being hampered by the taboos, orders, or requirements of salesmen, advertisers, or business magnates.

In the field of international news, especially, television and radio net-work executives would have the people of America believe a remarkable job is being done. This job is "proved" in terms of how many correspon-dents they have overseas, how many "direct reports" are used, and so on. Equating the job done in terms of dollars, bustle, and numbers, a quantifi-cation of quality, is characteristic of present network leadership. But it seems to deserve to be challenged as valid criteria. As a result of emphasis on quantity, distance, numbers, and expense, broadcast news becomes a flood of occurrences, reports, and stories. Many people are busily hurrying back and forth. Correspondents rush back and forth by jet. Cars crash, rushing films to planes. Thousands of feet of film are being used. Hundreds of people are being interviewed. Huge expense accounts are approved. Hundreds of news personnel are pushing each other aside to scoop each other daily. But is this the way news should be measured? I think not.

6. Giving people what they want. One of the attitudes of station manage-ment which seems to this writer to violate the meaning of news most flagrantly is the philosophy that broadcasting should give people what they want, in news as well as in other programs. This concept requires closer examination if its full implications are to be understood.

The Communications Act speaks of "the public interest, convenience and necessity." A person's needs are often quite different from his desires. There is a vast difference between reporting the truth, which may or may not be pleasant, and telling the people what they want to know, or know

about, which may or may not be the truth or the whole truth. There is also
a great difference between what is to a person's interest and what is to his
liking, just as there is a difference between the real *need* which the word
hunger describes and the *desire* for something, possibly harmful, which the
word *appetite* describes. Most critics acknowledge that people do not
know what to expect of broadcasting as a news source except as broadcasting itself has instructed them in what is news, what they have a right to
expect, and what the electronic media are capable of providing.

Information or news about any subject, by the very act of being broadcast, generates interest in the topic involved. Supply is not merely shaped
by demand; demand is equally created by what the media supply, and by
the latent appetites awakened. Likes and interests can no longer be considered as innate. They are bred and developed by the media. What will result
in highest profits rather than in the greatest good has recently come all too
often to dominate value judgments about what to broadcast. This can be
as dangerous in the news field as it is in nutrition or medicine. For an
editor or publisher to follow majority appetites in news selection is to
reduce to meaninglessness the profession of journalism. Men and societies
must be told when their houses are on fire, or their children dying of
malnutrition, whether or not that is what they wish to hear. John Q.
Public, given a choice, of course would certainly rather not hear about the
growing power of Communist China. But to fail to tell him is neither
responsible journalism nor operation in the public interest; it is a violation
and evasion of both.

Several responsible newsmen and editors have indicated what use they
think should be made of ratings. If the people know little about *international news*, such editors say, they consider low ratings, or low readership,
a challenge to do *more*, and work *harder* to make international news vital
and interesting—not to *give up covering* international news. Such is the
kind of guidance that "what the people want," as compared to what they
need, would seem to offer responsible journalists. In TV, low ratings are
generally used either to cause or to rationalize dropping or de-emphasizing
whatever is rated. This practice, surely, should not be applicable to news.

Democracy must place certain needs ahead of appetites. To select news
on the basis of "what the people want," or ratings, or any extraneous
values is to destroy the meaning of news. If news meant no more than this,
a long line of distinguished American journalists would not have dedicated
their lives to it.

7. Misleading or neutralizing by other techniques. There are several practices in the handling of certain kinds of facts, evidence, and statistics which
seem to have developed peculiarly in broadcast journalism. This should
not be surprising since in commercial TV and radio, claims and counterclaims, "evidence" and contrary evidence, so dominate the environment in

which news is placed. One such practice is the "leveling" of values or evidence in such a way that the trivial and the great, the urgent and the unimportant, are presented as of equal weight. This perhaps grows out of desire to avoid favoring one sponsor over another. The lie and the truth are given the same prominence. A few "antis" or fabricated authorities, with the help of public relations agents, can be amplified by TV or radio to sound as numerous and qualified as thousands of scholars and such specialists as chemists, dentists, doctors, or lawyers. On almost any subject someone who "thinks otherwise" can be found and cited to equal or neutralize the expert or specialist. By what clues can the listener or viewer tell which is the real expert? A sort of objectivity which equates quantity with quality, as if any fifty words were equal to any fifty others, or any speaker were as good as any other, prevails not only in broadcasting but also in other media which must compete with it today more and more. This appears to have dangerous consequences in the production of confusion or indifference of public opinion, whether deliberate or unintentional. How many citizens are restrained from legitimate action as a result of being neutralized by "evidence" presented in the media as if it were valid, rather than merely intended to preserve the status quo, or to confuse the opposition? What are the social and political effects of such practices? Certainly great care should be taken to insure against such practices becoming more widespread, consciously or deliberately. The consequences for decision-making are too great.

8. Fragmentation and discontinuity. Some of the consequences of firstness and emphasis on speed were noted earlier. Left until now, however, is an analysis of the extent to which these practices lead to fragmentation and discontinuity as characteristics of broadcast news as a whole.

If an item started yesterday, and was mentioned then, it usually is considered as having been "covered." Fewer listeners and viewers than one would wish write to stations to ask: "Whatever happened to——?" There is simply not time enough under present practices, nor are records generally kept (in TV or radio, in contrast to newspaper morgue practices and "tickler" files) of *continuing* developments, to be sure the whole story about any one item mentioned is ever heard. Consequently, historical processes are too often lost sight of, and treated as of no interest. Instead of keeping us up to date on what is happening, however slowly and gradually, in all fields of human endeavor such as politics, commerce, science, education, religion, aviation, medicine, law, labor, conservation, communication, transportation, and so on, television and radio news seems to have become rather a fragmented listing of isolated accidents and acts of violence and abnormality without apparent causes or explanation, hanging in space. One of the dangers of this approach is that reporting events without background or cause gives an impression of fatalism to history. That slums or poor educational facilities or unemployment, or the use of alcohol or certain drugs may be the causes of the crime or accident reported is all too rarely examined. Snippets of discontinuity proliferate in a plethora of confusion.

9. Rigging. Another all too common characteristic of news presentation as now practiced is *rigging*, not too dissimilar to that used on quiz programs. In world news roundups, networks go through the motion of a direct report, whether it is needed or not. If the "direct report" from Hong Kong fails, however, the anchor man can generally report as much and as adequately as the man-on-the-spot, or perhaps more. As in quiz shows, he "has the answer" all the time. The "remotes" are often rigged up and staged largely for show. To view news as something to be "rehearsed" and then "put on" in this sense is not a news but a showmanship practice.

Television and radio practices, by their power, then come to be copied in other media as well. A young reporter at New York University, who did a biography of Kim Novak, tells how she got Miss Novak on the phone and had her describe the room from which she was speaking. The reporter then wrote the story as if *she* herself had actually been there. This is of course a technique used for years by TV and radio newsmen in "You Are There" type re-creations and documentaries. In the co-existence of reality and fantasy within news departments many dangers arise which have so far had too little attention. Whether space shot coverage is real or by "animation" comes to be irrelevant. Whether programs are live or prerecorded, actual or "enacted," all come to have effects—and dangers, when labeled "news" or said to be the product of a news department. When such news standards and criteria begin to be adopted by the other news media in order to compete with television and radio and the new pressures they bring with them, the need for adoption by the latter of criteria which take into account and clearly identify significance, truth, and other real values, becomes obvious. Present criteria of television news selection and presentation, thus viewed, seem overdue for revision.

One aspect of *rigging*, less within than *about* news, arouses special concern. In statements of networks and stations regarding the amount of news broadcast as compared to the amount of entertainment presented, we read repeatedly that 25 per cent or more of a network's time is devoted to news department offerings. Besides overlooking the fact that most of these broadcasts contain advertising often taking up to 10 or more per cent of this time, several other essential facts are concealed by such claims. A quick review of the principal problems involved would be useful at this point.

Because television and radio are evanescent media, it is difficult for the public to check on them or to tell how *much* news, if equated in terms of newspaper column inches, for example, our vaunted "complete newscasts" contain. As much as three thousand words (or picture and film equivalents) of solid news appears to be considerably above the average available daily from most stations, if we exclude repetitions on successive newscasts, and non-news items.

Any reader or observer who cares to use a stop watch and pencil can himself check to see how many minutes of a newscast on TV or radio are really devoted to news; how many to commercials; and how many to what may be considered pseudo events or public relations releases which are sometimes difficult to identify. Once openers, closers, commercials, and other extraneous elements are timed and noted, the complaints of the best newsmen in the country that they do not have enough time, in uninterrupted segments, to do the news job the nation requires, can be more fully appreciated.

When human interest, sports, and weather stories (which are often duplicated elsewhere), fashion and celebrity notes, and so on are deducted, many 30-minute newscasts are found to average not over ten to fifteen minutes of solid local, national, and world news. At average reading rates this is perhaps two thousand words, which would take very little space, if seen in print. Martin Agronsky once estimated that the average 15-minute newscast did not contain more than two minutes of Washington news. Only rarely is there any more international news than that on many stations, as has been found by stop-watch monitoring of news programs each year by university students in radio and television courses.

Another kind of rigging is found in trade association brochures and ads which list the total hours of news available on all networks or stations. The rigging lies in the implication that the viewer can watch or hear this much news, whereas nearly all these programs are scheduled within the same few hours, and thus overlap. There may be six hours of news, additively computed, on six stations in a given area, but since the viewer must miss the other five if he selects one, he can watch the number of hours of these different newscasts for a given day as listed in the ads only if he has several television receivers and several sets of ears, eyes, and attention. If one wishes television news between 7:00 P.M. and 10:00 P.M. in most sections of the Midwest (or 8:00 and 11:00 in the East), one finds *none*, no matter how many hours of news a day the published figures seem to indicate as "available." If you are unable to watch at 10:00 P.M. on weekdays or 10:30 P.M. on Saturdays in a given area, you miss not one but *all* the evening news broadcasts. The long list of programs missed is impressive but of little consolation or help to the viewer unable to view at those hours. Furthermore, viewers are often scolded for "missing" a larger number of hours of good programs than it is physically possible to view because such programs are scheduled simultaneously. This is of course an entertainment practice. (Many viewers would like to have supported both the *Danny Kaye Show* and ABC's *Stage 67* in the fall of 1966. But to choose one meant to "vote against" the other, although many *other* hours of the week offered these same viewers nothing of interest, or a choice only of one of several game shows, Westerns, comedies, or fine news or documentary programs.) Some opportunity for listening to more than one news program and documentary, and comparing them, using one to complement the other, should be found. . . .

Who Forgot Radio?

Edward P. Morgan

. . . By and large, I suggest, radio reporting from Washington—and from almost everywhere else, for that matter—suffers most from what might be called instant spasms. Pour hot water over a dehydrated concentrate and you get instant coffee. Bring a processed cereal to a boil and you have instant oatmeal. Grind a news story down to a palmful of facts, pour on the audio for forty seconds and serve. The quality of this journalistic spasm does not compare with instant food and is likely to cause mental indigestion. I am not arguing that you cannot impart a lot of information in intervals of a minute or less. Sentences such as "I love you" or "drop dead" can transmit a world of meaning in less than two seconds. I am arguing that the frenetic framework into which most broadcast news is now compressed produces a dangerously superficial picture.

There are at least a couple of other abominations. One comes under the heading of "actualities." The other could be labeled the compulsive monster of microphone-itis. Radio is sound, but to justify itself in a broadcast, sound must have meaning. That includes the sound of voices. A tape recorder is a marvelous electronic butterfly net in which to capture the noises of the news, but too often the process is carried to lengths that are utterly absurd. A stunned victim's halting phrases may give an on-the-scene sense to the report of an accident. There may be a legitimate measure of disaster in the noise of a hurricane, a mark of authority to the warden's description of a prison break in his own words and accent. But too often these actualities, while audible, are unintelligible. I would rather get my facts on a story from a trained newsman than have the information impeded by the mumbling voice of a so-called eyewitness butchering

From *The Press in Washington* by Ray E. Hiebert. New York: Dodd, Mead & Company, 1966. By permission of Mr. Hiebert.

the English language. How many times have you heard a forest lookout, a traffic cop, or a passerby drone out a completely unilluminating version of an event that an experienced broadcast reporter, once he had the facts, could have put more clearly in half the time?

I'm not talking about documentaries or interviews in which there is time to turn around with questions and answers, but about these quick and interruptive splices of strange voices to establish the mobility of datelines: radio has a portability that TV may never be able to match. I have had the good fortune to cover Richard Nixon's vice-presidential trips to Africa and the Soviet Union, President Eisenhower's extraordinary journey to India, and President Kennedy's historic visit to Berlin. Thanks to patient engineers who applied their special talents to unusual circumstances and were able to put the right circuit jacks in the right holes on the right wave-lengths, I was able to maintain my nightly quarter-hour program with hardly a hitch. I was even able to get through from such unlikely places as Monrovia, Liberia; Tripoli, Libya; and Sverdlovsk in Siberia.

The so-called actualities could indeed embellish a newscast far more than they do if we Americans on the whole didn't have such abominable diction or enunciation and could speak a simple sentence. While we're on the subject, interviews and panel shows could be far more lively and "listenable" if the protagonists could articulate more lucidly their thoughts, if any. What is there about the American way of life, upbringing, and education that makes so many men speak in monotones and so many women squeak like shrill shrews? We could learn a thing or two from our British cousins in the art of speech and expression, and I'm neither demanding nor expecting a nation of Winston Churchills or Lawrence Oliviers when I say this. At the risk of sounding both pretentious and presumptuous, I long ago gave up the use of inserted interviews on my radio program because I found it easier to translate the gist of the interviews into my own scripts— thus minimizing persistent problems of sounds, length, and content of the interviewees' expressions.

This brings us, in some respects, to the more urgent matter of compulsivitis of the microphone. On stepping down from his lofty role as Secretary of State, Dean Acheson once told James Reston of *The New York Times*, in effect, that there was a basic incompatibility between the press and the government, that reporters were constantly trying to find out what officials were trying to conceal, with the implication being that the higher the involvement of the story at hand with national security, the more intense the incompatibility. There is a basic truth here, but in an open society like ours there are two honest interpretations of it, one by a responsible press and one by responsible officials; and out of the tension between them flows, erratically sometimes, a current of information vital to an informed public opinion. That is the theory, at least. Sometimes it does not work. Paradoxically, the addition of radio and television to the media of communications has often made it harder rather than easier to make this system work. The reason is the ubiquitous microphone and its companion tool, the TV camera.

An important caucus breaks up at a political convention and some hapless official is waylaid in the corridor to say something, at gun-point, in a manner of speaking, with the heavy artillery of radio and television zeroed in on him. Out comes banality or evasion. What else is the victim likely to say under such circumstances? The Secretary of State flies off to a crucial conference. Before his plane leaves, he has to run the bristling gamut of the thrust microphones. He says he is confident that the conference will produce a useful exchange of views. After his plane lands he goes through the same ritual all over again. He has high hopes that the conference will produce a useful exchange of views. After the conference is over a communiqué is issued and a spokesman assures the microphones that there *has* been a useful exchange of views.

This dubious travelogue is news? It is an exercise in the thinnest and most synthetic kind of journalism. The interviewee, a past master at the art of manipulation of the meaningless expression by now, has long since ceased to become the victim. The public is the dupe and broadcast journalism is an accessory before, during, and after the crime.

When the tense three-hour confrontation between President Johnson and Alabama's Governor Wallace ended on that sunny but chilly Saturday afternoon of March 13, 1965, the President guided the governor through a writhing waiting-room full of reportorial flesh to a cluster of microphones outside the executive west wing of the White House not for a news conference but for a statement for the electronic gear, deployed and waiting. They had an exchange of views, the governor said, not with notable agreement, but the President, he added, behaved, as he always does, like a gentleman and the governor hoped that his deportment had been gentlemanly too. Then he flew back to the state of Alabama, where there seems to be a conflict over the codes of what makes and who is entitled to be not a gentleman necessarily but merely a voting citizen. This kind of hi-jinx is substantive information?

Questions can be as ridiculous as answers—another liability of the actualities and ubiquitous microphone techniques. I caught one broadcast from Travis Air Force Base in California of interviews with some of the first service families to be evacuated from South Vietnam after President Johnson had expanded American counterstrikes against the Communists. Obviously desperate to get *something* on tape, one reporter asked a returning army wife, "and do you feel your husband will be okay there, now that you've gone?"

While we're attacking the clumsy query and the cliché, I soberly suggest that we working broadcasters all sign a pledge of abstinence and never again ask a candidate's wife how it feels to have her husband nominated.

I'd be willing to break the pledge, naturally, if there was reason to believe the lady would reply, "What a stupid question," or "This is the last straw. I've been trying to get Horace to quit politics for years. Now I'm leaving him."

These perhaps slightly ulcerated criticisms should not be taken as justifying the free and untrammeled transit of men and women who make the news to and from their appointments without any attempt by the press to find out the score, but there is a distinction, or should be, between news and nonsense. The old-fashioned shoeleather approach of the reporter patrolling his beat is still valid and for the most part is still the best way to dig out the facts. On the other hand, live coverage of certain events can be unbeatable, not just for immediacy but for dimension.

If the principals and broadcasters can train themselves—restrain themselves, it might be better said—to concentrate on substance, not just the sensational, then congressional committee hearings will be even more newsworthy and instructive to the public. It is possible that live coverage of the sessions of House and Senate themselves would be a benefit to the country and maybe even improve the quality of Congress, or at least its debate. Let us not go overboard with optimism on these prospects, however, for if we are candid with ourselves, live radio and television coverage of national political conventions has not improved the function of those cumbersome events at all.

The thoughtful, conscientious broadcast reporter is probably the most frustrated member of the Washington press corps. He makes his rounds, as do his colleagues of the newspapers and magazines. He goes to hearings, background briefings, filibuster sieges, news conferences at the White House, the State Department, and the Pentagon. He goes endlessly to lunches and dinners with people in or behind the news. He seeks key officials out in their bureaucratic lairs for interviews. He reads mountains of material, from handouts to *The New York Times*. And when he has his story he has to squirt it through a tiny hole of time in a five-minute or a fifteen-minute news roundup on the air.

The CBS "World News Roundup," at eight o'clock every morning on radio, used to be one of the most vital sources of intelligence in Washington. The government, especially the executive branch, listened for news that might beat—or set in clearer perspective—the diplomatic dispatches from our embassies abroad. It wasn't nationally sponsored, however, and the local ad spots sold by affiliates on a "co-op" basis were not profitable. So at one point, when I happened to be director of news for CBS, the network brass decided to take that fifteen-minute journalistic gem off the air. I sounded the alarm in Washington and thanks in large part to James Hagerty, then White House news secretary for President Eisenhower, we got some high-level testimonials, some of which were almost threatening in their emphasis on the program's value. It stayed (and that is the only accomplishment I can think of worth remembering in my brief tenure as a junior broadcasting executive). The "World News Roundup" continues and so do counterparts on ABC and NBC, but they are all so loaded with disconcerting commercials now that it is hard to separate the news from plugs for liver pills, laxatives, body deodorizers, and cigarettes, filtered and unfiltered.

New York Herald Tribune columnist John Crosby once wrote that I had "one of the more enviable jobs around." He was talking about my five-nights-a-week assignment of fifteen minutes of news and comment, on ABC Radio, sponsored by the AFL-CIO. I am well into my eleventh year at that same job, and as far as I am concerned, Crosby's words are truer than ever. I wish, in a way, that that weren't so.

That is to say, I wish there were more competition. Not just in the fifteen-minute time segment. The eclipse of the quarter-hour by these five-minute bursts that are called newscasts is bad enough. (They are nearer to three minutes when you subtract the commercial time.) But I am free to voice opinion and critical comment, even including criticism of broadcasting and organized labor. I wish that journalistic phenomenon were not so unique. If the trade union movement, with all its warts, dares encourage it, why can't General Motors, or the National Association of Manufacturers, or the American Medical Association, or the organized groups of the radical right, sponsor broadcasts that report the news and in addition paint arrows of responsible criticism that point inward as well as outward? The sinews of our society would be stronger and Washington would be a livelier place for the electronic journalist to ply his trade if they did. . . .

III. Critiques
and
Cases

In recent years, newspapers, magazines, radio, and television have been subjected to constant and close analysis, not only of their general performance in conveying information and opinion, but also of specific performances. With a variety of approaches, these critiques have examined the performances of individual publications, programs, or types of programs as well as media-wide performances in treating specific events or situations.

One such ongoing problem situation for the media is the complex and influential interaction between media and government. In criticizing both media and government for the dangers he sees in the current situation, James McCartney introduces one of the chief issues in media journalism today, objective versus interpretive reporting.

Irwin Ross touches on another much-debated trouble spot, media coverage of trials. While emphasizing the problems arising from certain specific cases, he also suggests the broader issues that these cases reflect.

John C. Merrill and Reo M. Christenson provide two differing approaches to the close content analysis of a periodical. Merrill focuses on one limited subject—the rhetoric employed in referring to the actions of three presidents—to illustrate the general methods and approach of *Time*. Covering a wider area, Christenson cites examples of a number of subjects to indicate the general direction in bias of *The Reader's Digest*.

Using vivid, concrete detail from his personal experiences in covering the war in Vietnam, Michael J. Arlen builds a general critique of the treatment of news in the media, and particularly in television.

Audience participation phone-in shows are among the most popular of radio programs; they are also the most extensive effort so far in all the media to effect a two-way interchange of information and opinion. In discussing their qualities, allures, and limitations, Jessica Mitford finds them a mixed blessing at best, but nonetheless a vibrant force amidst the hardening uniformity of media performance.

Must the Media Be "Used"?

James McCartney

Not long ago columnist and associate editor Tom Wicker of the New York *Times* mused at a casual lunch that he believed the Washington press corps had flopped miserably in reporting the Vietnam War. "Our failure on Vietnam is an indictment of the entire press corps," he said. "It was our greatest failure." In his opinion, Lyndon Johnson might not have been able to escalate the Vietnam conflict into a full-scale war had the press more skillfully dramatized the Administration's misrepresentation and the shortcomings of what Wicker calls its "Munich psychology"; a Tet Offensive then would not have been necessary to show the public that Mr. Johnson's version of what was happening in Vietnam was false.

"I am convinced that we did our historic job in reporting it all accurately," said Wicker, who was *Times* Washington bureau chief during the period of the escalation. "We knew what the Government was up to. I suppose I was one of the few people in Washington who could get the President of the United States on the phone if I had to, to check an important point. But that wasn't enough. I'm not sure in looking back now that sometimes we didn't do more harm than good by just telling it as the Administration said it was."

In retrospect, examples of Pentagon misrepresentation now seem almost inconceivable. Take Defense Secretary Robert McNamara's misrepresentations on the troop buildup. On October 14, 1966, McNamara returned from his eighth "fact-finding" mission to South Vietnam and declared, "I see no reason to expect any significant increase in the level or tempo of operations in South Vietnam, nor do I see any reason to believe that deployments of U.S. forces to that country will change significantly in the future." The number of U.S. troops at that time was 331,000. In the months to come the troop level steadily rose at a rate of more than 10,000 a month—a massive effort. By the following April—six months after McNamara's flat statement—more than 100,000 new troops had been sent to Vietnam. McNamara's remarks were made just three weeks before the 1966 Congressional elections.

The *Times* and other papers, in the traditional manner of the press,

Reprinted from the *Columbia Journalism Review* (Winter 1969–70). By permission of the author and the *Columbia Journalism Review*.

reported the statements and the figures. They held a mirror up to Lyndon Johnson's declarations and sought to report accurately all that was said. What more could one ask of the press? Wicker, among others, today asks more. It could be that the families of more than 40,000 Americans killed in Vietnam would ask more, too. For it is apparent that the press was often used by the Johnson Administration to merchandise its Vietnam policies—policies a majority of the public now believe were a mistake.

The surface story of other aspects of Mr. Johnson's salesmanship is now well known: the highly publicized "peace offensives" while more and more troops were plunged into the war, right up to his last day in the White House; the troops that would be starting home by Christmas; the light at the end of the tunnel; the innumerable "turning points" that never came. This process went on from 1965, when the President began to escalate the war, until 1968—when Senator Eugene McCarthy and the reality of the Tet Offensive provided catalysts to begin to stop it. It took almost three years for public opinion to form and to make itself felt.

The Vietnam War is only Exhibit A, the classic, still under-researched case of the using of the press by a powerful government in the 1960s. But it illustrates what the U.S. Government—or any other determined and talented body of men—can do with modern media if they put their minds to it and employ proven techniques.

The press is often used. The federal government is so accustomed to using it for its own ends that Presidents become annoyed and irritable when they find, to their surprise, that on some occasions they cannot do so. This is the context in which Vice President Spiro Agnew's remarks about the news media belong. Agnew was frustrated and angry because some analysts and commentators criticized President Nixon's November 3 speech on Vietnam. Agnew had nothing to say about the fact that day after day, week in and week out, most White House ploys designed to build a favorable image of the President and his administration, are dumped undigested on a public which often does not have sufficient time or information to evaluate them on its own.

The immense prestige of the U.S. Presidency today leads the media to make a giant of any man who holds the job, regardless of his personal limitations. The most innocuous statement from President Nixon is often treated as though it were a pronouncement of intrinsic worth from on high.

Nixon announces a campaign against crime in the District of Columbia. It draws huge headlines, but is not implemented. In the press, Nixon is a battler against crime. Nixon tells a meeting of governors that drug addiction is a "national problem" requiring a nationwide campaign of education. His program has no teeth and represents little change. In the press, Nixon is a battler against the evils of dope. Nixon tells a White House conference that hunger must end. He has no news program, and resists efforts of conference moderates to obtain a declaration of a national hunger emergency. Says the Washington *Star*, in an eight-column streamer: NIXON PRESSES DRIVE ON HUNGER. Nixon states in his campaign for the Presidency that "the war in Vietnam must end." As it turns out, his program for Vietnam is not to end the war at all, but rather to turn it over to South Vietnam so it can continue, perhaps indefinitely. This is explained many months later by Defense Department witnesses before a Congressional committee. The distinction is essentially lost in the press.

Nixon, in a nationally televised speech on Vietnam in May, claims to have taken "new" initiatives to try to break open the Paris peace talks with an eight-point proposal. White House National Security Adviser Henry Kissinger describes the proposal as "new" and "important." Five of the eight points had been proposed, in essentially the same form, by the Johnson Administration as early as 1966. The other three were repetitions of positions stated by Peace Negotiator Henry Cabot Lodge four months earlier. But the press blithely conveys the deception.

No one knows this game better than Richard Nixon, whose talents for using the press, if he could be graded, would range somewhere between B-plus and A-minus. But he still must rank behind former President John F. Kennedy, who perfected some of the techniques Mr. Nixon is using today. Kennedy created a sense of movement and excitement in Washington that persists in the Kennedy legend—and defies all logic when judged by legislation actually passed or changes actually achieved.

But it is not just the President who uses the press. So does anyone else who has a cause to plead and has the talent and imagination to calculate how it can be done. A nation can be escalated into war, but so also can an administration be toppled. The anti-war demonstrators have learned their lessons. Their use of the press at the 1968 Democratic National Convention in Chicago belongs in an anthology of masterworks.

The role of TV in this drama has often been discussed. Hubert H. Humphrey is a convert to the theory that his campaign was mortally damaged on the nation's picture tubes by a cruel juxtaposing of violence in Chicago streets with convention hall proceedings. The net impression, he has said, was that Humphrey was the candidate of violence; he never lived it down. This bit of artful staging was intentional enough on the part of the leaders of the demonstrations, although they could hardly have predicted the active cooperation of the Chicago police department, whose members responded to the plot as though they had been rehearsed.

An equally impressive feat of stage-managing, however, was performed for the written press in the weeks and months before the convention. The objective of at least some of the demonstration leaders was to create a confrontation with police. This would dramatize the Establishment's "support" of the Vietnam War. If troops could be enticed to the scene, the convention could provide televised evidence of a militaristic society. But to

234 CRITIQUES AND CASES

create this confrontation, it would be necessary to have police in large numbers and, if possible, troops. Somehow city officials would have to be convinced that terror was in the wind. They would also have to be convinced that massive numbers of demonstrators would be descending—so massive as to be unmanageable by normal forces.

The campaign began across the country early in June. Predictions, freely given, were that as many as half a million demonstrators would be moving on Chicago. Some of the most effective ploys were products of the Yippies—the Youth International Party. They dreamed up bizarre plots: LSD would be put in Chicago's drinking water; carpet tacks would be scattered at major interchanges of the expressway system; power stations would be threatened; the city would be brought to its knees.

Chicago's *American*, owned by the *Tribune*, proved particularly susceptible to outrageous predictions. The more egregious they became, the more serious the *American* took them in its news columns. For months before the convention, it reported that hundreds of thousands of "revolutionaries" were coming to Chicago. Thus a tiny minority of virtually unknown, youthful revolutionaries used the press to spark the idea that the *entire* group of demonstrators would be bent on tearing the city down. A few agitators who understood the predispositions of the press toward over-simplification and sensational predictions made a major contribution to an atmosphere of fear and tension. In particular, the demonstrators understood the passion of TV for action shots. On the eve of the convention one group obligingly staged rehearsals—for the cameras—showing how they would break police lines. No statement or prediction seemed too eccentric to get TV attention.

All of this had its effect on Mayor Richard J. Daley. The Mayor panicked. The degree to which he was baited is perhaps best illustrated by his decision to reject a request from anti-war demonstrators for a permit to use Soldier Field, a lake-front amphitheater that seats 100,000. Had the Mayor granted that permit he would have called the bluff of the demonstrators; the crowd they eventually assembled in Chicago numbered fewer than 15,000. It would have been lost in Soldier Field.

In the city's official televised report on convention-week rioting, "daily press reports" were cited as major elements in justifying security measures. Counting police, national guardsmen, and regular Army troops, Daley assembled a security force of more than 25,000 men. They outnumbered the demonstrators almost two to one. Just as some of the demonstrators during convention week baited the police into violence with obscene language, or by throwing human feces, some of their leaders baited Mayor Daley before the convention through the press.

As Max Ways has written in *Fortune*, "the demonstration has become the dominant form of social action" in modern American society "rather than the petition, the political debate, or the lawsuit." A demonstration provides movement and action for the cameras that no petition can. The demonstrators showed in Chicago that they can be just as adept at using the media as can the White House.

Moreover, just as a case can be made that the media were used by Lyndon Johnson in the buildup and perpetuation of the war, and by demonstrators to play a major role in driving Johnson's party from power, still another case can be made that Richard Nixon used the press more cleverly than any Presidential candidate before him to find his way to the White House. This is perhaps the third side of the triangle.

Here we have the phenomenon of a Presidential candidate who, early in the 1968 political year, came to a deliberate and calculated decision to bypass the writing press and carry his cause directly to the public via the imagery of TV. Like no Presidential candidate before him, he was packaged as though he were a bar of soap. The quiet genius behind all this was Harry Treleaven, onetime creative director of the J. Walter Thompson Agency, with generous help from Frank Shakespeare, onetime vice president of the Columbia Broadcasting System. The two decided on the image they wanted as early as the New Hampshire primary in February: they wanted a friendly, homey Richard Nixon, personable, experienced, well informed. Their vehicle was the TV tube, operating from a completely controlled studio situation. They would present their candidate, live and in color, being questioned by "average Americans"—handpicked by the GOP.

This was the Studio Campaign, directed to the nation's living rooms and conducted right up to election day. Only rarely was the candidate exposed to questioning from the working press that made up most of his campaign entourage. Reporters were treated to a repetition of the same, basic campaign speech in various parts of the country. The major sop thrown to them was a few extra, contrived paragraphs, to be inserted into the basic speech—a "release" for a.m.'s on a typical day, and another few paragraphs for p.m.'s. The press, as though following Wendell Willkie on a 1940 campaign train, faithfully tried night after night to make stories out of the same, repeated basic speech. And the real campaign went on over their heads, on the packaged, electronic airwaves.

Thus the candidate's major pronouncement on the crucial issue of the election—the Vietnam War—was made in a prepared statement at the Republican Convention in July in Miami. "We must end the war in Vietnam," he said. But he never was required to explain even broadly how he would do it, and throughout the campaign he was allowed to escape questioning on the subject by any sophisticated, informed panel. Indeed, the Nixon image-makers would not even let the writing reporters sit in the studios where the packaged TV programs were made. "Press Rooms" were set up in the TV studios so that reporters could have the privilege of seeing exactly what any TV set owner could see on his set at home.

The Nixon campaign for the Presidency was another classic case of using the press. He used it by ignoring it, bypassing it. He used it on his own terms, and, of course, he used it effectively, from his point of view. He raised the technique of not answering legitimate questions to an art form.

These illustrations, of course, are only a sampling. J. Edgar Hoover had been spreading his personal philosophy of life and crime through release of FBI uniform crime reports for years. The fine print candidly acknowledges that uniform crime statistics are, in fact, impossible because reporting techniques and customs vary from city to city. Still, Hoover issued press releases splashed liberally with quotations from J. Edgar Hoover, representing a view of the causes of crime straight out of the nineteenth century —and the statistics are faithfully reported month after month in the nation's finest papers. An official-looking press release from the FBI is all the platform required.

Across the ideological fence, meanwhile, black militants have found an infallible formula to gain attention: the stronger the criticism of society, the harsher the judgment, the bigger the threat, the more likely it is to be on the tube. Or in the papers. Stokely Carmichael and Rap Brown became masters of the technique. By using the media carefully to build national images and reputations, they have distorted the image of America's black community, prompting many a member of the white middle class to cower in his suburb waiting for the revolution—while in-depth studies universally indicate that the overwhelming majority of the black community is deeply committed to the preservation of the established social system.

In fact, in this age of media manipulation, reporters at times seem to beg to be used. The "background" session, in which government officials decline to be identified or quoted directly, continues to thrive, not only in Washington but now in the provinces as well. By the standard Washington rule the reporter is permitted to use information thus imparted "on his own authority." He is permitted, in other words, to report the government line as though it were Gospel without mentioning that it is the government line. There even are regular "background breakfasts," organized like social clubs, which compete for officials' favor. The most successful current group is operated by Washington reporter Godfrey Sperling, Jr., of the *Christian Science Monitor*, who had the wisdom to assemble a blue-ribbon panel of newspapermen when he initiated the enterprise in 1966. It is successful in the sense that top government officials accept invitations to the breakfasts. As a result, Sperling is having trouble restricting membership. At least two other breakfast groups have been formed since, at least partially as competitors.

The breakfasts are a useful way of allowing reporters to get to know officials and to question them at some leisure and in some depth outside the formal confrontation of a press conference. Many reporters who participate have deep-seated reservations about the "background" syndrome, but feel that they must take advantage of the only opportunities they may have to question officials. For the Government, the backgrounder can be an invaluable propaganda tool. Government officials are often anxious to take advantage of the platform. Anonymity, however, rarely seems to breed either courage or candor.

Must the media be used? Are they, like a Greyhound bus, a public carrier that should accept all, equally, who wish to ride? What, if anything, can the media do to avoid being used?

Various newsmen believe that "using" of the media can be reduced, but their approach to achieving this probably would give Spiro Agnew insomnia. For they believe, in effect, that rather than having too many analysts and commentators, the media have too few. Rather than doing too much analysis, the media do too little. If so, newspapers must hire reporters and writers with the background and brains to qualify as independent analysts in major fields of government. Then if a president stands up and says that it is important to the nation that it fight a war in Asia, the reporter will have the background and training to challenge the president. Hence, the future role of newspapers would be to supply more criticism, examination, and questioning.

"We once did the hard news," says Tom Wicker. "But TV has taken that over. Our job now must be in the area of depth, questioning, and analysis."

If there was a media failure on Vietnam, what exactly was it? Was it a failure to interpret and analyze available material, or was it a failure to discover and report—and possibly dramatize—what was really happening? Joseph Goulden, former Washington bureau chief for the Philadelphia *Inquirer*, in a book called *Truth Is the First Casualty*, examines the story of the Gulf of Tonkin incident of 1964, which Lyndon Johnson seized upon to gain a Congressional blank check to wage war in Vietnam. Through personal interviews with participants, Goulden makes a convincing case that the incident was a fraud. One key witness had never talked to a reporter until Goulden traced him; then his story exposed the incident as a sham. What might have happened if reporters had found that witness in 1964?

In the same way, David Kraslow and Stuart H. Loory of the Los Angeles *Times* have exposed Johnson's diplomatic strategy. The two were given eight months' reportorial time, and an unlimited budget, to try to piece together the behind-the-scenes story of Johnson's Vietnam diplomacy. Their series of articles in the *Times* and their book, *The Secret Search for Peace in Vietnam*, leave little doubt that Johnson's strategy was to talk peace and make war. His objective was a military victory, and it was not abandoned until the very end of his administration. Kraslow and Loory, both top reporters, were not able to complete their research and publish it until Spring, 1968—after the Tet Offensive and Clark Clifford had changed the complexion of the war. What might have happened if some other great news organization had undertaken a mission similar to Kraslow's and Loory's a year earlier?

A "used" press is in many ways a passive and timid press whose staff members take the statements and explanations and rationalizations and handouts and background sessions and passes them along to the reader or the viewer and then go home to the suburbs to watch *Laugh-In*. If the Vietnam War could indeed have been reversed or slowed by the media, it is hard to believe it could have been done without aggressive, challenging, controversial reporting. It certainly could not have been done on the back pages. It would have to have been done at the tops of front pages, with stories for which reporters had excavated facts to show that the Administration was lying. It is hard to believe it could have been done by a press corps that could adopt a phrase like "credibility gap."

If the media are to avoid being used, they must recognize that the most common technique employed by those who would use them, in or out of government, is the staged or pseudo-event—what some have called the "media event." The speech, the announcement, the statement by the Secretary of Defense, the antiwar demonstration, the press conference called by the black militants, the press release from J. Edgar Hoover, even the appearance at breakfast by a Cabinet member—all share one thing in common. All are a way in which a salesman for a point of view may present his case. The problem in this fast-moving society is to put hundreds of these pseudo-events, staged daily, into a context that bears a relationship to their importance.

Here is a prominent way in which the media fail. They continue to be victimized by the old "hard-news" formula in which not enough is said about who is doing the talking—and why. As one newsman put it, "A Congressman can still get up on the floor of the House and make a cogent argument that we ought to recognize Red China and the wires still put it out with a tone of shock that suggests the man is probably a red. The world has changed, but the hard-news reporters haven't."

No rule of journalism forbids a reporter from attempting to set the scene for what he is reporting. Some newsmen in Washington will identify information as coming from a "backgrounder" in which the source declined to be identified. That helps. But it would also help if stories went deeper in suggesting a President's motivation, or even the possible motivation of the director of the FBI. It would have helped in Chicago had more effort been invested in determining who was whom among potential demonstrators, and who spoke for how many. It would have helped if reporters covering the Nixon campaign had taken time to investigate and explain his image-making techniques, which Joe McGinniss so adroitly exposed in *The Selling of the President*. With more and more pseudo-events becoming legitimate news, the necessity for providing background for an event becomes greater and greater.

It is necessary to recognize, too, that the nature of news—or what is called news—is changing. Because of the infinite complexity of modern society, many things are "news" that can't be learned in police stations: attitudes in the black community or among youth; the influence of the military; the economics of hunger; the adequacy of public education or health care; the will of the people in South Vietnam; the way images are made. All these may bear directly on the lives of readers and, having importance to them, may be "news," though not events.

The news media still must try to hold up a mirror to the world, to reflect it as accurately as possible to readers or viewers. But the picture can hardly be accurate if the media are largely occupied with reflecting the views of pleaders of causes, or dramatizing "happenings," or blandly transmitting the official Government line. The press must not turn itself over to those who would use it. Editors and writers must seek out the questions that require answering and set out to find the answers for themselves.

Trial by Newspaper

Irwin Ross

On April 24, 1964, police in Brooklyn, New York, picked up a semiliterate nineteen-year-old Negro named George Whitmore, Jr., on suspicion of attempted rape. The next day, after Whitmore had been continuously questioned for twenty-two hours, the police announced that he had confessed to three crimes—the attempted rape, the murder of a char-woman in Brooklyn, and the killing of Janice Wylie and Emily Hoffert, young career girls who had been brutally stabbed to death in their Manhattan apartment eight months before. The gruesome Wylie-Hoffert case had shocked New Yorkers as few crimes of violence do; the police, under great pressure to solve the murder, had floundered helplessly. Now their professional honor was vindicated.

The newspapers hailed the coup. The *World-Telegram*'s headline, "Wylie Murder Solved: Drifter Admits Killing 2," was typical. All the

From *The Atlantic Monthly* (September 1965). Copyright © 1965 by The Atlantic Monthly Company, Boston, Massachusetts. Reprinted with permission.

papers set forth details of Whitmore's confession, as authoritatively furnished by Chief of Detectives Lawrence J. McKearney—how Whitmore had been wandering around New York that summer morning, how he had casually entered the girls' apartment when he found the door unlocked, how he had been surprised by one of the girls while "rummaging around" in the kitchen, and how he had successively murdered each of them. The *Journal-American* interviewed the father of one of the victims, its story beginning with his characterization of Whitmore: "An animal . . . obviously deranged . . . a horror . . . should be imprisoned with no chance of parole."

At his arraignment, however, Whitmore repudiated his confession, his court-appointed lawyer arguing that it had been exacted under duress. The newspapers were unimpressed, and in rebuttal published further details of the confession, endorsing the police contenion that Whitmore had such intimate knowledge of the crime that he had to be the murderer. Reading all this, the average citizen could only agree with Chief McKearney that "we got the right guy. No question about it."

A great many questions subsequently arose, however, as well as evidence that Whitmore had been 120 miles away on the day of the crime. Nine months after his arrest, District Attorney Frank S. Hogan cleared Whitmore of the Wylie-Hoffert murder charge. Another suspect was arrested for the crime. The delayed exoneration was welcome, but Whitmore had meanwhile suffered grievous damage, for he had been tried, convicted, and damned in the newspapers long before he had his day in court.

In the intervening period, he had also stood trial in Brooklyn on the lesser charge of attempted rape and had been convicted, partly on the basis of the same contested serial confession. But it soon became clear that he had not received a fair trial, owing to the prejudicial atmosphere created by the press. In March, Brooklyn District Attorney Aaron E. Koota joined the defense in asking that the verdict be set aside and a new trial scheduled. The court agreed.

Trial by newspaper is not a new phenomenon in the United States. Recently, renewed debate on the subject has been stimulated by the Warren Commission's criticism of the way the press covered the initial police investigation of President Kennedy's assassination. The Commission put most of the blame on the Dallas police department for its amazing lack of restraint in releasing information; item after item of evidence against Lee Harvey Oswald, as well as hearsay and unverified leads, were announced to the world at a series of frantic impromptu press conferences. As for the news media, they were criticized for badgering the police beyond the call of normal journalistic diligence.

"A fundamental objection to the news policy pursued by the Dallas police," the Commission wrote, "is the extent to which it endangered Oswald's constitutional right to a trial by an impartial jury. . . . The disclosure of evidence encouraged the public, from which a jury would ultimately be impaneled, to prejudge the very questions that would be raised at trial."

Partly as a consequence of the events in Dallas, the American Bar Association launched an intensive study of how the requirements of fair trial can be reconciled with the demands of a free press. Committees of the American Society of Newspaper Editors and the American Society of Newspaper Publishers went to work on the same question. The Justice Department, after months of deliberation, issued a policy directive limiting the kinds of information to be released to the press by the FBI and U.S. attorneys. Late last December, the Philadelphia Bar Association got in ahead of the crowd with a set of guidelines that would drastically restrain police, prosecutors, defense counsel, and the news media. For its pains, the Bar Association found itself denounced by the Philadelphia press for trying to subvert the First Amendment.

In law, the accused is presumed innocent until proved guilty. The press pays formal obeisance to this principle but frequently betrays it in practice. In a variety of ways, news stories tend to convey a presumption of guilt. If the police announce that the accused has confessed, the press usually accepts the assertion as proof of guilt, even though the confession may later turn out to be false. If no confession is mentioned but the police provide a lengthy chronicle of what the accused is supposed to have done, the newspaper account usually reads like a statement of fact rather than merely an elaboration of the charge. The occasional qualifying phrase "as the police allege" or "the police charge that" is likely to be lost on the average reader

Moreover, the news media often report incriminating evidence which the judge may rule to be inadmissible at the trial. And inevitably, prominent attention is given to the defendant's prior criminal record, if he has one, which cannot be mentioned in court unless the accused takes the stand in his own defense.

The endless elaboration of detail about what the accused supposedly did or confessed or was previously convicted of readily creates an impression of guilt. Moreover, even the rhetorical devices of journalism favor acceptance of an accusation as a fact. Thus, "Malcolm X Assassin Charged" is a more effective, though far less accurate, headline than "2nd Muslim Seized in Malcolm Killing." It is a commonplace when an unprepossessing suspect is arrested for him to be referred to as "hoodlum," "thug," or even "killer."

In routine criminal cases, especially in large cities, prejudicial pretrial publicity may not matter: by the time the defendant goes on trial, weeks after the crime, prospective jurymen will have forgotten the half-column news story, if indeed they ever read it. But in sensational crimes, which agitate the entire community, memories are longer, and the cascade of one-sided news accounts usually begins again on the eve of trial. Only an illiterate shut-in who does not listen to radio or watch television could avoid any acquaintance with the case.

In *The Innocents,* a recent book about celebrated miscarriages of justice, Edward D. Radin tells of the weird case of James Foster, a hapless itinerant worker whose unfavorable press notices almost led him to the electric chair. Late in the spring of 1956, a burglar shot a prominent merchant, Charles Drake, in the living room of his home in Jefferson, Georgia. Mrs. Drake, who had been hurt, was able to give the police a description of the intruder. Some days later, detectives found a likely suspect in Foster—then in jail in Gainesville, Georgia, on a traffic violation—for he vaguely fitted the killer's description.

Foster was brought to Jefferson and identified by Mrs. Drake in a confrontation in her home. Colorful newspaper accounts described the bereaved widow as demanding "Why did you kill my husband?" The newspapers also pointed out that Foster had previously served time in Florida for armed robbery. Unmentioned was the fact that his complicity was meager and the judge had let him off with a light sentence.

Soon afterward, the newspapers presented even more conclusive "evidence." Foster's cell mate in jail stated that he had spoken of murdering a man in Jefferson. The newspapers now had a "confession" with which to hang Foster; they did not ask whether the cell mate was telling the truth or merely trying to curry favor.

When Foster went on trial for murder a few weeks later, his lawyers asked for a change of venue because of the pervasive atmosphere of prejudice in the community. It is a standard motion when a trial by newspaper seems to preclude a fair trial by jury. The judge denied the motion. The case against Foster consisted of Mrs. Drake's identification and the "confession" related by his former jail mate. Foster's defense, supported by several witnesses, was that he had been with Gainesville friends throughout the entire evening when the murder took place in Jefferson. He was convicted and sentenced to death.

Then a strange thing happened. A group of townspeople who had been convinced by his defense raised money for an appeal, and while it was making its way through the higher courts—a period which lasted for two years and resulted in successive defeats for Foster—the true killer was found and confessed. Foster was freed.

Even where pretrial publicity does not result in a conviction, its inequity can be painful. A few years ago in a park in San Francisco, a young nurse and her escort were assaulted by a knife-wielding maniac. The escort was bound and gagged, after which the nurse was raped, beaten, burned with a cigarette, and shorn of her hair. The girl got a good look at the rapist, whose most prominent feature was buckteeth, which led to the headline tag "Fang Fiend."

A few days later, the police picked up a twenty-three-year-old ex-convict on suspicion of the assault. He had no buckteeth, and he kept protesting his innocence, but the distraught girl identified him in her hospital room. "That's Him!" the headlines quoted her, and the papers went on to detail the suspicious evidence which the police found in his quarters: surgical tape, scissors, rubbing alcohol, and vaseline. "These common items took on added significance," one newspaper noted, "since the park rapist used surgical tape to bind his victims and he carried a kit of various medical supplies."

The papers made great play with the suspect's prior criminal record, including "two sex arrests." These were actually less damning than they sounded, for in one instance, the youth, then seventeen, had been convicted of statutory rape (intercourse with a girl below the age of eighteen), and in the other the police had dropped the charge as "unfounded." Even the suspect's alibi—that on the night of the crime he was at home tape-recording some of his writing—was used against him, with the press quoting a police inspector as commenting that the tapes revealed him to be a "sexual psychopath and sadist." The inspector went on to suggest that the poet-sadist had become so intoxicated with his own words that he had rushed from his apartment to turn fantasy into horrible fact.

By the time the papers were finished with the "park rapist," it would have been difficult to find a prospective juror in San Francisco who was unacquainted with the case against him. Then, unexpectedly, the police arrested another man for the crime and released the poet. He had been as innocent as he claimed, and on examination, his verse showed no evidence of sadism or sexual psychopathy.

In recent years, the federal courts have taken a stern view of prejudicial reporting. In *Marshall v. United States,* one Howard R. Marshall was convicted of illegally dispensing pep pills. At his trial, the prosecutor had tried to introduce evidence that Marshall had previously practiced medicine without a license. The judge cut off this approach, saying that "it would be just like offering evidence that he picked pockets or was a petty thief . . . and I think would be prejudicial to the defendant."

Thereafter, two newspapers published the inadmissible evidence while the trial was still on. The judge questioned each of the jurors privately and discovered that seven of them had read one or both articles, but they all assured the judge that their impartiality had not been damaged, and he allowed the trial to proceed. In 1959, the Supreme Court reversed Marshall's conviction, stating, "The prejudice to the defendant is almost certain to be as great when the evidence reaches the jury through news accounts as when it is a part of the prosecution's evidence. It may indeed be greater for it is then not tempered by protective procedures."

A 1961 Supreme Court decision, *Irvin v. Dowd,* vividly documented the impact of pretrial publicity on jury attitudes. Six murders had been committed in the vicinity of Evansville, Indiana, in a four-month period. After the suspect was arrested, both prosecutor and police officials issued press releases saying that he had confessed to all six killings, though he was subsequently brought to trial for only one.

As Justice Tom Clark summarized the press campaign: "A barrage of newspaper headlines, articles, cartoons and pictures was unleashed against him during the six or seven months preceding his trial. . . . These stories revealed the details of his background, including a reference to crimes committed when a juvenile, his convictions for arson 20 years previously, for burglary. . . . The headlines announced his police line-up identification, that he faced a lie detector test, had been placed at the scene of the crime. . . . Finally, they announced his confession. . . ." Before the trial, a roving reporter even solicited man-in-the-street opinions about the accused's guilt and appropriate punishment, and broadcast these interviews over local radio.

The defendant's lawyers initially won a change of venue from Vanderburgh County, where Evansville is located, to adjoining Gibson County. They then tried to get a second change of venue, on the grounds that public prejudice was as great in Gibson County, but it was refused. Of the 430 people on the jury panel, 370 stated on examination that they thought the accused was guilty, their opinions ranging from suspicion to outright certainty. Of the twelve jurors finally selected, eight admitted that they believed the defendant to be guilty but claimed that they would be fair and impartial. The Supreme Court was unwilling to take them at their word, stating, "With his life at stake, it is not requiring too much that petitioner be tried in an atmosphere undisturbed by so huge a wave of public passion." It reversed the conviction and ordered a new trial.

Crime-reporting that is heavily weighted against the defendant is a difficult problem to eradicate because the police, the prosecutor's office, and the press all have a stake in the present system. The police have an understandable desire to show they are doing an effective job. More than vulgar headline-grabbing, though there is a good deal of that, can be involved here. As Police Chief W. H. Parker of Los Angeles has rather ponderously put it, "The commission of heinous or serious crimes in a community invariably results in the public demand for an enumeration of police efforts directed toward a solution. . . . This includes, of course, the apprehension of suspects and an explanation of the basis for such arrests." In the absence of effective restraints, explaining the basis of arrests often involves trying the suspects in the public prints.

The District Attorney's office faces similar pressures. Rarely is a prosecutor in the position of New York's Frank S. Hogan, who has held office for over two decades, invariably being elected with major all-party support. Hogan could take a principled position eleven years ago that he would no longer release confessions by defendants, but most D.A.'s have to fight for their political lives at every election and continually face the temptation to sacrifice a bit of the punctilio of due process in order to burnish their public image.

The press is under compulsions of its own. There is, first of all, its purely commercial interest in purveying crime news; few stories sell papers as well as a sensational murder does. But tendentious crime-reporting can also be the consequence of a crusading zeal that is genuinely disinterested: in an effort to bring criminals to book or to prevent a political "fix," it is all too easy to prejudge the guilt of defendants against whom the weight of evidence seems overwhelming.

The British arrange things much better. When a suspect is arrested, almost nothing can be published except his name, age, address, occupation, and the charge against him. If he has made any admissions to the police, they cannot be alluded to in print; nor can the press indicate how he is supposed to have committed the crime; publication of any evidence is forbidden, as is prior criminal record or any expression of belief in his guilt or innocence. Even the defendant's photograph cannot be printed if there is any likelihood that the question of identification will be a relevant point at the trial. These restrictions are enforced by the contempt powers of the British courts. Infractions result in fines and even jail sentences imposed on the offending journalists.

While the British press occasionally grumbles, it hardly suffers from the court-imposed restraints. Once a case comes to trial, newspapers are free to publish anything that transpires in the courtroom; if anything, the popular press plays up crime news even more sensationally than in the United States. All that happens is that the commercial exploitation of crime is postponed from the arrest to the trial stage. Nor does the British system produce public relations problems for the police; after the case is over, there is plenty of occasion for the police to take their bows. On the other hand, in Britain there is no problem about politically ambitious district attorneys, for full-time prosecutors are not employed. One week a barrister will be retained as a prosecutor, the next as defense counsel.

In this country, the results of the British system are more admired than its methods; few reformers propose adopting them here. For one thing, the Supreme Court has shown extreme reluctance to uphold contempt proceedings against the press, on grounds of infringing the First Amendment. That problem aside, it is felt that it would be unwise to allow so vast an expansion of a judge's contempt powers. We have too many political hacks and incompetents on the bench; the possible caprice and vindictiveness of judges, suddenly capable of fining and imprisoning editors, are rightly feared. "We know that judges as well as editors can be tyrants," Mr. Justice Douglas has tartly observed.

On the other hand, our present methods of dealing with prejudicial publicity are clearly inadequate. Adjournments sometimes provide time for passions to die down, but not in celebrated cases, where press attention resumes as the trial date approaches. A change of venue can be useful only when a case is of purely local interest. Reversals of conviction in general provide an ineffective remedy; if the defendant is innocent, he may have been victimized by a long stay in jail; if he is guilty, society may be victimized, for after the long lapse of time it may be difficult to secure a conviction in a new trial.

As a consequence, various proposals have been made to curb publicity before a defendant's rights have been prejudiced. The most moderate approach is cooperative self-restraint; in Oregon and in Massachusetts, representatives of the news media and the bar have adopted voluntary codes of good behavior. Since Oregon's "Statement of Principles" was adopted in 1962, no substantial complaints of press excesses have occurred, but Oregon does not have an especially sensational press. The "Massachusetts Guide for the Bar and News Media," now two years old, has been adopted by twenty-six daily and thirty-one weekly papers, but except for the *Christian Science Monitor*, all Boston papers have rejected it. The problem with voluntary codes, it is clear, is simply their voluntarism.

Legal authorities have made a number of proposals for compulsory restrictions. In a speech before the American Bar Association last year, Dean Erwin N. Griswold of the Harvard Law School suggested that the bar's canon of ethics be amended to prohibit both prosecutors and defense counsel from releasing a wide range of prejudicial information. The restrictions would be clearly spelled out; infractions could then be dealt with by the grievance committees of the local bar associations and by disbarment proceedings in the courts. "Until we take this step," Griswold said, "we cannot really criticize the news media very severely if they publish the information which lawyers give them."

As for enforcing more restrained behavior on the police, Griswold proposed that it be done through the rule-making and contempt powers of the courts. Imposing contempt penalties on garrulous cops, he argued, did not involve the same constitutional problems as punishing a newspaper for contempt. Federal legislation along these lines has been proposed by Senator Wayne Morse. Morse's bill would levy fines of up to $1000 on any federal investigator or prosecutor, as well as defendant or counsel in the federal courts, who released for publication information that was not part of the court record "which might affect the outcome of any pending criminal litigation."

A more far-reaching proposal by New York Supreme Court Justice Bernard S. Meyer has aroused considerable interest. Meyer advocates passage of a law which would prohibit both the release and the publication of prejudicial material; thus the press as well as police and lawyers could be punished. The restrictions would apply only to jury trials, for judges in any event have to be exposed to prejudicial material when they rule on the admissibility of evidence.

In Meyer's proposed statute, certain matters would be specifically prohibited, such as publication of prior criminal record, or of a confession, or of the offer of a settlement in a civil case, or of opinions about the credibility of a witness or the guilt of the accused. In addition, there would be a second category of material which might or might not be prejudicial, such as interviews with the victims of a crime, statements about the expected testimony of a witness, publication of the addresses of jurors. Whether the printing of such matters substantially endangered a fair trial would have to be determined by a jury, evaluating all the circumstances of the case.

The press, understandably, is apprehensive about all such proposals. Any suggestion of court-enforced restraints raises fears of full-blown censorship. Many journalists, though by no means all, also oppose restricting the utterances of the police and the D.A.'s office, on the grounds that the public's "right to know" would be infringed. While the right to know, unlike the right to print, has no constitutional sanction, it is clearly in the public interest that the police, prosecutors, and courts be subject to continual journalistic scrutiny. This goal can be achieved, however, without the press's inquisitiveness being satisfied at so premature a stage in a criminal proceeding as to victimize a defendant. The right to know is not an absolute, in the police station any more than in the Pentagon or the State Department. While unnecessary secrecy in any area of government is to be avoided, the press can hardly demand instant candor.

On the other hand, proposals like Meyer's, Morse's, and Griswold's, while pointing in the right direction, all share a common defect: they admit of no exceptions. To ensure that a jury is uncontaminated by extraneous impressions, they would prohibit virtually all statements to the press, before and during a trial, by both defense counsel and prosecutors.

Such a sweeping approach assumes that justice is always done in the courtroom, that throughout the fifty states we always enjoy an equitable and efficient judicial system. The truth is that on occasion pretrial publicity serves the ends of justice; instead of damaging the case of an innocent defendant, it may ensure fair treatment. It has not been unknown in some parts of this country for trade-union organizers occasionally to be run on trumped-up criminal charges; what would be gained if defense lawyers were prevented from saying that the real crime was organizing a union?

Similarly, during the civil rights upsurge in the South, the ostensible charge on which arrests are made is usually far removed from the real offense—an assertion of constitutional rights which the local authorities regard as intolerable. It would certainly be a perversion of justice if defense attorneys (and newspapers, under Justice Meyer's proposed statute) were to be punished for stating that their clients were being unfairly harassed.

Some of the most celebrated civil liberties cases of the past could never have been effectively fought if Dean Griswold's or Justice Meyer's proposals had been in effect. In the Scottsboro case, back in 1931, nine Negro youths who had been riding a boxcar through Alabama were falsely charged with rape by two white girls (one of whom later recanted) who were on the same train. Eight of the boys were convicted and sentenced to death in a judicial atmosphere that would have dismayed an English court. The case remained a *cause célèbre* throughout the thirties. There were endless trips to the appellate courts, two reversals by the U.S. Supreme Court, and several jury trials in Alabama; in the end, most of the youths were released. But had some of the restraints currently proposed been operative, the campaign for the Scottsboro nine would have had to halt every time a new trial was pending. It is difficult to see how such restrictions would have furthered justice; and they would certainly have made it more difficult to raise money for the defense.

The George Whitmore case, with which this article began, ironically illustrates not only the inequities of the present system but also how the engines of mass publicity can aid a hapless defendant. On the basis of false information from the police, the New York press initially damned Whitmore beyond the point where he could get a fair trial. On the other hand, long before District Attorney Hogan exonerated him of the Wylie-Hoffert killings, a number of newspapermen became suspicious of the charges and launched a press campaign in his behalf. It is true that an assistant district attorney had also begun to doubt the validity of Whitmore's confession, and in the end (partly aided by journalistic investigators), turned up the crucial evidence that cleared him. But no one who has followed the case doubts that relentless newspaper attention has had much to do with the scrupulous concern for Whitmore's constitutional rights now manifested by all the authorities.

What would have happened to Whitmore if the British rules or Dean Griswold's rules had been in effect? At the outset, his false confession would not have been published; he would unquestionably have been tried on the initial charge, that of attempted rape, by as close to an impartial jury as one can get in a sensational case. Once the press began to doubt his guilt, the papers would either have been prevented from saying anything in print or would have at least been denied access to Whitmore's lawyers while the two additional trials were pending. Whitmore has clearly gained by the present arrangements.

Obviously, some balance must be struck between total lack of restraint and restrictions so severe as to defeat, under some circumstances, the very ends they seek to secure. As a practical matter, it is unlikely that any legislation could pass that would penalize the press for derelictions in crime-reporting. The only approach that has a chance to work is one that would stop the flow of prejudicial material at its source: the police department and the prosecutor's office, which routinely furnish the press with the bulk of information about confessions, incriminating evidence, "bombshell" witnesses.

As a general rule, the defense counsel should be put under the same restraints, for it is clearly as unfair for one side as for the other to try its case in the newspapers. But one escape clause should be provided, wide enough to accommodate the exceptional case like the Whitmore affair or the Scottsboro boys—defendant's option. The defendant already has the option in criminal trials of deciding whether to testify. Under the present proposal, the defendant who thought he was being framed could take his case to the press; his lawyer could talk. In that event, of course, the prosecutor would have the right to respond. One would anticipate that only under unusual circumstances would the defendant exercise the publicity option; in most cases he would be better off avoiding all but the most neutral press comment.

This may not be a perfect solution, but it is one which is likely to prevent the excesses of trial by newspaper without relinquishing the safeguards of a crusading press. In the vast majority of cases, it would sweep away the fog of prejudice that frequently clouds the jury's vision. It would, in short, return the trial to the courtroom.

How *Time* Stereotyped
Three U.S. Presidents

John C. Merrill

The suggestion that *Time* magazine selects, aligns and explains (*i.e.,* "subjectivizes") information will certainly not startle many persons. In fact, its editors have insisted from the magazine's founding in 1923 that objectivity in news presentation is impossible and that *Time* writers should "make a

From *Journalism Quarterly* (Autumn 1965), p. 563. Reprinted by permission.

judgment" in their articles.[1] This study investigates some of the techniques used by the publication to subjectivize its news and to try to determine what stereotyped pictures of three American Presidents were presented. The study is not concerned with the "ethics" of a news magazine's "subjectivizing" its news content, although some writers have been critical in this respect.[2]

This study[3] was undertaken primarily to answer this question: What kind of stereotyped image of each of the Presidents—Truman, Eisenhower, and Kennedy—was presented by the magazine? Rather cursory and non-analytical reading of *Time* had given the impression that the magazine was anti-Truman and pro-Eisenhower. And during the Kennedy administration, there were many surface indications that *Time* was at least more objective (or neutral) toward the late President. What would be the stereotypes of the three Presidents presented by *Time* and how would the magazine go about creating them?

Would the "newsstories" in the magazine indicate political bias? Would the stories provide clear-cut examples of subjective, judgmental or opinionated reporting? If so, what were these techniques of subjectivizing? This study would at least be a beginning in a systemized critique.

THE METHOD

Ten consecutive issues of *Time* were chosen for study from each of the three Presidential administrations. The beginning date of each consecutive issue period was chosen by the random method of selection. First, the years of each administration were chosen: for Truman, 1951; for Eisenhower, 1955; for Kennedy, 1962. Successive procedures determined the month and the week which would be used as the beginning date for the 10 issues in each administration. The Truman beginning date was April 2, 1951; the Eisenhower date was January 24, 1955, and the Kennedy beginning date was November 23, 1962.

It was decided that there was no need to compare space treatment given the three Presidents, since space in itself has no necessary bearing on subjectivity or bias. What was considered important was the language used to describe each President, with special emphasis on the presence or ab-

[1] John Kobler, "Luce: The First Tycoon and the Power of His Press," *Saturday Evening Post* (Jan. 16, 1965), pp. 28–45. Cf. James Playsted Wood, *Magazines in the United States* (New York: Ronald Press, 1956), pp. 205–6, and *The Story of an Experiment* (New York: Time, Inc., 1948).

[2] Almost the entire first issue of *FACT* (Jan.-Feb., 1964) was devoted to a series of highly critical essays by important personages, all deploring the practices of *Time*. Another criticism of *Time*, even more harsh, perhaps, was the entire issue of *UAW Ammunition* (December 1956). Yet another, couched in more intellectual though hardly less cutting language, was "Time: the Weekly Fiction Magazine" by Jigs Gardner in *The Nation* (August 15, 1959), pp. 65–67.

[3] Sponsored in part by the Fund for Organized Research, Texas A&M University.

sence of "loaded" words and expressions and on general contextual impressions presented.

Six *bias categories* were set up: 1) attribution bias, 2) adjective bias, 3) adverbial bias, 4) contextual bias, 5) outright opinion, and 6) photographic bias. In considering these categories, as they related to the 30 issues of *Time* studied, instances of bias were noted either as *positive* (favorable) or as *negative* (unfavorable). Advanced journalism students served as an evaluative panel. Indications of bias (either positive or negative) thought dubious (borderline cases) were not counted as bias in this study.

THE BIAS CATEGORIES

ATTRIBUTION BIAS designates bias which stems from the magazine's means of attributing information to the President. In other words, this is bias which is contained in the synonym for the word "said" used by the magazine. An attribution verb such as "said" is neutral (not opinionated and evokes no emotional response) and was ignored in the study. An attribution verb such as "snapped" (negatively affective) is a word designed to appeal to the reader's emotions, to give a judgmental stimulus. An attribution verb such as "smiled" is counted as a "favorable" term, for it is positively affective.

ADJECTIVE BIAS is a type which, like attribution bias, attempts to build up an impression of the person described; this is accomplished by using adjectives, favorable or unfavorable, in connection with the person. While use of adjectives is quite common in news reporting, they must be used with extreme care or subjectivity will creep in and the mere use of the adjectives will create a favorable or unfavorable impression. Or, as Rudolf Flesch points out, "the little descriptive adjectives" of *Time* "tend to blot out" the other words because of their "overpotency." This results, says Flesch, in the reader getting "a wrong impression or, at least, an emphasis that isn't there."[4]

An example of "favorable" bias in adjective use: "*serene* state of mind." An example of "unfavorable" bias in adjective use: "*flat, monotonous* voice." Not only do these adjectives tend to prejudice the reader for or against the person described, but they are actually *subjective* in nature; they are opinions of the writer. They might be called "judgmental" adjectives; at any rate they are quite different from adjectives which might be called "neutral" or "objective"—such as "the *blue* sky."

[4] *How to Write, Speak and Think More Effectively.* New York: Signet Books, 1963, pp. 68-9. Dr. Flesch says that these adjectives, according to *Time* editors, help the reader get a better picture of what's going on. Dr. Flesch takes issue with this and says that it is "quite obvious that *Time* readers are apt to learn a lot about the faces, figures, hands, lips and eyes of world leaders, but are liable to misread or skip what these people do" (p. 69).

ADVERBIAL BIAS depends on qualifiers or magnifiers—adverbs—to create an impression in the reader's mind. Often this adverbial bias is a sort of reinforcing of another bias expression already present (*e.g.,* when an adverb reinforces an attribution bias as in this case: "He barked *sarcastically.*") This is a technique by which the magazine creates a favorable or unfavorable impression in the mind of the reader by generally telling *how* or *why* a person said or did something.

CONTEXTUAL BIAS cannot be notated in neat lists. It is the bias in whole sentences or paragraphs or in other (and larger) units of meaning, even an entire story. The purpose is to present the person reported on in a favorable or an unfavorable light by the overall meaning or innuendo of the report, not by specific words and phrases alone. The whole context must be considered. Since one's own biases or interpretations might very well determine what he considers contextually biased, it was necessary to get the opinions of a panel.[5] Contextual bias was counted *only* when there was agreement among the panelists.

OUTRIGHT OPINION, of course, is the most blatant and obvious type of bias or subjectivity in newswriting. The expression of opinion by the publication might be called "presenting a judgment," which S. I. Hayakawa says should be kept out of reports.[6] Dr. Hayakawa defines "judgments" as "all expressions of the writer's approval or disapproval of the occurrences, persons, or objects he is describing." Readers do not expect to find the judgments or opinions of the writer in a newspaper or a news-magazine except in a signed column or editorial. *Time* does use outright opinion. Examples: "His (Eisenhower's) powers of personal persuasion are strong" and "He has an aversion to stirring up unnecessary national crises."

The expression of opinion is sometimes disguised. In other words, through semantic tricks *Time* permits someone else (or the whole United States) to say or believe something about the President, thus presenting its own opinion indirectly. Example: "Few at home in the U.S. seemed to begrudge the President his trip, however inauspicious the timing." In addition, *Time* projects its opinion by explaining *why* people in the news do as they do. As one writer puts it: *"Time* reads men's motives—good for friends, bad for enemies—with that Olympian supremacy and aloofness which prompted Commager to speak of the period 'before *Time* became omniscient.' "[7]

PHOTOGRAPHY BIAS, it is granted, might possibly result from inability to get other photographs or from no real desire to prejudice the reader. In other words, it could be unintentional. However, intention is not consid-

---

[5] Six advanced journalism students at Texas A&M composed the panel to decide on these cases of possible contextual bias.

[6] *Language in Thought and Action.* New York: Harcourt, Brace and Company, 1940, pp. 38, 42–44.

[7] Garry Wills, "Timestyle," *National Review* (August 3, 1957), p. 130.

ered in the treatment of this or any other category, for there is no real way to know intent. These questions were asked in trying to determine this bias: What overall impression does the photograph give? How is the President presented in the picture—dignified, undignified; angry, happy; calm, nervous, etc.? What does the caption say/imply?

TABLE 1

BIAS CATEGORY BREAKDOWN FOR THE THREE
PRESIDENTS IN EACH 10-ISSUE PERIOD

BIAS CATEGORY	TRUMAN	EISENHOWER	KENNEDY
Attribution Bias	9	11	5
Adjective Bias	21	22	3
Adverbial Bias	17	7	4
Contextual Bias	33	20	13
Outright Opinion	8	17	12
Photographic Bias	5	5	8
Total Bias	93	82	45
Total Positive Bias	1	81	31
Total Negative Bias	92	1	14

A SELECTED WEEK: TRUMAN

Issue of April 23, 1951: Of the 10 weeks of *Time* studied from the Truman administration, this issue of April 23 contains more obvious indications of bias and subjectivity than any of the others. It is one of the several issues which dealt with Truman's relieving General MacArthur of his post as Supreme Commander in the Far East. *Time* is obviously in sympathy with the general, and in this week's issue makes some of its more biased statements. Some examples of the magazine's opinions can be seen in the following paragraph (p. 24):

Seldom had a more unpopular man fired a more popular one. Douglas MacArthur was the personification of the big man, with the many admirers who look to the great man for leadership, with the few critics who distrust and fear a big man's domineering ways. Harry Truman was almost a professional little man, with admirers who like the little man's courage, with the many critics who despise a little man's inadequacies.

Not satisfied with the then-current issue, *Time* quickly and in broad strokes presents the readers with a "flash-back" to an administration filled with six years of "shabby politicking and corruption" and "doubts about his State Department" coupled with "distaste for his careless government-by-crony."

Time in this issue, *however,* does not stop here; it goes further and gives the impression that the nation shares its opinion of President Truman. Says *Time* (p. 25): "A few days later, over the morning coffee, the nation read of Harry Truman's reply and fumed." (This followed a report by the magazine that Truman had "replied curtly" to a critic of his MacArthur action.) Also in this issue readers were reminded that "probers were still unearthing new evidence of skulduggery in the RFC" and that Truman was a President who "stubbornly protected shoddy friends."

A SELECTED WEEK: EISENHOWER

Issue of Feb. 7, 1955: In this week's issue, *Time* quite typically provides vivid examples of subjective and biased reporting and evidences a strong pro-Eisenhower slant. According to the magazine: "The strong leadership of President Eisenhower and the near-unanimity of the Congress in backing him in the Formosa resolution undoubtedly retrieved much of the U.S. prestige and influence that had been recently lost in Asia." As described by *Time,* Ike's resolution that the U.S. would fight was "evidence of the President's patience and peacefulness" (p. 9).

A few further quotes from this story might serve to indicate the magazine's bias toward *Eisenhower* and give good examples of subjective reporting:

A few days before the President's message to Congress last week, the whole anti-Communist position in the Far East seemed to be coming apart. Ike stopped the rot, and the U.S. emerged in a better light than it had enjoyed in several weeks. (P. 9)

He (Eisenhower) wanted to demonstrate national unity behind the policy; he wanted to keep his 1952 campaign promise that he would submit to Congress any proposed steps to use U.S. forces in combat. (P. 10)

For Dwight Eisenhower, the week's events were demonstration of forceful and skillful presidential leadership. He had used his prestige to score a political and policy victory, and placed Capitol Hill—its Republicans and Democrats alike—in the position of sharing the decision. (P. 10)

A SELECTED WEEK: KENNEDY

Issue of Dec. 28, 1962: Again in this issue *Time* presented the President as a confident person, one who "bluntly voiced his growing impatience with British and European bellyaching about U.S. contributions to the common defense," one who was behind the ransom payments to Castro's government, and one whose TV interview "from the rocking chair" showed the President "at his informal confident best" (pp. 13-15). Over in the "Business" section (pp. 50-55), the Presidential image turned more unpleasant. Recounting the business year of 1962, *Time* dealt at some length with JFK's part in the steel crisis. The magazine referred to "John F. Kennedy's hasty and whitelipped counterattack" against U.S. Steel Chairman Roger Blough, who was trying to raise steel prices $6 a ton. According to *Time,* "virtually all U.S. businessmen were outraged by the tactics Kennedy used against Blough." But, added the magazine later in the story, "in board rooms around the country, businessman were impressed that President Kennedy had talked even tougher to Khrushchev than to Roger Blough" (p. 62).

THE PRESIDENTIAL STEREOTYPES

It was found in this study that from week to week *Time,* through the skillful use of devices described earlier, creates and reinforces a stereotype of the President in office. The personality of the President gets more emphasis through the colorful and subjective language of the magazine than does his news activities. As Jigs Gardner wrote in *The Nation,* it is the "reduction of news to emotional conflicts of personalities."[8] One reason for this, obviously, is that "conflicts of personalities" make strong appeal to emotions. This appeal is far greater for the general reader than is the appeal of straight, neutralist reporting.

The following paragraph from *Time* (June 16, 1952) serves as an example:

> They saw Ike, and liked what they saw. They liked him for his strong, vigorous manner of speech . . . and for an overriding innate kindliness and modesty. But most of all, they liked him in a way they could scarcely explain. They liked Ike because, when they saw him and heard him talk, he made them proud of themselves and all the half-forgotten best that was in them and the nation.

This example is typical of the way *Time* creates and develops its presidential images and stereotypes. Below, in brief profiles taken from *Time*-treatment, are re-created the stereotypes of the three Presidents which the reader of the magazine had developed for him week by week during the three administrations. These stereotypes, although naturally abstractions even of *Time*-images, picture each president as seen through the verbal lenses of the "weekly newsmagazine."

> TRUMAN: A bouncy man, sarcastic and shallow. A very unpopular man, a "little" man with many inadequacies. A President who condoned all types of "shabby politicking and corruption" in his administration. A man who practiced "careless government-by-crony." A petulant President who "stubbornly protected shoddy friends," one who had "grown too touchy to make

8 Gardner, *op. cit.,* p. 66.

judicious decisions." A President who failed to give firm leadership to the country. A man whose State Department was full of homosexuals. A man who evaded issues and refused to face an argument. A President who "breathed cocky belligerence," and bounced on his heels while he launched off-the-cuff oratory. A President whose every action was motivated by shabby politics. A President, who when he spoke, generally sputtered, barked, cracked, droned, or "popped a gasket." A person who "grinned slyly," and "preached the Truman sermon" and "probed with a blunt finger." A man whose speeches had a "thin, overworked and flat quality" as he spoke with a "flat, monotonous voice." A man who stirred up national crises and who left the nation's nervous system "jangled and jumpy." A man who was blunt, sarcastic, belligerent, cocky, petulant, irascible, harried, lazy, vain, angry, sly, curt, and cold.

EISENHOWER: A smiling, warm-hearted, sincere leader. A man of "earnest demeanor." A President whose strong leadership brought united determination. A patient and peaceful man, and one who wanted to keep his campaign promises. A skillful leader who was a statesman rather than a politician. One who was humble and who took his duties very seriously. One who was "on top of his job." A President who when he moved, moved "quietly." One who was sensitive to "the mood of the nation," and who did not like to stir up crises. A person who loved children, one who was forgiving and religious. One who brushed away misunderstandings and insisted on facts and the truth. A President who was cautious, warm, charitable, modest, happy, amiable, firm, cordial, effective, serene, frank, calm, skillful, and earnest. A person who talked with a happy grin, who pointed out cautiously, spoke warmly, and chatted amiably.

KENNEDY: A President who was wealthy but generous in charity. A man who liked much social life in the White House, and who travelled extensively. A versatile man—who wore "many hats." A President who fostered a kind of "forced togetherness of New Frontier society." A man whose mistake it was not to censor the press, but "to talk out loud" about it. A confident person, usually pleasant. A happy man with a "cheery look." A man who seldom showed irritation, but who could launch a "hasty and white-lipped counterattack." A President who would bring full force of his power to bear to get his way. A President who talked tough to Khrushchev. A man whose presence had great impact on crowds, one who was willing to take risks, who had a "conviction of correctness." A speaker who, when he spoke, said, reaffirmed, announced, promised, concluded, and insisted. He usually simply "said." A man who was usually confident, informed, emphatic, cheery, social, versatile, energetic, youthful, impressive, determined, and well-informed.

EXAMPLES AND COMMENTARY

Following is a group of selected examples of subjective and biased reportorial quotations taken from the sample study periods. After each example is the author's comment[9] on the example. These examples offer insight into the kind of techniques used by *Time* in its reporting during the periods studied:

If the Administration had ever toyed with the idea of appeasement, it had been forced to a public renunciation. (May 21, 1951, p. 19.)

Here is the case of implicating somebody of something where nothing—so far as Time *knew—really existed. This is possibly the most questionable type of reporting used by the magazine.*

Harry Truman had worn a harried and rumpled air during General Mac-Arthur's three days of testimony before Congress. (May 21, 1951, p. 19.)

Here there is an insinuation of a guilty conscience, of someone afraid something unpleasant will leak out about him. A case of implication by appearance.

History would remember this day and this man, and mark him large. (April 30, 1951, p. 23.)

Here is a case of pure opinion and doubtful syntax. The quote relates to MacArthur.

It was a neat bit of off-the-cuff campaigning, and was calculated—like his "hope" of making a cross-country give-'em-hell speaking tour this spring or summer—to gladden the hearts of Democrat bigwigs who met in Denver last week to beat the drums for '52. (June 4, 1951, p. 19.)

Here is the case of Time *telling the reader why Truman greeted a group of young people at the White House; this is purely the magazine's conjecture stated as fact.*

The State Department was still clearing homosexuals out of its woodwork. . . . Total number of homosexuals dismissed as bad security risks since 1947: 146 men and two women. (May 7, 1951, p. 26.)

Here is a case of imputing corruption to an administration by pointing out and playing up a certain "scandal" in one department.

---

[9] These comments by the author dealing with the examples from *Time* are certainly themselves "subjective." But there is one thing in their favor: they are *said to be comments* and are not hidden in a factual context.

A few days later, over the morning coffee, the nation read of Harry Truman's reply and fumed. (April 23, 1951, p. 25.)

Time here projects its omniscience over the entire nation and tells the reader what the country read and even how it reacted after reading it.

The strong leadership of President Eisenhower and the near-unanimity of the Congress in backing him in the Formosa resolution undoubtedly retrieved much of the U.S. prestige and influence that had been recently lost in Asia. (Feb. 7, 1955, p. 9.)

This example is interesting not only for the clever way positive bias is packed in, but for the use of the subjective key-word "undoubtedly."

He (Eisenhower) has an aversion to stirring up unnecessary national crises, has deliberately tried to soothe the nation's nervous system—left jangled and jumpy by an unbroken procession of Truman crises. (Feb. 28, 1955, p. 13.)

Here is the implication that other presidents might like to stir up trouble, but not Ike. Also Truman's "crises" are dragged in and the reader is informed that this is the reason for the "nation's nervous system" being "jumpy."

TABLE 2

SUBJECTIVE EXPRESSIONS USED BY *Time* IN REPORTING
SPEECHES OF THE THREE PRESIDENTS

TRUMAN:	EISENHOWER:
"said curtly"	"said with a happy grin"
"said coldly"	"cautiously pointed out"
"barked Harry S. Truman"	"chatted amiably"
"cracked Harry Truman"	"said warmly"
"with his voice heavy with sarcasm"	"paused to gather thought"
"preached the Truman sermon"	"equanimity and inner ease"
"flushed with anger"	"sensitive to the mood of the nation"
"grinning slyly"	"devastatingly effective"
"petulant, irascible President"	"serene state of mind"
"had worn a harried and rumpled air"	"calm and confident"
"made his familiar, chopping motions"	"frankness was the rule"
"cocky as ever"	"skillfully refused to commit himself"
"publicly put his foot in his mouth"	"obviously a man with a message"
"with a blunt finger he probed"	"brushing aside misunderstanding"

KENNEDY:

"President Kennedy said" (10 t.)
"President Kennedy announced"
"Concluded the President"
"stated the case in plain terms"
"the President urged"
"Kennedy argued"
"concluded Kennedy"
"he suggested"
"President Kennedy recommended"
"Kennedy insisted"
"Kennedy contended"
"Kennedy maintained"
"The President promised"

CONCLUSIONS

Because of its racy style, its clever use of captions and pictures and its smooth integration of separated (in space and time) incidents and speeches, *Time* is understandably a popular publication for the general reader. However, the careful and thoughtful reader who is looking for proper perspective and serious backgrounding instead of entertainment and polemic will probably not find the magazine very satisfying.[10] This is not to imply that *Time* contains no *facts*; certainly its pages abound with facts. But it is the popularization of these facts, the constant weaving of these facts into semi-fictionalized language patterns and the constant evidence of preferential or prejudicial treatment of news subjects that would probably be unpalatable to the reader seeking the "true picture."

This study indicated that *Time* editorialized in its regular "news" columns to a great extent, and that it used a whole series of tricks to bias the stories and to lead the reader's thinking. Mostly, in its Presidential treatment, the magazine presented the reader with highly loaded essays of a subjective type.

In addition to isolating several interesting types of subjectivizing procedure, the study showed that *Time* 1) was clearly anti-Truman, 2) was strongly pro-Eisenhower, and 3) was neutral or certainly moderate toward Kennedy. Stereotypes of the three Presidents built up by the magazine during the periods studied were quite vivid—especially in the cases of Truman and Eisenhower.

---

10 It should be noted, however, that some critics seem to feel that *Time* in 1965 has become more responsible in its news reporting; see, for example, William Forbis, "The March of Time; Curt, Clear and More Complete," *Montana Journalism* Review (Spring 1965), pp. 6–8. This article contrasts sharply with the negative criticism about *Time* made by David Halberstan in his *The Making of a Quagmire*. New York: Random House, 1964, pp. 35–37.

By way of summary, the following principal techniques were used by *Time* in subjectivizing its reports: 1) deciding which incidents, which remarks, etc., to play up and which ones to omit completely or to play down; 2) failing to tell the whole story; 3) weaving opinion into the story; 4) imputing wisdom and courage and other generally admired qualities by use of adjectives, adverbs and general context and by quoting some friend of the person; 5) dragging into the story past incidents unnecessary to the present report; 6) using one person's opinion to project opinion to this person's larger group—the "one-man cross-section device."

7) Imputing wide acceptance, such as "the nation believed" without presenting any evidence at all; 8) transferring disrepute to a person by linking him or his group to some unpopular person, group, cause or idea; 9) playing up certain phrases or descriptions which tend to point out possible weaknesses, paint a derogatory picture or create a stereotype (e.g., "small-town boy," "off-the-cuff oratory").

10) Creating an overall impression of a person by words, an impression which is reinforced from issue to issue (e.g., to show an active and healthy President when the nation was concerned about his health, *Time* would have him "yelling tirelessly," "playing a wicked game of golf," "enjoying himself tremendously," "waving happily," and "stepping lightly"); 11) explaining motives for Presidential actions, and 12) telling the reader what "the people" think or what the nation or public thinks about almost anything.

Report on the *Reader's Digest*
Reo M. Christenson

In 1944, the editors of *Commonweal* wrote: "The *Reader's Digest* is today the most powerful vehicle for the printed word in the American hemisphere . . ." Today, with the *Digest's* circulation up threefold to 25,000,000 (more than 15,000,000 in the United States), there is no reason to revise that judgement.

In that same issue of *Commonweal,* James Rorty observed that "the millions of people who depend largely on the *Digest* are in danger of in-

Reprinted from the *Columbia Journalism Review* (Winter 1965). By permission of the author and the *Columbia Journalism Review*.

tellectual malnourishment and ideological deficiency diseases." Twenty years later, there is no reason to revise that judgment, either.

The *Digest* does not claim to offer readers a true cross section of magazine opinion, although millions may believe that it does. About 70 per cent of its articles, including a high percentage of those dealing with public affairs, are either staff-written for the *Digest* or planned and planted by the *Digest* in other magazines, then reprinted in the *Digest*. These practices help insure that the *Digest* offers its own philosophy, not a sampling of American opinion.

The philosophy is avowedly conservative. In the *Digest*'s public-relations book, *Of Lasting Interest* (1958), James Playsted Wood writes that the *Digest* "believes in social and political change through orderly development." He continues: "It believes in the traditions which are the heritage of the race, in religion, in the social codes which have taken man most of his history to develop. Critical attacks on the *Digest* have come naturally from sources swayed by opposing philosophies."

Thus is the *Digest*'s philosophy stated. How has it worked out in practice? This report is an effort to describe the political and economic editorial policies of the *Digest,* as revealed in an examination of the public-affairs articles carried in the magazine over the last twenty years. It is also an effort to assay the reportorial accuracy of the magazine.

It takes precious little political awareness to recognize that the *Digest* takes a bilious view of goings-on in Washington. Years ago, Richard Rovere wrote that while DeWitt Wallace, the editor, based much of his editorial judgment on the belief that the American people want hope, he apparently regarded the federal government as hopeless. Although there is much truth in this assertion, the *Digest* actually finds it much more hopeless when Washington is in the grip of Democrats.

A dominant editorial theme of the *Digest* is that federal officials are congenitally extravagant, that deficit spending and the national debt threaten disaster, that federal taxes are an unsupportable burden, that the federal bureaucracy bungles and botches as it bloats, and that federal power is a menace to the liberties of every American, great and small. Since November, 1944, the *Digest* has published more than 300 articles that develop these themes.

Even filler material in the *Digest* is attuned to the theme: "While you're reading these two lines, the U.S. Government will have spent $110,000— if you're a fast reader." "Bureaucracy is a giant mechanism operated by pygmies." "Our Federal Government probably spends as much accidentally now as it did on purpose 30 years ago." "Politicians and wives agree on one thing—if you postpone payment until some time in the future, it's not really spending." "After his stay in the U.S. in 1831-1832, French philosopher Alexis de Tocqueville had this to say: 'Democracy in the U.S.

will last until those in power learn that they can perpetuate themselves through taxation'." The newspaper editorials reprinted in the *Digest*'s "Press Section" reflect the same type of view.

The life of a *Digest* article does not end with its appearance in the magazine. The *Digest* offers reprints, at less than 2 cents each for quantities, of many of its assaults on Washington. About a million reprints are sold each month—some dealing, of course, with non-political subjects. To take a recent issue: In June, 1964, the *Digest* advertised reprints of Senator Frank Lausche's "The Dangerous Failings of Our State Department," as well as "One Man's Crusade for Everybody's Freedom," a laudatory article by Henry J. Taylor about the owner of Knott's Berry Farm. (Sample comment by Mr. Knott: "We've seen government grow until it is all out of proportion. Every time it grows, it takes bits of freedom out of our lives, and we become more dependent on it and less on ourselves.") Finally, *Digest* attacks on federal policies have been used in its television and radio documentary, "All America Wants To Know."

It is revealing that the favorite postwar *Digest* non-staff writers on political and economic subjects have been Henry Hazlitt (sixteen articles and a book condensation, *Will Dollars Save the World?*); Herbert Hoover (sixteen articles, some non-political); John T. Flynn (twelve articles and a condensation of his book, *The Road Ahead*); Henry J. Taylor (sixteen articles, some non-political); David Lawrence (five articles); and Barry Goldwater (five articles). Mr. Hazlitt is one of the most right-wing economists extant; some of John T. Flynn's diatribes were in the blood-line of *None Dare Call It Treason*; and Messrs. Lawrence and Goldwater are known, too, as pillars of something often called conservatism.

That every government needs informed, accurate, hard-hitting criticism goes without saying. But in its eagerness to discredit Washington, the *Digest* frequently prints staff-written articles that cast doubt on the professional competence or scrupulousness of the editors. One recent example was the lead article in the May, 1963, issue—"The Real Truth About the Federal Budget" by Charles Stevenson, who is listed on the masthead as a department editor. It allegedly presented the "shocking facts that taxpayers have not been told" about the national budget for fiscal 1964.

As it turned out, the most shocking thing about the article was the kind of repeated distortion and misinformation employed by the author. In the necessarily restrained language of the Bureau of the Budget, the article was "essentially a compilation of half-truths which together sum up a very misleading view of the Federal financial situation. An extravagant use is made in the article of color words, and many things are left unsaid which would not serve the writer's purpose."

The October, 1964, *Digest* carried a lead article called "The Great Manpower Grab," which provided another instructive example of *Digest* reporting. The sub-heading read: "Almost unnoticed, the U.S. Employment Service is undermining one of our basic freedoms—the right to choose one's life work."

This sounds frightfully totalitarian; who wants the government to decide whether you or your children will become doctors, merchants, die-casters, or fishermen? The charge, when examined, turns out to be as absurd as it is improbable. The author, Representative Frank T. Bow, is able to provide no evidence whatever that the USES or anyone else has such a goal in mind, except that the service is helping counsel many high-school students about careers!

The *Digest* did not inform its readers that Representative Bow has close relations with private employment agencies, who have a special interest in restricting the USES. In 1962, the private agencies, joined in the National Employment Association, issued a statement to members saying they planned a campaign against USES. Representative Bow told a convention of the association, "I take great pride in carrying a musket in your ranks in this battle." Yet who in the association could have hoped that he would be able to carry the musket into the pages of America's most widely read magazine.

This was not the first time the *Digest* had attacked the USES. In September, 1961, James Daniel had an article called "Let's Look At Those 'Alarming' Unemployment Figures," in which he charges USES with manipulating statistics to make the unemployment situation appear more serious than it really was. The director of the Bureau of Labor Statistics, Ewan Clague, declared, "I cannot recall ever having read a short article in which so many inaccurate statements were presented in support of such unwarranted conclusions." He then proceeded to document his case. Meanwhile Secretary of Labor Arthur Goldberg asked the *Digest* for the chance to write an article setting the facts straight. His request was ignored. When a subcommittee on economic statistics of the Congressional Joint Economic Committee asked Mr. Daniel to testify before it, he refused. A study during the Kennedy administration by an independent committee of economists and statisticians of the methods used by the Bureau of Labor Statistics found the Daniel charges to be without foundation in fact.

This sequence of events illustrates what is perhaps the most disturbing *Digest* policy—its refusal to allow rebuttal or correction. That the *Digest* prefers not to have a conventional letters column is its privilege, but its failure to give individuals and agencies attacked in its pages an opportunity for reply is indefensible by any professional standard. Representative Elmer J. Holland of Pennsylvania properly criticizes the *Digest* for its "hit-and-run journalism."

Many other agencies have felt the sting of the *Digest*'s criticism. A May 1964, lead article by Charles Stevenson called "Is This the Way to Fight the War Against Poverty?" indicted the Area Redevelopment Administration on fourteen counts that were factually inaccurate or misleading. (The ARA contends that half a dozen additional distortions exist, but while its defense is plausible, the facts are not clear in those instances.) The March, 1964, *Digest* contained an article, "The Mounting Scandal in Urban Renewal," which was inaccurate in at least thirteen instances. (The agency alleges six additional misstatements, which—again—are difficult to verify.) Many other instances could be cited. When the *Digest* blasts a federal agency or program, the prudent reader would do well to conclude that the account represents the *Digest*'s attitudes, not necessarily a dispassionate account.

Over the years, the *Digest* has shown a remarkable consistency in its attitudes when a "welfare state" agency was involved. It has criticized the Social Security system or some aspect of it five times. Five articles have dwelt on abuses of unemployment compensation. Minimum-wage laws have twice come under fire. In 1950, Harold Stassen wrote four articles attacking British socialized medicine and warning against the camel's nose under this country's tent. Other articles praised voluntary health insurance as the answer to Federal medical programs. Medicare has been attacked three times. Still other articles deplored welfare abuses or attacked the entire idea of government responsibility for welfare. In none of these categories was I able to find a single article since 1945 presenting "welfare state" activities or concepts in a generally favorable light.

The *Digest* attitude toward labor unions is hard to determine statistically. Many articles have centered on abuses in the labor movement while simultaneously praising individuals who were trying to correct those abuses. One thing is clear, however: There has been a decided shift toward a more critical attitude since 1953. From October, 1945, through 1952, my analysis showed, there were ten articles primarily friendly to unions, eight that could be termed neutral, and nine primarily critical. After 1952, eight articles could be regarded as friendly (including only two after 1956), five neutral, and forty-nine primarily critical. Eight in the last category dealt only incidentally with unions, but carried passages derogatory to labor powers and policies.

Attacks on the Teamsters leader, James M. Hoffa, constituted almost a fourth of the forty-nine critical articles. Yet the inescapable conclusion is that the *Digest* is not eager to show that unions meet their responsibilities. The *Digest*'s attitude toward unions crops up in its articles on right-to-work laws and the role of labor in politics, and in advocacy of application of antitrust laws to unions. In each instance the *Digest* takes the position opposed by the AFL-CIO.

In yet another area of governmental controversy, the *Digest* has published five articles friendly to the House Committee on Un-American Activities or to other Congressional committees investigating Communist or other radical political activities. No *Digest* article has focused on abuses of the investigatory power. As to Senator Joseph McCarthy—one of the most controversial men in postwar America—the *Digest* chose to ignore him altogether.

Throughout the past two decades, the *Digest* has repeatedly printed articles favorable to the rights, potentialities, and accomplishments of American Negroes. Yet when it chose to deal with the 1964 civil-rights bill, it confined itself to two articles from *U.S. News & World Report,* in which its editor, David Lawrence, denounced the proposed Equal Employment Opportunities Commission. The *Digest* carried no defense of the commission.

Despite its consistent tone, it should not be thought that the *Digest* has been monolithic. It has, in fact, printed a number of articles that would please many of its critics. It has backed the United Nations on a number of occasions, although its support has cooled in recent years. It once tended to defend the foreign-aid programs. It has consistently fought for conservation. It has usually supported antitrust activities. It has opposed highway billboards. Individual articles have proposed self-government for Washington, D.C., statehood for Alaska, and repeal of the Connally Amendment restricting American participation in the World Court. The *Digest* has supported reapportionment and has defended civilian control of the Joint Chiefs of Staff. Stuart Chase was given space to attack the concept of guilt by association. Censorship has been opposed and the First Amendment praised. And the *Digest* has even opened its pages to pleas for higher salaries for federal officials and military personnel, more spending on national parks, and federal aid for improving prenatal care.

Reading the *Digest* for 1945 and early 1946, one is struck by the difference between its tone in those years and its attitudes today. Considering current editorial policy, it seems almost incredible that the *Digest* should have condensed Henry A. Wallace's postwar tract, *60 Million Jobs,* in which he spoke out for farm supports, increased minimum wages, extended social security and health insurance, housing and hospital-construction programs, TVA-like river developments, and a federal full-employment program. Other articles in that era praised governmental planning in Britain and lauded the vigor and reforms of the British Labor Party. At least five articles or book condensations between November, 1945, and May, 1946, urged the United States toward world government.

But the *Digest* repented with a vengeance, and the change is evident not only in domestic policy but in its adoption of a "hard line" foreign policy. For years its favorite writer on international affairs was William Bullitt, former ambassador to Russia and France, whose once favorable attitude toward Russia eventually shifted to belligerence. His latest *Digest* articles urged the United States to bomb strategic locations in China and to support a Chiang Kai-shek attack on the Chinese mainland.

Since 1961, the *Digest* has taken an ever tougher line. In 1964, the

Digest published such articles as Richard Nixon's "Needed in Vietnam: The Will to Win"; Senator Lausche's attack on the State Department, mentioned before; Allen Drury's "The Dangerous Game of Let's Pretend," in which he charges the United States government with timidity and says it is "fantastic that we should so consistently argue ourselves out of the unflinching firmness which may well be our salvation."

In November, 1964, the *Digest* published a long piece by Mr. Nixon, "Cuba, Castro and John F. Kennedy," which declared that a small group of "liberal" White House advisers persistently give "incredibly bad advice" that strengthens the enemy, that the United States has followed a "weak-kneed foreign policy" in Cuba, that "we have been humiliated, frustrated, outguessed and outmaneuvered at every turn," and that we must fight the cold war more grimly rather than follow the Kennedy-Johnson course. Nixon's article, reaching 15,000,000 readers about a week before the 1964 election, backed Senator Goldwater's foreign policy proposals almost to the letter. (The senator must also have been pleased with two other major pieces in the same issue by Walter Judd, keynote speaker at the Republican convention in 1960, that faithfully and eloquently expounded Goldwater views on domestic and foreign policy.)

Senator Goldwater was not the first Republican candidate to receive timely support in the *Digest*. Richard Nixon has been given royal treatment. In October, 1952, the magazine printed "I Say He's a Wonderful Guy," by Pat Ryan Nixon. The following issue, distributed just before the election, carried a long interview with Mr. Nixon about the Hiss case. During his tenure as Vice President, Mr. Nixon wrote about his Latin American travels for the *Digest*. Later, when he was fighting for his political life in the gubernatorial campaign in California in 1962, the *Digest* published three long installments from his book, *Six Crises*.

General Eisenhower, too, has fared well in the *Digest*. Before 1952, the magazine carried five articles friendly to or written by the general; in 1952, four more appeared (there were none about Adlai Stevenson in that year). During the Eisenhower terms, fifty-eight articles extolling the President or members of his cabinet, were written by members of his administration, or otherwise depicted the administration favorably. (The lead article in January, 1956, was entitled, "Run Again, Ike.")

In the same years, eighteen articles could be termed critical of administration policies or performance, with the bulk of these centering on defense or foreign aid. Even these articles were general, rather than specific criticisms of the administration.

How did the Truman administration fare? During his seven years and seven months, the *Digest* carried friendly articles about Mr. Truman only in his first year—in June, 1945, and in March, 1946. After the 1948 election, the *Digest* mounted continual attacks on the administration's farm program, its health plan, its public-power policies, its extravagance, its relations with business, its trend toward socialism, and its corruption. On the last-named, the *Digest* carried eight articles from 1950 to 1952, the last being Henry J. Taylor's "Was Corruption As Bad Under Harding?" Mr. Taylor's answer: "No."

During President Truman's last four years, forty-four articles could properly be labeled critical of the administration, and only fourteen friendly. The friendly pieces were primarily personality sketches of such prominent government figures as Philip Jessup, Paul Hoffman, Matthew Ridgway, Robert Lovett, and Stuart Symington. (In his 1945 analysis of the magazine, *Little Wonder,* John Bainbridge estimated that *Digest* articles in the Franklin Roosevelt era had run 3 to 1 against the administration.)

The Kennedy administration was treated somewhat more gently, although President Kennedy's domestic policies received a steady pummeling—partly from General Eisenhower, writing for the *Digest* as an elder statesman. Moreover, the failure at the Bay of Pigs was followed by a series of aricles critical not only of that fiasco but of other administration foreign policies as well. After Lyndon B. Johnson assumed the presidency, the *Digest* republished an earlier article by Mr. Johnson offering noncontroversial principles, and carried a friendly appraisal of him by Stewart Alsop. These were the only articles (through November, 1964) friendly to his administration. In the same period, twenty-three were published that could be called unfriendly to policies advocated by or executed by the administration.

It is not suggested here that there is something reprehensible about being a Republican journal. Every magazine has a right to follow its own editorial preferences. The preceding evidence was presented only to establish beyond cavil that the *Digest* is staynchly Republican—a fact that readers and educators have a right to know.

Almost half a million copies of the *Digest* are used regularly in United States classrooms, mostly secondary schools. On two occasions in the 1940's the National Council of Teachers of English appointed committees to evaluate the suitability of the *Digest* for classroom use. Twice the committees recommended against the *Digest* and twice the recommendation was rejected on ground that the reports lacked objectivity and documentation.

The record of the *Digest* in the postwar years would certainly offer the council, it would seem, good reason to reconsider its decision. However, if the *Digest* is to continue being used in the classroom, teachers at least owe it to their students to warn them of its bias, its partisanship, and the dubious character of its reporting on the Washington scene.

An historian, Dixon Wecter, wrote in 1944 that compared with many of his competitors DeWitt Wallace "has shown considerable restraint, fair taste, and good intentions, with a not unwholesome effect on American life." In many respects, this judgment may still be valid. Perhaps the typical *Digest* reader is exposed to more worthwhile literature than would be the case if the *Digest* were not on the scene. After all, it has published many writers one might not ordinarily associate with the *Digest*: in recent issues, it has had such contributors as Marya Mannes, Robert Heilbroner, John F. Kennedy, John Steinbeck, Barbara Ward, John Fischer. And it helps youngsters develop reading habits—a service of no mean importance.

It is a pity, though, that a magazine that in so many respects has demonstrated its ability to meet the states and needs of millions of Americans should have its usefulness so seriously impaired by editing so obsessed with the wickedness of Washington under Democrats that it countenances or encourages shoddy and politically biased reporting.

It is unfortunate moreover that the *Digest* cannot bring itself to permit competent spokesmen to conduct regular, spirited debates in its pages on controversial public issues. A magazine that takes pride in its educational role, and in its widespread use by schools, should not be averse to playing host to diversity.

TV and the Press in Vietnam; or, Yes, I Can Hear You Very Well— Just What Was It You Were Saying?

Michael J. Arlen

. . . People often refer to television's coverage of Vietnam as "television's war" (as one could probably describe television's coverage of civil rights as "television's civil war"), and although it seems fair to say that in general television has done very well strictly in terms of what it has set out to report about Vietnam—in terms of those usually combat-oriented film clips that appear on the morning and evening news programs—it also seems fair to say that for the most part television in Vietnam has operated on a level not much more perceptive than that of a sort of illustrated wire service, with the television crews racketing around the countryside seeking to illustrate the various stories that are chalked on the assignment boards in Saigon ("4th Div. Opn.," "Chopper story," "Hobo Woods Opn.,"

From *Living-Room War*, by Michael J. Arlen. Copyright © 1967 by Michael J. Arlen. Originally appeared in *The New Yorker*. Reprinted by permission of The Viking Press, Inc.

"Buddhist march"), constantly under pressure to feed the New York news programs new stories (ideally, combat stories), moving in here, moving out, moving in there the next day. Recently, the major effort of the military war has been taking place up north in the I Corps area, and, as a result, many of the television and newspaper correspondents are now working out of the DaNang press center. Ordinarily, though, much of the work is done almost in bankerish fashion from Saigon, and one says "bankerish" not to disparage the factor of risk-taking in their covering of various operations (a factor that ranges from slight to very considerable), but as an indication of how difficult it is to get close to a strange war in an unfamiliar country by a process that more often than not consists in your having breakfast at the Hotel Caravelle at seven-thirty, driving out to a helicopter base, going by chopper to where some military operation is occurring (say, a search of an area where a Vietcong ammunition dump supposedly exists, possible picture value being in the blowing up of the ammo dump), wandering around in the woods taking pictures until three-thirty, maybe getting shot at a bit and maybe not, then taking the chopper back, doing all your paperwork and film-shipment arrangements, and meeting friends in the Continental bar at seven o'clock. The correspondents tend to have mixed feelings about all this themselves. Many of them, to be sure, are older men with families and are not crazy about spending more time than necessary out in the field, and, doubtless like journalists everywhere, they complain of not having enough time to cover the "right stories," and of the pressure from New York to provide combat coverage. Of the newspapermen and magazine correspondents, in fact, except for a couple of people like Peter Arnett and Henri Huet of the AP, and David Greenway of *Time,* and Dana Stone of UPI, virtually none are doing the combat work that television is now doing almost on a routine basis (a seemingly routine basis, anyway). And although it's true that the Vietnam story is more than the story of men shooting at one another (the television people themselves refer to it as "bang-bang" coverage, and have a healthy respect for what goes into the getting of it), it's also true that American men (and Vietnamese men) are indeed getting shot and killed, and are shooting and killing others, and one would have to be a pretty self-indulgent pacifist to say that it wasn't somebody's job to record and witness something of that. The trouble is that television doesn't do much more than that. It doesn't try. There are the highly structured news programs, with correspondents from around the world coming on for a few minutes at a time. And then, as a way of circumventing this limitation, there are the "news specials," which up to now have generally been done with the same hasty, unfeeling, technically skillful professionalism that (more justifiably) characterizes the shorter film clips. For the most part, "television's war" is a prisoner of its own structure, a prisoner of such facts as that although television is the chief source of news and information for the majority of the people, the

News & Information act is still just another aspect of the world's greatest continuous floating variety show; that the scope and cost of television news require an immense weight of administrative managing from above; that for TV the newsworthiness of daily events is still so restrictively determined by visual criteria. For example, people watching an evening news show about an ammo dump being blown up in the Hobo Woods might reasonably conclude, on a day, say, when a nationwide strike was averted in San Diego, when a rebel army was captured in Nigeria, when the Pope fell sick, and when Indonesia broke relations with Red China, that there was some special significance to the blowing up of this particular ammo dump, or not even anything special about it, just some significance—that its presentation on the screen in front of one said something useful about the war. In all too many cases, though, what the blowing up of the ammo dump says is that when you blow up an ammo dump it goes boom-boom-boom and there is a lot of smoke, and that is about it.

Daily journalism in general seems to be virtually rooted in its traditional single-minded way of presenting the actuality of daily life, as if some invisible sacred bond existed between the conventional structures of daily journalism and the conventional attitudes of so many of the people whom daily journalism serves. This has been increasingly noticeable in journalism's severely conventional covering of most of the major matters of our time—covering civil rights, for instance, with its technically proficient battle-action accounts of rioting, and its distracted, uncomprehending, essentially uninterested sliding over of the dark silences that fill the empty spaces in between the riots. It is now especially evident, and damaging, in Vietnam, where, for the most part, American journalism has practically surrendered itself to a consecutive, activist, piecemeal, the-next-day-the-First-Army-forges-onward-toward-Aachen approach to a war that even the journalists covering it know to be non-consecutive, non-activist, a war of silences, strange motions, where a bang on the table gets you nothing and an inadvertent blink causes things to happen in rooms you haven't even looked into yet, where there is no Aachen, and "onward" is a word that doesn't seem to translate very well into the local language. The journalists reorder the actuality of Vietnam into these isolated hard-news incidents for the benefit of their editors. The editors say that that's what the public wants, and, to a great extent, the editors are right about that. The public does indeed want and need hard news, something concrete amid the chaos, something you can reach out to over the morning coffee and almost touch —a hill number, for example. Hill 63. Hill 881. It's a truism, especially among wire-service reporters in Vietnam, that if you can somehow get a hill number attached to a military operation (most operations start at one latitude-longitude point and move to another), regardless of the number of casualties, regardless, especially, of the relevance of this operation to the rest of the war, the story will run on for days, particularly in the pages of the small-to-medium-circulation newspapers that buy most of the wire-service copy. The public also presumably wants and needs a sense of progress, and since this is a public that tends to measure progress numerically—so many yards gained rushing, so many villages pacified, earnings per share up, body counts down, carloadings steady—there is a tendency on the part of the dispensers of information, the military and the government, to scour Vietnam for positive statistics and dole them out to newsmen, who are always under pressure to supply copy, and who know that there is nearly always a market back home for these firm-sounding stories that seem to be about numbers, which in turn seem to mean something, but in fact are often just about the numbers. One of the better *Catch-22* effects over here is to pick up the daily *Stars & Stripes* and read the wire-service lead, datelined Saigon—"Hurtling out of an overcast sky, warplanes of the United States Seventh Fleet delivered another massive air strike against the port city of Haiphong," and so on—and try to recall the atmosphere and the phrasing when the source information was delivered in the course of the daily briefing, the famous "five-o'clock follies" held each day at the Mission Press Center. A couple of dozen correspondents are slouched in chairs in the briefing room, a bored Air Force major is reading aloud in a flat, uninflected voice the summary of the various air strikes conducted that morning and earlier that afternoon: "Airplanes of the United States Seventh Fleet flew 267 missions against targets in the south. . . . Airplanes of the 12th Tactical Fighter Wing flew 245 missions and 62 sorties against selected targets, including the warehouse system outside Hanoi and bridges in the Loc Binh area. . . ." Everybody has been dozing along, except that now someone asks, "Say, Major, isn't that Loc Binh just five miles from the Chinese border?" The major will acknowledge that it is. "Say, Major, isn't that the closest we've yet come to the Chinese border?" The major will acknowledge that it is. "Major," another voice will ask, "wouldn't you say that was a 'first'—I mean in proximity terms?" The major looks thoughtful for a moment. "In proximity terms," he will reply, "I would say 'affirmative.' "

Television correspondents try to get around the limitations, not of their medium but of what they are structurally required to cover (at least, the more political and thoughtful among them do), by inserting some sort of verbal point of view in the taped narrative they send off with their brief film reports, as though to say, Okay, fellows, here's your bang-bang footage, but if I put a little edge in my voice maybe it will come out a bit closer to the way things were. Morley Safer used to do this with a vengeance on CBS, and CBS's David Schoumacher and NBC's Dean Brelis do it to a certain degree now, and in some ways it's effective—it sharpens a point of view, if there should be one to begin with, and it allows for a slight intrusion of irony into a war that most news organizations are attempting to report without irony. (Trying to report a war without irony is a bit like trying to keep sex out of a discussion of the relations between men and women.) The fact is, though, that if you show some film of, say, half a dozen helicopters whirring in onto the ground, our men rushing out with rifles at the ready amid sounds of gunfire here and there, a platoon commander on the radio, men running by with stretchers amid more gunfire, what you are really doing is adding another centimeter or millimeter to what is often no more than an illusion of American military progress (our boys rushing forward, those roaring helicopters, the authoritative voice of the captain). And to stand up there afterward, microphone in hand, and say, with all the edge in your voice you can muster, as Safer used to do, "Another typical engagement in Vietnam. . . . A couple of battalions of the Army went into these woods looking for the enemy. The enemy was gone. There was a little sniper fire at one moment; three of our men were hit, but not seriously. It was pretty much the way it usually goes," doesn't pull the picture back quite straight—or perhaps, to be a bit more accurate, it focuses one's eyes on a picture that may not really have any useful connection with the situation it claims to be communicating about. Communications. One is so terribly serious about some things. One has a direct circuit installed between Rockefeller Center and the Hotel Caravelle. One can whoosh eight cans of 16-millimeter film two-thirds of the way around the world in less than twenty hours. For around seventy-five hundred bucks, one can buy thirty minutes' worth of satellite time and relay the film in from Tokyo. The television people work like hell in Vietnam—Saturdays, Sundays, all the time, really. Many of the journalists there work like hell—able men, responsible men, pasting detail upon detail into some sort of continuing scrapbook of stories about bombing raids, and pacification programs, and bombing raids, and about the Buddhist march, and the new infrared searchlight, and bombing raids, and about the fact that forty thousand Vietcong defected in the last six months. And the detail accretes, day in, day out; paragraphs clatter out over the cable, film by the bagload heads home for processing, detail, detail, detail, and people back home, who have been fed more words and pictures on Vietnam than on any other event in the last twenty years, have the vague, unhappy feeling that they still haven't been told it straight. And, of course, it's true. When President Johnson stands behind the podium in the East Room, looks into the cameras, and declares that he has "read all the reports" and that the reports tell him "progress is being made," it isn't that he's lying. He doesn't need to lie for the situation to be potentially disastrous; all he needs to do is defer to the authority of a reportorial system (one is thinking especially of the government's) that, in terms of the sensitivities, the writing skill, and the general bias of the reporters, is unlikely to be automatically accurate, or anywhere near it. Patriotism doesn't have much to do with it, any more than inaccuracy or distortion has much to do with whatever it is that gives old Fred—after three years in which he has read 725,000 words about

Vietnam—the feeling that he couldn't write three intelligible sentences about the subject on a postcard to his mother.

There are a couple of things one could probably do to improve the situation. In television, the most likely would be to loosen up and expand the evening news programs so that the correspondents could handle larger themes, and then be less restrictively visual about the assignments. (The networks might also get some correspondents whose interest in daily events wasn't entirely confined to hustling 450 feet of film into a can.) In newspapers (the best of which are far less limited, obviously, than television), one might conceivably do the same sort of thing—loosen the paper up, get some new writers, encourage them to at least allow themselves the possibility of breaking through the barriers of the orthodox good-newspaper-writing declarative sentence ("McCormick Place, the huge exposition center that draws more than a million visitors a year to Chicago, was ravaged by fire today. Damage was estimated at $100 million" is the way *The New York Times* sings it). In television, again—although this, admittedly, isn't very likely, at least in this Golden Age—it might even happen that a network official would someday have the nerve and imagination to call on a few of the really inventive movie-makers, like Godard, Antonioni, and Richardson, or, since they might be a bit hard to get, some of the young inventive movie-makers like Stan Vanderbeek, Shirley Clarke, Donn Pennebaker, and say, "How about you and you and you going in there for a while, to Vietnam, Harlem, Texas, and bringing back some film of what you think is going on?" After all, there *are* these really inventive movie-makers, and one of the reasons they're in movies, and not TV, is that TV tends to remain so consistently nerveless and conventional in its use of film. And both the papers and TV could stand being a great deal more investigative, because if the emperor doesn't have any clothes on you're surely not doing the empire much of a favor by saying he does.

Right now, for example, there's a big public-relations push going on among the military and the embassy people here to get across the idea that the ARVN is a fine, competent, reliable modern army, which it certainly isn't—partly because we spent three years (between 1959 and 1961) training it to be an old-fashioned army, and partly for reasons having to do with corruption and such matters. With the exception of Peter Arnett of the AP, and Merton Perry of *Newsweek,* and a very few others, however, nobody has really gone into the ARVN story, which isn't to say that everyone has been praising the ARVN; even *Time* qualifies its statements about it to the extent of acknowledging that the ARVN hasn't yet fully "found itself." Still, it's an important story to do (many of the things you find out about the ARVN are inextricably connected with the rest of Vietnamese life), and it's here, it's here all the time (maybe a bit the way

Negro slums are there all the time back home), and nobody really looks into it until something happens—a victory, a defeat, a campaign. Or, when somebody does, he does it the way ABC looked into the ARVN the other day, which was to run a three-minute film clip on one of its few decent battalions receiving a Presidential citation from General Westmoreland, concluding with a few well-chosen words from the general on the great improvement he had lately detected in the South Vietnamese Army—all presented absolutely straight. The thing is, one takes note of these various deficiencies, inabilities, disinclinations; one dutifully nudges forward one's little "constructive suggestions"—but they're no more than that. We're all prisoners of the same landscape, and it hardly seems realistic to expect that we'll ever derive a truly intelligent, accurate, sensitive reflection of actuality from a free-market communications system that is manned and operated by people like us, and that will, inevitably, tell us for the most part what we want to know.

In Vietnam recently the war has shifted—superficially, maybe, but shifted anyway—up into the I Corps area, where, just below the DMZ, we have some batteries of Marine artillery, which were placed there last February in an aggressive move to fire upon the enemy infiltration routes, and which have now become exposed, potentially isolated, and subjected to extremely heavy shelling from the enemy's guns, these being in the main well camouflaged, dug in behind the hills within the DMZ, and hard to hit. The other day, after a month-long period in which Con Thien in particular had taken as many as a thousand rounds of artillery fire in a single day, the military headquarters in Saigon (four hundred miles to the south) suddenly announced that the enemy had pulled back from his positions, that we had in fact won at Con Thien, had punished him too severely with our artillery and bombers, and instantly there was a great outpouring of cables and messages back home. U.S. GUNS BATTER REDS AT CON THIEN, headlined the *New York Post*. REDS FLEE GUN POSTS; CON THIEN SIEGE ENDS, said the *Denver Post*. The AP put a big story on the wire which began, "Massive American firepower has broken the back of the Communists' month-long artillery siege of Con Thien," and went on to quote General Westmoreland as having said, "We made it a Dien Bien Phu in reverse." One of the few exceptions was Charles Mohr of the *Times*, who had recently been up there and who filed a long piece to his paper two days later to the effect that Con Thien was still extremely exposed, that "aerial photos confirmed a limited withdrawal but did not necessarily prove that the bulk of the gun pits—most of which have never been located—were hit by B-52 bombing raids and United States arillery," and that "few sources believe that more than a respite has been gained." There is disagreement among journalists here as to the real likelihood of our suffering a military defeat in I Corps, at a place, say, such as Con Thien. There are those who point out that two weeks ago eighteen inches of rain fell on Con Thien in two days, that air strikes could not get in, that trucks could not supply the base with ammunition, or even with water, that it is not totally implausible, considering the fact that the enemy has superior forces in the area, for a combination of circumstances to occur in which the enemy might indeed overrun Con Thien, destroy the guns, raise hell, get out—and then you really would have a sort of mini-Dien Bien Phu disaster. There are also those—the majority—who regard a successful enemy attack on Con Thien as very unlikely, who think that Con Thien could never get that exposed, and who cite as evidence the fact that the enemy is as impeded by monsoon weather as we are. The majority view is probably right. ("The United States Command disclosed today that about 4000 men of the First Air Cavalry Division had been moved north to within 20 miles of DaNang," the AP filed a few days later, forgetting perhaps to disclose that DaNang is the central staging area for I Corps and the outposts near the DMZ, or that the reinforcement of the Marine Corps by the Army is not yet an everyday occurrence in Vietnam or anywhere else.) But, in either case, most journalists who have been up north (some of the same men, indeed, who seem to have so blithely passed along those "Victory at Con Thien" announcements) recognize that the shifting situation in I Corps, and notably around Con Thien (where for the first time Vietnam has turned into a conventional war; in fact, not just a conventional war—a small-scale replica of the First World War), not only says a great deal about the military possibilities in Vietnam right now but, even more important, raises a good many questions about the limits of technology as a cure-all in every modern military situation, about the hazards of trying to fight what appears increasingly to be a ground war with insufficient troops, about the possibilities of negotiating a peace settlement with an enemy who seems to be able to effectively increase his infantry capabilities more than we can. ("Long-range Communist artillery and Red mortars opened up again yesterday and today on U.S. Marine positions south of the Demilitarized Zone," the AP dispatch began on October 11, as if the previous ones had never existed.) Con Thien—lately, anyway—raises these sorts of questions, but, with few exceptions, such as Mohr, and Lee Lescaze of the *Washington Post,* nobody seems to even hear the questions, let alone try to pass them on. (Television, it should be pointed out, first broke the Con Thien story, first took note of the fact that the situation had shifted from an aggressive gun emplacement last February to a defensive battery holding on for dear life in the fall, but, in terms of the three-minute film clips on the evening news, it hasn't done much beyond showing what the place is like—no mean trick itself.)

Back home now, one gathers, the tide of impatience and unhappiness with the war keeps growing. Governor Reagan, one reads, advises that we should use the "full technological resources of the United States" to win the war. An eminent Midwestern senator visiting Saigon the other day slammed his thick hand upon the table and declared in anguish and frustration (the special anguish and frustration of eminent people) that he could see "no alternative remaining" except that we "step up the bombing" or "pack up and leave." A journalist was talking here recently, a young man who works for television and who has been up to Con Thien. "The real hazard about Con Thien," he was saying, "is that we'll get so frustrated trying to win a ground war without enough troops that we'll indeed step up the technology, whatever that means. I hate to think what that means." There are so many real and possible tragedies connected with Vietnam—the tragedies of men and women dead, of men and women dying, of nations dying. (Perhaps there's no worse tragedy than people dying.) But sometimes, listening to the note of anger and impatience that arises above the towns and cities in our country, that hovers over daily life, feeling the growing swell of semi-automatic hawkishness and doveishness that pushes so many people nowadays, and seems to say less for what they rigorously, intelligently believe is right than for the inability of many persons to stand in uncertainty much longer when there are firm choices to be seen on either side, sometimes one has the sense that maybe as great a tragedy as any other will be that we will indeed *do* something shortly (this nation of men and women that always has to be doing something to keep sane), distracted, numbed, isolated by detail that seemed to have been information but was only detail, isolated by a journalism that too often told us only what we thought we wanted to hear, isolated, in fact, by communications—expressing pieties, firmness, regrets, what you will, citizens patting each other on the back ("We did the right thing, Fred"), and not know what we did. Or why. And, once again, will have learned nothing.

Hello, There!
You're on the Air

Jessica Mitford

Radio listeners in Dayton, Ohio, were recently treated to one of the most spirited debates ever aired in that city. It occurred on Phil Donahue's "Conversation Please" program over Station WHIO, and was triggered by

Reprinted by permission of the author and her agents, James Brown, Associates, Inc. Copyright © 1966, by Minneapolis Star and Tribune Co. Reprinted from the May, 1966, issue of Harper's Magazine by permission of the author's agent.

a woman who telephoned in to raise the question, should a husband's underpants be ironed? "Am I remiss? I don't," she said. So many calls followed that comment that the lines were jammed for hours. Examples: "It depends whether he wears jockey shorts or boxer style." "I don't, it's a waste of time." "I do, it makes me feel as though I've accomplished something when I see how comfortable he looks when he puts them on in the morning." "I iron them, but I don't put a crease in the front." "I don't, and I think women who do are those who feel inadequate, and have to seek fulfillment by ironing their husbands' undershorts." Finally, an irate caller complained that the whole undershorts controversy was a waste of time, a ridiculous subject for a radio program, and an indication of the immaturity of women who would participate in such trivia. Asked by Donahue if she herself ironed her husband's undershorts, she held forth for a solid six minutes on this absorbing topic.

The audience-participation program, though it may not always manage to stir passions on such basic issues as this one, has emerged in the past few years as the brightest hope of the beleaguered radio industry. Threatened throughout the 1950s by the towering specter of television competition, radio is making a sensational comeback—and the reason may well be the success of the telephone "talk shows." Soap opera has moved on to television and has all but vanished from radio, displaced by the more gripping drama of real-life situations and dilemmas.

Words, words, words—they pour over the airwaves by the millions, night and day. If a housewife tells her husband at dinner, "Guess who I talked to today? Bobby Kennedy!" (or Martin Luther King, Jr., or Billy Graham, or Guy Lombardo) she may not be kidding. The guest-star program—in which a public personality consents to be Aunt Sally, a target for bricks and bouquets from anonymous callers—is one of the many forms taken by the talk shows. Others are straight question-and-answer shows, like that conducted by Dr. Rose Franzblau in New York, who advises parents on child upbringing. More often, there is no guest star and no set subject, just an endless stream of irrelevancies, misinformation, conjecture, opinion, punctuated by the beckoning voice of the announcer: "Just pick up your phone and call this number. . . . Hullo, there! You're on the air."

The radio industry seems to have stumbled on this astonishingly successful format almost by accident. According to Paul Kagan, in charge of the talk programs for all the CBS-owned radio stations, the earliest origins of the telephone response program are lost in antiquity somewhere in the early 'fifties. Radio stations in California, Florida, and Colorado claim the prototype but such boasts are difficult to document because records are often sketchy and the men who created the programs have usually moved on.

It is within the past two or three years that the format has spread fast and wide in all directions. Some stations, such as the CBS group, have virtually converted to talk-telephone all day. Of some 5,000 radio stations in the country, almost all except for the strictly music stations now offer some type of talk program. While the earlier talk shows were all of the "night-owl" variety, beamed to shut-ins, insomniacs, lonely people with nobody but the radio to talk to, they now fill the daytime hours as well.

Listening to a random selection of talk-telephone shows from all over the United States, I often felt like an invisible guest at a huge cocktail party where nobody knows anyone else and at which there are too many women. One is alternately bored, irritated, amused, perforce instructed in all sorts of miscellaneous and unconnected matters. Snatches of conversation assail the ear: an amateur pundit is holding forth authoritatively about international affairs; a weepy matron is relating her marital troubles; others are quietly getting drunk and making no sense at all. We are not likely to be introduced to anyone because most stations do not permit the callers to give their names, on the theory that discussion will be freer and franker if they remain anonymous. No doubt the caller's anonymity also makes it safer for the program host to liven up the show by slanging the guests. "Lady, I'd like to paste a stamp on the end of your nose and mail you to a forest fire," Joe Pyne of KLAC, Los Angeles, recently told a caller.

Topics, styles of delivery, opinions expressed by the callers are as various as human nature itself. Although the dominant voices are those of the clearly deranged, the far-right hate-peddler, the religious nut, and the loquacious bore, an occasional witty or well-informed caller gets through to provide moments of comedy or legitimate comment. The advocate of radical social change may also be on hand to inject an unorthodox viewpoint. It is the anticipation of the unexpected that makes it hard to shut off these programs. After all, who wants to leave before the end of the party? Something interesting might still happen.

Some indication of the popularity of the programs is afforded by those stations that have installed a monitor system to record the number of incoming calls. Mr. Kagan says that a run-of-the-mill half-hour talk program will attract between three and five hundred calls but often, if there is something of special interest, this may run far higher. A program featuring two nuns just returned from the Selma march drew 20,000 calls. An offer of free Beatles tickets drew more than 120,000—which is strange, since industry surveys show that the audience for talk-telephone is overwhelmingly adult, with less than 7 per cent under eighteen.

One might have assumed that a great advantage of the talk show, in which the listeners double as unpaid performers, would be that it costs little to produce. Quite the contrary is true. The talk show is one of the most expensive kinds of radio production—a music program costs half as much, and the expense of soap opera, a network operation, is small because it is divided between many stations. The talk show will typically require a secretary, a writer-producer, a head producer, and the "air personality" himself; their combined salaries may run upwards of $50,000 a year. To this must be added an engineer's salary and extensive engineering costs—perhaps a dozen extra incoming telephone lines, and a six-second delay device which permits the producer to eliminate obscene or libelous remarks by pushing a button.

The outlay has proved well worth it, for the talk programs have been rewarded by the approval of the advertisers, who have discovered that this format is made to order for their purposes. While music is often used by listeners merely as a background against which they may converse, read, or otherwise occupy themselves, the talk shows attract what is known in the industry as the "foreground audience"—listeners who are hanging on every word that is spoken and who are therefore unlikely to miss the message conveyed in the commercial. Radio stations all over the country report huge increases in advertising revenue since the advent of the talk shows—in the past three years, radio-time sales for local stations has risen by almost 30 per cent. Thus the merry tinkle of the cash register chimes in harmony with the ringing telephone.

There is as yet no universally-accepted appellation for the host on these programs. "Commentator" or "moderator" is not quite accurate. "Talk jockey" is disliked in the trade as being somewhat derogatory, too flip to describe the serious role some are trying to carve out for themselves. No doubt in the near future, with the American genius for upgrading status through the use of high-sounding titles, somebody will come up with "conversation engineer," "talk counseler," or "spokestonian." In the absence of a distinctive and acceptable title, I shall steer a safe middle course and call them "talkicians."

The talkician, then, is alternately bull baiter, confidant, and highest authority on any subject that may be thrown his way by a caller. His only qualifications may be a pleasant voice, a glib tongue, and a background as radio sports announcer. Yet he deals handily with topics ranging from the threatened suicide of a caller to the Vietnam war, from the possibilities of life in outer space to the problems of Mexican farm workers, from juvenile delinquency to Zen Buddhism. He freely tenders advice on medical, legal, political, and religious subjects. Having established his omniscience in the minds of listeners, he then proceeds to deliver the commercials, thus adding his own prestige to the claims of the pet-food manufacturer or vacuum-cleaner outlet whose product he is selling.

Not all talkicians fit all aspects of this composite picture. Some are intelligent and well-informed men (very few women have found their way into this line of work) who do their best to steer the program into the direction of sanity. Some are modest, easygoing types who readily admit ignorance of a topic flung out by a caller, and who are too principled to give random, possibly harmful advice off the top of their head. Still others are driven, tormented spirits, the captive of their métier which has swallowed them whole. . . .

According to Phil Donahue, whose highly successful "Conversation Please" in Dayton, Ohio, has the biggest audience of any program in its time slot, most talk shows are plagued by two major problems: the "regular" caller, and the Radical Right. The regular caller is apt to be an exhibitionist who asks questions on the air, not to get answers, but to hear himself ask. The Radical Right, he said, make a business of "exposing" people.

"The best way to kill a talk show is to cram it with callers who read, and the 'exposers' always read," Donahue explained. "They come on the air shuffling their pamphlets and editorials; they are speakers not with notes in their heads but with their heads in their notes. In the show-biz sense, they are deadly. Cut them off and you arouse their zeal. They thrive on martyrdom." He added, "Collectively, I believe these people do more to curse the cause of conservatism in this country than the overwhelming defeat of Barry Goldwater—and I believe a strong conservative force in this country is a healthy thing."

Donahue's remarks about the Radical Right were echoed by other talkicians across the country. Les Vogel of WQAM, Miami, regularly crosses swords with members of the John Birch Society. His complaint is that he finds it impossible to induce them to appear in person on his program: "They can write letters and make phone calls, they can lie about this station, lie to my sponsors, but we can't get them to come into the station and take a position on the air." (However, admitted Birchers have made occasional rare appearances on other talk shows). . . .

Conclusions about the talk shows? It would be easy to dismiss them as so much vacuous drivel beamed to idle minds. Yet that is not the whole story. They do offer a lively change from the bland output of much of the mass media. Newspapers across the country are becoming more and more uniform as they substitute the canned syndicated column for original writing. Television, cowering further and further away from controversial or disturbing issues, has retreated into its own wishy-washy fantasy land. In contrast, the talk shows thrive on controversy and actively encourage the uncensored airing of nonconformist ideas. They at least offer the potential of uninhibited discussion and rough-and-tumble debate. Perhaps, in an overtranquilized land, this is the key to their success.

For Further Study, Analysis, and Research

I. Topics and Questions

PART 1: MASS MEDIA AND SOCIETY

I. Backgrounds and Perspectives

1. Which of the media has the strongest impact? Which is the most influential in shaping the opinions, attitudes, values, beliefs, or basic assumptions of its audience? Why? What is it about this particular media and its workings that achieves this impact? Is this also the most valuable media?

2. What has been the single most significant experience you have had as a member of the audience of a mass media presentation? What effect, influence, or both did it have on you and what were the reasons for this?

3. Has the image-making of the mass media affected your life personally? Which of your values, concepts, attitudes, assumptions have been influenced by the media? How?

4. Does the television audience get what it wants to see? Does it get what it should see? Should it get what it should see or what it wants to see?

5. Do the media tend to harden conformity or encourage diversity in a society? In what ways?

6. What problems are created by the fact that the media are both private business enterprises and public services? How can we best move toward solving these problems? How are these problems related to the laws and regulations governing the various media?

7. Focus on one area of change discussed by Paul Baran and argue why, or why not, and in what ways, one or several of his interpretations or predictions seem valid.

II. Critiques and Cases

1. Analyze the advertisements of one issue of a publication or compare the advertisements in two publications in terms of the following: implied or stated values, kinds of appeals, use of connotation, audience, style and level of language, relation to contents of the publication.

2. Analyze the image of a group or type of person projected by media advertising, whether in a single medium like television or in several. What stereotypes of personality characteristics and values are projected? Why would these be felt to be useful in selling products?

3. Create two different ads to sell the same product or service, adapting your approach to suit the style and audience of two different publications.

4. What motives, needs, or fears are appealed to in advertising? Select several specific ads or commercials to illustrate your claims.

5. Research and analyze some recent arguments about whether or not violence in the media actually affects people and in what ways. What kinds of evidence are presented? Which arguments seem more convincing?

6. Compare violence on television and in movies. Which seems most extreme? Which is most influencing? What are the differences in the situations?

7. What are the reasons for continued acceleration of violence in the media, especially in movies?

8. More explicit treatment of sex and more graphic depiction of violence tend to go together in recent movies. Do you think these have made movies more valuable? More entertaining? Why?

PART 2: MASS MEDIA AND CULTURE

I. Backgrounds and Perspectives

1. Do the mass media tend to alienate people from personal experience and impoverish responsiveness, or do they tend to enrich consciousness and experience? Approach this subject in terms of either a personal response to specific media situations or an investigation of the writings of authorities in the field, such as those cited in Gans' article.

2. Is there a conflict between entertainment and art in the media today? What is the effect of the size of the audience involved?

3. Apply Marshall McLuhan's concept of hot and cold media to your own experience of a particular form of media presentation or one specific film, program, or performance. Do you agree with McLuhan's definition of the differing psychological demands and responses of different media?

4. How have the forms and contents of media affected the younger generation's attitudes? How does James W. Carey's position on this relate to your own?

5. Do you agree with Susan Sontag that the way new art affects our sensory responses and sensibility is as important as or more important than the way it influences our moral values?
6. What changes have occurred in the media's treatment of black and other minority groups?

II. Individual Media

1. What differences in culture, in life-styles and manners, are illustrated by the differences between a standard newspaper and an underground newspaper?
2. Is the kind of "trivialization" discussed by Abrams a serious problem for radio and television audiences? How is it related to sensationalism and standardization?
3. How varied are the cultural opportunities offered by television? How are these affected by audience size and ratings?
4. Analyze the differences in the degree of realism and the treatment of love situations in films and television? Can these differences have any effect on the personal emotional lives of the audiences?
5. How do current movies or certain types of movies reflect contemporary ideas and feelings about people and life? Respond through personal experience or by an examination of secondary sources that have made this kind of analysis.
6. What is the image projected by the personality and typical roles of a popular actor or actress? What is the appeal, the influence?
7. Compare developments in popular music of the seventies with the interpretation of the music of the sixties made by Robert A. Rosenstone.
8. What is your own interpretation of the appeals and influences of contemporary popular music?
9. Do you agree with Kauffmann, with Bickel, or with a different position toward pornography?
10. Should there be different regulations governing private and public vicarious sex experiences?

III. Critiques and Cases

1. Compare and contrast the treatment of the sexes in the contents and advertisements of two different magazines.
2. What is the basis for the popularity of certain basic genres or types of television programs or movies—such as the Western, the family drama or comedy, the secret agent or science fiction thriller, the hospital or legal drama? What do the elements of these popular genres reveal about the audience?
3. The mass media provide a wide variety of comedy and comedians, each

with different bases and approaches to humor, and different social significance. Define and analyze one type of comedy, one particular comedian or comedy series, or one comic film. Discuss the basis of the humor and reasons for its popularity, and show its relationship to society and the times. Or compare two different types of comedians or comedies in these same terms.

4. Write a review of a film or television program. Be sure to go beyond a mere citation of plot and characters. Analyze and evaluate the themes. Describe the techniques used to dramatize them.

5. Analyze two or more works by a single movie director by tracing the unifying threads of situation, theme, character analysis, social comment, and technique. Or research and report on differing professional critics' interpretations of the work of a director.

6. Analyze several newspaper and/or magazine critics' reviews of a particular movie or television program. What are the agreements and disagreements? Note, for example, the differing views of *A Clockwork Orange* and *Straw Dogs* in Morgenstern's article in Part 1 and Pechter's in this section.

7. What common denominator do you find in the central heroes or heroines of several recent films? What do they reveal about current psychological attitudes and current values?

8. What are the central qualities of a current popular music performer? What are the characteristics of his or her kind of song? What do they seem to represent for the audience? What is their appeal?

9. Compare and contrast a popular black magazine, like *Ebony*, with a popular white magazine, like *Life*.

10. What is the appeal of science fiction? What social comment is involved?

PART 3: MASS MEDIA AND INFORMATION

I. Backgrounds and Perspectives

1. What are the differences between freedom of the press and responsibility of the press? What effects on conveying news and opinion do these differences entail?

2. In what ways does government seek to influence public opinion? What problems does this create for the mass media?

3. In what ways can the coverage by the mass media actually influence public events? What changes, for example, in political campaigning have been produced by media coverage?

4. Survey a variety of opinions on the influence of the media on public opinion. In what kind of situations can the media exert more influence? What is the extent of slanting of news to influence opinion?

5. What are the differences in the regulations over reporting news and giving opinions between the electronic and print media?

II. Individual Media

1. Analyze the differences in the handling of the news as typically practiced in two of the media—such as television and newspapers.
2. Apply one or several of Harry J. Skornia's categories of trouble spots to the way the news is handled on a local television station.
3. How has television affected the conduct of political affairs and campaigns? Are the results harmful or beneficial?
4. Analyze the similarities and differences among the variety of magazines published in a single field—such as news and opinion magazines, sports magazines, entertainment magazines, men's or women's magazines.
5. In what ways does the fact that the media are privately operated businesses influence the performance of any one form of media in presenting news and opinions?
6. Is news coverage on local radio satisfactory? What differences are there among stations? What changes would be beneficial?

III. Critiques and Cases

1. Compare and contrast the differences in news and opinion found in an underground newspaper and a standard newspaper.
2. Can media objectivity become a problem? Is more interpretive journalism needed to balance the limitations of completely objective reporting?
3. Compare and contrast the treatment of a single event or situation in two different magazines, in a magazine and a newspaper, or in a magazine and on television.
4. Analyze and evaluate the purposes, format, functions, coverage, and techniques of a particular magazine as it presents news and opinions. Or compare the approaches of two differing magazines.
5. Do research to determine the main complaints about government secrecy and/or publicity in the field of information and opinion.
6. Compare the immediate treatment of a significant news event, individual or situation in magazines with the later treatment in books or magazines.
7. Study a number of issues of a single newspaper or magazine. What kind of slanting, stereotyping, or bias is discernible in its treatment and selection of news? Or focus on a single subject, such as the Vietnam war, and compare the treatment at two different times, say 1968 and 1972.
8. What problems are created by media coverage of trials? What are some of the alternatives to these problems? What is your position?
9. How are Michael J. Arlen's complaints about the coverage of the Vietnam

war related to the trouble spots defined by Harry J. Skornia in the previous section?

10. What are the chief problems in the media presentation of news and opinion about minority groups? What progress has been made in solving these problems?

11. What are the chief values and drawbacks of two-way talk shows that you have heard? What are some other possibilities for active audience participation in the media process?

Bibliography

PART 1: MASS MEDIA AND SOCIETY

I. Backgrounds and Perspectives

Bauer, R. A., and H. A. Bauer. "America, Mass Society, and Mass Media," *Journal of Social Issues*, 16, 3 (1960), 3–66.

Boorstin, Daniel. *The Image*. New York: Atheneum, Publishers, 1962.

Brucker, Herbert. "Mass Man and Mass Media," *Saturday Review*, 48 (May 29, 1965), 14–16.

Chaffee, Zechariah. *Government and Mass Communication*, 2 vols. Hamden, Conn.: The Shoe String Press, 1947.

Clark, David G., and Earl R. Hutchison. *Mass Media and the Law*. New York: John Wiley & Sons, Inc., 1970.

Clark, W. C., "Impact of Mass Communication in America," *Annals*, (July 1968), 68–74.

DeFleur, Melvin L. "Mass Communication and Social Change," *Social Forces* (March 1966), 314.

———. *Theories of Mass Communication*, 2d ed. New York: David McKay Co., Inc., 1970.

Dexter, James Anthony, and David Manning White. *People, Society, and Mass Communication*. New York: The Free Press, 1964.

Fontaine, Andre, "Mass Media—A Time for Greatness," *Annals* (May 1967), 72.

Gerald, J. Edward. *The Social Responsibility of the Press*. Minneapolis: University of Minnesota Press, 1963.

Gerson, Walter M., "Alienation in Mass Society," *Sociology and Social Research*, 49 (January 1965), 143–152.

Johnson, Nicholas. *How to Talk Back to Your Television Set*. Boston: Little, Brown and Company, 1970.

Kelley Jr., Stanley. *Public Relations and Political Power*. Baltimore: The Johns Hopkins Press, 1956.

Klapper, Joseph T. *The Effects of Mass Communications*. New York: The Free Press, 1960.

Loevinger, Lee. "The Ambiguous Mirror: The Reflective-Projective Theory of Broadcasting and Mass Communication," *Journal of Broadcasting* (Spring 1968), 110.

Marx, H. L. *Television and Radio in American Life*. New York: The H. W. Wilson Co., 1953.

Olson, Philip, ed. *America as a Mass Society*. New York: The Free Press, 1963.

Rivers, William L., Theodore Peterson, and Jay W. Jensen. *The Mass Media and Modern Society*, 2d ed. New York: Holt, Rinehart and Winston, Inc., 1971.

Rose, Arnold M., "Reactions Against the Mass Society," *Sociological Quarterly*, 3 (October 1962), 316–330.

Wertham, Fredric. "The Scientific Study of Mass Media Effects," *American Journal of Psychiatry*, 119 (October 1962), 306–311.

White, David Manning, and Richard Averson, eds. *Sight, Sound, and Society: Motion Pictures and Television in America*. Boston: Beacon Press, 1968.

II. Critiques and Cases

Berkowitz, Leonard, and Edna Rawling. "Effects of Film Violence on Inhibitions against Subsequent Aggression," *Journal of Abnormal and Social Psychology*, 66 (1963), 405–412.

Bogart, Leo, "Violence in the Mass Media," *Television Quarterly* (Summer 1969), 36.

Clor, Harry M. *Obscenity and Public Morality*. Chicago: The University of Chicago Press, 1969.

Elliot, George P. "Against Pornography," *Harpers* (March 1965), 55.

Gerbier, G. "Cultural Indications: The Case of Violence in Television Drama," *Annals*, 388 (March 1970), 69–81.

Greyser, S. A., and R. A. Bauer. "Americans and Advertising," *Public Opinion Quarterly*, 30 (Spring 1966), 59–78.

Halloran, James D., "Television and Violence," *The Twentieth Century* (Winter 1964–1965), 61–72.

Knopf, Terry Ann. "Media Myths on Violence," *Columbia Journalism Review* (Spring 1970), 17.

Krugman, Herbert. "The Impact of Television Advertising; Learning without Involvement," *Public Opinion Quarterly* (Fall 1965), 349.

Lacy, Dan. *Freedom and Communications*. Urbana, Ill.: University of Illinois Press, 1965.

Larsen, Otto N., ed., *Violence and the Mass Media*. New York: Harper & Row, Publishers, 1968.

Randall, Richard S. *Censorship of the Movies: The Social and Political Control of a Mass Medium*. Madison: The University of Wisconsin Press, 1968.

Robischon, Tom, "The Supreme Court and the Redemption of Pornography," *Arts in Society*, 2 (1967), 210.

Ruszkowski, *et al.* "Screen Censorship: Three Views," *TV Quarterly*, (Winter 1967), 31–46.

Schramm, Wilbur, *et al. Television in the Lives of Our Children*. Stanford: Stanford University Press, 1961.

Seldin, Joseph J. *The Golden Fleece: Selling the Good Life to Americans*. New York: The Macmillan Company, 1963.

Shickel, Richard. "Pornography and the New Expression," *Atlantic* (January 1967), 48.

Steiner, George. "Night Words: High Pornography and Human Privacy," *Encounter*, 25, 4 (October 1965), 14.

Tebbell, John. "Journalism—Public Entertainment or Private Interest?" *Annals* (January 1966), 79–86.

Tynan, Kenneth. "Dirty Books Can Stay," *Esquire* (October 1968), 168–170.

Van den Haag, Ernest. "Is Pornography a Cause of Crime?" *Encounter* (December 1967), 52–56.

Wertham, Fredric. *A Sign for Cain: An Exploration of Human Violence*. New York: The Macmillan Company, 1966.

Zielske, H. A. "The Remembering and Forgetting of Advertising," *Journal of Marketing* (January 1959), 239–243.

PART 2: MASS MEDIA AND CULTURE

I. Backgrounds and Perspectives

American Scholar, The. "The Electronic Revolution—Special Issue," (Spring 1966).

Arts in Society. "The Electric Generation, Special Issue," Vol. 7, 2 (Summer-Fall 1970).

Browne, Ray B., Larry Landrum, and William Bortorff, eds. *Challenges in American Culture*. Bowling Green, Ohio: Bowling Green University Press, 1970.

Carpenter, Edmund, and Marshall McLuhan, eds. *Explorations in Communication*. Boston: Beacon Press, 1960.

Gowans, Alan. *The Unchanging Arts*. Philadelphia: J. B. Lippincott Co., 1971.

Hall, Stuart, and Paddy Whannel. *The Popular Arts*. New York: Pantheon Books, 1965.

Innis, Harold. *The Bias of Communication*. Toronto: University of Toronto Press, 1951.

Jacobs, Norman. *Culture for the Millions*. Boston: The Beacon Press, 1962.

Kristol, Irving. "High, Low, and Modern," *Encounter*, 15, 2 (August 1960), 33.

Lowenthal, Leo. *Literature, Popular Culture, and Society*. Englewood Cliffs, N.J.: Prentice-Hall, Inc., 1961.

Nye, Russell B. *The Unembarrassed Muse—The Popular Arts in America*. New York: The Dial Press, 1970.

Rosenberg, Bernard, and David Manning White. *Mass Culture*. New York: The Free Press, 1957.

————. *Mass Culture Revisited*. New York: Van Nostrand, 1971.

Rosenthal, Raymond, ed. *McLuhan, Pro and Con*. Penguin Books, 1968.

Seldes, Gilbert. *The Public Arts*. New York: Simon and Schuster, Inc., 1956.

Shils, Edward A. "Mass Society and Its Culture," *Daedalus*, (Spring 1960).

Slater, Philip E. *The Pursuit of Loneliness: American Culture at the Breaking Point*. Boston: Beacon Press, 1970.

Smith, Alfred G., ed. *Communication and Culture*. New York: Holt, Rinehart and Winston, Inc., 1966.

Stearn, Gerald Emanuel, ed. *McLuhan: Hot and Cool*. New York: The Dial Press, 1967.

White, David Manning. *Pop Culture in America*. Chicago: Quadrangle Books, 1970.

Wilensky, Harold L. "Mass Society and Mass Culture: Interdependence or Independence," *American Sociological Review*, 29 (April 1964), 173–197.

II. Individual Media

Belz, Carl I. "Popular Music and the Folk Tradition," *Journal of American Folklore*, 80, 316 (April–June 1967), 130.

Bestor, Alfred. "The New Age of Radio," *Holiday*, 33 (June 1963), 56–65.

Carey, James T. "Changing Courtship Patterns in the Popular Song," *American Journal of Sociology*, Vol. 74, 1 (May 1969), 720.

Casty, Alan. *Development of the Film: An Interpretive History*. New York: Harcourt, Brace Jovanovich, Inc., 1973.

Cunliffe, Marcus. "Periodical Culture," *Encounter* (August 1965), 82.

Eck, Robert. "The Real Masters of Television," *Harper's* (March 1967), 45.

Feiffer, Jules. *The Great Comic Book Heroes*. New York: The Dial Press, Inc., 1965.

Felker, Clay S. "Life Cycles in the Age of Magazines," *Antioch Review*, 29 (Spring 1969), 7–13.

Gillette, Charlie. *The Sound of the City*. New York: E. P. Dutton, 1970.

Homan, W. H. "The New Sound of Radio," *New York Times Magazine* (December 3, 1967), 56–58.

Knight, Arthur. *The Liveliest Art*. New York: Crowell, Collier and Macmillan, Inc., 1957.

Linneck, Anthony. "Magic and Identity in Television Programming," *Journal of Popular Culture* (Winter 1969), 644.

Marcus, Greil, ed. *Rock and Roll Will Stand*. Boston: Beacon Press, 1970.

McCann, Richard Dyer, ed. *Film: A Montage of Theories*. New York: E. P. Dutton & Co., Inc., 1966.

Mehling, Harold. *The Great Time Killer*. Cleveland: The World Publishing Company, 1962.

Meyersohn, R. "Television and the Rest of Leisure," *Public Opinion Quarterly* (Spring 1968), 102–112.

Mooney, H. F. "Popular Music Since the 1920's," *American Quarterly* (Spring 1968), 319.

Mowat, David. "The Cinema's New Language," *Encounter* (April 1970), 64.

Robinson, John P. "Television and Leisure Time: Yesterday, Today and (maybe) Tomorrow," *Public Opinion Quarterly*, 33 (Summer 1969) 210–222.

Robinson, W. R., ed. *Man and the Movies*. New Orleans: Louisiana State University Press, 1967.

Shickel, Richard. "Movies Are Now High Art," *New York Times Magazine* (June 5, 1969), 12.

Shillaci, Anthony. "Film as Environment," *Saturday Review* (December 28, 1968), 111.

Singer, Aubrey. "Television: Window on Culture or Reflection in the Glass?" *American Scholar*, 35, 2 (Spring 1966), 303.

Smith, Desmond. "American Radio Today," *Harper's Magazine*, 229 (September 1964), 58–63.

Stephenson, Ralph, and Leon R. Debrix. *The Cinema as Art*. Baltimore: Penguin Books, Inc., 1965.

Whale, John. *The Half-Shut Eye*. New York: St. Martins Press, Inc., 1969.

White, David Manning, and Robert Abel, eds. *The Funnies: An American Idiom*. New York: The Free Press, 1963.

Wolseley, Roland E. "The Black Magazine," *Quill*, 57 (May 1969), 8–11.

III. Critiques and Cases

Bailey, Margaret. "The Women's Magazine Short-Story Heroine in 1957 and 1967," *Journalism Quarterly*, 46, 2 (Summer 1969), 364.

Bellone, Julius, ed. *Renaissance of the Film*. New York: Crowell, Collier and Macmillan, Inc., 1970.

Brissett, Dennis, and Robert P. Snow. "Vicarious Behavior: Leisure and the Transformation of *Playboy Magazine*," *Journal of Popular Culture* (Winter 1969), 428.

Cannon, G. "Age of Aquarius," *Partisan Review*, 36: 2 (1969), 282–287.

Carey, James W. "Variations in Negro/White Television Preferences," *Journal of Broadcasting*, 10 (Summer 1966), 199–212.

Clarens, Carlos. *Horror Movies*. Berkeley: University of California Press, 1968.

Chenoweth, Lawrence. "The Jimi Hendrix Experience and The Jefferson Airplane," *American Quarterly* (Spring 1971), 125.

Connell, F. M. "Rough Beast Slouching: A Note on Horror Movies," *Kenyon Review*, 32 (1970), 42.

Cripps, Thomas R. "Death of Rastus: Negroes in American Films Since 1943," *Phylon*, 28 (Fall 1967), 267–275.

Davies, E. "Psychological Characteristics of Beatles Mania," *Journal of the History of Ideas*, 30, 273 (April 1969), 80.

DeMott, Benjamin. *Supergrow*. New York: E. P. Dutton Co., Inc., 1970.

Denisoff, Serge R. "Folk-Rock: Folk Music, Protest or Commercialism," *Journal of Popular Culture* (Fall 1969), 214.

Dye, Robert Paul. "The Death of Silence," *Journal of Broadcasting*, 12 (Summer 1968), 225–228.

Eisen, Jonathan, ed. *The Age of Rock*. New York: Vintage, 1969.

Gans, Herbert J. "The Rise of the Problem-Film: An Analysis of Changes in Hollywood Films and the American Audience," *Social Problems*, 11 (Spring 1964), 327–336.

Harley, N. P. "Toward a Sociology of Jazz," *Thought*, 44 (Summer 1969), 219–246.

Harper, Ralph. *The World of the Thriller*. Cleveland: The Press of Western Reserve University, 1969.

Hemphill, Paul. *The Nashville Sound: Bright Lights and Country Music*. New York: Simon and Schuster, 1970.

Kael, Pauline. *Going Steady*. Boston: Little, Brown and Company, 1970.

Kauffmann, Stanley. *A World on Film*. New York: Harper & Row, Publishers, 1966.

Lewis, George H. "Dylan, The Pop Artist and His Product: Mixed-Up Confusion," *Journal of Popular Culture* (Fall 1970), 327.

Macdonald, Dwight. *Dwight Macdonald on Movies*. Englewood Cliffs, N.J.: Prentice-Hall, Inc., 1969.

Mims, Grace A. "Soul: The Black Man and His Music," *Negro History Bulletin* (October 1970), 140.

Nussbaum, Martin. "Sociological Symbolism of the 'Adult Western,'" *Social Forces*, 39 (October 1960), 25–28.

Reddick, Glenn E. "Deception as a TV Comedy Tool," *The Christian Century* (September 29, 1965), 36.

Rorem, Ned. "The Music of the Beatles," *The New York Review of Books*, January 18, 1968, 23.

Sarris, Andrew. *Confessions of a Cultist: On the Cinema; 1955–1969*. New York: Simon and Schuster, 1971.

Simon, John. *Private Screenings: Views of the Cinema of the Sixties*. New York: The Macmillan Company, 1967.

Smith, Desmond. "American Radio Today—Listener Be Damned," *Harper's* (September 1964), 58–63.

Taylor, John Russell. *Cinema Eye, Cinema Ear: Some Key Film Makers of the Sixties.* New York: Hill and Wang, Inc., 1964.

Warshow, Robert. *The Immediate Experience.* New York: Doubleday & Company, Inc., 1962.

PART 3: MASS MEDIA AND INFORMATION

I. Backgrounds and Perspectives

Bagdikian, Ben H. *The Information Machines—Their Impact on Men and the Media.* New York: Harper & Row, Publishers, 1971.

Bauer, Raymond. "The Limits of Persuasion," *Harvard Business Review* (Sept.-Oct. 1958), 105–110.

Chester, Edward W. *Radio, Television and American Politics.* New York: Sheed & Ward, 1968.

Childs, Harwood. *Public Opinion: Nature, Formation, and Role.* New York: Van Nostrand, 1965.

Davies, R. T. "American Commitment to Public Propaganda," *Law and Contemporary Problems*, 31 (Summer 1966), 452–457.

Festinger, L., and N. Macoby. "On Resistance to Persuasive Communication," *Journal of Abnormal and Social Psychology*, 68, 4, (1964), 359–366.

Gross, Gerald. *The Responsibility of the Press.* New York: Fleet Publishing Company, 1966.

Hohenberg, John. *The News Media.* New York: Holt, Rinehart and Winston, Inc., 1969.

Minor, Dale. *The Information War.* New York: Hawthorn Books, Inc., 1970.

Rivers, William. *The Opinion Makers.* Boston: The Beacon Press, 1965.

Schramm, Wilbur. "The Nature of News," *Journalism Quarterly* (September 1949), 128.

Sears, David O., and Jonathan L. Freedman. "Selective Exposure to Information: A Critical Review," *Public Opinion Quarterly*, 31, 2 (Summer 1967), 194.

II. Individual Media

Bagdikian, Ben. "The Newsmagazines," *New Republic*, 40 (February 2, 16, and 23, 1959), 11–16.

Blumler, Jay G., and Denis McQuail. *Television in Politics.* Chicago: University of Chicago Press, 1969.

Boylan, James, and Alfred Balk, *et al.*, eds. *Our Troubled Press.* Boston: Little, Brown and Company, 1971.

Brachman, Jacob. "The Underground Press," *Playboy*, 14 (August 1967), 83.

Casey, Ralph D., ed. *The Press in Perspective*. Baton Rouge, La.: Louisiana State University Press, 1965.

Cox, Kenneth A. "Can Broadcasting Help Achieve Social Reforms?" *Journal of Broadcasting*, 12 (Spring 1968), 117–130.

Day, Robin, "Troubled Reflections of a TV Journalist," *Encounter* (May 1970), 76.

Gans, Herbert J. "How Well Does TV Present the News?" *New York Times Magazine* (January 11, 1970), 31.

Glessing, Robert J. *The Underground Press in America*. Bloomington: Indiana University Press, 1970.

Hulting, Joseph L., and Ray Paul Nelson. *The Fourth Estate*. New York: Harper and Row, Publishers, 1971.

Johnson, Michael L. *The New Journalism*. Lawrence, Kansas: University of Kansas Press, 1971.

Kintner, Robert E. "Broadcasting and the News," *Harper's Magazine*, 230 (April, May 1965), 49–55.

Lang, Kurt, and Gladys Engel Lang. *Politics and Television*. Chicago: Quadrangle Books, 1970.

McCombs, Maxwell E. "Negro Use of Television and Newspapers for Political Information, 1952–64," *Journal of Broadcasting*, 12 (Summer 1968), 261–266.

MacNeil, Robert. *The Influence of Television on American Politics*. New York: Harper & Row, Publishers, 1968.

Wagner, Philip. "What Makes a Really Good Newspaper?" *Harper's Magazine*, 224 (June 1962), 12.

III. Critiques and Cases

Bernstein, Victor, and Jesse Gordon. "The Press and the Bay of Pigs," *Columbia Forum* (Fall 1967), 5.

Ely, J. J. "Trial by Newspaper and Its Cures," *Encounter*, 28 (March 1967), 80–92.

Fairlie, Henry. "Anglo-American Differences in the Press," *Encounter*, 26, 6 (June 1966), 73.

Felsher, Howard. *The Press in the Jury Box*. New York: The Macmillan Company, 1966.

Friedrick, Otto. "There are 00 Trees in Russia: The Function of Facts in News Magazines," *Harper's Magazine*, 229 (October 1964), 59–65.

Greenberg, Bradley S., and Edwin S. Parker, eds. *The Kennedy Assassination and the American Public*. Stanford: Stanford University Press, 1965.

Hirsch, Paul M. "An Analysis of *Ebony*: The Magazine and Its Readers," *Journalism Quarterly*, 45 (Summer 1968), 261–270, 292.

Klein, Woody. "The Racial Crisis in America: the News Media Respond to the New Challenge," *Quill*, 57 (January 1969), 8–12.

McGoffin, William, and Erwin Kroll. *Anything But the Truth: The Credibility Gap: How the News Is Managed in Washington.* New York: G. P. Putnam's Sons, 1968.

Mead, Margaret. "Our Leaders Do Not Understand Television," *TV Guide* (December 6, 1969), 16.

Paletz, D. L., and R. Dunn. "Press Coverage of Civil Disorders: A Case Study of Winston, Salem, 1967," *Public Opinion Quarterly*, 33 (Fall 1969), 328–345.

Schiller, Herbert. *Mass Communication and American Empire.* New York: Augustus M. Kelley, Publishers, 1969.

Schwartz, Harold. "Covering the Foreign News: News Agencies, Print, and Electronic Media," *Foreign Affairs* (July 1970), 741.

Seldin, Joseph J. "Public Relations and the Public Interest," *The Progressive* (January 1964), p. 33.

Tannebaum, Percy H. "The Effect of Headlines on the Interpretation of News Stories," *Journalism Quarterly*, 30 (Spring 1953), 189–197.

Welles, Chris. "Newsweek (a fact) is the new hot book (an opinion)," *Esquire* (November 1969), 152.

Wright, James D. "Life, Time and The Fortunes of War," *Trans-Action* (January 1972), 42.

Indexes

Indexes

Index of Authors

Index of Titles